ENCYCLOPEDIA OF TRADITIONAL BRITISH RURAL SPORTS

Compiled by leading researchers, the *Encyclopedia of Traditional British Rural Sports* is a comprehensive guide to the games, recreational activities and competitive events that emerged from the rural society of Britain's past. The first reference work on the subject to be published in a century, it provides an authoritative record of Britain's indigenous sports, and full discussion of the issues surrounding rural sports today, covering:

- The cultural origins and development of today's competitive sports (such as **football, rowing, horseracing,** and **athletics**).
- Field and animal sports (including the **hunting** debate).
- Celtic sports (such as **shinty, Gaelic football** and **hurling**).
- The first sports festivals (including the **Llandudno Grand Olympic Festival,** the **Much Wenlock Games**).
- Pub games (**darts, skittles, Aunt Sally, road bowling**).
- And a few curiosities (such as **copsole pulling** and **lark singing**).

Entries focus on the social, political and economic aspects of the sports described. Taken together they represent a compelling and authoritative social history of sport in Britain.

With extensive cross-referencing, suggestions for further reading and relevant internet links, the *Encyclopedia of Traditional British Rural Sports* is both an essential reference and a fascinating store of information.

Tony Collins is a Research Fellow at the International Centre for Sports History and Culture at De Montfort University, UK. **John Martin** is Principal Lecturer in Economic and Social History at De Montfort University, UK. **Wray Vamplew** is Professor of Sports History and Director of Research in Sports Studies at the University of Stirling, UK.

ENCYCLOPEDIA OF TRADITIONAL BRITISH RURAL SPORTS

Editors

TONY COLLINS, JOHN MARTIN
AND WRAY VAMPLEW

Associate Editors

JOHN BURNETT AND EMMA LILE

LONDON AND NEW YORK

First published 2005
by Routledge
2 Park Square, Milton Park, Abingdon, Oxon OX14 4RN

Simultaneously published in the USA and Canada
by Routledge
270 Madison Ave, New York, NY 10016

Routledge is an imprint of the Taylor & Francis Group

Typeset in Sabon by
Keystroke, Jacaranda Lodge, Wolverhampton
Printed and bound in Great Britain by
Antony Rowe Ltd, Chippenham, Wiltshire

Every effort has been made to ensure that the advice and
information in this book is true and accurate at the time of
going to press. However, neither the publisher nor the
authors can accept any legal responsibility or liability for any
errors or omissions that may be made. In the case of
drug administration, any medical procedure or the use
of technical equipment mentioned within this book,
you are strongly advised to consult the
manufacturer's guidelines.

British Library Cataloguing in Publication Data
A catalogue record for this book is available from the British Library

Library of Congress Cataloging in Publication Data
Encyclopedia of traditional British rural sports / editors, Tony Collins,
John Martin, and Wray Vamplew; associate editors, John Burnett and
Emma Lile.
p. cm. – (Sports reference series)
Includes bibliographical references and index.
1. Sports–Great Britain–Encyclopedias. 2. Country life–
Great Britain–Encyclopedias. I. Collins, Tony, 1960
II. Series.
GV605.E53 2005
796'.0941–dc22
2004027375

ISBN 0–415–35224–X

Contents

Introduction

When initially planning this book we outlined our working brief as looking at 'hunting, football and cheese rolling'. We have taken a fairly loose definition of sport, generally omitting children's games but including some recreational pastimes and pub games. Our aim was to bring together several distinct types of traditional rural sports, including those that involved the killing of animals, those in which humans competed against each other and those that eventually transformed themselves and became modern sports. Our objective was to present a wide-ranging social, economic and political study of rural sports, with particular emphasis on the social history and 'traditional' aspects.

It is hoped that the *Encyclopedia of Traditional British Rural Sports* will provide students, scholars and sports enthusiasts with a comprehensive and authoritative source of information on the history and culture of rural sport in Britain. It contains several hundred entries focusing on individual sports and others providing analyses of key concepts, themes and terminology. We hope that it will be the first port of call for readers or researchers wanting information on British rural sport, but we recognise that for many it will also be the last. Its objective, therefore, is to be as comprehensive as possible, both in its selection of subjects for inclusion and in its treatment of them. It also endeavours to provide guidance to those wishing to take the subject further. The entries aim to summarise the current state of knowledge; generally they are not meant to serve as a forum for scholarly debate or special pleading. We believe that most people use encyclopedias for quick answers to reference questions; they want to open the book and retrieve the needed information with a minimum of trouble. As a general rule people do not read encyclopedias cover to cover, but we hope that dipping into this volume might encourage them to browse further.

One thing that this encyclopedia reveals is that although many traditional sports and games were specific to a locality, others had variants throughout the British Isles. This raised the possibility that different names for what seemed to be similar activities might owe more to dialect than to actual practice. We have attempted to make this volume genuinely British by including entries on Irish, Scottish and Welsh traditional sports as well as English ones. Where a game was widespread across the different countries we have occasionally used Welsh, Irish and Scottish examples as reflecting what went on in Britain generally, but at other times we have integrated the Celtic material into entries focusing on the English situation. Post-independence Irish examples are included where they show what happened to the traditional sport over time. Both Scotland and Wales also have a specific entry on sports in those nations. We have also included an essay on a selected region of England, the county of Northumberland (or at least its eastern part). Context is provided by an essay on European traditional sports, though readers are cautioned that the views expressed are those of one specialist in the field.

Critics might argue that some of the sports we list may well be traditional but are not rural. Our response is that, generally, we have included sports that began in a rural setting even though they have evolved to become more urban-based. We also note that in the days when these sports began, the distinction between urban and rural was perhaps not so clear-cut as it is today. We have also extended the time period covered in many of the entries into the twentieth century to demonstrate that there was continuity as well as change in the history of British sport.

One major change in the British tradition is the decline in rough, barbaric animal-baiting sports, though some of these still continue as clandestine activities. The entries for these sports will contribute to the debate among both sports historians and scholars of contemporary sport as to whether sport reflects the society within which it takes place. Through their use of animals, competitive work-related activities and general disregard for health and safety issues traditional sports in Britain certainly mirrored the rural society and agricultural economy of the time!

The references and additional reading listed are drawn from a range of sources, but we must acknowledge a debt to pioneers in the field of collective works on traditional sports, games and customs. In particular, we draw attention to Alice Gomme's *The Traditional Games of England, Scotland and Ireland*, Christina Hole's *English Traditional Customs*, Compton Reeves's *Pleasures and Pastimes in Medieval England*, Pietro Gorini's *Encyclopedia of Traditional Games*, Brian Day's *A Chronicle of Folk Customs* and William Hone's *Everyday Book*.

For those readers who want to apportion blame and praise, the respective responsibilities of the editorial panel were as follows: John Martin looked after hunting, shooting, fishing and other field sports, Tony Collins saw to most other English rural sports, Emma Lile and John Burnett took charge of Welsh and Scottish sport respectively, and Wray Vamplew oversaw the Celtic entries generally and edited the volume overall. As editors, we are grateful to our contributors, most of whom delivered on schedule and within word limits! We are also appreciative of the proofreading efforts of Brian Lile, who is in no way to blame for the final product not matching his exacting standards.

A final note concerns measurements. Traditional sports emerged – and indeed many disappeared – before Britain went decimal. We have used imperial (and earlier) measurements where they were central to the sport being discussed (though usually with metric equivalents provided), but modern measurements when heights, weights and distances simply need to be recorded.

JOHN BURNETT, TONY COLLINS, EMMA LILE
JOHN MARTIN, WRAY VAMPLEW

List of Entries

List of Contributors

Jess Barker
Research Officer
League Against Cruel Sports

John Burnett
Curator of Scottish Ethnology
National Museums of Scotland

Robin N. Campbell
Department of Psychology
University of Stirling

Timothy J. L. Chandler
Kent State University, Ohio

Patrick Chaplin
Anglia Polytechnic University

Ian Clarke
International Centre for Sports
History and Culture
De Montfort University
Institute for Cornish Studies

Tony Collins
International Centre for Sports
History and Culture
De Montfort University

Christopher Dodd
River and Rowing Museum
Henley-on-Thames

Heiner Gillmeister
University of Bonn

Nicholas Goddard
Anglia Polytechnic University

Steve Greenfield
University of Westminster

David Hamilton
Wellcome Centre for the History of
Medicine
University of Glasgow

Mark Hathaway
Kellogg College
Oxford University

Tom Hayes
Mary Immaculate College
University of Limerick

Win Hayes
University of Edinburgh

Roger Helmer
East Midlands MEP

Grant Jarvie
Department of Sports Studies
University of Stirling

Martin Johnes
St Martin's College
Lancaster

Joyce Kay
Department of Sports Studies
University of Stirling

Rob Light
International Centre for Sports
History and Culture
De Montfort University

Emma Lile
Museum of Welsh Life
St Fagans, Cardiff

Malcolm MacCallum
Curator of the History of Sport
National Museums of Scotland

John Martin
Department of International and
Historical Studies
De Montfort University

Richard McBrearty
Scottish Football Museum

Gordon T. Mellor
De Montfort University

Alan Metcalfe
University of Windsor
Canada

Guy Osborn
University of Westminster

Catriona M. Parratt
University of Iowa

Roland Renson
Chairman Flemish Folk
Games Central
Chairman of the Sport Museum
of Flanders
Faculty of Physical Education
and Physiotherapy
Katholieke Universiteit Leuven,
Belgium

David B. Smith
Research Associate
National Museums of Scotland

John Tolson
Biggleswade

Mike Tripp
College of St Mark and St John
Plymouth

Wray Vamplew
Department of Sports Studies
University of Stirling

Annette Walsh
Department of Sports Studies
University of Stirling

Contextual Essay
Traditional Rural Sports in Europe

Introduction

One of the most successful cultural products of Great Britain is its legacy of standardised games. These British sports, which did not even require the preceding designation of 'British', were exported and – together with the Union Jack – implanted into the most remote corners of the Empire by colonial explorers, missionaries and entrepreneurs (McIntosh 1968; Holt 1989; Guttmann 1994; Mangan 2003). British sports were also eagerly imitated and adopted by Anglophile dandies on the Continent who called themselves sportsmen (Thibault 1976).

The term 'football' was never translated into French. The Spanish and Portuguese used the onomatopoeic words *futbol* and *futebol*. The Germanic languages adopted a neologist translation, which became *fussball* in German, *voetbal* in Dutch, *fotboll* in Swedish, etc. Only the Italians stuck to their own renaissance terminology of *calcio*.

By a strange turn of history, however, it was a French baron, Pierre de Coubertin, who turned this British sporting craze into the largest international social movement of the twentieth century, recapturing the term 'Olympic' from the ancient Greek past. The founder of the modern Olympic Games glorified Thomas Arnold (1795–1842) of Rugby College as the inventor of modern sport (Boulongne 1975; Ulmann 1997: 326–9). Coubertin, who was a moralist not a scholar, needed a link between, on the one hand, his ideal to reform France's society and school system and, on the other hand, athletic games: '. . . and he needed that link embodied in a single, distant, exotic, kind, and fatherly figure of patriotic and progressive genius to serve him as an imago and the new France as a model. Because he needed Arnold to be this man, so he made him to be' (MacAloon 1981: 79).

Coubertin – like many of his contemporaries – believed in unilinear progress, expressed in the 'citius, altius, fortius' ideal, borrowed from Dominican father Henri Didon (Arvin-Bérod 1994). Cultural change in the realm of sports generally operates in one direction, from traditional to modern. Nevertheless every step on the road to modernity is contested by the traditionalists, who see, rightly, that 'a succession of minor adjustments culminates eventually in a major transformation' (Guttmann 1994: 158). This essay focuses on the reception, adoption or rejection of British sports on the Continent and on the survival and revival of traditional sports and games.

Coming to Terms with Terms:
Tradition, Rural, Sport

In an attempt to clarify why British islanders and continental Europeans still disagree – or simply misunderstand each other – when they bandy words about terms such as 'traditional rural sport', we will try to dig down to the roots of these different cultural perceptions.

Tradition

The word 'tradition' comes from the Latin verb *tradere*, which means 'to hand over' or 'to hand down'. It lies also at the origin of the English word 'trade', originally meaning to make an exchange with or doing business with.

The German historians Johann Gustav Droysen (1868) and Ernst Bernheim (1889) defined *tradition* as the conscious process of preserving something for posterity. By contrast, *relics* are remains that were not consciously intended. Many traditions are, moreover, not very ancient but are in fact phenomena often quite recently invented, as shown by Eric Hobsbawm and Terence Ranger (1992) in a collection of articles. One of these articles, by Hugh Trevor-Roper on the invention of the Highland tradition of Scotland, focuses particularly – and not without irony – on the origin of the kilt in the eighteenth century.

At the end of the nineteenth century and during the period before the First World War, all over Europe ethnographers and pedagogists collected and tried to preserve the play customs of their regions. Folklorists such as Ter Gouw for the Netherlands (1871), Gomme for England, Scotland and Ireland (1894/1898), Boehme for Germany (1897), De Cock and Teirlinck for Belgian Flanders (1902–8) and D'Allemagne (1903) for France devoted themselves to inventory the 'lore' of traditional games. They mainly focused on children's games because children were considered by the evolutionists as primitive beings and their behavioural patterns were supposed to reflect survivals of adult activities in so-called earlier societies (see Renson 1984). That descriptive ethnographic tradition was continued by Iona and Peter Opie for England (1969).

Scepticism about economic progress and about the modern sports movement, which was accused of a colonial and imperialist ideology, emanated from the culture of student revolt and protest in the late 1960s (Eichberg 1984). This contestation movement also contributed to the traditionalist revival in ecological, historical and cultural spheres (Renson 1984, 1997; Eichberg 1991). 'Make love not war' was paraphrased as 'play folk games not sports'. Moreover, the macroscopic process of globalisation in sport, which has been characterised by Joseph Maguire (1999: 212–13) as 'a balance and blend between diminishing contrasts and increasing varieties', also appears to reawaken and promote traditional national or regional habitus codes. Globalisation thus seems to go hand in hand with localisation. Symptomatic of this tandem operation of 'glocalisation' were two European seminars on traditional games, which used the slogan 'think global, act local'. The first was organised in Vila Real (Portugal) in 1988 and the second in Leuven (Belgium) in 1990. The unification of Europe has thus not only stimulated claims for more autonomy on regional levels, it has also revitalised festivals and societies of local traditional games, which were dormant or might have died out completely (Renson 1997). The concept of 'ludodiversity' (Renson 2004) has been introduced to explain the mechanisms of extinction, survival and invention of movement cultures and to warn against a modern sport monoculture.

An exponent of this heightened awareness of local sporting knowledge was the creation of the European Traditional Sports and Games Association (ETSGA) in Lesneven (Brittany) in 2001. The founding members represented national or regional traditional sport federations from Aragon (Spain), Brittany (France), Cantabria (Spain), Flanders (Belgium), France, Ireland, Italy, Picardy (France), Spain, Scotland, and Valle d'Aosta (Italy). At the 2003 meeting in Doornzele (Flanders/Belgium) the Netherlands and Catalonia (Spain) joined the association.

Sports and games and their paraphernalia have in the meantime become salient items of the so-called heritage cult and found their way to museums and halls of fame. David Lowenthal, who has written a critical and provocative work entitled *The Heritage Crusade and the Spoils of History*, says that from about 1980 'All at once heritage is everywhere . . . It is the chief focus of patriotism and a prime lure of tourism . . . Every legacy is cherished, from ethnic roots to history theme parks' (Lowenthal 1998: xiii). Lowenthal asserts that patrimony ceases everywhere to be exclusive to elites, but that for the working class heritage is more likely to mean folkways (faiths, foods and forms of music and dance). Strangely, in the whole book, which is richly documented with source references and with hundreds of examples of the heritage craze, sports and games are never mentioned. This is surprising, but it seems to prove Lowenthal's (1998: 156) own contention that 'What heritage does not highlight it often hides'.

Finally, one will notice that when sport is linked with tradition, most nations of continental Europe – unlike Great Britain – prefer the terms 'games' or 'play forms' instead of 'sports'. This is due to the fact that on the Continent the term sport has been associated with modern standardised games and athletic competitions, imported from Great Britain, and not with the local traditional movement culture. This is analysed further during the discussion on the concept of 'sport'.

Rural

The word 'rural' stems from the Latin term *rus*, meaning the country, the field or a rural estate, and stands in contrast to *urbs*, the town.

Contrasts between rural and urban originated when large-scale agriculture enabled efficient food production. This technological development, around 3000 BC, enabled humans to live in permanent settlements. This led in turn to 'civilisation', which literally means that people became city dwellers. *Civitas* is Latin for city and 'civilised' points at the lifestyle of the citizen, the civilian or burgher, in contrast to the lifestyle of the farmer. The origin and growth of the medieval towns in Europe is linked with the conquests of the raiding Norsemen at the end of the ninth century and then with the Crusades (Evans 1969). The medieval merchants and craftsmen who flocked together for economic and military purposes surrounded their settlements with walls. They strove to become independent for the defence of their lord's castle or the abbey and developed their own urban militia. The origin of the archery gilds of the cities dates back to the fourteenth century (Renson 1976, 1980). Industrial life within the city walls and agricultural life in the country became another marked medieval contrast.

Historian Slicher van Bath (1977: 215) has pointed out that after the peasant wars in the first half of the sixteenth century the social perception of the peasants underwent a drastic change. From then on they were depicted in grotesque postures, drinking, dancing and playing games during village fairs and festivals (Renson and De Vroede 1986–7). This 'genre' of peasant drinking and sporting scenes became very popular through the oeuvre of Pieter Bruegel the Elder (1525/30–69) and his sons and was later continued by David Teniers (1610–90). It pleased the burghers to look down at the uncivilised behaviour of the country folk, thus keeping their social distance, but also expressing their envy because of the rise in corn prices. This class of well-to-do burghers became more and more important and developed a lifestyle 'apart'. The proud burghers of Bruges not only challenged the legal privileges of feudal mobility, these nouveaux riches also imitated their sports. They organised, for instance, a tournament with English merchants in 1305 (Van Winter 1974: 590–9). It seems that the members of this city patriciate acted according to the principle 'we live a noble life, therefore we are nobility' (Van den Abeele 2000: 59–67).

The concept of civilisation has been analysed by Norbert Elias (1939, 1978) as a dynamic process of technological, social, scientific and ideological accomplishments which characterise Western nations and of which they are proud. These are the results of a long-term, all-encompassing process, which accompanied the rise of the major European cities in Italy, France, the Low Countries and Germany. The Latin concept of *civitas*, *civilité* in French, gained its new specific meaning and function in the second half of the sixteenth century. This new interpretation, from 'citylike' to 'well behaved', started with the publication of Erasmus's *De Civilitate Morum Puerilium* in 1530. The book became a bestseller on the polite manners (civility) of boys. The first chapter focuses on bodily functions and the sixth (out of seven) chapter deals with play. Norbert Elias and Eric Dunning (1986) have further analysed the civilising process in sport and qualified it as 'a quest for excitement'.

Peter McIntosh (1968: 29–30) pointed out that when Joseph Strutt wrote his comprehensive survey of British sport in 1801, he classified sports under three broad headings: 'rural exercises practised by persons of rank', 'rural exercises generally practised' and 'pastimes usually exercised in towns and cities, or places adjoining them'. These were geographical and social distinctions, which fitted the social situation at the end of the eighteenth century, but they allowed Strutt to trace – throughout history – the fundamental distinctions between rural and urban and between aristocratic and plebeian.

It is striking that the eighteenth-century *New English Dictionary* defined a *sportsman* as: 'a man who follows, engages in, or practises sport, esp. one who hunts, or shoots wild animals or game for pleasure' (in Hirn 1936: 22). This rural connotation of sport also resounds from D. P. Blaine's *An Encyclopaedia of Rural Sports*, published in London in 1840. Football was at that time still so slightly regarded that it was not even mentioned by Blaine, whereas badger-baiting was included. Hunting and fishing also completely dominate in the artistically illustrated work of E. D. Cuming (1909), *British Sport: Past and Present*.

When the Earl of Suffolk and Berkshire edited the new and enlarged edition of *The Encyclopaedia of Sports and Games* in 1911 he was well aware that the word 'sport' had a far larger meaning than ten years before. His encyclopedia attempted to bring together 'information essential to the different sports and games which constitute the pastimes of civilised man' (Suffolk and Berkshire 1911: preface). Whereas an article on bicycling had been included in the original edition (of 1900) 'with some hesitation', now all kinds of locomotion, on land and in the air, found their proper place in the new edition. Still, however, out of the 229 entries, 198 (73 per cent) dealt with hunting and fishing, especially the sorts of animals and fishes that can be hunted or caught. The other 61 entries ranged from aeronautics to yachting and covered such topics as 'lassoing' and 'obsolete sports', such as badger, bear and bull baiting, and cockfighting. The Chief Scout, Robert Baden-Powell, wrote the entry on 'pig sticking or hog-hunting': 'a sport unique of its kind; it is the first sport of India, and one which especially commends itself to the Briton, owing to the fact that it includes the use of a horse in bringing to terms a fast, bold, and dangerous quarry' (pp. 314–9).

The notion of *rural sports* is not a very common descriptor in historical or sociological sport research in continental Europe. However, significant differences in sports participation in rural and urban areas appear in surveys in Europe. In 1969 the percentages of sport participation in Belgium still differed strongly, ranging from 34 per cent to 62 per cent for men and from 9 per cent to 40 per cent for women, between extreme categories of rural villages on the one hand and big cities on the other (Renson *et al.* 2004). In the meantime, however, the differences have gradually faded and a general increase in sports participation has been noticed for the years between 1969 and 1999. Sport participation percentages for the rural and urban extremes are now 51 per cent versus 84 per cent for men and 68 per cent versus 77 per cent for women. These drastic changes cannot only be attributed to the impact of 'sport-for-all' campaigns, but also to major socio-geographical changes over the past 30 years. Rich city dwellers moved to the countryside and poor immigrants settled mainly in the big cities. Of even greater importance than the participation figures were the contrasts in sports participation preferences between rural and urban dwellers. In 1969, korfball, field hockey and basketball appeared as the most frequently practised sports in urban milieux. The rural population was characterised by its preference for 'the world game', soccer, and traditional sports, such as angling, archery and 'kaatsen' (traditional handball) (Renson and Vermeulen 1972). Thirty years later, basketball has lost its urban character and the typical city sports are now – apart from korfball – kayaking, rowing, posture training and yoga. Road and cross-country cycling, dance, hunting and archery are now the most popular rural sports (Scheerder *et al.* 2002: 81–3).

The practitioner of traditional games in Flanders is commonly stereotyped as an elderly lower-class male from the countryside. When this stereotype was confronted with survey data from the Flemish Folk Games File in 1981 (Renson and Smulders 1981), these prejudices were confirmed, except for the rural characteristic. It seemed indeed that Flanders still had a strong tradition of folk games deeply rooted in town and city life (Renson, De Cramer and De Vroede 1997). In 2002 a new Flemish survey was conducted, which has brought to light some conspicuous changes in the profile of the 'common traditional gamester' over the past two decades. Several forms of traditional games have shown a decrease in their numbers of practitioners, as with both vertical and horizontal popinjay shooting, and others have almost disappeared or are on the verge of extinction, such as *struifvogel*, a kind of darts. In contrast to 20 years ago, most traditional games are no longer exclusively male 'game preserves'. The participation rate of women rose, and varied from 6 per cent to 42 per cent, according to the kind of game. However, the mean age of the practitioners has increased by almost ten years. The already low socio-professional status of the practitioners has dropped even lower and the socio-geographical status has become definitely more rural than urban. At first sight, these observations appear to be bad omens for the future of traditional games (Renson *et al.* 2004).

Sport

John Arlott wrote in his *Pageantry of Sport* (1968) that games are truly part of the history of a nation and reflect the social life of the people and the changes in economy, religion and politics:

> There are some games of which history barely makes mention. Until they made some deep impact on events, and affected the law, taxation or finance, they were accepted as part of life, but not considered worthy of the attention of serious historians.
>
> (Arlott 1968: 14)

Alas, Arlott erred when he wrote that 'what is now generally called "sport" – a word which existed in no other language except English . . . now has been adopted into many' (Arlott 1968: 17). The etymology of the word 'sport' goes back to the Latin verb *de(s)portare*, which literally means to 'carry away'. Nowadays millions of people all over Europe are indeed 'carried away' by their favourite sport, either as a participant or as a spectator. The verb first occurred in thirteenth-century France as *desporter* in the sense of to amuse, entertain, divert, distract oneself. It made its appearance in early fourteenth-century England as 'disporter'. A 'disporteress' was, for instance, the name for a female acrobat in the fifteenth century. In the sixteenth century one finds 'sporter' and 'sporteer', and from then onwards the abbreviated term *sport* begins to dominate (Hirn 1936: 22).

In the 1542 edition of *Gargantua and Pantagruel*, François Rabelais described how Panocrates made his pupil Gargantua read for three hours, then they '*se desportoient*' (diverted themselves) in a nearby tennis hall where they played ball, tennis and the triangle ballgame, 'elegantly exercising their bodies like they had exercised their souls before' (Rabelais 1542: 118).

In *The Compleat Gamester* by Charles Cotton (1674), no distinction was made between activities that demand physical effort (such as bowls and archery) and those that are played indoors and sedentary (such as chess and card games). The term game is derived from the Saxon word *gamen*, meaning 'play', 'pleasure', 'sport' or 'gaming'. For Cotton, the term 'game' was virtually synonymous with gambling, as shown in his description of cock fighting: 'Cocking is sport or pastime so full of delight and pleasure, that I know not any game in that respect is to be preferred before it' (Cotton 1674: 206).

Gambling means 'indulging in those games, or exercises, in which chance assumes a more important character and where the money motive increases, as chance predominates over skill' (Ashton 1899: 2). Dennis Brailsford (1969: 214–19) has pointed out that in the later seventeenth century 'sport' and 'exercise' were considered as two quite different and separable things and that no awareness of evil in cruelty towards animals troubled men before the second half of the eighteenth century.

Throughout the ancien régime the majority of British sports and pastimes did not differ fundamentally from those on the Continent. Joseph Strutt (1801: 1) admitted that 'many of them originated on the continent' and Jean-Jules Jusserand (1901: 1) commented exactly 100 years later that 'Athletic exercises are fashionable these days in France; this is not a new fashion, nor is it an English fashion, it is a renovated French fashion'.

Henry Alken described in the amply illustrated publication *The National Sports of Great Britain* of 1821 the following activities: hunting on horseback, hawking, gun shooting, angling, horse racing, animal fights, pugilism and dressage. The common feature of all these pastimes was that they were practised by aristocratic gentlemen, so-called sportsmen: 'C'est au classes opulentes de la société que cet amusement est surtout nécessaire puisque n'ayant ne le besoin, ni la volonté de faire du travail un plaisir, elles se font du plaisir une occupation' (Alken 1821: preface).

The first signs of the revolutionary change in the nature of sport appeared during the first half of the nineteenth century in the public schools and in the universities of Oxford and Cambridge, where the association between sport and character-training was taken for granted. The public schools were the workshops where some specific forms of traditional (football) games were modernised. The peculiar balance between freedom and control of the schoolboys in these institutions formed the necessary conditions for the occurrence of this process (McIntosh 1968: 57–79; Dunning 1976; Dunning and Sheard 1979; Mangan 1981).

Thoroughbred horse races were the harbingers of the modern sport movement from Great Britain on the Continent. They made their very first appearance in the elite health resort of Spa in the Belgian Ardennes in 1773. Significantly, the English term sport, the shortened version of French *desport*, first appeared in France in 1828 in the *Journal des Haras* (Journal of the Stud Farms) (Thibault 1976). Louis Barron commented in 1891 (p. 175) that 'Those privileged by fortune, who have adopted sport, gave it an air of elegance. It is "bon ton" now, but the games are dead certain old games.' Thibault (1976) has claimed that French sport originated from two different currents: a national one based on the traditional *desport* (amusements and games) of the popular classes, and an aristocratic one borrowed from England at the start of the nineteenth century. Le Havre Athletic Club was the first English sports club in France and was founded in 1872 by British expatriates. But it was young Anglophile Frenchmen, so-called 'dandies', who founded the first and most important clubs in 1882: the Racing Club and its rival Stade Français. Lord Seymour, France's most famous 'dandy', became the first president of the Jockey Club, founded in 1833. Its motto was *Faire le bien en s'amusant*. Only gradually did a distinction occur between 'turf' and 'sport', between 'sportsman' and *sportif* (Thibault 1976).

Georges de Saint-Clair (1845–1910) and later Pierre de Coubertin (1863–1937) were the pioneers who aligned British sport with the cause of social renewal in France after the defeat of 1870. Coubertin (1889) wrote, for instance, a treatise on *L'Éducation Anglaise en France*. Others, such as Paschal Grousset (*fl*.1880s) and Philippe Tissié (1852–1935), felt that the new sporting Anglomania was too much a slavish imitation of the English. Therefore in 1888 they founded organisations of their own: the Ligue Nationale d'Education Physique and the Ligue Girondine de l'Education Physique, respectively. They advocated a revival of traditional forms of French sport, such as *barette* (a rugby variant), *mail* (pall mall) and other ancient ball games (Thibault 1976; Holt 1981, 2001; Arnaud and Camy 1986; Meunier 1989). Grousset published a sport encyclopedia, under the pseudonym of Philippe Daryl (1894), in which he presented a *mélange* of relatively new British ball games (such as rugby, soccer and lawn tennis) and traditional French ones (such as *soule*, *paume* and *crosse*).

Horse races were also the first symptoms of the British sports invasion in Germany in the 1820s. The English Rowing Club was founded in Hamburg in 1830 by members of the English colony. Their example was followed by local merchants of the Hansa, who created the Hamburger Ruderclub in 1836 (Eichberg 1980; Langenfeld 1988). The aficionados of modern British sports clashed with the apologists of German *turnen* in a *kulturkampf* between new and old bourgeoisie. Christiane Eisenberg (1999) has presented the thesis that modern sport is a cultural expression of the competitive principle, which is, historically speaking, a universal principle of the middle class. This explains why sport in Germany was adopted and propagated by the bourgeoisie from the large cities, the latter in contrast to the sport's country of origin. The so-called *Spielbewegung* (Games Movement) propagated from its foundation in 1891 onwards the rediscovery, invention and popularisation of games and outdoor activities. These also included British sport games, which were, however, often criticised for their competitiveness or brutality. The Games Movement thus occupied a more moderate position, in-between the extreme standpoints of the 'Turners' (the practitioners of *turnen*) on the one hand and the sportsmen on the other (Preising 1980; Steins 1982; Hamer 1989; Prange 1996; Pfister 1997).

In Belgium the struggle against modern British sport was fought – and eventually lost – by a strange entente 'non-cordiale' of Flemish nationalists, socialists,

Christian-democrats and the advocates of the rival *Turnen* and Swedish gymnastics systems. They each had their own arguments for rejecting this 'English illness' (as modern sport was sometimes called). Flemish nationalists rejected British sports as non-indigenous; socialists considered them snobbish; Christian-democrats considered them undemocratic; German Turners blamed them for not being educational; and Swedish gymnasts accused them of not being scientific (Renson 1998a, 1998b)

Allen Guttmann (1978), who analysed the modernisation process of sport, has distinguished seven characteristics of modern sports, as contrasted with those of primitive, ancient and pre-industrial eras. These seven characteristics are secularism, equality of opportunity to compete and the conditions of competition, specialisation of roles, rationalisation (research, training methods, etc.), bureaucratic organisation, quantification (sports 'stats') and the quest for records. Guttmann's taxonomy came under heavy fire in a coordinated attack by John Marshall Carter and Arnd Krüger (1990) in which they brought together evidence that both the quantification and the record mania had precursors in primitive times, in ancient and medieval Europe. Although Guttmann's analysis took a few blows, it was largely upheld and still proves to be a valuable tool for comparing, for instance, traditional rural sports with modern sports in Europe or elsewhere.

Unity and Diversity of Traditional Sports in Europe

As already mentioned, interest in traditional sports has revived in recent years, and they have received official encouragement from the Council of Europe and from national, regional or local authorities. This is reflected in a series of recent publications on traditional sports, summarised in Table 1. Only books that direct their attention more to what has survived than to what once existed and that have been published since 1970 were selected. For this reason, some interesting historical contributions were excluded, such as *Man at Play: Nine Centuries of Pleasure Making* (Armitage 1977), *Fun and Games in Old Europe* (Endrei and Zolnay 1988), *Popular Recreations in English Society 1700–1850* (Malcolmson 1973), *Den Folkliga Idrotten* [Folk games in Sweden] (Hellspong 2000) and *Der Wettkampf in Der Alten Eidgenossenschaft* (Schaufelberger 1972).

The works listed in Table 1 are all books that include descriptions of a variety of traditional games, either from one region or a country, or from all over Europe or all over the world. Works on individual traditional games or on children's games, of which there are many, are not included.

Rather than looking at traditional games by country or region, the following sections follow the typology adopted during the second European Seminar on Traditional Games (Renson, Manson and De Vroede 1991). The typology is helpful because both countries and traditional games can be influenced by wider social and political changes, as for instance indicated by the title *Old Yugoslavian Games* (Cvetković 1982), a term which has in the meantime become anachronistic. This overview is a revised version of the chapter on traditional sports in Europe by Renson (1996).

Table 1 Recent books on traditional games in Europe (since 1970)

Coverage	Publication
International	Pfister, Niewerth and Steins 1996 Gounot, Niewerth and Pfister 1996 Levinson and Christensen 1996 Liponski 2003
Europe	Gorini 1994 Barreau and Jaouen 1998, 2001
Aragon	Maestro Guerrero 1996
Basque region	Aguirre Franco 1971
Brittany	Beaulieu and Ronné 2002 Ferré 2002
Canary Islands	Navarro Adelantado, Noda Gomez and Hernandez Auta 1994
Denmark	Møller 1990–1
England	Finn 1981
	Taylor 1992
Flanders	Jespers *et al.* 1982a, 1982b De Vroede 1996
France	Trémaud 1972
Galicia	Veiga 2001
Ireland	Healy 1998
Low Countries	Botermans, Visser and Burrett 1991
Nord and Pas de Calais	Delporte 1981 Dupuis and Dhote 2000
Picardy	Loubère 2000
Portugal	Cabral 1981
Scotland	Webster 1973
Spain	Moreno Palos 1992
Valle d'Aosta	Daudry 1981
Yugoslavia	Cvetković 1982

Ball Games

There is a rich variety of traditional ball games. They can be played by hand or foot or with a batting device. Traditional European team handball games include *pärkspel* on the Swedish island of Gotland, *kaatsen* or *balle pelote* in the Dutch province of Frisia and in Belgium and France, *pallone elastico* in Italy, and *pelota* in Spanish Valencia or in the Basque country. Most of the ancient and violent football forms have disappeared and have been replaced by modern soccer or rugby, except for the traditional *calcio fiorentino* in Florence (Italy). Some ball games, such as Gaelic football in Ireland, are played with both hands and feet.

All kinds of batting devices are used, from racquets, as in real tennis and in France's *longue paume* game, to the sticks that are used to play *crosse*, a variant of golf played in northern France and Belgium, or in the rather rough team games of shinty in Scotland and hurling in Ireland. In the game of *tsan* in Valle d'Aosta, the ball is launched from a bent wooden pole with a bat. It is related to the Swiss game of *hornuss*, where the balls are intercepted with large bats, thrown in the air. Other ball games make use of a tambourine (France and Italy), a forearm cover, or *bracchiale*, as in the Italian *pallone*, or a *chistera*, as in the spectacular *jai alai* of the Basques.

Bowl and Pin Games

Bowl games are played with a solid spherical object that is either rolled or thrown at a target. In pin games, targets are knocked down. Italian *bocce* and the French *jeu de boules* are now also played far from their original home countries. A special case is the game of *closh*, which at the time of Erasmus (1469–1536) and Bruegel the Elder (1525–69) was popular all over Europe. In this game, a shovel-shaped bat is used to roll a heavy round bowl through an iron ring fixed in the ground. The game is still frequently played in the Belgian and Dutch provinces of Limburg, where it is known as *beugelen*, and in the adjacent region in Germany. Moreover, the same type of game has a variant in Portugal (*jogo do aro*) and on the Lipari Islands near Sicily (*pallaporta*).

Apart from the well-known flat green bowls, which spread from England to the former British colonies, a wide variety of bowling games are found in Britain and in the central and southern European countries. *Ruzzola* is a form of 'cheese rolling' played in central Italy, where heavy wooden discs are rolled for distance in a number of throws. The game of skittles or nine pins has several variants, some of which are highly standardised or mechanised, such as *kegeln* in Germany and *quilles* in France and bordering countries. Other pin games range from *Karelian pins*, in which a stick is thrown instead of a bowl, to *pendelkegeln* (Germany and Hungary), in which the bowl swung at the pins hangs on a wire. *Eisschiessen* in Austria and curling in Scotland are variants of bowling, but played on ice.

Throwing Games

In Sweden's traditional *varpa* game the projectiles are heavy discs. Smaller discs or coins, or sometimes stones, are used in both children's and adult's throwing games, such as quoits in England and *malha* in Portugal. *Barra*, a particular type of javelin throwing, is practised in northern Spain; an iron bar weighing 3.5 kilograms and measuring 1.5 metres is launched after several body rotations. Hammer throwing and tossing the caber are typical events of the well-known Scottish Highland Games. A log-throwing event virtually identical to caber-tossing is found in Portugal, where it is known as *jogo do panco*, and in Sweden, where it goes by the name of *stang-störtning*. The latter game was demonstrated at the occasion of the 1912 Olympic Games in Stockholm, together with *pärkspel*, *varpa* and *glima-wrestling*. Stone-putting is practised in the traditional festivals of Swiss farmers in the Alps and stone lifting and stone dragging in the Basque region. In Brittany, strong men show their skill in pole lifting and cart-axle lifting. The *levantamiento del arado* on the Canary Islands consists of lifting the pole and yokes of an ox-cart. Bretons and the Irish compete in tossing a sheaf or bale of hay over a high cross-beam with the help of a pitchfork.

The game known as road bowls in Ireland, *klootschieten* in the Netherlands and *bosseln* or *klootschiessen* in East Frisia (Germany) is an interesting example of both the expression of regional ethnic identity and the growing international awareness of traditional games. In 1969, three independent groups of bowling enthusiasts representing the three games joined together to form the International Bowl Playing Association. *Tiro de bola* is a Spanish variant of the same type of game and is played in the Aragon region.

Toad in the hole is an English pub game, which has several continental variants. The French version is *jeu de grenouille*, which in turn is called *la rana* in Spain, *jogo do sapo* in Portugal and *pudebak* in Flanders. In these continental games the 'toad' – actually a frog – is a bronze replica of the animal, and its open mouth is the main target to throw at. In England, however, the toad is a thick, heavy, brass disc which is thrown. The target hole is enshrined within a specially made wooden box on four legs.

Shooting Games

Shooting games have flourished in all cultures and have evolved into modern high-tech sports. Popinjay shooting, in which the target is a 'jay' or set of 'jays' attached to a tall mast, is depicted in many medieval and Renaissance paintings and prints and is still a very popular traditional sport in Flanders (Belgium). It was even featured in the 1900 Paris Olympic Games and the 1920 Antwerp Olympic Games.

Some present-day crossbow guilds in Flanders originated in the fourteenth and fifteenth centuries and can thus be considered as the oldest sports clubs in Europe. The impressive crossbow-shooting festivals of the Italian *balestrieri* (crossbow-men), such as are held in the cities of Gubbio, San Sepolcro and San Marino, also have a long historical pedigree. Witnessing the pageantry of such competitions of crossbowmen competing to win a *palio* (flag) is like stepping back into the past. When firearms were introduced, many archery and crossbow societies replaced their traditional weapons with culverins or carbines. These associations of riflemen, especially in Germany and Austria, but also in Denmark, are highly organised and have preserved to a notable extent their character as patriarchal men's clubs, especially in rural areas.

Fighting Games

Wrestling is probably the oldest and the most universal traditional sport of human-kind. So-called Greco-Roman wrestling, which has acquired official Olympic status, has no connection with the wrestling styles of Greek and Roman antiquity. The type of wrestling practised during the ancient Olympic Games has much more in common with present-day *pelivan* (Turkish wrestling) or even with modern judo. In Europe, international competitions have been staged, in which *glima* wrestlers from Iceland were matched with adepts of the *lucha canaria* (Canary wrestling) style practised in the Canary Islands. Moreover, an International Federation of Celtic Wrestling was founded in 1985, bringing together Icelandic *glima*, Scottish backhold and Breton *gouren*.

In *savate*, also called French boxing, both fists and feet are employed to hit the opponent; this traditional sport is structurally related to Thai kickboxing. *La canne* (stick fighting) was also once popular in France. *Jogo do pau* is a Portuguese version of stick fighting with some similarities to Japanese kendo.

Tilting, the favourite sport of the knights of medieval Europe, was officially abolished in France in 1559 when King Henry II was mortally wounded in a confrontation with his captain of the guard, Montgommery. However, some of its variants have survived. They include ring tilting and quintain, which can be practised either on land or water. Ring tilting is still very popular in the Dutch province of Zealand, and quintain is practised at the yearly festival of Foligno in Italy. Similar jousts are held on water, as in the case of the *joutes girondines* (jousts from the Gironde area) in France and the *fischerstechen* (fishermen-tilting) in Ulm in Germany. *Kufenstechen* is an equestrian game in Feistriz in Austria in which the rider must break a barrel, fixed to a post, with a short iron lance.

Forms of swordplay have been practised throughout Europe for centuries. Many of these sports have been highly ritualised and stylised in an endeavour to make them less lethal. Special protective gear is worn by practitioners of sports such as fencing, which has had Olympic status since the first modern Olympic Games were held in Athens in 1896.

Tug of war was practised for the last time as an Olympic event during the Antwerp Games in 1920, but international competition is still organised by the Tug of War International Federation (TWIF).

Animal Games

Several animal games have gained a reputation as 'blood sports' in the course of history and have been officially banned in many countries. Such cruel sports as bull baiting and bear baiting were popular in medieval and sixteenth- and seventeenth-century England, but these baitings, in which specially trained bull-dogs were used, have not survived the so-called civilising process. Cockfighting, however, is still very popular in the north of France. In Belgium and other countries where cockfights are illegal, these games still have their clandestine but loyal supporters.

Animals are also matched in fair competitions, as in pigeon racing and dog racing. In most of these animal competitions, people train and coach the animals.

In cock crowing and finch warbling, the birds compete more peacefully in singing competitions, crowing or warbling as many times as possible in a set time period.

In other cases, people engage in direct and hazardous confrontation with animals, as in bull-running in France and Spain, and bull-fighting in France, Portugal and Spain. Goose-riding and other similar 'games', in which animals such as geese, ducks or cocks are decapitated, survive in most of the Catholic regions of Europe.

Locomotion Games

Some traditional hill races are part of the Scottish Highland Games and of the Grasmere sports festivals in the English Lake District. *Fierljeppen* (jumping for distance with a fen-pole) has survived in the Dutch province of Frisia as a spectacular form of pole vaulting over smaller rivers. Even more spectacular, however, is the *salto del pastor* (shepherd's jump) practised on the Canary Islands, in which a leaping pole is used to jump off cliffs and hill slopes.

Among the Sami people of Norway, Sweden and Finland, who depended almost entirely for their subsistence on their reindeer, traditional sports tend to highlight riding skills, such as during reindeer-sledge races. The famous *Palio* of Siena, a traditional annual horse race in the very heart of the old Italian town, attracts so many visitors that it is now an internationally known tourist attraction.

Traditional rowing contests (for men and women) are held yearly during the *regatta storica* (ancient regatta) of Venice in Italy and during the *regattas de traineras* (whaling boats) in the bay of San Sebastian in the Spanish Basque country. In Cornwall, the Falmouth Working Boat Association was formed some years ago to regulate the old style regattas for the river Truro oyster-dredgers.

Acrobatics

In all cultures, people try to keep in good physical shape by performing coded sets of physical exercises. Because of the limitations of the human neuromuscular system, which has hardly changed since the emergence of *Homo sapiens*, acrobatic performances are strikingly similar regardless of historical period or culture. The acrobatics that we see in the modern circus are, for example, very similar to those performed in the arenas of ancient Rome. Nor are the vaults and somersaults of modern gymnastics very different from the tumbling exercises described in 1599 by the Italian professional acrobat Tuccaro (1536–1604). Vaulting and acrobatics on real horses were performed during the 1920 Antwerp Olympic Games. *Salto del caballo* (horse jumping) is still practised in the Aragon region of Spain.

The *Cong-Fou* gymnastic exercises of the Chinese Taoist monks described by the French Jesuit Amiot in 1779 had so much in common with the Swedish gymnastics system of Per Henrik Ling (1776–1839) that the French author Nicolas Dally (1857: 155) was tempted to believe that Ling had simply copied them.

Turnen, the special German apparatus gymnastics created by Friedrich Ludwig Jahn (1778–1852), has evolved into the internationally established discipline of

Olympic gymnastics. The early Turner movement nevertheless also cherished so-called *volkstümliche spiele* (ethnic games) as a part of its nationalist philosophy. A striking example of traditional acrobatics is the *castells* or human pyramids formed by amateur gymnasts in Barcelona (Spain) as towering symbols of their Catalan identity.

Conclusions

A first observation is that traditional forms of play and physical activity are generally not qualified as 'sports' in continental Europe. Neither are they qualified as 'rural', with the only exception of an anthology on rural games from Aragon in Spain (Maestro Guerrero 1996). They are usually referred to in terms of popular or traditional play forms or games: *jeux* (Belgium and France), *jogos* (Portugal), *juegos* (Spain), *lege* (Denmark), *lekar* (Sweden), *spelen* (Belgium and Netherlands) and *Spiele* (Germany). Scandinavians use the idiosyncratic term *idraet/idrett/idrott* (movement activity), or combinations such as *gamle idraetslege* (Danish for 'old movement play forms') or *folkliga idrotten* (Swedish for 'folk movement activities'). An exception is the neologist term *volkssport* (Dutch for 'folk sport'), introduced in Flanders to distinguish the traditional games of adults from *volksspel* (Dutch for 'folk play') which is commonly associated with traditional children's games (Renson and Smulders 1981). On the rare occasion that the term 'sport' is used, it is then associated with the adjective 'old' or 'popular'.

The reasons for these terminological confusions are twofold. The first is of a semantic nature, namely the fact that most European languages – unlike English – have no word for 'game'. Dutch, French, German, Italian, Spanish, Portuguese and Swedish have only one word for both concepts of 'play' and 'games': *spel, jeu, Spiel, gioco, juego, jogo* and *lek*. The second reason is of an historical-political nature; on the Continent the term 'sport' was always associated with the modern competitive physical activities imported from England.

A second observation is that traditional games vary widely in Europe, both in terms of frequency and appearance. This variation has been demonstrated by a comparative analysis of the types of games in four different regions in Europe. A great variety and high frequency of traditional games was found in the Basque region and in Flanders, and although both Gotland (Sweden) and Scotland cherish their local traditions, they have less variety in their heritage of games. Further, if one looks at the skills required for the games, it appears that physical strength is of great importance in the Basque region and Scotland. Strength is of less importance in Gotland and never seems to play a significant role in the traditional games of Flanders, where precision and agility are emphasised.

As final conclusion, it must be said that this regional gaze at the European landscape of traditional games points more towards diversity than unity (De Vroede and Renson 2004). Let us therefore become aware of and take care of this rich European 'ludodiversity'.

ROLAND RENSON

References

Aguirre Franco, R., *Juegos y Deportes Vascos* (San Sebastian: Auñamendi, 1971).

Alken, H., *The National Sports of Great Britain with Descriptions in English and French* (London: Thomas McLean, 1821).

Arlott. J., 'Pageantry of Sport', in Arlott, J. and Daley, A. (eds), *Pageantry of Sport: From the Age of Chivalry to the Age of Victoria* (London: Paul Elek, 1968), 12–53.

Armitage, J., *Man at Play: Nine Centuries of Pleasure Making* (London: Warne, 1977).

Arnaud, P. and Camy, J., *La Naissance du Mouvement Associatif en France* (Lyon: Presses Universitaires de Lyon, 1986).

Arvin-Bérod, A., *Et Didon Créa La Devise des Jeux Olympiques* (Enchirolles: Scirolius, 1994).

Ashton, J., *The History of Gambling in England* (London 1899; reprinted 1968, New York: Burt Franklin).

Barreau, J. J. and Jaouen, G. (eds), *Les Jeux Populaires: Eclipse et Renaissance* (Karaez: FALSAB, 1998).

Barreau, J. J. and Jaouen, G. (eds), *Les Jeux Traditionnels en Europe: Education, Culture et Société au XXIe Siècle* (Colloque de Plouguernau, 1999; FALSAB, 2001).

Barron, L., *Les Jeux: Jeux Historiques, Jeux Nationaux, Sports Modernes* (Paris: Laurens, 1891).

Beaulieu, F. and Ronné, H., *Les Jeux des Bretons* (Rennes: Ouest-France, 2002).

Bernheim, E., *Lehrbuch der Historischen Methode und der Geschichtsphilosophie* (Leipzig: Duncker, 1889).

Blaine, D. P., *An Encyclopaedia of Rural Sports: or a Complete Account, Historical, Practical and Descriptive of Hunting, Shooting, Fishing, Racing and Other Field Sports and Athletic Amusements of the Present Day* (London: Longman, 1840).

Boehme, F. M., *Deutsches Kinderlied und Kinderspiel* (Leipzig: Breitkopf-Härtel, 1897).

Botermans, J., Visser, N. and Burrett, T., *Timpelen, Hinkelen & Pierebollen: Spelen in de Lage Landen* (Van Holkema & Warendorf, 1991).

Boulongne, Y. P., *La Vie et L'Œuvre Pédagogique de Pierre de Coubertin 1863–1937* (Ottawa: Lemeac, 1975).

Brailsford, D., *Sport and Society: Elizabeth to Anne* (London: Routledge and Kegan Paul, 1969).

Cabral, A., *Jogos Populares Portugueses* (Porto: Domingo Barreira, 1981).

Carter, J. M. and Krüger, A. (eds), *Ritual and Record: Sports Records and Quantification in Pre-Modern Societies* (New York: Greenwood Press, 1990).

Cotton, C., *The Compleat Gamester* (London: A.M. for R. Cutler, 1674; reprinted 1972, London: Cornmarket Reprints).

Coubertin, P. de, *L'Éducation Anglaise en France* (Paris: Hachette, 1889).

Cuming, E. D., *British Sport: Past and Present* (London: Hodder & Stoughton, 1909).

Cvetković, J., *Stari Sportovi Jugoslavije* [The Ancient Sports of Yugoslavia] (Osijek: Stampa, 1982).

D'Allemagne, H. R., *Sports et Jeux D'Adresse* (Paris: Hachette, 1903).

Dally, N., *Cinésiologie ou Science du Movement dans ses Rapports avec L'Éducation, L'Hygiène et La Thérapie* (Paris: Librairie Centrale des Sciences, 1857).

Daryl, P., *Jeux de Balle et de Ballon: Football, Paume, Lawn Tennis par un Juge de Camp: Encyclopédie de Sport* (Paris: Librairies-Impr. Réunies, 1894).

Daudry, P., *Documenti di Sport Popolare* (Val d'Aosta: Federaxon Esport Nohtra Tera, 1981).

De Cock, A. and Teirlinck, I., *Kinderspel en Kinderlust in Zuid-Nederland* (Gent: Siffer, 8 vols, 1902–1908).

De Vroede, E., *Het Grote Volkssportenboek* (Leuven: Davidsfonds, 1996).

De Vroede, E. and Renson, R. (eds), *Proceedings of the Second European Seminar on Traditional Games* (Leuven: Vlaamse Volkssport Centrale, 1991).

De Vroede, E. and Renson, R., 'Unity or Diversity in Traditional Games in Europe? A Regional Approach', in Pfister, G. (ed.), *Games of the Past – Sports for the Future* (ISHPES seminar; TAFISA symposium; Duderstadt 2000) (Sankt Augustin: Academia, 2004).

Delporte, L., *Jeux D'Hier et D'Avant Hier dans le Nord Pas-de-Calais* (Roubaix: G.E.P., 1981).

Droysen, J. G., *Grundriss der Historik* (Leipzig: Veit, 1868).

Dunning, E., 'Industrialization and the Incipient Modernization of Football', *Stadion*, 1 (1976), 136–8.

Dunning, E. and Sheard, K., *Barbarians, Gentlemen and Players: A Sociological Study of the Development of Rugby Football* (Oxford: Martin Robertson, 1979).

Dupuis, V. and Dhote, S., *Jeux, Fêtes et Traditions dans le Nord et le Pas-de-Calais* (Rennes: Ouest-France, 2000).

Eichberg, H., 'Sport im 19. Jahrhundert: Genese Einer Industriellen Verhaltensform', in Ueberhorst, H. (ed.), *Geschichte der Leibesübungen* vol. 3/1 (Berlin: Bartels & Wernitz, 1980).

Eichberg, H., 'Olympic Sport: Neocolonization and Alternatives', *International Review for the Sociology of Sport*, 19 (1984), 97–106.

Eichberg, H., 'A Revolution of Body Culture? Traditional Games on the Way from Modernisation to "Postmodernity"', in Barreau, J. J. and Jaouen, G. (eds), *Eclipse et Renaissance des Jeux Populaires* (Rencontre International de Berrien 1990) (Rennes: Institut Culturel de Bretagne, 1991), 101–29.

Eisenberg, C., *English Sports und Deutsche Burger: Eine Gesellschaftsgeschichte 1800–1939* (Paderborn: Schöningh, 1999).

Elias, N., *The Civilising Process* (Oxford: Blackwell, 1978) (English translation of *Ueber den Prozess der Zivilisation*, 1939).

Elias, N. and Dunning, E., *Quest for Excitement: Sport and Leisure in the Civilizing Process* (Oxford: Blackwell, 1986).

Endrei, W. and Zolnay, L., *Fun and Games in Old Europe* (Budapest: Corvina, 1988).

Evans, J., *Life in Mediaeval France* (London: Phaidon, 1969).

Ferré, D. (ed.), *Les Jeux Traditionnels de Bretagne* (Rennes: Terre de Brume, 2002).

Finn, T., *Pub Games of England* (Cambridge: Oleander, 1981).

Gomme, A. B., *The Traditional Games of England, Scotland and Ireland* (two volumes) (London: Nutt, 1894/1898).

Gorini, P., *Encyclopedia of Traditional Games* (Rome: Gremese, 1994).

Gounot, A., Niewerth, T. and Pfister, G. (eds), *The World of Games: Political, Social and Educational Aspects* (ISHPES Studies 2) (Sankt Augustin: Academia, 1996).

Guttmann, A., *From Ritual to Record: The Nature of Modern Sports* (New York: Columbia University Press, 1978).

Guttmann, A., *Games and Empires: Modern Sports and Cultural Imperialism* (New York: Columbia University Press, 1994).

Hamer, E. U., *Die Anfänge der 'Spielbewegung' in Deutschland* (London: Arena, 1989).

Healy, P., *Gaelic Games and the Gaelic Athletic Association* (Dublin: Mercier, 1998).

Hellspong, M., *Den Folkliga Idrotten: Studies i Det Svenska Bondesamhällets Idrotter Och Fysiska Lekar Under 1700-Och 1800-Talen* (Stockholm: Nordiska Museets Förlag, 2000).

Hirn, U., *Ursprung und Wesen des Sports* (Leibesübungen und körperliche Erziehung in Theorie und Praxis 1) (Berlin: Weidmannsche Buchlandlung, 1936).

Hobsbawm, E. J. E. and Ranger, T. O., *The Invention of Tradition* (Cambridge: Cambridge University Press, 1992).

Holt, R., *Sport and Society in Modern France* (London: Macmillan, 1981).

Holt, R., *Sport and the British: A Modern History* (Oxford: Clarendon, 1989).

Holt, R., 'English Influences on French Sport: "Anglomania" and National Revival, 1870–1914', *Stadion*, 27 (2001), 179–188.

Jespers, J., De Meyer, P., De Schepper, P., Schwartz, C., Van Dam, M. and Vanhaeren, N., *Volkssporten Spelen: de Volkssportkoffer* (Serie der Vlaamse Volkssport Dossiers 3) (Brussels: Bloso, 1982a).

Jespers, J., De Meyer, P., De Schepper, P., Schwartz, C., Van Dam, M. and Vanhaeren, N., *Volkssporten Spelen: Speltradities uit Eigen Streek* (Serie der Vlaamse Volkssport Dossiers 5) (Brussels: Bloso, 1982b).

Jusserand, J. J., *Les Sports et les Jeux D'Exercice Dans L'Ancienne France* (Paris: Plon, 1901).

Langenfeld, H., 'Wie Sich der Sport Seit 200 Jahren Organisatorisch Entwickelt Hat', in Digel, H. (ed.), *Sport im Verein und im Verband* (Schorndorf: Hofmann, 1988), 18–34.

Levinson, D. and Christensen, K. (eds), *Encyclopedia of World Sport* (three volumes) (Santa Barbara: ABC-CLIO, 1996).

Liponski, W., *World Sports Encyclopedia* (Poznan: Atena, 2003).

Loubère, J. R., *Picards, Faites Vos Jeux* (Amiens: Ligue de Picardie de Longue Paume, 2000).

Lowenthal, D., *The Heritage Crusade and the Spoils of History* (Cambridge: Cambridge University Press, 1998).

MacAloon, J. J., *This Great Symbol: Pierre de Coubertin and the Origins of the Modern Olympic Games* (Chicago: University of Chicago Press, 1981).

Maestro Guerrero, F., *Del Tajo a la Replaceta: Juegos y Divertimentos en el Aragon Rural* (Zaragoza: Ediciones 94, 1996).

Maguire, J., *Global Sport: Identities, Societies, Civilizations* (Cambridge: Polity Press, 1999).

Malcolmson, R. W., *Popular Recreations in English Society 1700–1850* (Cambridge: Cambridge University Press, 1973).

Mangan, J. A., *Athleticism in the Victorian and Edwardian Public School: The Emergence and Consolidation of an Educational Ideology* (Cambridge: Cambridge University Press, 1981).

Mangan, J. A., *The Games Ethic and Imperialism* (London: Frank Cass, 2003).

McIntosh, P. C., *Sport in Society* (London: Watts, 1968).

Meunier, R., 'Les Jeux, une Innovation dans les Projets d'Amélioration du Régime des Lycées en France à la Fin du XIXe Siècle', in Bonhomme, G., Dinety, R., Le Guiner, A. and Meunier, R. (eds), *La Place du Jeu Dans L'Éducation: Histoire et Pédagogie* (Paris: F.F.E.P.G.V., 1989), 83–92.

Møller, J., *Gamle Idraetslege i Danmark* (four volumes) (Kastrup: Danish Rifle, Gymnastics and Sports Association, 1990–1991).

Moreno Palos, C., *Juegos y Deportes Tradicionales en España* (Madrid: Alianza Editoral, 1992).

Navarro Adelantado, V., Noda Gomez, T. and Hernandez Auta, J. M., *Juegos Deportivos Tradicionales* (Tenerife: Centro de la Cultura Popular Canaria, 1994).

Opie, I. and Opie, P., *Children's Games in Street and Play-Ground* (Oxford: Oxford University Press, 1969).

Pfister, G., Niewerth, T. and Steins, G. (eds), *Games of the World: Between Tradition and Modernity* (ISHPES Studies 1) (Sankt Augustin: Academia, 1996).

Pfister, G., 'Research on Traditional Games: The Scientific Perspective', *Journal of Comparative Physical Education and Sport*, 29: 2 (1997), 53–64.

Prange, K., 'Die Diskussion über den Nutzen der Turn- und Sportspiele um 1900', in Gouno, A., Niewerth, T. and Pfister, G. (eds), *The World of Games: Political, Social and Educational Aspects* (ISHPES Studies 2) (Sankt Augustin: Academia, 1996), 83–8.

Preising, W., 'Die Spielbewegung in Deutschland: Die Entwicklung Einer Gesellschaftlichen Bedeutung des Spiels', in Ueberhorst, H. (ed.), *Geschichte der Leibesübungen* (volume 3/1) (Berlin: Bartels & Wernitz, 1980), 413–42.

Rabelais, F. [under the pseudonym Alcofribas], *La Vie Treshorrificque du Grand Gargantua, Père de Pantagnmel* (Lyon: F. Juste, 1542; re-published by F. Jonkovsky, Paris: Flammarion, 1993).

Renson, R., 'The Flemish Archery Guilds: From Defence Mechanisms to Sports Institutions', in Renson, R., De Nayer, P. P. and Ostyn, M. (eds), *The History, the Evolution and Diffusion of Sports and Games in Different Cultures* (Proceedings of the 4th International HISPA Seminar, Leuven, 1975) (Brussels: Bloso, 1976), 135–59.

Renson, R., 'Leibesübungen der Bürger und Bauern im Mittelalter', in Ueberhorst, H. (ed.), *Geschichte der Leibesübungen* (volume 3/1) (Berlin: Bartels & Wernitz, 1980).

Renson, R., 'The "Traditionalist" Renascence: The Revival of Traditional Forms of Sports, Games, Dance and Recreation Around the World', in Simri, U., Eldar, D. and Lieberman, S. (eds), *Health, Physical Education, Recreation and Dance Education in Perspective* (Wingate Institute: Emmanuel Gill, 1984), 149–59.

Renson, R., 'Traditional sports, Europe', in Levinson, D. and Christensen, K. (eds), *Encyclopedia of World Sport* (volume 2) (Santa Barbara: ABC-CLIO, 1996), 1070–5.

Renson, R., 'The Reinvention of Tradition in Sports and Games', *Journal of Comparative Physical Education and Sport*, 29: 2 (1997), 46–52.

Renson, R., 'Sport and the Flemish Movement: Resistance and Accommodation 1868–1914', in Derez, K. and Vos, L. (eds), *Nationalism in Belgium, Shifting Identities* (London: Macmillan, 1998a), 119–26.

Renson, R., 'Sport Historiography in Europe: A Comparative Perspective and Heuristic Model', *Sport History Review*, 29 (1998b), 30–43.

Renson, R., 'Ludodiversity: Extinction, Survival and Invention of Movement Culture', in Pfister, G. (ed.), *Games of the Past – Sports for the Future* (ISHPES seminar; TAFISA symposium; Duderstadt, 2000) (Sankt Augustin: Academia, 2004).

Renson, R., Comeyne, H., De Vroede, E., Huysmans, K., Troch, I., Vandecasteele, S. and Verswyfelt, B., *Social and Cultural Dynamics of Traditional Games in Flanders 1982–2002* (research project aided by the King Boudewijn Foundation), 2004.

Renson, R., De Cramer, E. and De Vroede, E., 'Local Heroes: Beyond the Stereotype of the Participants in Traditional Games', *International Review for the Sociology of Sport*, 32 (1997), 59–68.

Renson, R. and De Vroede, E., 'Folk Games at the Fair: Kermis Scenes in the Work of Pieter Bruegel the Elder', *Stadion*, 12–13 (1986–1987), 87–99.

Renson, R., Manson, M. and De Vroede, E., 'Typology for the Classification of Traditional Games in Europe', in De Vroede, E. and Renson, R. (eds), *Proceedings of the Second European Seminar on Traditional Games* (Leuven, 1990) (Leuven: Vlaamse Volkssport Centrale, 1991), 69–81.

Renson, R. and Smulders, H., 'Research Methods and Development of the Flemish Folk Games File', *International Review for the Sociology of Sport*, 16 (1981), 97–107.

Renson, R. and Vermeulen, A., 'Sociale Determinanten van de Sportpraktijk bij Belgische Volwassenen', *Sport* (Brussels) 15 (1972), 25–39.

Schaufelberger, W., *Der Wettkampf in der alten Eidgenossenschaft: Zur Kulturgeschichte des Sports van 13. bis in 18. Jahrhundert* (two volumes) (Bern: Haupt, 1972).

Scheerder, J., Taks, M., Vanreusel, B. and Renson, R., *30 Jaar Breedtesport in Vlaanderen: Participatie en Beleid* (Gent: Publicatiefonds voor Lichamelijke Opvoeding, 2002).

Slicher van Bath, B., *De Agrarische Geschiedenis van West-Europa 500–1850* (Utrecht: Spectrum, 1977).

Steins, G. (ed.), *Spielbewegung – Bewegungsspiel: 100 Jahre Gossler'scher Spielerlass* (Berlin: Forum für Sportgeschichte, 1982).

Strutt, J., *The Sport and Pastimes of the People of England* (Bath: Firecrest Bath, 1801; new enlarged edition, 1969).

Suffolk and Berkshire, Earl of, *The Encyclopaedia of Sport and Games* (four volumes) (London: Heinemann, 1911).

Taylor, A. R., *The Guinness Book of Traditional Pub Games* (Enfield: Guinness Publishing, 1992).

Ter Gouw, J., *De Volksvermaken* (Haarlem: De Erven, 1871).

Thibault, J., 'Du Dandysme au Sport', in Renson, R., De Nayer, P. P. and Ostyn, M. (eds), *The History, the Evolution and Diffusion of Sports and Games in Different Cultures* (Proceedings of the 4th International HISPA Seminar, Leuven, 1975) (Brussels: Bloso, 1976), 248–55.

Trémaud, H., *Jeux de Force et d'Adresse* (Paris: Ed. des Musées Nationaux, 1972).

Ulmann, J., *De la Gymnastique aux Sports Modernes* (Third edition) (Paris: J. Vrin, 1997).

Van den Abeele, A., *Het Ridderlijk Gezelschap van de Witte Beer: Steekspelen in Brugge Tijdens de late Middeleeuwen* (Brugge: Walleyn, 2000).

Van Winter, J. M., *Ridderschap: Ideal en Werkelijkheid* (Haarlem: Fibula-Van Dishoeck, 1974).

Veiga, P., *O Libro dos Xogos Populares Galegos* (Santiago de Compostela: Sotelo Blanco, 2001).

Webster, D., *Scottish Highland Games* (Edinburgh: Reprographia Edinburgh, 1973).

Alcohol

Rural sport and alcohol have been long-standing companions. Sport during fairs, festivals and holidays was part of the process of release from the rigours of the winter, the toil of the summer or demands of the harvest. It was a time for the relaxing of inhibitions and cultivation of indulgence. This sense of the complementary relationship between alcohol and sport in a rural environment meant that drink was an inextricably interwoven strand in the fabric of the sporting experience. Whether it was the drinking booths at horseracing, the inns which staged cockfighting or the individual beer-sellers who lined the routes to major sporting events, attendance at a sports event was accompanied by almost limitless opportunities to imbibe. At the larger horse-racing events, drunken revelry was a constant source of concern for the authorities and a vital part of the sport's appeal to not inconsiderable sections of its crowd. Moreover, most alcohol was, of course, a product of the rural economy.

It was not just spectators who imbibed. Many athletes resorted to alcohol as a perceived aid to stamina and courage. Sir John Sinclair's views on training, published in his *Code of Health and Longevity* in 1807, argued that the drinking of red wine, and especially beer (up to three pints a day), should be part of training regimes. There was some debate as to whether or not spirits were also strength-giving, but, in contrast to modern sports-medicine advice, there was no discussion as to whether alcohol should be proscribed.

There are many references to alcohol being consumed during long-distance running and walking performances. Lieutenant Fairman of the Royal Lancashire Militia went 60 miles in 13 hours 33 minutes in 1804 and *en route* took a piece of bread steeped in Madeira wine. Foster Powell, famous for his walks from London to York and back in less than six days, was reported usually to take wine and water, or brandy and water, during his journeys.

Bottleholders at prizefights often used a mixture of brandy and water to stimulate their champion after long exertion. No doubt at times alcohol was also consumed to provide the fighters with extra 'bottom' or courage, which is perhaps the origin of the phrase of courageous sportsmen 'having bottle'.

The use of alcohol by athletes should be seen in the context of a society in which much of the population utilised alcoholic drinks as thirst quenchers or for physical stamina. Such drinks were seen as less dangerous than water, which was both scarce and unsafe in rural areas; at least alcoholic drinks contained water either drawn from unpolluted deep wells or which had been boiled as part of the brewing process. Moreover, it was generally believed that intoxicants imparted stamina: whenever extra energy was needed, as at harvest time, the best resort was to use alcohol to fuel the exertion.

Sources and Reading:
Collins, T. and Vamplew, W., *Mud, Sweat and Beers: A Cultural History of Sport and Alcohol* (Oxford: Berg, 2002).

See also Church Ales, Pubs and Sport

Wray Vamplew

Alnwick Football

This survivor of pre-industrial folk football played in Alnwick in Northumberland is more organised and less of a free-for-all than the other remnants of folk football played today.

Like the other forms of the game it is played on Shrove Tuesday. It takes place on a field called the Pasture, which is specially reserved for the game, between men of the St Michael's and St Paul's parishes of the town, each team having around 100 players. Two goals in the field are around a quarter of a mile apart.

Before the game, the ball is brought from Alnwick Castle by a piper in the service of the Duke of Northumberland. The game ends after three goals have been scored, and there is then a struggle between the players to get the ball to the castle. The player who does so wins a prize. If no result is reached on Shrove Tuesday, the game continues on Ash Wednesday.

As with many other local football matches, attempts were made to ban the game from being played in the town in the 1820s. These were countered by the Duke of Northumberland, who offered the field for the game to be played upon and began the practice of presenting the match ball before the kick-off.

Sources and Reading:

Day, B., *A Chronicle of Folk Customs* (London: Hamlyn, 1988).

Garnham, N., 'Patronage, Politics and Modernization of Leisure in Northern England: The Case of Alnwick's Shrove Tuesday Football Match', *English Historical Review*, CXVII: 474 (2002), 1228–46.

Hole, C., *English Traditional Customs* (London: Batsford, 1975).

See also Football

Tony Collins

Ancient Welsh Feats

– *see* Welsh Feats (Ancient)

Angling

The pursuit of fish with a rod and line – hence the term angle from the geometric shape created – has been undertaken in Britain since the late Middle Ages. It evolved from an activity undertaken principally by the wealthy upper classes and today angling is the most important mass-participation sport in Britain. Its enhanced popularity has been accompanied by successive waves of technological innovations, which have

led to the adoption of more sophisticated methods and techniques, although the principles on which it is based, namely the use of a rod, line and hook, remain the same. The sport has developed into two main branches, coarse and game, which are differentiated by the type of species pursued. Many variations in technique and methods are employed, principally float fishing, fly-fishing and lure fishing, which, whilst strongly associated with a single branch of the sport, are not exclusive to it.

In the fifteenth century, angling was established as a sport, as opposed to being a complement to the net and the spear as a means of catching fish for food. One of the first accounts of the subject was *Treatyse of Fysshynge wyth an Angle* incorporated as an appendix in Dame Juliana Berner's *The Boke of St Albans* (1496). This set forth the then novel argument that among the four main rural sports, hunting, hawking, fowling and fishing, it was the latter that ranked the highest. It described the use of fishing rods twenty feet long, with lines made from horsehair and the use of live flies as bait. Angling at this time was mainly for carp, using a crude home-made hook and a swan's quill or cork float on a horsehair line attached to a loop at the end of a wooden rod. The text, which focuses exclusively on the use of rod, line and hook, constitutes the first known codification of the sport of fishing. Other methods of catching fish, including trapping or netting of fish for food, were not deemed to be sport. Such practices are still used in commercial sea fishing, and were used in areas such as the Fens where, until the mid-twentieth century, a small number of fishermen continued to make a precarious living by catching eels, pike and other edible species of coarse fish for human consumption.

The popularity of the sport was significantly enhanced by the publication of Izaak Walton's (1593–1683) classic work *The Compleat Angler* in 1653. Walton is widely regarded as the patron saint of angling, with most writers eulogising the way his text epitomises the enjoyment derived from fishing in the idyllic seventeenth-century countryside. Much of his work, however, was derived from earlier writers on the subject. Another angling writer of note was James Chetham (1640–1692), whose text *The Angler's Vade-Mecum* was published in 1689. His reputation as the author of an informative and influential account of the sport would have been far greater if the text had been published in his own name rather than simply issued under the pseudonym 'Lover of Angling'.

The growing interest in the sport was accompanied not only by improved, more-effective rods, but also, and more importantly, by the development of specialised, distinctively shaped fish hooks. Using a more scientific approach, specialist craftsmen began to manufacture hooks from tempered steel, incorporating a gut eye to which the line was attached. The most famous pioneer of these improvements was Charles Kirby of London, who, in the 1650s, developed a distinctive style of more-effective hook, which became known as the 'Kirby bend'.

In the Victorian period the sport expanded rapidly as a result of the railways, which initially provided opportunities for richer members of urban society to escape to the more rural areas of the countryside in search of adventure, and then allowed the urban artisan and labouring classes to participate in fishing expeditions. Angling was particularly attractive to many of the more-prosperous Victorian tradesmen who wished to participate in field sports but could not afford the cost or the time entailed in activities such as fox-hunting. As the hallmark of their superior status, and to differentiate themselves from the working masses who went fishing, there was a tendency to concentrate on the pursuit of game or specimen fish, to dress elaborately in tailored waistcoats beneath tailored jackets, to wear top hats or to use more expensive tackle, such as split-cane rods and the improved multiplier reels. In contrast, working-class anglers were distinguished by their focus on less expensive and less prestigious coarse fishing, and were required by financial considerations to use much cheaper bamboo rods known as roach

poles, where the line was fixed to the top of the rod rather than to a reel.

The modern-day structure and organisation of the sport are important legacies of the Victorian era. Anglers went to extreme lengths to unite into clubs and national organisations to coordinate the sport, to rent water from riparian owners and to organise competitions, a progression that culminated in 1869 with the formation of the Angling Association. By this time there were over 80 anglers' clubs with in excess of 50,000 members. On 1 July 1880, the first national fly-fishing competition took place at Loch Leven, Scotland. This competition later developed into the prestigious Scottish fly-fishing championship, and was the precursor of all modern international, commonwealth and world events. The rapid expansion of coarse fishing was also accompanied by the establishment of clubs and organisations to coordinate the sport. Local pubs frequently became the headquarters of angling clubs, where sweepstake matches, in which the winner took all the money, were organised. These sweepstakes were later complemented by cups, medals and other prizes, being competed for on either an individual or team basis.

The enhanced popularity of the sport led to the establishment of specialised tackle manufacturers producing rods and reels and a host of other technological innovations. Rods, which had traditionally been produced from locally available types of woods such as crab apple or ash, were increasingly made out of the more pliant greenheart wood imported from South America and the West Indies. In the 1840s, William Blacker developed the practice of fashioning rods from split-cane, which was bamboo split lengthwise into strips and glued together. Rods of this type were considerably lighter, more flexible and more durable than their wooden counterparts. These more-expensive rods, used for game fishing, became increasingly popular with the wealthier middle classes. Improved centre-pin reels made of wood, with a free-running, ungeared, wide drum as a centre, also became widespread, particularly in the

Nottinghamshire area where they originated. Metal hooks with eyes, which had been invented around 1850, were widely adopted after 1890. In the case of fly-fishing, artificial lures became considerably more ornate due to the importation of brightly coloured feathers from exotic species of birds – species that are now protected.

Britain was regarded as the Mecca of angling, and it continued to export the sport, in terms of its techniques and practices, to the rest of the world. Even fish were exported; brown trout were transported as ova to the streams of the Kashmir in India, the blue mountains of South Africa and the lakes of New Zealand and Tasmania. The publication of *The Field* in 1855 with its fishing reports heralded the emergence of angling journalism. This was followed by the establishment of the *Fishing Gazette* (1877–1966), which focused more directly on the needs of the angling fraternity. These developments heralded the start of angling's long-term association with literature intended not only for anglers but also for those who were interested in rural life.

The rapid expansion of the sport continued virtually unabated until the outbreak of the First World War, when the effects of mass enlistment of men into the armed forces, coupled with a multitude of wartime controls and restrictions, reduced opportunities to participate in the sport. The industrial depression and mass unemployment of the interwar period led to a revival in the sport, with growth in the number of anglers and the amount of time devoted to inexpensive activities such as coarse fishing. By the late 1920s there were more than 600,000 members of the Working Men's Anglers' Association, which increasingly became more assertive in dealing with conservation and pollution issues. Environmental concern fostered the establishment of the Pure Rivers Association and the Anglers' Cooperative Association, which became a leading anti-pollution organisation and took legal action against all types of offenders. Following the outbreak of military hostilities in 1939, the trend of increased participation was rapidly reversed due to the imposition of petrol rationing for leisure purposes and restrictions on public access to designated areas of the countryside.

In the aftermath of the Second World War the revival of angling's popularity reflected the need to escape the rigours of wartime regimentation and the austerity measures that enveloped people's work and social lives. The advent of the motor car provided many families with their first real opportunity to travel as a group to fishing venues of their own choice. In this period, a generation of young anglers was captivated by the exploits of 'Mr Crabtree goes fishing', graphically illustrated by Bernard Venables and published in the mass-circulation *Daily Mirror*. The popularity of the sport peaked in the mid-1980s, with in excess of 3.7 million participants. By 1996 this had declined to about 3.3 million, the majority of whom were men employed in manual jobs. By this time, family fishing outings had for many been replaced with other forms of mass entertainment.

Since the Second World War, the sport has been revolutionised by a number of technological innovations that have changed the techniques and methods, although not the principles, of fishing. Hollow glass-fibre rods introduced from America offered many advantages over split-cane rods in terms of cost and weight. These were gradually replaced by more precisely tapered carbon-fibre and aramid rods, which enabled very accurate casting due to their light, positive action. The most significant change was the advent of fixed-spool reels, having the spool set at right angles to the axis of the rod; the basic principle of its mechanism is similar to that utilised for cotton bobbins in the textile industry. The subsequent use of graphite composite in reels reduced their weight and made them resistant to corrosion. Fixed-spool reels gave every angler the opportunity to cast and fish at much greater distances than previously. This was particularly significant for those new to the sport, who had not mastered the skilled intricacies of using centre-pin reels. The sport has also been transformed by the reintroduction of fishing poles. Use of ultra-light materials in the construction of poles now enables poles of up to 15 metres to be used. More recent developments have included the use of high-protein baits (commonly known as 'boilies'), the mass use of these supplements having contributed increases in the sizes of fish such as carp and tench.

Angling has spawned an industry in its own right, characterised by the development of central federations and competitive networks, frequently sponsored by large, multinational corporations. The industry has been supported by a bludgeoning array of magazines, books, television programmes and institutional videos, and an increasing number of individuals who secure their living from the sport. It is estimated that annual expenditure on the sport exceeds £3.5 billion. For the vast majority of anglers, however, angling remains an activity they indulge in simply for the pleasure and enjoyment it provides.

Sources and Reading:

Bailey, J., *Where to Coarse Fish in Britain and Ireland* (London: New Holland, 2002).

Lowerson, J., 'Brother of the Angle: Coarse Fishing and English Working Class Culture 1850–1914', in Mangan, J. A. (ed.), *Pleasure, Profit Proselytism: British Culture and Sport at Home and Abroad 1700–1914* (London: Frank Cass, 1988), 105–27.

Lowerson, J., 'Angling', in Mason, T. (ed.), *Sport in Britain: A Social History* (Cambridge: Cambridge University Press, 1989), 12–43.

Miles, T. and Vaughan, B. (ed.), *The Practical Guide to Coarse Fishing* (London: Southwater, 2000).

National Coarse Fishing Federation of Ireland: http://homepage.eircom.net/~ncffi/

Pope, N. (ed.), Arbery, L. (Foreword), *Specimen Hunting* (London: Boxtree, 1993).

See also Coarse Fishing, Fishing (Wales), Game Fishing

Nicholas Goddard and
John Martin

Archery

During the late eighteenth and nineteenth centuries, archery was an exclusive sport whose appeal was rooted in its historic and rural associations and the opportunities that it provided for socialising and flirtation. Archery evolved as a sport as the development of guns marginalised the longbow as a military weapon. At the end of the eighteenth century the sport became a popular aristocratic fashion thanks to a nostalgic taste for the gothic and medieval. Archery societies were set up across the country, each with its own strict entry criteria, outlandish costumes and extravagant dinners. They were conspicuous displays of wealth, havens of exclusivity and a way of reinforcing and reassuring one's own position in society. In the midst of urban development and social and political change, the social association archery offered was an important way of forging new solidarities and identities. Furthermore, women could not only compete in the contests but could also retain and display their 'feminine forms' while doing so, and thus the clubs also acted as a forum for introductions, flirtation and romance. Archery's aesthetics were historic, rural, picturesque and elegant. It appealed to exactly the same sentiments that made the contemporary Romanticist movement so popular among the leisured classes. As the nineteenth century progressed, archery gained a more middle-class following, but it continued to be a forum for exclusive social interaction and bonding. In the middle years of the century, the sport also developed a more scientific and rational element through the establishment of a national championship and standardised rules.

The use of the bow in hunting and in conflict dates back into prehistory, but it was the Welsh who, after the Norman Conquest, first used a longbow effectively in war. The longbow quickly became a standard weapon in medieval warfare and subsequently the implement used for target archery. During the medieval period, archery was practised by men of all classes, not as a sport but in preparation for war. In the twelfth century, bowmen who accidentally killed someone while practising were absolved from legal charges. Archers played decisive roles in the battles of Crécy (1346) and Agincourt (1415). So important was the longbow to military needs that, from the fourteenth century, various kings of England actively prohibited other sports because of fears that they distracted men from practising shooting their bows. Archery competitions first evolved as a way of enlivening such practice and became a feature of fairs and holidays. During the sixteenth and seventeenth centuries, the longbow was slowly rendered redundant as a weapon of war by technological developments, such as the musket. The bow's use in hunting also largely died out in this period.

With the decline of the bow's military use, archery became a pastime. Perhaps the first archery society in Britain was the Guild of St George, formed in London in 1537 by Henry VIII. From it grew the Finsbury Archers, who met in London until the late eighteenth century, when the land on which they traditionally shot was enclosed. Drawing upon medieval European and Scottish traditions, the Kilwinning Papingo, which required archers to dislodge a wooden parrot from the top of an abbey tower, was established in 1688. The papingo shoot was an annual event until 1870 and was revived in 1948. Today, the target is a model dove. The Company of Scottish Archers was formed in 1676 and is possibly the oldest sporting body in Britain today. It was granted a royal charter by Queen Anne and drew its membership from the aristocracy, gentry and professional classes of Edinburgh. Archery took place at Harrow school until 1771, when a new headmaster ended the practice. In Yorkshire and Teesside, the Scorton silver arrow has been shot for since 1673, and encouraged the formation of local archery societies in Richmond in 1755 and Darlington in 1758.

By the middle of the eighteenth century, archery was thus little more than a scattered and peripheral pastime. The revival of

archery as a fashionable pursuit owed much to Sir Ashton Lever, an antiquarian and collector, who was famous for his aviary and museum. He formed the Toxophilite Society in London in 1781. The society soon attracted the patronage of George, Prince of Wales. Royal favour encouraged imitation, and so in an age of novelty and fashion archery was soon immensely popular with the nobility and gentry, for whom it provided an excuse to socialise, eat and drink. Members of the aristocracy had considerable time and money on their hands and they indulged in extravagant and competitive displays of wealth. Archery prize meets were lavish, festive and ceremonial affairs, where the shooting often seemed secondary to the socialising. In north Wales and the borders, for example, the Royal British Bowmen toured around the country houses of its members, complete with its own marquee and servants. Members marched on to the shooting ground, waving flags and banners, to the accompaniment of specially composed music and a 21-gun salute. (However, the Royal British Bowmen actually regarded its shooting more seriously than most and took steps to limit the excessiveness and expense of the festivity; its rules placed time limits on meals in order to ensure sobriety and specified that dinners should only consist of cold meats.) Many societies sounded bugles when an arrow struck the target's gold centre and presented prizes to the champions, such as laurel leaves, medievalesque titles, and silver bugles, arrows and medals. Shooting days naturally included gambling and were followed by dinners, balls, patriotic poetry recitals and singing. The wealthiest societies built their own lodges to host the celebrations, while the smaller societies utilised marquees or local taverns. From 1789 to 1793, a series of general meetings were held at Blackheath and Dulwich for the leading archery societies of Britain.

Public display and ceremony were important elements in the aristocracy's affirmation of its own status. The Woodmen of Arden built their Forest Hall, designed by an Italian architect, on the estate of its president, the Earl of Aylesford. Its interior, decorated with the coats-of-arms of various members, must have acted as a self-affirmation and expression of status and lineage. Like some hunts, dress codes added to the sense of status, identity and cohesion. The uniform of the Yorkshire Archers was typical: a plain green frock and velvet cape, with uniform buttons, white waistcoat and breeches and a round black hat with a white ostrich feather. Most societies fined their members for not turning up in the correct attire. The cost of such uniforms ensured that they developed the wearer's sense of status and reinforced the exclusiveness of the society. The well-cut green archery uniforms combined the display of dazzling contemporary military uniforms with the elegant but more sombre civil dress that was becoming fashionable in the wake of the anger of the French Revolution's mobs at their powdered peacock elite. When an array of such uniformed aristocracy shot in the landscaped grounds of country houses (which themselves were potent symbols of taste, status and power) to the accompaniment of bands, marquees, banners and beautiful women, the picturesque spectacle reflected the self-vision of the aristocracy.

Such scenes had the cultivated feel of a medieval tournament. Medievalism, antiquity and gothic romance were highly fashionable in polite culture across Europe in the late eighteenth century, and archery was both shaped and promoted by such tastes. It was believed that in the medieval period, custom, hierarchy and inherited rank enjoyed greater significance than they did in contemporary society. The fashion for all things medieval thus provided the aristocracy with some reassuring roots, stability and a sense of continuity in the face of the uncertainty of the Industrial Revolution, a demographic explosion and the political upheaval and sense of crisis engendered by the French Revolution and the loss of the American colonies. Archery's central place in the popular legends of Robin Hood and medieval English victories meant that the sport also boasted a patriotic twist. In an age of increasing European tensions, this fulfilled the ruling classes' desire for new patriotic forms of cultural expression that had British

roots. The revival of archery was thus part of the invention of new patriotic traditions and myths in which Britain could seek solace, unity and greatness. Advocates of archery were never slow to emphasise the pastime's historic credentials. Eighteenth- and nineteenth-century works on the sport featured long historical sections, and *Toxophilus* (1545) by Roger Ascham, tutor to Elizabeth I and her half-brother, was reprinted in 1788.

As industry and commerce increasingly created new men of money, the aristocracy could no longer rely on wealth alone as a signifier of social status. By the late eighteenth century, the aristocracy was deliberately excluding men of new money from the realms of social and cultural power. Archery societies demonstrated these elitist concerns by limiting the number of members and having strict entry criteria that were operated by systems of balloting and blackballing. The Royal Foresters took such criteria to extremes by demanding that prospective members prove the gentility of their descent on their father's side for at least three generations. The social aspirations of the English bourgeoisie meant that the culture of the wealthy middle class often imitated that of the aristocracy and a number of archery societies were set up by the business elites of provincial towns. These societies offered the middle classes their own opportunity to socialise and assert their local status.

After the Napoleonic wars and subsequent domestic tensions had disrupted archery and aristocratic life across Britain, the 1820s saw the sport being revived again, with old societies being reformed and new ones established. Royal patronage again gave archery some fashionability and prestige. Edinburgh's Royal Company of Archers was appointed as the King's Bodyguard in Scotland in 1822 and its captain-general took part in Queen Victoria's coronation procession. Queen Victoria had shot before her accession, and later created a master of archery among her household officers. New heights of opulence were reached in the revived meets, as the landed gentry and aristocracy's obsession with competitive and ostentatious display continued. With show and sociability the prime concerns, handicaps were often devised to ensure that the better archers did not spoil proceedings. At the Mersey Archery Society, established in 1821, shooting partners were drawn by lot, and there was a stipulation that no one was allowed to win more than twice in any season.

The revived popularity of archery again owed much to the taste for medievalism. This fashion peaked in the second quarter of the nineteenth century, partly in reaction to the unprecedented industrial growth of the 1820s. Grounded in the fashion for medievalism, but also hugely influential in developing its popularity, were the novels of Sir Walter Scott and, in particular, his hugely popular *Ivanhoe* (1819). One chapter of *Ivanhoe* depicted the winning of an archery competition by a heroic, manly and chivalrous Locksley, who was based upon on the ever-popular Robin Hood. Sir Walter Scott himself became a member of Edinburgh's Royal Company of Archers.

The fashion for medievalism and archery was now particularly prevalent among the urban middle classes, who were attracted by archery's combination of rural overtones and urban fashion. The crisis that preceded the 1832 Reform Act revealed the deep-seated divisions that existed between the upper and middle classes. The increasing adoption of archery by the middle classes no doubt made the pastime less palatable to its upper-class adherents. The cost of the extravagance that accompanied archery did not help and the aristocratic fashion for conspicuous displays of status slowly declined. Less-ostentatious provincial archery societies thus became more common and aristocratic excess more unusual. Between 1840 and 1860 archery perhaps reached its peak of popularity, with the number of clubs trebling.

The Royal British Bowmen had admitted women members in the late eighteenth century, but most other archery societies were not quite so progressive towards their female guests and relatives. Women's roles in the eighteenth century were usually limited to shooting at the invitation of their male counterparts, or to traditional symbolic positions, such as the lady patroness who would present the winning archer with his prize. However, the archery of the early nineteenth century was notable for the involvement of women. The presence of women, as either participants or just dinner guests, added to the whole conviviality of archery. Among women themselves, archery could be a most popular and rare physical and social antidote to their sedentary lives. The social acceptability of women practising and watching archery was rooted in their contribution to the pastime's aesthetics. The stance required to shoot a bow involved no unseemly exertion, but it did require women to stand gracefully upright with their chests protruding. The male archers no doubt admired and enjoyed such elegant feminine postures. Yet archery was not simply an excuse for voyeurism. Marriage and motherhood were a respectable woman's overriding vocation and preoccupation and, despite the growing consideration given to personal compatibility, rank was still a fundamental consideration in the choice of marriage partners among the middle and upper classes. Archery offered men and women an opportunity to view, meet and enjoy their social equals, away from the prying eyes of their social inferiors. Indeed, some women's preoccupation with the male archers and lack of ability and interest in the sport was often a source of some amusement. There was, however, nothing to stop men or women shooting on their own and so archery also offered entertainment and physical recreation when polite company was not available.

In the 1840s, a decade when the ethos of rational recreation was on a significant upturn, archery developed more modern and sporting characteristics. In 1844, the first Grand National meeting was held in York, marking the increasing encouragement of archery as a rational, healthy and scientific pastime. The beginning of this annual national championship also represented a conscious break with the older extravagant and festive practices of display.

Nonetheless, the taste for the medieval was not anti-modern and celebrations of the past took forms that did not interfere with the working week. Thus an increasingly competitive approach to the sport was not at odds with its essential antique and rural appeal. The promotion of the Grand National also owed something to a desire to promote friendship among archers across the country. The annual Grand National archery meets, usually held in provincial towns, were convivial occasions that drew together the local gentry and were accompanied by other social functions, such as dances and fairs.

The Grand National was decided by a series of shoots over 60, 80 and 100 yards, which became a standard format for competitions and was known as the 'York Round'. This development of consistent rules was in line with gradual moves in other sports to codifying and unifying ways of playing. Women first shot at the Grand National in 1845, but shot over shorter distances than the men. With the founding of the *Archer's Register* in 1864 by James Sharpe, a freemason and editor of county newspapers, archery also gained its own press. The embodiment and leading practitioner of this new serious and scientific sport of archery was Horace Alfred Ford, a Cheltenham solicitor (1822–80). He did much to help improve archery standards and won the Grand National eleven times in succession between 1849 and 1859, often completely out-shooting his competitors. He was a pioneer in technique and berated those who were not willing to learn how to improve their skill. His book *Archery: Its Theory and Practice* was first published in 1856 and remains influential today.

Competitive and scientific archery perhaps diverted some interest from the traditional festive societies, but archery did continue as a forum and excuse for flirtation and socialising on the lawns of country houses, manors and vicarages. However, it was increasingly on a much smaller, less ostentatious and more informal scale. The fashion for medievalism had dropped away by the 1860s and with it went some of the customs of archery. Archers continued to shoot in green, but only a small minority of isolated societies kept up the hats, elaborate uniforms and festive traditions. Thus rather than being the plaything of the aristocracy, archery became more common among modest provincial gentlemen and their lady friends, for whom it played a role in bonding together the country gentry.

The rifle volunteer movement appears to have reduced the number of male archers in the 1860s, but the number of female archers temporarily upheld the popularity of the sport. By the mid-1870s, female competitors at the Grand National were outnumbering their male peers. There were around 130 archery clubs in 1881, but the more active and faster, but still feminine and respectable, games of croquet and tennis were becoming hugely fashionable and marginalising the popularity of archery among the middle classes. By 1889, there were only approximately 50 archery clubs left in Britain.

In the twentieth century, archery did retain some popularity, and its inclusion in the 1900 Paris Olympic Games signalled the pastime's acceptance as a serious sport. In 1922, the private archery field of the Royal Toxophilites in Regent's Park was surrendered to make way for public tennis courts at the demand of the park owners. This perhaps symbolised how the old exclusive, festive and picturesque tradition of archery was coming to an end in a modern and perhaps more democratic age. In the post-1945 period, archery continued as a competitive and serious sport. It also found a new lease of life as a sport for the disabled. Some of the traditional societies do still exist today and exhibit a significant degree of pride in their history and heritage. However, technology has revolutionised the bow and, as a sport, archery has left its traditional and rural roots and been absorbed into a wider modern sporting culture.

Sources and Reading:

Burnett, J., 'Sport and the Calendar: Archery and Rifle Shooting in Scotland in the Nineteenth Century', *Scottish Studies*, 33 (1999), 110–31.

Burnett, J. and Urqhart, R. H. J., 'Early Papingo Shooting in Scotland', *Review of Scottish Culture*, 11 (1998), 4–12.

Credland, A. G., 'The Grand National Archery Meetings, 1844–1994 and the Progress of Women in Archery', *Journal of the Society of Archery Antiquaries*, 43 (2000), 68–104.

Heath, E. G., *History of Target Archery* (Newton Abbott: David & Charles, 1973).

Longman, C. J. and Walrond, H., *Archery* (London: Longmans, 1894).

Lowerson, J., *Sport and the English Middle Classes, 1870–1914* (Manchester: Manchester University Press, 1993).

Websites:

Archery Library: www.xs4all.nl/~marcelo/archery/library/books/

Grand National Archery Association: www.gnas.org

See also Archery (Scotland), Archery (Wales), Grand Wardmote, Royal British Bowmen, Scorton Silver Arrow

Martin Johnes

Archery (Scotland)

Archery was an art of war in the Middle Ages, and men practised it in their leisure time, particularly on Sunday after the church service. The point at which it was clearly seen to be a leisure activity in the Scottish Lowlands, and nothing more, was when the burgh of Musselburgh, four miles east of Edinburgh, put up a full-size silver arrow as a trophy within a year or two of 1600. In the next century, at least a dozen burghs followed Musselburgh's example. They took up the continental practice of each winner adding a token of his own victory, a silver medal engraved with his name and his heraldic achievement, with some suitable image or motto on the reverse. Archery also survived in educational institutions. In the same way that the English public schools sustained traditional forms of football and fives, archery continued at St Andrews University and Aberdeen Grammar School when it had little appeal to other people in these towns.

The Company of Scottish Archers was founded in 1676 on the model of the archery guilds of the Low Countries. The exiled Charles II had been a member of the Gilde Saint-Sebastiaan at Bruges in 1656–8, and both he and his queen, Catherine of Braganza, were enthusiasts. Archery thus became fashionable in Britain, though the bow was still an implement of war in the Scottish Highlands in the second half of the seventeenth century and was also used for hunting in the Scottish Lowlands. Royal patronage was granted to the Company of Scottish Archers by Queen Anne in 1704, making it the Royal Company of Archers. Ironically, for much of the eighteenth century its membership had leanings towards the House of Stuart. Particularly around the time of the rebellion of 1745–6, it had a strongly Jacobite flavour, and John Murray of Broughton, winner of the Musselburgh Arrow in 1735, was Prince Charles Edward Stuart's secretary during the Jacobite rebellion. In time, the political leanings of the membership changed, and on the occasion of George IV's visit to Edinburgh in 1822, the Royal Company was appointed as the King's Bodyguard in Scotland. In the eighteenth century, the Royal Company's shooting does not seem to have been particularly competitive, but it kept the sport alive. Its membership was sufficiently large and wealthy that in 1777 it was able to afford to build a clubhouse, Archers' Hall, on what was then the southern outskirts of Edinburgh. A bowling green was laid out beside it.

The Kilwinning Papingo was started in 1688 by members of the Company of Scottish Archers who owned land near this small Ayrshire town. In papingo or popinjay shooting, archers shot vertically upwards at a wooden model of a popinjay or parrot. At Kilwinning, the bird is placed on a pole projecting from the top of the abbey tower. Colloquially, the aim is to *ding doon the doo* (knock down the dove) and the parrot has been replaced by a wooden pigeon. Since the Middle Ages, competitions of this kind have been quite common in French Flanders, Belgium, the Netherlands and in the adjacent parts of Germany. The Kilwinning Papingo always had a little more than local status; even in the eighteenth century it was from time to time reported in the Glasgow newspapers. With the growing popularity of archery the Papingo thrived, and it was given a further boost in 1840 by the opening of the railway line from Glasgow. The Papingo declined with the rest of archery, and it was last shot in 1870. It was, however, revived in 1948, and is still held in July each year. The spurious claim that it has been held since 1488 still appears from time to time in print and on the Internet; this claim was, however, authoritatively dismissed by William Lee Kerr in 1894.

As in England, there was a revival of archery in Scotland in the last two decades of the eighteenth century, although it was on a small scale north of the Border. For example, a club was formed in Dumfries in 1794 and a local cabinet maker advertised bows he had obtained from England, but no further evidence has emerged of the club's activity. Between 1820 and 1860, archery was a comparatively popular sport among the wealthier people, particularly in the cities. At its peak in the 1840s there were 30 or 40 clubs in Scotland, though most seem to have had no more than a couple of dozen members. Women's events paralleled those for men, though they had their own distinctive prizes. At the inaugural meeting of the Ayrshire Archers' Club at Ballochmyle House in 1838, Miss McLeod of McLeod won a brooch in the form of 'a splendid arrow tipped with topaz and feathered with precious stones'. Archery was also enjoyed outside these clubs, on the lawns of the mansions of the landed gentry and middle classes.

Archery has also acquired a literary background. James Hogg, 'the Ettrick Shepherd', started the St Ronan's Games at Innerleithen in 1826, under the inspiration of Sir Walter Scott, particularly the novel *Ivanhoe* (1819) in which Robin Hood is a central character. The Marchmont Arrow was the archery trophy at Innerleithen from 1830 to 1845. Hogg, a Borderer with deep sympathy for the falling quality of life suffered by Border people as farmers set themselves above their workers and increasing numbers were forced into textile mills, consciously wished to recreate the past, and, along with football and feats of strength, archery was part of his programme. Hogg himself took up archery.

Archery in this period had a feel of the Middle Ages, along with Gothic architecture and medieval romances. It was partially a reaction against the grimy modern world that industrialisation had produced; archery clubs were most common around Glasgow and Ayrshire, the Scottish centres for textiles, engineering and mining. Part of the appeal of the Papingo was the medieval venue of Kilwinning Abbey (though the tower had collapsed in 1803 and had been rebuilt), and other romantic ruins, such as Linlithgow Palace, were also the sites of meetings.

The increasing popularity of target archery, and the establishing in 1859/60 of the military Volunteer Movement, brought a rapid decline in the traditional archery competitions. By 1870, the Middle Ages no longer offered an appealing vision to the British middle classes, and the Volunteer could claim to be using his leisure time to be an active patriot. Women who had been archers took up the new game of croquet. Target archery remained a minority sport.

Scots were involved in Grand National archery meetings from the beginning in 1844, and in 1850 the annual meeting was held in Edinburgh. During this period emerged the most significant single figure in Scottish archery, Peter Muir. He came from Kilwinning and is said to have been a descendant of David Muir, the first known winner of the Kilwinning Arrow (1697). He was an archer of great skill, for many years the best in Scotland, and for a period second only to Horace Alfred Ford in British competitions. His greatest fame, however, was as a bow maker, in which role he served the Royal Company for more than 50 years. Even Ford used arrows made by Muir.

Sources and Reading:

Buchanan, M., *Archery in Scotland: An Elegant and Manly Amusement* (Glasgow: Glasgow Art Galleries and Museums, 1979).

Burnett, J., 'Sport and the Calendar: Archery and Rifle Shooting in the Nineteenth Century', *Scottish Studies*, 33 (2000), 111–31.

Burnett, J. and Urquhart, R. U., 'Early Papingo Shooting in Scotland', *Review of Scottish Culture*, 11 (1998), 4–12.

Ker, W. L., 'The Papingo', *Transactions of the Glasgow Archaeological Society*, n.s., 2 (1891–6), 325–39.

Longman, C. J. and Walrond, H., *Archery* (London: Longman, Green, 1894).

Paul, J. B., *The History of the Royal Company of Archers* (Edinburgh: Blackwood, 1875).

See also Archery

John Burnett

Archery (Wales)

Archery in Wales can be traced back to early times. The tenth-century Laws of Hywel Dda refer to the cost of buying a bow and arrow, while the twelfth-century traveller and writer Gerald of Wales described the arrows used by the Welsh when at battle. Archery was one of the activities included in the 24 ancient Welsh feats, and medieval poets praised their patrons' archery skill in a period when youths were legally obliged to master the longbow for military purposes.

When guns superseded longbows as major weapons of war, the latter began to be used by the gentry as a means of entertainment. From the seventeenth century, archery was fashionable among the social elite and in Wales the first society dedicated to the sport was the Royal British Bowmen, founded in 1787. Many other clubs were formed in its wake, and, judging by the number in existence at any one time, archery peaked in Wales between the 1860s and 1880s. Membership of the societies was restricted to the upper classes who, following the archery contests, enjoyed an evening's entertainment, usually in the form of a dinner or a ball. Indeed, the convivial element was just as important as the sporting, and wealthy families viewed such occasions as valuable opportunities to mingle with fellow aristocrats and gentry.

Most of these societies, which had largely been based in south Wales, had been dissolved by the end of the nineteenth century, and all had disappeared by the onset of the First World War. Archery's fortunes were severely affected by the rise of modern sports, and the appeal of such activities as croquet and tennis seems to have hastened its decline.

Sources and Reading:
Hansard, G. A., *The Book of Archery* (London: Henry G. Bohn, 1841).

Lake, F., 'Royal British Bowmen 1787–1880', *British Archer*, 25: 3 (1973), 132–5.

Usher, G., 'The Society of Royal British Bowmen (1787)', *Denbighshire Historical Society Transactions*, 4 (1955), 85–90.

See also Archery, Royal British Bowmen, Welsh Feats (Ancient)

Emma Lile

Arrow Throwing

Arrow throwing was an informal sport common in industrial Lancashire and Yorkshire in the late nineteenth and early twentieth centuries, in which a pointed shaft of ash or deal was thrown as far as possible. About a yard long, the shaft was plain with no flights or feathers to assist it, although in the version played in south Yorkshire feathers were attached to the arrow. However, a taut string attached to the shaft was used to aid the propulsion of the arrow. Arrow throwing resembled javelin throwing, and the distance thrown was measured in 'scores' (twenty yards); the longest throws recorded were of around 280 yards. Culturally, the sport was part of the same continuum as knur and spell. Perhaps naturally, gambling on the eventual winner and the length of individual throws was a key part of the attraction of the sport.

Sources and Reading:
The Encyclopaedia of Sport (London: The Sportsman, 1912).

See also Knur and Spell

Tony Collins

Articles of Horseracing

The organisation of a horse race requires a set of rules to demonstrate fairness to all competitors and to prevent anarchy on the course. There was no central governing body in horseracing in the eighteenth century and so the organisers of each meeting devised their own set of articles, which were a legally binding code of conduct between the owners of the horses entered and the givers of any prizes. Although the articles were partly determined by local conditions and opinions, they usually followed a similar pattern in showing the basic details of place and date, financial arrangements, officials, weights to be carried, types of horses allowed, distance, number of heats, route to be run and dispute resolution. The articles shown below, which were for a race at Malton in 1713, are typical.

Articles agreed by the founders for a plate to be run for on Langton Wolds, near New Malton, on Thursday, the 1st day of October next:

1. Every horse that runs to carry 10st. weight besides saddle and bridle.
2. That any horse that wins two heats and saves his distance the third shall have the plate. And if three horses win each of them one heat, then those three horses are only to run in the fourth heat: and the horse that wins that heat shall have the plate.
3. That every person that enters a horse shall subscribe or bring an authority from his master to subscribe that he will abide and be determined by these articles.
4. That unless three or more horses run, the plate shall not be run for.
5. That every founder that enters a horse for this plate shall pay over and above his subscription one guinea, and all other fower guineas apiece.
6. Every rider shall leave the posts on the right or left-hand according to the original articles of this course.

7. That every person that enters a horse shall name the rider and three tryers.
8. That it shall be lawful to change any rider that is by accident disabled in any heat, provided the weight be carried according to the articles.
9. That every horse that runs shall be entered on Saturday, the 28th day of this instant September, at Mr. John Dunns, New Malton, and every person that enters shall pay 5/- for entering.
10. That every horse shall be ready to start between the hours of two and three in the afternoon on the day appointed to run, and shall have halfe an hour allowed for rubbing after every heat; and no horse shall start before notice of the clarke.
11. That if any difference shall arise upon account of this plate, it shall be referred to Sir William Strickland, Bt., or, in his absence, to the majority of the founders then present, who hereby have power to determine the same.

Signed: Will Strickland,
Hugh Cholmley,
W. Strickland, Jn.

Sources and Reading:

Fairfax-Blakeborough, J. *Northern Turf History: Extinct Race Meetings* (London: J. A. Allen, 1949).

Kay, J. and Vamplew, W., 'A Modern Sport? "From Ritual to Record" in British Horseracing', *Ludica* (2003).

Wray Vamplew

Artillery Sports (Wales)

Welsh artilleries sometimes hosted rural sports-days in which a range of activities were contested by officers and watched by large crowds. While the Aberystwyth Artillery Sports of May 1895 included familiar throwing, jumping and running events, it also included a more unusual bandsmen's boot race and a menagerie race, in which competitors wore fancy dress and led various farm and domestic animals.

Sources and Reading:
Cambrian News (31 May 1895).

Emma Lile

Ashbourne Football

A form of folk football played every Shrove Tuesday in the Derbyshire village of Ashbourne in the Peak District, the Ashbourne game is an example of mass football played over a large area. The goals are two mills around three miles apart, separated by Henmore Brook, and the teams, which can be of any size, are known as 'upp'ards' and 'down'ards', depending on whether players were born north or south of the Henmore. Much of the play takes place in a huge scrum, or 'hug' as it is known locally. A goal is scored when the ball is tapped three times against a board attached to the stone goal-plinth.

The leather ball, which is filled with cork and made in the village, can be kicked, carried or thrown, although, in recognition of modern transportation, it cannot be carried in a car. The game starts with the 'turning-up' (throwing into the air) of the painted ball at the local Shaw Croft car park at 2 p.m. and continues until 10 p.m. If there is no winner on Shrove Tuesday the game continues on Ash Wednesday. In 1928, the ball was 'turned-up' by the Prince of Wales (later to become Edward VII), which has allowed the town to call the game 'royal'.

The game was first mentioned in 1683, but it appears to have been played well before that. As with other football games, attempts were made in the 1850s and 1860s to suppress it, including prosecutions under the Highways Act in 1860, but in 1862 an agreement was reached between players and the police. The game was then moved out of the town's market square and on to a field on the outskirts of the town called Shaw Croft, where it has continued up to today.

Sources and Reading:
Corbishley, G. J., *The Ashbourne Custom of Shrovetide Football* (Yeldersley: Wood, 1953).
Day, B., *A Chronicle of Folk Customs* (London: Hamlyn, 1988).
Morris, D., *The Soccer Tribe* (London: Cape, 1981).
Porter, L., *Shrovetide Football and the Ashbourne Games* (Ashbourne: Ashbourne Landmark, 1999).

See also Football

Tony Collins

Atherstone Shrovetide Football

A form of folk football played every Shrove Tuesday in the north Warwickshire town of Atherstone. Although a form of mass football, it differs from other versions in that it is played without teams or goals, the competition being based on an 'every man for himself' principle.

Allegedly dating back to 1199, the game begins at 3 p.m. when the ball, which is roughly the size of a cricket ball, filled with water and decorated with red, white and blue ribbons, is thrown from the top floor of a local bank (although it was originally thrown from a pub window). Play takes place along the town's Long Street, which was originally part of the Roman-built Watling Street. The game ends at 5 p.m., although after 4.30 p.m. it is legal to deflate the ball, and the winner is the player holding the ball at the end of the match.

Originally, according to local custom, the prize was a bag of gold and a year serving in the army, sought after because it carried a guaranteed wage for a year, but today the winner is entitled to keep the ball and receive free beer from some of the town's pubs.

Sources and Reading:
Brace, M., 'When push comes to Shrove . . .' *The Guardian*, 13 February 1999.

Day, B., *A Chronicle of Folk Customs* (London: Hamlyn, 1988).

Hole, C., *English Traditional Customs* (London: Batsford, 1975).

See also Football

Tony Collins

Athletics

The origins of all modern running, jumping and throwing athletics events can be found in the myriad of sporting activities of the pre-industrial era. Indeed, most can trace their antecedents back to the ancient Greek Olympics. Many are obviously related to military training. Javelin throwing, for example, is clearly derived from the throwing of spears, while the shot put reputedly began with the throwing of cannon balls. Running acquired additional prestige because of its importance for military communications, as highlighted by the story of the runner at the battle of Marathon. Hammer throwing is said to derive from a Viking method of laying claim to land, although this would appear to be unlikely given the relatively small distances, relative to the size of a smallholding or similar piece of land, that even the best hammer throwers can achieve.

Despite the widespread belief that all sports originated in the British Isles, many modern jumping sports have been shown to have developed in Germany. The high jump stand used today can be traced back to the invention of J. F. Simion in Dessau in 1776. The earliest recorded pole vault stand was used in Schnepfenthal in 1791, and both the triple jump (known as *dreisprungen*) and the long jump appear to have been significant in fifteenth-century and late-eighteenth-century Germany respectively.

The origins of modern athletics meetings can be traced back to the town and village fairs and festivals of early modern Britain, in which various athletics contests were often the centrepiece. By the nineteenth century, these events had become a focus for noted athletes to compete at a high level. The Highland and Border Games, the Egremont Crab Fair and the Grasmere Sports were among the prominent athletics carnivals that derived from these fairs. Unlike pedestrianism, most of the events that took place at these games were contests between men, and occasionally women, rather than being endurance, time or distance challenges.

As with most sports, the second half of the nineteenth century saw the organisation and codification of athletics by the middle classes. The Royal Military Academy at Woolwich began organising athletics competitions in 1849, swiftly followed by Oxford University's Exeter College in 1850. In the north of England, the Liverpool Athletic Club was founded in 1862. In 1865, the Amateur Athletic Club was founded in London based on rigid social exclusivity and in 1880 it extended its authority across Britain by transforming itself into the Amateur Athletic Association. It was not only working-class professional athletes who found themselves excluded from the new amateur athletics: initiatives such as William Penny Brooks' Much Wenlock Games found themselves marginalised by the evangelists of amateurism.

The common athletic club appellation 'harrier' has its origins during this period, due to the popularity of cross-country running. In 1867, a cross-country race was organised in south London by the Thames Rowing Club and the London Athletic Club in which runners, the 'hounds', would follow a paper trail left by two leading runners, the 'hares'. Known at the time as a 'paper chase', the success of the event was such that the following year saw the formation of the Thames Hare and Hounds club, from which the word harrier derived. The first cross-country championships were held in 1876 at Epping Forest.

Perhaps more than any other contemporary sport, the history of athletics has been reinvented as having little or no connection to its prehistory, which was that athletics was a universal and common form of sporting activity. Traditionally, athletics historians have concentrated on the origins of clubs with military, university and socially exclusive origins, while forgetting that for centuries running, jumping and throwing activities were enjoyed and organised by people of all social classes. This is not simply due to social prejudice; much of modern athletics depends on the highly accurate measurement of time and distance, a technological development that was not available until late Victorian times. The achievements of runners, jumpers and throwers of earlier generations simply could not be recorded with the accuracy that record-keepers now require. If, as suggested by historian E. P. Thompson, it was the fate of the working classes of the early nineteenth century to suffer the condescension of posterity, then it is perhaps also the fate of athletes of that era to have to contend with the disdain of digitally-measured time.

Sources and Reading:

Goulstone, J., 'English Folk Games and Sports', *British Society of Sports History Newsletter*, 10 (1999), 34–8.

Lovesey, P., *The Official Centenary History of the AAA* (London: Guinness, 1979).

Quercetani, R. L., *Athletics: A History of Modern Track and Field Athletics: Men and Women* (Milan: Vallardi & Associati, 1990).

Terry, D., 'Track and Field: Jumps and Throws', in Levinson, D. and Christensen, K. (eds), *World Encyclopedia of Sport* (volume 3) (Santa Barbara: ABC-CLIO, 1996), 1050–6.

See also Bar Throwing (Wales), Casting the Bar, Egremont Crab Fair, Fell Running, Grasmere Sports, Highland Games, Jumping, Leaping Pole, Liverpool Olympics, Morpeth Olympic Games, Much Wenlock Games, Pedestrianism, Stone Throwing

Tony Collins

Aunt Sally

Aunt Sally is a throwing game played outside public houses throughout Oxfordshire, south Warwickshire and around Abingdon, in what was north Berkshire. Pubs are organised into a series of local leagues, mostly established after 1918. Some pubs, such as The Fishes at North Hinksey and The Plough at Wolvercote, both near Oxford, are famous for the sport. The annual Aunt Sally Championships, contested by teams from the pub leagues of Oxford and Abingdon, are held in late August and early September. Clearly, Aunt Sally is closely related to skittles, but, given the lack of documentary evidence, its origins are obscure. It might have evolved from a game in which sticks were thrown at tethered chickens. Popular belief is that the Royalists brought the game to Oxford during the English Civil War. Another version of the game, now defunct, seemingly originated in America.

Several alternative explanations can be advanced for the genesis of the game's name. Sally is an English dialect word for the hare, and the use of throwing-sticks for poaching hares was not uncommon during the nineteenth century and earlier. However, the simplest explanation based on English dialect is that 'sally' means to pitch forward or totter and that 'aunt' refers to an old woman, or one of bad character. (The shape of the dolly at which throws are aimed clearly suggests a feminised figure.) Similarly, when Aunt Sally was popular in America, from the 1850s, 'aunt' was a nickname for an elderly black woman. This is significant because the American variant, apparently imported into England around 1855, entailed pitching batons (or balls) from nine yards at a black doll's head on a stake, attempting to hit a pipe held in the mouth, or which substituted for the nose, without striking the head. Like the coconut shy, Aunt Sally quickly became commonplace as a commercial sideshow at country fairs and racecourses, especially in southern England, with four throws per bout. This game was also known in France, as *jeu de massacre* ('wholesale slaughter').

In 1858, Aunt Sally received attention for its role in a *cause célèbre*. At Brighton races, the Duke of Beaufort assaulted a vet who rode across the Aunt Sally pitch the duke was playing on, spoiling his aim. The vet was awarded £100 damages. *The Times* wrote a leader about the case and *Punch* published a suitably caustic poem that stressed the impropriety of an aristocrat playing such a plebeian sport:

> Of all the games for Peers to play
> There's none that beats 'Aunt Sally;'
> Although 'tis fitter, some may say,
> For small boys in an alley.
> . . .
>
> 'Aunt Sally' is a doll, like one
> Of those which ragmen hang up:
> The nobs pronounce her 'rawther fun,'
> The snobs declare she's 'bang up!'
>
> Between her lips a pipe is set,
> Stout sticks are thrown to break it;
> The game is slightly vulgar, yet
> E'en Dukes their pastime make it.
> . . .
>
> 'Tis sweet to see Peers condescend
> With 'prentices to rally,
> And Dukes their lordly leisure spend
> A-playing of 'Aunt Sally'!

During the 1860s Aunt Sally became more socially acceptable, and was even a popular entertainment at garden parties in the Home Counties. Until the 1890s, it lingered as an attraction at resorts, pleasure fairs and grounds, such as that at Rosherville on the River Thames in Kent. Thereafter, fashion dictated that it retreat to what is now its heartland.

In the modern (post-1900) variant of the pub game, players take turns to throw six wooden truncheons (sticks), 18 inches long and 2 inches round, at a bulbous white skittle (dolly) with a small head, 8 inches high and 4 inches wide. The dolly is put on a small, slim bar that projects horizontally from the top of a vertical, four-foot high, metal rod (the iron), placed in the ground ten yards from the line (hockey) that each player tosses from. A pairs match consists of four legs (horses); a point is scored for a direct hit on the dolly. A score of 20 points or over, out of a player's 24 sticks, is outstanding. The eight-a-side team game normally consists of three horses, with each player throwing once per horse, making 144 sticks per team.

Sources and Reading:

Anon., 'A Morning Party', *Cornhill Magazine*, III (1861), 734–5.
Anon., 'A Trip on a Collier', *Pall Mall Gazette* (15 August 1884), 4.
Halliwell, J. O., *A Dictionary of Archaic and Provincial Words, Obsolete Phrases, Proverbs, and Ancient Customs, From the Fourteenth Century* (Fourth edition) (London: J. R. Smith, 1860), 112, 703.
Honey, D., *An Encyclopaedia of Oxford Pubs, Inns and Taverns* (Usk: Oakwood Press, 1998).
Jackson's Oxford Journal (11 July 1868), 1.
Punch (25 December 1858), 254.
Walsh, E. G. (ed.), *The Poacher's Companion* (Woodbridge: Boydell Press, 1983).
Wright, J. (ed.), *The English Dialect Dictionary*, V (Oxford: Oxford University Press, 1905), 207.

Mark Hathaway

Backsword

– *see* **Cudgelling and Singlestick**

Bad

A nineteenth-century version of informal cricket played in Yorkshire, using a bat, ball and a wall for a wicket.

Sources and Reading:

Gomme, A.B., *The Traditional Games of England, Scotland and Ireland* (London: Thames and Hudson facsimile edition, 1984).

See also Cricket

Tony Collins

Baddin

A name used for hockey-type games in Cheshire.

Sources and Reading:
Gomme, A. B., *The Traditional Games of England, Scotland and Ireland* (London: Thames and Hudson facsimile edition, 1984).

See also Hockey

Tony Collins

Badger Baiting

A particularly gruesome form of animal baiting in which a badger was tied by its tail to a stake in the ground and attacked by dogs. In another form, the badger was placed in a box and a dog sent in to fight with it. Badger baiting was outlawed in 1835 yet proved difficult to suppress, even after the Badgers Act of 1973, which specifically protected badgers from persecution.

Indeed, the sport experienced an upsurge in popularity in the late 1990s. In 2002 it was estimated that more badgers were killed by badger baiting than foxes were killed through fox-hunting. In the modern version, terriers are fitted with tracking devices to hunt down badgers in their underground setts. When a badger is captured, a pit is dug and terriers are dropped in to fight it. Often the badger's claws and teeth are removed to make the struggle easier for the dogs.

The work of the National Federation of Badger Groups, founded in 1986, has done much to bring to public attention the cruelty that badgers still face, and its work played a major part in the passing of the Badger Protection Act 1991.

Sources and Reading:
Blaine, D. P., *An Encyclopaedia of Rural Sports* (London: Longman, 1870).

The Encyclopaedia of Sport (London: The Sportsman, 1912).
Townsend, M., 'Badgers Fall Prey to Blood Sport Revival', *The Observer* (16 June 2002).

See also Bear Baiting, Bull Baiting

Tony Collins

Balloon

Also known as 'balloo' and 'pat ball', this was a game popular from the fourteenth to the seventeenth centuries. Players used their arms to strike back and forth an inflated leather ball, in a similar way to modern volleyball. Its first recorded mention dates back to 1580, and it is also mentioned in works by both John Donne and Ben Jonson. It was reputedly a favourite game of Prince Henry, the son of James I of England.

Sources and Reading:
Gomme, A. B., *The Traditional Games of England, Scotland and Ireland* (London: Thames and Hudson facsimile edition, 1984).

See also Handball

Tony Collins

Bando (Wales)

Popular across Wales, especially in Glamorgan, until the late nineteenth century, bando resembled the modern game of hockey or hurley; it involved striking a ball with a curved club (called a 'bando') across a fixed area of play before attempting to drive it into the opponents' goal. Matches were traditionally held between parishes, and the players of the two teams, which were generally all male, were known to train in advance in their quest to achieve victory. The prominence of the game at Margam, west Glamorgan, accounts for a ballad, probably early nineteenth-century, entitled *The Margam Bando Boys*, celebrating the team's proficiency and wide renown.

'Bando' derives from the French *bande*, meaning 'bent stick', and the clubs used were made of hard local woods, such as ash or elm. The ball, similar in size to today's hockey ball, was often carved from holly or box. Lacking a set of standardised rules, games varied depending on the area; there was also no specific time limit to the matches or restrictions on the number of players. Violence was commonplace, and even the presence of a referee could not deter athletes from hitting the opposition with their sticks. The large crowds placed bets on the final score, and with local innkeepers ensuring a continuous flow of alcohol, it was almost certainly the lethal combination of gambling, drink and boisterous behaviour, both on and off the pitch, that eventually drove bando out of existence.

Sources and Reading:

Lewis, H. (ed.), *Morgannwg Matthews* (Cardiff: University of Wales Press, 1953).

Lloyd, H., 'Tri o Hen Chwaraeon', *Transactions of the Honourable Society of Cymmrodorion* (1960), 97–108.

Redwood, C., *The Vale of Glamorgan: Scenes and Tales Among the Welsh* (London: Saunders and Otley, 1839).

Emma Lile

Bandy

Also known as 'bandy ball', the sport was a forerunner of hockey (in both its field and ice versions). The name derives from the name of the stick used by players, the 'bandy', which, like a modern hockey stick or golf club, was long with a curved end. Two teams would endeavour to drive a small wooden ball towards goals, the natures of which were, as in football, dependent on local custom and geography.

In his 1830 *Vocabulary of East Anglia*, Robert Forby describes the bandy as being 'made of very tough wood, or shod with metal, or with the point of the horn or the hoof of some animal. The ball is knob or gnarl from the trunk of a tree, carefully formed into a globular shape. The adverse parties strive to beat it with their bandies through one or other of the goals.' In contrast to the bandy, a straight stick was known in Old English as a 'crick'.

Popular in Devon in the sixteenth century, bandy was also commonly played in Wiltshire on Palm Sunday, although this game involved a ball being hit to the top of a hill by men and boys. Thomas D'Urfey mentions the sport in his 1693 comedy, *A Richmond Heiress*. Similar games in Norfolk and Suffolk were known as 'bandy-hoshoe' and as 'hawkey' respectively. Nottingham Forest Football Club was formed in 1865 by players of the game and was originally titled Nottingham Forest Football and Bandy Club.

Other variants of the sport included 'bandy cad', which was also known as 'bandy gad', in which a type of wooden puck was used rather than a ball, and 'bandy-wicket', a form of cricket played with a curved bandy bat and which was popular in Norfolk and Suffolk in the eighteenth century.

Bandy was also the name given in the late nineteenth century to a form of ice hockey, which used a rubber ball instead of a puck and whose rules resembled those of soccer. The first organised match between teams from London took place in 1875. A National Bandy Association was founded in 1891 to regulate the sport and clubs existed in Virginia Water, Camberley and Northampton, as well as in Holland and Norway. Today, the game is played indoors in Holland and outside in Finland, Norway, Sweden and the Baltic states of the former Soviet Union.

From a modern perspective, ice bandy's importance lies in its role as a precursor to ice hockey, which was first played in Ontario, Canada, by British troops in around 1867, although the first rules were drawn up at McGill University in Montreal in 1879.

Sources and Reading:

Encyclopedia of Sports, Games and Pastimes (London: Fleetway, 1935).

The Encyclopaedia of Sport (London: The Sportsman, 1912).

Gomme, A. B., *The Traditional Games of England, Scotland and Ireland* (London: Thames and Hudson facsimile edition, 1984).

Whitlock, R., *A Calendar of Country Customs* (London: Batsford, 1978).

See also Cashornie, Crick Ball, Hockey

Tony Collins

Barclay, Captain Robert

Captain Robert Barclay achieved national prominence and a place in athletics posterity in the summer of 1809 when he achieved the phenomenal feat of walking 1,000 miles in 1,000 hours. Walking a course set out with great precision on Newmarket Heath, he began his walk on 1 June and ended it successfully at 3.37 p.m. on 12 July. As well as nationwide fame, his feat won him an estimated 16,000 guineas (£16,800); although the original wager was for 1,000 guineas, side-bets had swelled the purse substantially. *The Times* estimated that a total of £100,000 had been bet on the event.

The attempt attracted huge public interest. Thousands flocked to the heath to see him walk his daily quota of miles, lending the event a carnival-like atmosphere. Given the amount of money at stake, and the dangers of physical exhaustion, Barclay's course and routine were meticulously planned. Seven gas lamps were erected one hundred yards apart to illuminate the course. A bodyguard was appointed to ensure that nothing untoward happened to Barclay to prevent him finishing the course and collecting the money. Barclay's attendant, William Cross, was responsible for treating injuries and ensuring that the captain did not fall asleep before or during the walk. Unsurprisingly, the walk took a tremendous toll on Barclay's body; he lost 32 lbs (14.5 kilograms) during his endeavours.

Born Robert Barclay Allardice on 25 August 1779 at Ury in Scotland, Barclay was one of eight children. His father, Robert senior, was a Scottish laird who became an MP in 1788. The son obviously inherited his hardiness and athleticism from his father, who had once walked the 510 miles between Ury and London in ten days. These were attributes that could be put to good use by an enterprising athlete in the late eighteenth century, a period that witnessed a craze for improbable feats of endurance.

In 1789, Donald MacLeod walked 1,680 miles, despite the fact he was allegedly 100 years old, and many other similar walking feats were reported with enthusiasm by the press. Gambling was crucial to all such events. Large stakes were wagered on the success or failure of such high-profile walkers, and even relative unknowns could make money if their attempted feats captured the public imagination. The young Barclay began his walking career at the age of 17, when he won a bet of 100 guineas that he could walk six miles in an hour from his home village of Brixton.

Just eight days after he had completed his mammoth walk, Barclay set out on another task of physical endeavour. He left with the 23rd Regiment for Europe to fight Napoleon in the Walcheren expedition, in which he served as aide-de-camp to the marquis of Huntly. Much of his subsequent life was spent in unsuccessful attempts to claim the Scottish earldoms of Airth, Strathern and Montieth. He died in 1854.

Sources and Reading:
Radford, P., *The Celebrated Captain Barclay: Sport, Gambling and Adventure in Regency Times* (London: Headline, 2002).

Tony Collins

Barley-Break

Also known as the 'last couple in hell', barley-break was a recreational game played by six people, three of each sex, on an area divided equally into three, the middle section being known as hell. Its name was supposedly derived from it being played among stacks of barley. After having drawn lots, the couple in the middle section had to catch the other players as they crossed from one outer section to the other in order to change partners. Once caught, a couple would take their place as catchers in the middle section. The middle couples faced the disadvantage of having to hold hands while the others, who did not, attempted to get by them. The aim of the game was to be the last couple to be caught.

The earliest reference to the game is in Henry Machyn's diary entry of 19 April 1557, in which he mentions the playing of 'barle breyke'. It features in Sir Philip Sidney's *Arcadia*, a poem about Strephon's courtship of Urania, and is also mentioned in Fletcher and Shakespeare's *Two Noble Kinsman*.

Popular throughout England and Scotland up until at least the eighteenth century, the game was denounced in 1607 in a booklet entitled *Barley Breake; or, A Warning for Wantons*, presumably for encouraging high spirits among mixed-sex groups. Primarily a game for young people, it is closely related to 'tag' and the game called 'prisoner's bars'. In Scotland, it was known as 'barla-breikis'.

Sources and Reading:
Gomme, A. B., *The Traditional Games of England, Scotland and Ireland* (London: Thames and Hudson facsimile edition, 1984).
Hone, W., *The Every-Day Book* (London: Thomas Tegg, 1830).
Opie, I. and Opie. P., *Children's Games in Street and Playground* (Oxford: Oxford University Press, 1969).

See also Prisoner's Bars

Tony Collins

Bar Throwing (Wales)

Throwing a heavy bar, most-likely made of metal, was an ancient Celtic pastime, common throughout Wales and frequently mentioned in medieval verse. Fifteenth- and sixteenth-century poets, such as Dafydd Llwyd (*c.* 1395–*c.* 1486) and Tudur Aled (*c.* 1465–*c.* 1525) often exalted their patrons' ability to hurl the bar great distances, and Tudur Aled himself was a renowned champion at the pursuit. Churchyard bar throwing was customary at the numerous parish festivals during the eighteenth and nineteenth centuries, in which it usually formed part of a wide-ranging programme of athletic sports.

Sources and Reading:
Jones, T., *Y Darian* (22 December 1927).
Lile, E., Athletic Competition in Pre-Industrial Wales, M. Phil. thesis, School of Sports Sciences, University of Birmingham, 1994.

Emma Lile

Baseball

A traditional English game closely related to many bat-and-ball games in which the ball is hit with a bat, at which point the batter has to make their way to a 'base' while fielders attempt to catch the ball, hit the batter with the ball or hit the base with the ball before the batter reaches it.

There are few things more irritating to modern baseball followers than to be told that their game is just another version of rounders. In fact, references to baseball, often with a hyphen or space between the two words, in England predate those to rounders. The earliest is probably the Puritan Thomas Wilson's complaint in 1700 that he had seen baseball, along with other sports, being played in Maidstone on Sundays. John Newbery's *A Little Pretty Pocket Book* (1744) even contains a woodcut and rhyming instructions on how to play the game. Probably the most famous reference, however, is found in Jane Austen's novel *Northanger Abbey*, written in 1798, where it is cited as one of the heroine's favourite pastimes. In contrast, it appears that the first substantial reference to rounders is a chapter published in the 1828 edition of *The Boy's Own Book* by William Clarke.

By the mid-nineteenth century baseball had come to be seen as a game for young people; Delabere Blaine noting in 1870 that 'there are few of us of either sex but have been engaged in base-ball since our majority'. Indeed, it would have remained just one of many versions of bat, ball and running games had it not become the 'national pastime' of the United States in the late nineteenth century.

In 1874 the first US baseball teams toured Britain, but they were bringing a reinvented 'foreign' sport to a nation in which cricket held an unassailable grip on British sporting culture. Unsurprisingly, the formation of the National Baseball League in 1890 proved to be unfulfilled in its hopes of establishing the professional game in Britain.

The 1907 attempt of A. G. Spalding to prove that baseball was a uniquely American game that had been invented by Abner Doubleday at Cooperstown in 1839 was not only laughed off by serious historians but also sparked a quest, which continues to this day, to discover the true origins of baseball. Despite considerable effort, and the discovery of a few blind alleys, such as the confusion of variants of prisoner's base with baseball, little progress has been made. The reason is simple; like the relationship between the modern football codes and folk football, modern baseball is not directly derived from any single pre-modern bat-and-ball game, rather it owes its spirit to all of them.

Sources and Reading:

Blaine, D. P., *An Encyclopaedia of Rural Sports* (London: Longman, 1870).

Gomme, A. B., *The Traditional Games of England, Scotland and Ireland* (London: Thames and Hudson facsimile edition, 1984).

Henderson, R. W., *Ball, Bat and Bishop: The Origin of Ball Games* (New York: Rockport, 1947).

Johnes, M., '"Poor Man's Cricket": Baseball, Class and Community in South Wales c.1880–1950', *International Journal of the History of Sport*, 17: 4 (2000), 153–66.

Mason, T., 'When Professional Baseball Nearly Came to Britain', *Revue Française de Civilisation Britannique*, 10: 4 (2000), 37–46.

Website:

UK branch of the Society for American Baseball Research: www.sabruk.org.

See also Rounders, Stoolball, Stowball, Trap Ball

Tony Collins

Battledore and Shuttlecock

Also known as 'shuttlefeather', battledore and shuttlecock is a sport that dates back at least to the fourteenth century and became especially fashionable in the first decades of the seventeenth century. While a prisoner in the Tower of London for alleged involvement in the Gunpowder Plot, the Earl of Northumberland reputedly purchased shuttlecocks to keep himself amused. The game became popular with all classes and regions throughout England at least, and was connected to a number of children's rhymes and games.

It bore great resemblance to modern badminton, which was based on the older sport, with the exception that the older game did not use a net. The battledore, which was originally the name given to a wooden bat used for beating clothes during washing, was a small hand bat. It was initially made of wood, but later it was made from animal skin stretched over a frame, which was ultimately replaced by catgut stretched over the frame. The shuttlecock was initially a small cork into which feathers were pushed at equal distances. Game-play consisted, as it does today in badminton, of hitting the shuttlecock between the two or four players, with points being scored when an opponent let the shuttlecock hit the ground.

Badminton was first played in the 1870s, most notably at Badminton House, home of the Duke of Beaufort, where it may have been imported from India. The Badminton Association was formed by 14 clubs in 1893.

Sources and Reading:
Gomme, A. B., *The Traditional Games of England, Scotland and Ireland* (London: Thames and Hudson facsimile edition, 1984).

Tony Collins

Bear Baiting

A blood sport in which a pack of up to half a dozen dogs would be set on a bear, the 'sport' deriving from the betting which took place on the chances of survival of the dogs or the bear. It could also consist of a human prodding a bear with a stick to agitate it. Up until at least the fifteenth century, it was commonly viewed as a popular sport with schoolboys. Part of the appeal of bear baiting was based on the fact that a bear was an extremely rare sight in Britain; every bear had to be imported as the animal was no longer native to the British Isles.

References to the sport can be found in Henry II's time but it became a major public attraction in London during the mid-sixteenth century. Sir Walter Raleigh claimed that the Southwark Bear Gardens were one of London's principal sights, and Elizabeth I allegedly attended a bear baiting display featuring twelve bears in 1575. In 1583 over 1,000 spectators crammed into the Paris Garden in London to a see a bait, but the grandstand collapsed leaving many dead or injured. There was even a crown office under Elizabeth I, the Master of Bears, for which the holder was paid one shilling and fourpence per day.

Bear baiting flourished despite strenuous efforts by Puritans and others to have it out-lawed. Philip Stubbs, in his 1583 *Anatomy of Abuses*, denounced the sport, asking:

> Is not the baiting of a bear, besides that it is a filthy, stinking and loathsome game, a dangerous and perilous exercise? . . . What Christian heart can take pleasure to see one poor beast to rend and tear and kill another, and all for his foolish pleasure?

Others felt that enthusiasm for the sport was undermining the appeal of archery as a pastime and also attendance at church services. Bear baiting returned to popularity following the Restoration, and it is referred to in the diaries of both Samuel Pepys and John Evelyn. It was suspended during the Great Plague of 1665 and subsequently struggled to regain its former popularity, not least because bears became increasingly expensive to import.

However, despite an attempt to ban it in 1724, the sport continued in a limited form throughout the eighteenth century, as the following advertisement from His Majesty's Bear Garden makes clear:

> A mad bull to be dress'd up with fire-works and turned loose in the game place. Likewise a dog to be dress'd up with fireworks over him and turned loose with the bull amongst the men in the ground. Also a bear to be turn'd loose at the same time; and a cat to be ty'd to the bull's tail.

In the mid-eighteenth century, it was the practice in Liverpool to provide a bear for baiting at mayoral election times. Its appeal still extended across all classes of society; as a local commentator noted 'every house and window in the vicinity of the spot where the bear was baited, was adorned by the appearance of the most elegant ladies and gentlemen of the town'. The taste for the exotic in animal baiting could also be seen as late as 1825 when an exhibition of lion baiting took place in Warwick in which a lion was set upon by three dogs.

Bear baiting gradually became unfashionable by the end of the eighteenth century, partly due to the increased appeal of human blood sports, such as boxing, and partly because the tethering of the bear was seen as unfair in that it did not allow the animal a 'sporting chance' of escape. The chief reason for its eventual death was, however, the major campaigns waged against blood sports by Christian-inspired animal-welfare reformers in the early nineteenth century, most notably highlighted by the formation of the Society (later the Royal Society) for the Prevention of Cruelty to Animals in 1824. The campaign's first major legislative victory was the 1835 Cruelty to Animals Act, which banned all forms of animal baiting and signalled the final end of bear baiting.

Sources and Reading:
Encyclopedia of Sports, Games and Pastimes (London: Fleetway, 1935).
The Encyclopaedia of Sport (London: The Sportsman, 1912).
Hone, W., *The Every-Day Book* (London: Thomas Tegg, 1830).
Malcolmson, R., *Popular Recreations in English Society 1700–1850* (Cambridge: Cambridge University Press, 1973).
Reeves, C., *Pleasures and Pastimes in Medieval England* (Stroud: Sutton, 1995).

See also Badger Baiting, Boar Baiting, Bull Baiting

Tony Collins

Becher, Martin

Steeplechase jockey 'Captain' Martin William Becher (1797–1864) found lasting fame by taking refuge in a brook. Son of an army man turned Norfolk farmer and horse dealer, he secured a position in Brussels in the stores supplying Wellington's troops. His own rank of captain was an honorary one in the Buckinghamshire Yeomanry. On his return to Britain he worked initially as a horse dealer, but later he became first jockey for Thomas Coleman, proprietor of the Turf Hotel at St Albans. Coleman is generally credited with pioneering the commercial development of steeplechasing

when he promoted the St Albans Steeplechase in 1830. He encouraged Becher to take up riding over fences; not that the gallant captain required much persuasion for he had been taught to ride all manner of horses as a child and was a skilled horseman. Although qualified to ride in races restricted to gentlemen, Becher made a living from riding and from schooling horses over fences for their owners.

His name is indelibly associated with the Grand National steeplechase. In 1836, riding The Duke, he won William Lynn's inaugural chase at Aintree and came third on the same horse two years later. However, it was in the 1839 race, usually recognised as the first Grand National even though the title was not formally adopted till 1847, that Becher gained racing immortality. When running second in a field of 17, his mount, Conrad, fell at a specially constructed jump in which a brook had been dammed to make it 2.6 metres wide and a 0.9 metre wooden fence set about a metre in front of the water. The hazard was increased by the landing area being a metre or so lower than the take-off side. Becher landed in the water and sensibly crouched in safety in the deepest part of the brook until the rest of the horses had passed by. Less sensibly, perhaps, he remounted, only to take another soaking at the next water jump. Although he never again rode in a Grand National, such was his fame that the fence at which he fell became known as Becher's Brook. In 1990, Becher's Brook was filled in, but it remains a challenging fence on the Aintree circuit, a fitting memorial to a tough and intrepid rider.

Sources and Reading:
Munting, R., *Hedges and Hurdles* (London: J. A. Allen, 1987).
Seth-Smith, M., Willett, P., Mortimer, R. and Lawrence, J., *The History of Steeplechasing* (London: Michael Joseph, 1966).

Wray Vamplew

Billets

Also know as 'billeting', the game was similar to 'knur and spell' and played in north Yorkshire. The billet was a wooden puck, usually between 7 and 10 centimetres long. The billet was balanced on the end of the player's billeting-stick, and then flicked up and hit with the same stick. Unlike the pommel in knur and spell, the billeting-stick had no flat surface, making the hitting of the ball more difficult.

Distances were measured in 'scores', but in contrast to knur and spell each score was 10 rather than 20 yards. The player who hit the billet furthest – a hit of 100 yards would be considered an excellent hit – was the winner. The game was particularly popular on the Lancashire–Yorkshire border around Todmorden and Halifax.

Sources and Reading:
Day, B., *A Chronicle of Folk Customs* (London: Hamlyn, 1988).

See also Knur and Spell, Tip Cat

Tony Collins

Bittle-Battle

A Sussex version of stoolball. The implication of the name is that the stool used as the wicket was defended by the use of the 'bittle', a local dialect word for bat.

Sources and Reading:
Gomme, A. B., *The Traditional Games of England, Scotland and Ireland* (London: Thames and Hudson facsimile edition, 1984).

See also Stoolball

Tony Collins

Blow-Point

A game dating back to at least the sixteenth century in which an arrow or pin was blown, sometimes using a tube, at a target or at other pins.

Sources and Reading:
Gomme, A. B., *The Traditional Games of England, Scotland and Ireland* (London: Thames and Hudson facsimile edition, 1984).

See also Puff and Dart

Tony Collins

Boar Baiting

A rare variation on bull and bear baiting, boar baiting is mentioned as a popular sport in London by the twelfth-century writer William Fitzstephen.

Sources and Reading:
Reeves, C., *Pleasures and Pastimes in Medieval England* (Stroud: Sutton, 1995).

See also Badger Baiting, Bear Baiting, Bull Baiting

Tony Collins

Bodmin Riding

Dating back to at least the fifteenth century, this was a midsummer festival held at Bodmin in Cornwall and was related to the Julian calendar's Midsummer's Day of 5 July. It took place on the Sunday and Monday following St Thomas a Becket's Day on 7 July. Its central event was a horseback procession around the town (hence its name), and sports were held on the Monday; the sports included Cornish wrestling, cudgel-fighting and running races. It disappeared in the early nineteenth century, but was revived in 1974.

Sources and Reading:
Munn, P., *Bodmin Riding and Other Similar Celtic Customs* (Bodmin: Bodmin Books, 1975).
Whitlock, R., *A Calendar of Country Customs* (London: Batsford, 1978).

Tony Collins

Book of Sports

Issued by James I of England (James VI of Scotland) in a proclamation at Greenwich on 24 May 1618 and officially titled *The King's Declaration of Lawful Sports*, the *Book of Sports* sought to establish which sports and games could be played on Sundays.

The immediate reason for its publication was to respond to a ban by Puritan magistrates in Lancashire in 1617 on the playing of all sports on Sundays. However, it was actually a response to long-running campaigns for strict sabbatarianism by Puritans, many of whom believed that Sunday sports were part of a papist conspiracy. Bills outlawing Sunday games had been passed by the House of Commons in 1606 and 1614, although they and the two subsequent bills passed in 1621 and 1624 had not been ratified by either James I or the House of Lords. In addition to the overtly religious concerns about Sunday sports, there was also increasing disquiet at the time about the growing popularity of games among the labouring classes, which, it was felt by those in authority, distracted them from work and sober conduct.

In issuing the proclamation, James I also sought to protect himself from accusations of being sympathetic to Catholicism. Hence the book decreed that sports could only be played after evening church services and that anyone who did not attend evening service, who were by implication Catholics, could not participate in Sunday sports. It also argued that if amusements on the Sabbath were banned, people would simply cease going to church at all, and that efforts to convert Catholics would be hindered.

Archery, leaping and vaulting were explicitly endorsed, as were many other non-sporting recreations, such as dancing, May games and Whitsuntide ales. In fact, the only sports that the book actually forbade to be played on a Sunday were bowls and bear and bull baiting; bowls being forbidden on the by-then traditional grounds that it distracted the common people from practising archery. However, in order to restrict any attempts to use sports events as cover for seditious gatherings, the book restricted participation in or attendance at Sunday games to members of the parish in which they were staged, warned against large gatherings and forbade the bearing of arms.

The *Book of Sports* did little to stop agitation for strict observance of the Sabbath; indeed, many Puritans were outraged that James I condoned such activities on the Lord's Day. The Sunday Observance Act of 1625, despite appearing to conciliate the Sabbatarians, did little more than codify the proclamation. It was reissued by James's son, Charles I, in 1633 following an attempt by magistrates in Somerset to outlaw all Sunday sports, and succeeded only in adding more combustible material to the tinder that would ignite into the English Civil War.

Sources and Reading:
Birley, D., *Sport and the Making of Britain* (Manchester: Manchester University Press, 1993).
Brailsford, D., *British Sport: A Social History* (Cambridge: Lutterworth Press, 1992).
Hill, C., *Society and Puritanism in Pre-Revolutionary England* (London: Secker and Warburg, 1964).
Sul, H., 'The King's Book of Sports: The Nature of Leisure in Early Modern England', *International Journal of the History of Sport*, 17: 4 (2000), 167–79.
Underdown, D., *Revel, Riot and Rebellion: Popular Politics and Culture in England 1603–1660* (Oxford: Clarendon, 1985).

Tony Collins

Bourton
Water Games

Played during late August on the river at Bourton-on-the-Water in Gloucestershire, the games include football and other 'traditional' sports.

Sources and Reading:
Day, B., *A Chronicle of Folk Customs* (London: Hamlyn, 1988).

Tony Collins

Bowls

Rolling a ball at a target appears to be a fairly universal human pleasure, almost as much as kicking and throwing a ball, stretching across time and societies. There are numerous examples of various forms of bowls being played in ancient cultures. Certainly in Britain a wide number of games derived from the original principle were being played by medieval times. Indeed, it is claimed that the Southampton Bowls Club's Knight of the Old Green tournament, which is still played today, dates back to 1299.

Bowls, associated with lush green turf and warm summer days, carries with it an evocation of a long-gone pastoral England. It is perhaps immortalised in English culture by the fact that Sir Francis Drake was allegedly playing bowls on Plymouth Hoe when told of the approach of the Spanish Armada in 1588; 'there is plenty of time to win this game and thrash the Spaniards too', he is said to have replied before returning to his game.

The sport generically known as bowls appears to have been first played using a round bowl, often a stone, which was rolled across flat ground to knock over a target. The target was often several small cones, known as 'jacks'. Marbles seems to have been a miniature version of the game suit-able for children. Half-bowl used a bowl cut in half, which was slid across the ground at a target. Closh used a stick to move the bowl through a hoop or ring. Kayles used a stick instead of a bowl to knock down the targets and was similar to skittles. Billiards seems to be derived from the same group as kayles, but was originally played on grass, as is noted in *Antony and Cleopatra*. Long bowls, later known as 'road bowls', was a version of the game in which a certain distance had to be bowled in the fewest number of throws.

However it was played, the game was sufficiently popular among the mass of the population for the authorities to see it as a threat to sports that were based on military training, such as archery. Bowls of all types was banned in 1361 by Edward III. This ban was lifted in 1455 by Henry VI, which immediately led to bowling greens and alleys springing up all over London. This probably caused more consternation, and in 1477 an edict forbidding the playing of closh and kayles was issued by Edward IV. Bowls was again banned in 1541 by Henry VIII, once again because it was thought to interfere with archery practice. The act under which it was banned, which was not repealed until 1845, said that no person 'by himself, factor, deputy, servant or other shall for his or their gain, lucre, or living, keep, have, hold, occupy, exercise or maintain any common house, alley or place of Bowling'. However, it did allow bowls to be played at Christmas time and a licence for a bowling green used for private play only could be applied for by those worth over £100 per annum.

Perhaps because of this exclusivity, bowls became fashionable among the upper classes in the sixteenth and seventeenth centuries. Henry himself was a keen bowler, and it is recorded that in April 1532 he lost £35 wagering on games. The following month, Anne Boleyn, his wife of the time, lost over £12. The ambiguous relationship between royalty and bowls can also be seen in the fact that one of the earliest bowling greens was installed at Holyrood Palace in Edinburgh by James IV of Scotland. However Mary, Queen of Scots, banned bowls under the 1555 Gaming Act, which also tried to outlaw the use of bowling alleys and arenas in an attempt to reduce the opportunities for seditious gatherings against the Crown.

Despite royalty's efforts to restrict its playing, the sixteenth century saw two of the most important technological developments in the sport: the introduction of the smaller 'jack' ball as a target and the introduction of bowls which had an in-built bias. This made the game more skilful, as it became much harder to bowl accurately, and also more interesting because it meant that bowls could be curved around opponents' bowls on the way to the jack. This appears to have increased the popularity of bowls. Like his father, Charles II was a keen bowler and drew up a set of rules during his reign, one of which forbade interference with a played bowl on pain of decapitation – although this rule does not appear to have ever been used. Gambling was central to the sport, and it appears that it was possible for the very best players to make a living as professionals: for example, a match was played at Hampstead in 1756 for 20 guineas.

The Edinburgh Society of Bowlers codified the first rules of modern bowls in 1771. A silver jack, presented as a trophy by the society in 1781, is still in existence. The game became very popular in the west of Scotland, and in 1849 a new set of rules was drawn up by William Mitchell, a Glasgow solicitor, which became the standard set of rules for the region and helped to popularise the game. Some English clubs also adopted these rules as the organisation of the game spread from the 1850s onwards.

It is noticeable that even at this time bowls was a sport associated with the elderly. Stonehenge, writing in the 1850s, noted that bowls was a game for the 'steady old gentleman rather than his racketty son' and that '30 or 40 elderly gentlemen will often amuse themselves in this way every evening throughout summer without ever arriving at anything like an absolute control of their erratic instruments'.

The late nineteenth century saw an explosion in the growth of bowls. The Northumberland and Durham Bowling Association began in 1882 and the Scottish Bowling Association was formed in 1892, although a number of local organisations and competitions were founded before this. The English Bowling Association (EBA) was formed in 1903, and the Welsh and Irish associations in the following year.

Modern lawn bowls is divided into three distinct versions. The EBA version is played on a flat green, with the aim of getting bowls (or 'woods') nearer to the jack than any opposing wood. Most popular in the south of England, it has traditionally opposed professionalism, insisted on the wearing of whites for matches and, until 1985, did not allow competition between men and women.

The English Bowling Federation's version of the game is similar, the most important difference being that no wood counts unless it is less than two yards from the jack. This form of the game is played primarily in the English north-east and Midlands. The federation was formed in 1945 and is far less formal than the EBA; it has also allowed mixed contests since the 1920s.

The third version of the game is crown green bowls, which developed and became the dominant form of the sport in the north of England, and is closely associated with bowling greens near pubs. As the name suggests, the green is raised in the middle and the jack has a bias, making it, in the eyes of its supporters, a more skilful game. Unlike the EBA game, crown green bowls allowed professionalism and betting. For many years its premier competition was the Talbot Handicap, started in 1887 and named after the Blackpool pub where it was played, but later the Waterloo Handicap, also held in Blackpool, superseded it. The game's first governing body, covering Lancashire and Cheshire, was founded in 1888.

Sources and Reading:
Brailsford, D., *British Sport: A Social History* (Cambridge: Lutterworth Press, 1992).

The Encyclopaedia of Sport (London: The Sportsman, 1912).

Hone, W., *The Every-Day Book* (London: Thomas Tegg, 1830).

Piley, P. (ed.), *The Story of Bowls from Drake to Bryant* (London: Stanley Paul, 1987).

Reeves, C., *Pleasures and Pastimes in Medieval England* (Stroud: Sutton, 1995).

Stonehenge [J. H. Walsh], *Manual of British Rural Sports* (London: Routledge, 1857).

See also Closh, Kayles, Marbles, Road Bowls, Skittles, Troco

Tony Collins

British Association for Shooting and Conservation

The British Association for Shooting and Conservation (BASC) is the main organisation responsible for fostering and safeguarding shooting in Britain, with particular emphasis on wildfowling and rough shooting. It represents the interests of wildfowlers on numerous national and international committees. Until the 1970s, it was known as the Wildfowlers Association of Great Britain and Ireland (WAGBI), which had been founded in 1908 by Stanley Duncan. It has several hundred affiliated wildfowling clubs, which are responsible for controlling wildfowling on their local marshes.

One of the BASC's most important functions is to monitor political activity at local, national and European levels. It reviews draft legislation affecting land use, wildlife conservation or firearms and makes the appropriate representations. Its staff provide advice and services covering all aspects of shooting and practical conservation to both individual members and wildfowling clubs. Practical conservation measures have included the Duck Conservation Scheme in 1954, the establishment (with the Wildfowl Trust) of an experimental reserve at Sevenoaks in 1958, and assisting with the Icelandic government's research into pink-footed geese, threatened by a proposed hydroelectric development in the 1970s. The BASC's Wildlife Habitat Trust has provided resources for purchasing the freehold of some marshes. The designation of Sites of Special Scientific Interest (SSSIs) and Special Protection Areas (SPAs) has posed threats to the survival of wildfowling in many localities. Work by BASC's research staff includes investigations into the effects of harsh weather upon wildfowl, and projects jointly with other organisations into the effects on wildfowl of the ingestion of lead shot.

Until the 1980s, the rise of wildfowling clubs was not universally popular since some wildfowlers were reluctant to accept a degree of regulation. For most shooters, membership is now a necessary prerequisite to securing access to suitable wildfowling foreshore. There has been a gradual realisation that self-regulation and the voluntary acceptance of sensible and moderate codes of conduct are the most effective ways of avoiding more draconian statutory regulations.

Sources and Reading:
Wildfowl Conservation in Great Britain – The Story of a Triumvirate (WAGBI, Nature Conservancy and the Wildfowl Trust, 1970).

John Martin

Broadsword

A double-edged sword designed both for cutting and thrusting, the broadsword contrasts with the rapier sword which is used only for thrusting. It was the premier sword of English soldiers until the advent of firearms.

It was also used for fencing and the first instruction book on its use in a sporting context was George Silver's *Paradoxes of Defence*, published in 1599. Silver later wrote two more detailed instruction books, which were never published but are still extant in manuscript form.

By 1737 at least, there were a number of professional broadsword fencers in Britain who made a living from sword fights in a similar way to pugilistic prizefighters. Captain James Miller's book of engravings published in that year illustrates the tactics and techniques used by professional broadsword fencers.

Sporting broadswords were blunter than those used by the military, yet were still sharp enough to inflict serious injury on the fencer careless enough to let his guard slip.

By the 1820s, the era of the professional swordsman had effectively ended, but the broadsword can still be seen today as a prop in battle re-enactments and also in Scottish country dancing.

Sources and Reading:
The Encyclopaedia of Sport (London: The Sportsman, 1912).

See also Backsword, Fencing, Sword and Buckler

Tony Collins

Broughton's Rules

These rules 'produced by Mr Broughton, for the better regulation of Amphi-theatre, and approved of by the gentlemen, and agree by the pugilists, August 18th 1743' (Brailsford: 8) were ex-prizefighter Jack Broughton's summary of best practice for use in his venture as a promoter. These rules became generally accepted in the sport and lasted with little change for well over a century. Broughton's Rules were:

1. That a square of a yard be chalked in the middle of the stage; and on every fresh set-to after a fall, or being parted from the rails, each second is to bring his man to the side of the square, and place him opposite to the other; and till they are fairly set to the lines, it shall not be lawful for the one to strike the other.

2. That, in order to prevent any disputes as to the time a man lies after a fall, if the second does not bring his man to the side of the square within a space of half a minute, he shall be deemed a beaten man.

3. That, in every main battle, no person shall be on the stage, except the principals and the seconds. The same rule to be observed in bye-battles, except that in the latter, Mr Broughton is allowed to be upon the stage to keep decorum, and to assist gentlemen to get their places; provided always, he does not interfere in the battle; and whoever pretends to infringe these rules, to be turned immediately out of the house. Everybody is to quit the stage as soon as the champions are stripped, before they set to.

4. That no champion be deemed beaten, unless he fails coming up to the line within the limited time, or that his own second declares him beaten. No second is to be allowed to ask his man's adversary any questions, or advise him to give out.

5. That in bye-battles the winning man to have two-thirds of the money given which shall be publicly divided upon the stage, notwithstanding any private agreement to the contrary.

6. That to prevent disputes in every main battle, the principals shall, on the coming on the stage, choose from the gentlemen present, two umpires, who shall absolutely decide all disputes that may arise about the battle; and if the two umpires cannot agree, the said umpires to choose a third, who is to determine it.

7. That no person is to hit his adversary when down or seize him by the hair, the breeches, or any part below the waist; a man on his knees to be reckoned down.

Sources and Reading:
Brailsford, D., *Bareknuckles: A Social History of Prize-Fighting* (Cambridge: Lutterworth Press, 1988).

See also Prizefighting

Wray Vamplew

Buckle, Frank

Frank Buckle (1766–1832) was the first jockey to dominate British racing. Aged 16 and weighing only 3 stones 13 pounds, Buckle made his racecourse debut at Newmarket in May 1783. At the age of 65 he rode his last race, also at Newmarket, in November 1831, just three months before his death. Neither horse won, but in between times Buckle notched up 27 Classic victories, including the Epsom double twice and the Guineas double six times. This record number of Classic wins stood until 1984, when Lester Piggott won the St Leger on Commanche Run. Piggott, however, had five opportunities a year, but Buckle only three until the Two Thousand and One Thousand Guineas were established in 1809 and 1814 respectively.

The son of a Newmarket saddler, Buckle was orphaned at the age of 12 and apprenticed to a trainer, the Honourable Richard Vernon, who had been impressed by the boy's riding in private trials. Buckle then began to ride for the first Earl Grosvenor, for whom he won two Derbys and two Oaks. After Grosvenor's death he rode for Newmarket trainer Robert Robson, whose principal patron was the third Duke of Grafton. Buckle was dubbed the 'Pocket Hercules' on account of the power he could exert for his size, and his forte was the waiting race, where he held up his horse prior to a late rush to the winning post. Such a tactic paid off well in the many match races in which he was involved, most notably when he piloted Hambletonian to victory against Diamond, ridden by Dennis Fitzpatrick, for a purse of 3,000 guineas. Over the 4 miles, 1 furlong and 138 yards of Newmarket's Beacon Course, Buckle judged things to perfection to win by half a neck. One match that he did not win was a two-mile race against Alicia Thornton at York in 1805. Riding side-saddle, Thornton beat Buckle, who was, it should be said, giving her a considerable weight advantage.

Generally, he disliked making the running, preferring to hang back and then to make a late challenge, as he did successfully on both Scotia and Tyrant to win the Oaks and the Derby in 1802. In those days jockeys were allowed to bet, and it is said that Buckle won a tidy sum on that Epsom Classic double. Unlike many jockeys, he chose not to live in a major training area, settling as a farmer near Peterborough where he pursued breeding of cattle, greyhounds, bulldogs and fighting cocks. This often necessitated a 90 mile round trip to ride trials at Newmarket, which he undertook on one of his immaculately turned-out hacks (a matter of personal pride) with his riding saddle strapped across his back. Allegedly, he banned discussion of racing at home to deter his sons from following him into a riding career. The idea must have worked as they became a solicitor, a chemist and a brewer. One of his whips, silver coated and emblazoned with details of his Classic triumphs, became a racing trophy in Germany.

Sources and Reading:

Mortimer, R., Onslow, R. and Willett, P., *Biographical Encyclopaedia of British Flat Racing* (London: Macdonald & Jane's, 1978).
Tanner, M. and Cranham, G., *Great Jockeys of the Flat* (London: Guinness, 1992).

Wray Vamplew

Bull Baiting

Probably the most popular form of animal-baiting sport, bull baiting consisted of a bull being tied to a stake with a rope between 10 and 15 feet long. It was then baited – bitten, scratched and savaged – by dogs, usually bulldogs or mastiffs specially bred for the sport.

The first account of it in England can be found in William Fitzstephen's description of the City of London in 1174, but it clearly has a history stretching back much further. Bull baiting was a common sight at wakes, fairs and other festivals, both in urban and rural areas. Up until the seventeenth century at least, it was also a common part of church ales entertainments.

Certainly, by the end of the eighteenth century it was popular enough to support a number of itinerant bull-baiting professionals, who, rather like circus entertainers, toured various wakes and fairs with a bull and charged people to allow their dogs to take part in the baiting. Like so many other pre-modern sports, it was also closely associated with pubs and the entrepreneurial activities of publicans. Its appeal lay not only in its violence but also in the opportunities it presented for gambling on the performance of both the bull and the dogs. Owing to their great strength, bulls occasionally broke free from their ropes, and were known to have injured and even killed spectators.

Unlike other forms of animal baiting, there was a ritualistic element to bull baiting which provided its supporters with justification for their apparent cruelty. It was widely believed that baiting the bull would improve the taste of the beef when the animal was finally butchered, making the flesh tender and tastier. Indeed, in the sixteenth and seventeenth centuries some local authorities laid down that a bull had to be baited before being killed in order to thin out its blood (which was believed to be poisonous). An example of how deep-rooted this belief was can be seen from 1618 when a Weymouth butcher was fined for selling unbaited beef. It is therefore not surprising that many bull-baiting areas were situated next to butchers' shops.

The importance of bull baiting to many areas is shown by the number of towns, such as Darlington and Hornsea in east Yorkshire, that had an iron ring permanently fixed to the ground (with which to tether the bull) in the centre of the town. Perhaps the most famous example of this is the Bull Ring in Birmingham city centre; the West Midlands region as a whole had a significant tradition of bull baiting that continued almost to the mid-nineteenth century. Indeed, bulls for baiting were also sometimes provided by the local civic authorities. In Beverley, it was the tradition for the newly elected mayor of the town to provide a bull, and in 1821 the authorities at Lincoln provided two bulls for baiting. In

Wales, bull baiting was popular among all social classes until the mid-nineteenth century, with a town's corporation often providing and maintaining the ring and the ground. The sport was especially prevalent in Welsh market towns, where it was authorised by law.

Despite this support, by the late eighteenth century bull baiting, along with other traditional sports associated with the working classes, such as football, came under attack from Christian reformers and groups opposed to animal cruelty, most notably those organised in the Society for the Prevention of Cruelty to Animals, which was founded in 1824. Butchers no longer provided bulls, gentry patronage was harder to come by and many towns in the north of England saw the complete disappearance of bull baiting.

Two bills to outlaw bull baiting were introduced to Parliament in 1800 and 1802 but both failed narrowly, due in some part to vigorous campaigning against them by William Windham. During the 1820s, many strongholds of the sport, such as Lincoln, Aylesbury and Beverley, banned the sport. The 1822 Cruelty to Animals Act forbade cruelty to cattle and was initially interpreted by some as applying to bull baiting, but this interpretation was overruled in 1827 when the King's Bench sanctioned bull baiting on private land. It was only with the 1835 Cruelty to Animals Act that bull baiting was explicitly and finally outlawed.

Sources and Reading:

Dodd, A. H. (ed.), *A History of Wrexham* (Wrexham: Hughes, 1927).

The Encyclopaedia of Sport (London: The Sportsman, 1912).

Griffen, E., 'Bull Baiting in Industrialising Townships 1800–1850', in Hewitt, M. (ed.), *Unrespectable Recreations* (Leeds: Leeds Centre for Victorian Studies, 2001), 19–30.

Malcolmson, R., *Popular Recreations in English Society 1700–1850* (Cambridge: Cambridge University Press, 1973).

Reeves, C., *Pleasures and Pastimes in Medieval England* (Stroud: Sutton, 1995).

See also Badger Baiting, Bear Baiting, Boar
Baiting, Bull Running

Tony Collins and Emma Lile

Bull Running

Allegedly dating back to the time of King
John, bull running was practised primarily
in Stamford in Lincolnshire, where every 13
November people and dogs would chase a
bull through the streets of the town – the
reversal of the more famous form of bull
running in Pamplona, Spain, when the bulls
chase the people. Local legend has it that
the event started in 1209, when a dog was
sent by a butcher to break up a fight
between two bulls and chased one through
the town. William, Earl of Warenne, the
lord of the town, was allegedly so amused
by the event that he offered to the local
butchers the field in which the bulls had
been fighting, with the proviso that the
butchers provide a bull every year to run
through the town.

A description in William Hone's *The Every-
Day Book* of 1830 captures the scene:

> Hivie, shivie, tag and rag, men, women
> and children of all sorts and sizes, with
> all the dogs in the town, promiscuously
> run after him with their bull-clubs
> scattering dirt in each others faces, as
> when Theseus and Pirithous conquered
> Hell and punished Cerberus.

A break in the proceedings took place at
lunch-time, but the running recommenced
at one o'clock. The aim was to drive the bull
to a bridge that spanned the river Welland,
where participants would then throw the
bull into the river, known as 'brigging
the bull'. The bull would make his way back
to a meadow, where he would then be
baited by dogs before being led back into
the town to be slaughtered. The rare bull
that successfully resisted being thrown into
the river was usually spared his life.

Much concern was expressed about the
licentiousness which surrounded the event.

In 1829, a campaigner against bull running
commented about the bull runners that:

> many young women were among the
> number, whose conduct was anything
> but modest. Indeed, all classes seemed as
> if they had, on that day, licence to cast
> off all appearance of decency and order,
> and plunge into every excess of riot,
> without shame or restraint.

Although the first attempt to ban the event
occurred in 1788, huge popular support
for it meant that it was only finally suppressed after the 1839 run, four years after
it had been banned by the 1835 Cruelty to
Animals Act. In the intervening four years
it had been illegally staged in defiance of
a regiment of dragoons and hundreds
of special constables who had been sent
to suppress it. It had also been the subject
of one of the first successful prosecutions
undertaken by the Society for the
Prevention of Cruelty to Animals.

Bull running also took place from 1374 in
Tutbury, on the border of Staffordshire
and Derbyshire, the object of which was
for one half of the town to drive the bull
into Derbyshire and for the other half to
keep him in Staffordshire. Local folklore
has it that John of Gaunt, who rebuilt the
castle at Tutbury, started the event in order
to remind his Spanish wife of home. It had
originally been staged by a local body called
the Court of Minstrels, with the bull being
provided every year by the local priory.
Following the dissolution of the monasteries, the bull was provided by the Duke of
Devonshire. Before the running began, the
bull had the tips of his horns sawn off, his
ears and tail cut off, his body smeared with
soap and his nose filled with pepper, the
object of the event being to catch the bull
before sunset. It was finally abolished by
the Duke of Devonshire in 1774.

There appears to be no evidence of bull
running taking place in Birmingham, as is
claimed in the *Victoria County History:
Warwickshire* (1908).

Sources and Reading:
Blaine, D. P., *An Encyclopaedia of Rural Sports*
(London: Longman, 1870).

The Encyclopaedia of Sport (London: The Sportsman, 1912).

Hone, W., *The Every-Day Book* (London: Thomas Tegg, 1830).

Malcolmson, R., *Popular Recreations in English Society 1700–1850* (Cambridge: Cambridge University Press, 1973).

Reeves, C., *Pleasures and Pastimes in Medieval England* (Stroud: Sutton, 1995).

Simpson, J. and Roud, S., *A Dictionary of English Folklore* (Oxford: Oxford University Press, 2000).

See also Bull Baiting

Tony Collins

Butter-Making Contests

An international butter-making contest was held at the Agricultural Hall in London in 1886, in which fourteen contestants sought to win the £10 first prize. Each entrant was given 20 lb of cream for her churn with which to make the butter, and the Welsh dairy-maid, Gwenllian Morgan, from Penderyn, mid Glamorgan, was victorious, for the general excellence of her product. Following her success, Morgan was presented with a gold medal by Queen Victoria, in commemoration of her achievement.

Sources and Reading:
Davies, D., *Brecknock Historian* (Brecon: D. G. & A. S. Evans, 1977).

Emma Lile

Buzz and Bandy

A name used in Shrewsbury and Much Wenlock for hockey.

Sources and Reading:
Gomme, A. B., *The Traditional Games of England, Scotland and Ireland* (London: Thames and Hudson facsimile edition, 1984).

See also Bandy, Hockey

Tony Collins

Caiche

Another name for handball.

Sources and Reading:
Gomme, A. B., *The Traditional Games of England, Scotland and Ireland* (London: Thames and Hudson facsimile edition, 1984)

See also Handball

Tony Collins

Cairnie, John

John Cairnie (1769–1842) is the most significant figure in the history of curling. When he was elected the first president of the newly instituted Grand Caledonian Curling Club on 25 July 1838 he must have felt that his mission in life was accomplished, for the game he loved now had a national organisation.

He learned the game on the frozen ponds of west Stirlingshire where his father, Neil Cairnie, was principal partner of the firm of Thomas Shiels and Company, which ran the Herbertshire Printfield in Denny. To date, little is known about John Cairnie's early life, beyond that he was born at Dunipace, near Denny, in 1769, that he studied medicine at the University of Glasgow, qualified as a surgeon and entered the service of the Honourable East India Company.

His enthusiasm for the game, which is exemplified in the following anecdote, can have had little scope for fulfilment in the burning tropical sun.

On a certain occasion one of his own name, in spite of friendly warnings, played a rink of stones at Denny over ice that was much too weak, with the result that the whole lot went to the bottom of the pond. The accident would not have mattered had not the stones been required for an important match on the following day. Having reviewed the whole situation carefully, Mr Cairnie, all heedless of the biting blast that was blowing and the deep and dangerous character of the pond, calmly divested himself of his clothing and dived for the stones, one after another, until all were safely landed. It is pleasant to be able to add that Mr Cairnie was so little the worse of his adventure that he assisted in brilliant style to play the rescued *channel stanes* to victory on the morrow.

Cairnie first served for some years in Ceylon, and in 1802 he was promoted to surgeon and thereafter served with the 2nd Madras Native Cavalry. The nature of the incident that separated the good doctor from his left hand, and, therefore, from the practice of surgery, is unknown, but it is known that he retired to Scotland, settled in Largs on the Ayrshire coast about 1804, married Agnes Galbraith in 1805 and built an imposing villa which he named Curling Hall. Thereafter, he appears to have lived the life of a gentleman of private means, devoting himself to yachting and bowls in the summer and curling in the winter. He actively promoted curling in Ayrshire and for a period was the secretary of the Noddle Curling Club of Largs, whose minute book he treated as a sort of diary during the winter months.

The lack of enduring frost at sea level caused Cairnie to consider how to multiply the number of curling days. As early as 1820 he hit upon the idea of creating a rink, consisting of a level impervious surface onto which a thin skin of ice could be formed by spraying water from watering cans as soon as the temperature reached freezing point. He reported the inspiration for it thus:

We were led to think of this simple invention from a plan we, with many other boys, have practised in our younger days, that of making ice on pavement, which we have often done to the great annoyance of his Majesty's lieges.

In 1833, Cairnie felt the necessity of proclaiming this as his invention in the book *An Essay on Curling and Artificial Pond-Making*. This is a lively polemical treatise, full of curling lore; by reading it, one can get a good idea of the man. His invention quadrupled the number of curling days throughout Scotland.

In his testament, Cairnie made a specific bequest of his curling stones to his nephew, for he had no children, and he made the Grand Caledonian Curling Club, of which he was president, the ultimate beneficiary if all his other bequests failed.

Sources and Reading:
Smith, D. B., *Curling: An Illustrated History* (Edinburgh: John Donald, 1981), 119–24.

David B. Smith

Calendar of Sport

Before the middle of the nineteenth century, holidays were the times when sports were played and watched: sport was not a weekly event. The calendar of pre-industrial society, including its sport, was determined by the annual rhythms of the agricultural economy. Many festivals (with associated sports) therefore evolved to mark the beginning or end of various phases of the rural year, such as ploughing, sowing, harvesting, sheep shearing and the slaughter of livestock. These festivals were the pivotal points in the annual cycle of hard work followed by leisure time, and often abundance followed by scarcity. Overlaid on this economic pattern were the holy days of the Christian church, such as Christmas, Shrove Tuesday, Lent, Easter and Whitsun, and individual saints' days, which generally became the days on which local church feasts were celebrated. Local fairs and festivals often had their origins in the need to offer refreshments and entertainment to pilgrims visiting shrines or places of worship on holidays.

The cycle of the sporting year began on New Year's Day, a common day for many local forms of folk football. This was especially true in Scotland, where football and forms of handball were played in the Lowlands, and shinty (camanachd) in the Highlands. Perhaps most famously, it was the day of the Kirkwall Ba', a game of hand ba' played in the Orkneys.

The importance of various holidays differed between England, Wales, Ireland and, particularly, Scotland. The one day that was important for sport in all four countries between the medieval period and the middle of the nineteenth century was Shrove Tuesday (whose date is variable within the period 10 February to 16 March), and the sports in general were the same everywhere: football and cockfighting. In Wales, cockpits were common in villages, and 'thrashing at cocks', in which the animal was placed in a hole in the earth before being struck at with a flail by blindfolded adults, was practised. The awkwardness of the blows and the dipping of the bird's heads produced much hilarity, and whoever killed the cock took it home for supper. The sport was a kind of lottery in which the prize was a good meal: eating well was part of celebrating a holiday. In 'throwing at cocks', contestants had three throws from a distance of some ten yards, and whoever struck the bird and then caught it before it stood up again won the animal. Though widespread, cock throwing and thrashing were less common than cockfighting.

In nineteenth-century Leicestershire and Yorkshire, Shrove Tuesday was sometimes called Shuttlecock Day because children played battledore on that day.

All religious holidays were ended in Scotland at the Protestant Reformation because the reformers believed that they were associated with ritual and the worship of images. The Scottish Shrove Tuesday, usually called Fastern's E'en, was the one widespread holiday in the Christian calendar that survived the Reformation. The pattern of cockfighting was the same in every parish, Highland and Lowland; the contests were held in the school, each boy was expected to bring a cock, all the defeated birds were the perquisites of

the schoolmaster, and the boy who brought the winning bird was named 'king' and honoured by his fellows.

Ash Wednesday, the first day of Lent, which immediately follows Shrove Tuesday, was traditionally the day for sports such as Aunt Sally and the Ashbourne and Alnwick football games (if the match had not been won on Shrove Tuesday), and also marked the start of the marbles season.

Easter was a particularly important time for sports, despite its date moving from year to year – a 'moveable feast' in the Christian calendar. The fact that the holiday spanned a weekend and that, especially when held in April, it often coincided with the first signs of warmer weather, made it ideal for sporting activity. It was a popular period for jousting, quintain, egg and orange rolling, football (for example at Workington) and marbles. Like many other local games, Hallaton bottle-kicking was staged on Easter Monday. Cockfighting was common over the Easter period. At Hartland (Devon) there was a variation called cock-kibbit, a kibbit being a cudgel. The cock was placed under an earthenware milking pan, and the aim was to release the cock by throwing the cudgel to smash the pan. Other popular Easter sports in Wales included quoits, wrestling, displays of strength and stoolball. Football was also played at Easter, as in Anglesey in 1734 between the parishes of Llanbadrig and Llanfair-yng-Nghornwy before a crowd of several hundred. That game continued for over three hours and finished one goal (or 'end') each, and despite the rather boisterous nature of the encounter the sides parted, according to the diarist William Bulkeley:

as good friends as they came, after they had spent half an hour together in cherishing their spirits with a cup of ale . . . [before returning home] . . . having finished the Easter Holydays innocently and merrily.

Sport was, above all, a celebration of the existence of the community.

May Day, first referred to in the mid-thirteenth century, was closely associated with the beginning of spring, and was marked by flower gathering. As this activity often involved young people going into the woods during the night to pick flowers, by the sixteenth century it had become a focus for opposition from Puritans, who, probably with some cause, thought it was a licence for immoral behaviour. It was banned under Cromwell, but revived during the Restoration only to eventually fade out in the early nineteenth century. The earliest reference to the maypole is from the mid-fourteenth century, and by the following century the maypole had become a major focus of activity on May Day for many villages. Claims for its phallic symbolism do not stand up to serious scrutiny, and many of the features associated with it today, such as the plaiting of ribbons, are Victorian inventions. Informal and less-organised games were common on May Day; indeed, the term 'May Games' was regularly used in the seventeenth century. It was also a frequent date for wrestling tournaments in the west of England.

Ascension Day is the Thursday 40 days after Easter, the day on which Christ ascended to Heaven. In some parts of Ireland it was a day for sports; for example, hurling, cockfighting and, by the middle of the nineteenth century, cricket too at Callan in County Kilkenny. Until the beginning of the nineteenth century, an Ascension Day horse race was held at Carlisle.

Whitsunday is the seventh Sunday after Easter; it was the end of the cycle of holidays that depended on the date of Easter. In north Devon, Whit Monday revels, including wrestling, boxing, skittles, running and football, survived into the twentieth century. At Liskeard, in Cornwall, wrestling and cudgel-playing was promoted by innkeepers, who offered hats as prizes. Robert Dover's Cotswold Games, held from 1604 to 1852, were at Whitsuntide. It was also an important time for horseracing. Because of the effort required for its staging and the need to attract large crowds, racing was traditionally closely tied to local fairs and festivals.

Local holidays were scattered over the summer months, and in particular there was a loose group of holidays around mid-summer. The English parish 'wakes and ales' were originally celebrations of the local saint: *wake* comes from *awake*, meaning an overnight vigil. The Irish 'pattern day' was similar: the word pattern coming from *patron*. After the church service, people ate, drank and enjoyed sport; by the late eighteenth century the sports included a large number of different events, from wrestling and running to grinning in a horse collar. In England, by the eighteenth century events were usually organised by a publican, who offered prizes and took a profit from the sale of food and drink. The wakes in the Black Country and in Lancashire and Yorkshire grew in size as their areas became industrialised and much more heavily populated. Until they were suppressed or sanitised in the middle of the nineteenth century they were characterised not only by fighting and blood sports but also by a very wide range of other sports. After the Reformation, saints' days were not celebrated in Scotland, though it was on St Andrew's Day 1871 that the first international team game was held: Scotland played England at rugby at Raeburn Place, Edinburgh.

The day of a horserace was also a local holiday: in north Kerry, farm workers' agreements with their farmers included Listowel races as a day off. The fact that most courses had only one meeting, at the same time each year, meant that they were fixtures in the calendar. It also meant that the time away from work was insignificant, though in a few areas, such as Ayrshire, there were so many local races that concerns were voiced about the amount of idle time. Where the people started their own events, such as the curragh races at Ventry (County Kerry) before the First World War, which were so well described by Maurice O'Sullivan in *Twenty Years A-Growing* (1933), these too were an occasion for a general cessation of work.

Summer holidays, held on different days in nearby places, were important for the growth of sports because talented competitors could attend several events during the season. They also tended to favour individual rather than team games. Some of the most famous, such as the great cockfight at Llanbrynmair in Montgomeryshire in 1795, seem to have been isolated events; held on a holiday, but in one year only. The summer months of July and August were, and still are, the period during which large athletic festivals were held, especially in Scotland when most of the major Highland Games tournaments were staged, although the important Braemar Gathering is held in September. The athletic festivals of the Lake District, such as those in Grasmere, Ambleside and Cockermouth, are also held during the summer months.

August Bank Holiday, held on the last Monday in August, was a major holiday from the time it was created by Act of Parliament in 1871. One autumn holiday was a minor occasion for sport: bull baiting was held in Kilkenny on Michaelmas (29 September), the day for the election of the mayor, and there were horse races in the Hebrides on the same day.

Many sports were enjoyed in the period between Christmas and Twelfth Night. In Ireland, hurling was played after mass on Christmas Day. In County Limerick, a special ball was used which contained a small tin box of loose shot that made a hard noise every time it was struck. In County Donegal, the match was played between the men of the various townlands of the parish: after mass each group aimed to drive the ball to their own land.

Christmas sports often ended in violence, and some places had a particular reputation for it, such as Lampeter (Cardiganshire), where the annual Christmas football match was held between the young men of 'bro' and 'blaenau', who lived on the low and high ground respectively. Such unbridled energies highlighted the significance of victory, for a defeat severely dented the reputation of one's parish. At the same time, violence was seen as something that distinguished the holiday from an ordinary day.

There was a general belief that the game laws did not apply on St Stephen's Day (26 December), so all sorts of animals were pursued in England, Wales and Ireland. Boxing Day's current links with fox hunting is part of a much longer tradition of association with hunting of all types that dates back well before the development of fox hunting in the early nineteenth century. In post-Reformation Scotland, Christmas was not a holiday and sport was found instead on New Year's Day: shinty in the Highlands and wad (wager) shooting in the Lowlands.

For people who had leisure time, sport took place across seasons rather than on individual holidays, though it was still bounded by the practicalities of farming. For example, fox hunting started in October, after the corn had been cut, and in the eighteenth century, golf came to a stop in early summer if hay was grown on the course.

Seasons also gave particular sports their character. Flat racing took place on dry, fast summer ground, and steeplechasing on ground made heavier by winter rain. On summer evenings, people bowled, wrestled, played music and danced, as at Llansanffraid-ym-Mechain in east Montgomeryshire; sport was one element in the social life of the community. There is vividness in field sports in cold weather in open country: an obituary (1861) of that great Ayrshire sportsman, the thirteenth Earl of Eglinton, remembered him 'with the pack in cry across the stubble rigs [ridges] in the red December days'.

Sources and Reading:

Banks, M. M., *British Calendar Custom: Scotland* (three volumes) (London: Folklore Society, 1937–41).

Brailsford, D., 'Sporting Days in Eighteenth Century England', *Journal of Sports History*, 9 (1982), 41–54.

Brailsford, D., *Sport, Time and Society: The British at Play* (London: Routledge, 1991).

Danher, K., *The Year in Ireland: Irish Calendar Customs* (Cork: Mercier Press, 1972).

Day, B., *A Chronicle of Folk Customs* (London: Hamlyn, 1988).

Day, B., *A Chronicle of Celtic Folk Customs* (London: Hamlyn, 2000).

Hutton, R., *Stations of the Sun: A History of the Ritual Year in Britain* (Oxford: Oxford University Press, 1996).

Malcolmson, R. W., *Popular Recreations in English Society 1700–1850* (Cambridge: Cambridge University Press, 1973).

Middleton, I. and Vamplew, W., 'Sport and the English Leisure Calendar: Horse Racing in Early Eighteenth-Century Yorkshire', *Ludica*, 4 (1998), 259–76.

Strutt, J., *The Sports and Pastimes of the People of England* (London: J. White, 1801).

Wright A. R. and Lones, T. E., *British Calendar Custom: England* (three volumes) (London: Folklore Society, 1936–40).

See also Shrovetide

John Burnett, Tony Collins and Emma Lile

Cammock

Also known as 'cambuck' and 'cambuca', this was a game of around the fourteenth century in which a ball was propelled with a wooden stick. It is unclear whether it was a variant of a hockey-type game, such as bandy, or a precursor of golf, although Sir Guy Campbell for one argued that cambuca was a forerunner of golf. Like bandy, the word means 'curved stick', and has similar meanings in Irish, Gaelic and Manx. The game is known to us largely because it was among those expressly forbidden by Edward III in 1369.

Sources and Reading:
Birley, D., *Sport and the Making of Britain* (Manchester: Manchester University Press, 1993).

Campbell, G., 'The Early History of English Golf', in Darwin, B. *et al.* (eds), *A History of Golf in Britain* (London: Cassell & Co, 1952).

See also Bandy, Hockey, Golf

Tony Collins

Camogie

A fourteenth-century sport played in Ireland in which two teams sought to score goals by hitting a wooden ball with a stick that was curved at the end. In the twentieth century, 'camogie' became the name for the women's version of hurling.

Sources and Reading:
Birley, D., *Sport and the Making of Britain* (Manchester: Manchester University Press, 1993).

See also Bandy, Hockey, Hurling, Shinty

Tony Collins

Camp Ball

Camp ball is a version of football dating back to medieval times. The word *camp* in Old English meant a military contest or battle, which gives an indication of the nature of the game. It differed from many other types of folk football in that it was much more structured: it had two teams, usually small in number, a goal at either end of the pitch and a ball, which had to be propelled through a goal to record a score. The sport was particularly popular in East Anglia. The annual Shrove Tuesday football match at Dorking was referred to on occasions as 'camping'.

The version of the game that was played on the Suffolk coast resembled in many respects modern forms of rugby, albeit played with a small ball, in that the ball was carried and when the ball carrier was caught he had to throw it to a team mate. Throwing between the goals (that is, in a forward direction) was forbidden. A goal was called a 'notch' or 'snotch', and a team that was caught in possession of the ball lost a notch. A game was completed when one side had won seven or nine notches, making the length of the game between two and three hours.

The ball appears to have originally been a small leather one, similar to a cricket ball, but by the Middle Ages it was made from a pig's bladder and, initially at least, filled with dried peas. In most forms of the game kicking, carrying and throwing the ball were all permitted, although the few versions that were based on kicking the ball became known as 'kicking camp' and tended to use a larger ball. 'Savage camp' was a variation in which players could wear heavily shod boots in order to kick each other's shins; a forerunner of 'hacking', which was so beloved by nineteenth-century public-school rugby players. Other versions, which allowed the use of sticks, evolved into bandy and early forms of hockey.

Unsurprisingly, violence was a constant feature of the game and a number of deaths due to the game were recorded. Two men were allegedly killed during a match at Easton in Suffolk in the late eighteenth century, and it was claimed that nine died during a game between Norfolk and Suffolk in the early nineteenth century. Indeed, it has been speculated that this was one of the reasons for camp ball's decline. It appears that the last match took place at Norwich cricket ground in 1831.

David Underdown has argued that camp ball's high level of organisation (such as small, equally sized teams and recognised rules) reflected the more developed economy and more structured society of the eastern counties, compared with the open-field midland and western regions in which ordinary football was played.

In some regions, camp ball was a synonym for football. Survivals of the sport can be seen in the names of places where it was played; for example, Norton Woodseats has an Upper Campfield and a Lower Campfield. Campo Lane in Sheffield was originally known as Camper Lane. Gomme, writing in 1894, noted that in the fifteenth century there were several examples of land being appropriated for the playing of the game.

Sources and Reading:

Gomme, A. B., *The Traditional Games of England, Scotland and Ireland* (London: Thames and Hudson facsimile edition, 1984).

Magoun, F. P., *A History of British Football from the Beginnings to 1871* (Bochum-Langendeer: Pöppinghaus, 1938).

Marples, M., *A History of Football* (London: 1954).

Reeves, C., *Pleasures and Pastimes in Medieval England* (Stroud: Sutton, 1995).

Underdown, D., 'Regional Cultures?', in Harris, T. (ed.), *Popular Culture in England c. 1550–1850* (Basingstoke: Macmillan, 1995).

See also Football

Tony Collins

Capie Hole

A Scottish game in which players standing behind a designated line had to throw a ball into a hole, or in the version played in Angus into three holes. The player who successfully did so the most times was the winner.

Sources and Reading:

Gomme, A. B., *The Traditional Games of England, Scotland and Ireland* (London: Thames and Hudson facsimile edition, 1984).

Tony Collins

Cashornie

A variant of bandy in which the goals are holes, the object being for each team to hit the ball into the opponent's hole.

Sources and Reading:

Gomme, A. B., *The Traditional Games of England, Scotland and Ireland* (London: Thames and Hudson facsimile edition, 1984).

See also Bandy, Hockey

Tony Collins

Casting the Bar

This was a contest in which a bar was thrown, or 'cast', as far as possible. Contemporary accounts are not clear as to whether the bar was thrown in a style similar to modern javelin throwing, or in one akin to the tossing of a caber. It is more than likely that either style could be used, depending on the weight of the bar. Henry VIII was allegedly talented at casting the bar, although it appears that he cast it using an action similar to that of a hammer thrower.

Sources and Reading:
Lacey, R., *The Life and Times of Henry VIII* (London: Weidenfeld, 1988).
Stonehenge [J. H. Walsh], *Manual of British Rural Sports*, (London: Routledge, 1857).

See also Bar Throwing (Wales), Stone Throwing

Tony Collins

Cat and Dog

A form of cricket played in Angus and Lothian in Scotland in the seventeenth and eighteenth centuries.

Sources and Reading:
Blaine, D. P., *An Encyclopaedia of Rural Sports* (London: Longman, 1870).
Gomme, A. B., *The Traditional Games of England, Scotland and Ireland* (London: Thames and Hudson facsimile edition, 1984).

See also Cricket

Tony Collins

Catrin Cwmglas

– *see* **Thomas, Catrin**

Cheese Rolling

Taking place every Spring Bank Holiday at Cooper's Hill, Brockworth in Gloucestershire, cheese rolling appears to date back to medieval times, although there is little evidence to substantiate this claim (the event was first referred to in the early nineteenth century). Cheeses – Double Gloucester, of course – are placed in small round wooden cases and rolled down a hill, to be chased by competitors. Those who win can keep the cheeses they catch. For reasons of safety, the rolling was forbidden by the local council in 1998, but the ban was defied by early morning cheese-rollers and the event was re-established the following year.

Although Brockworth is the only surviving example, cheese rolling was not uncommon in other areas in at least the eighteenth and nineteenth centuries; Thomas Hughes refers to it taking place at Uffington in his *The Scouring of the White Horse* of 1859.

Cheese rolling of a different kind also took place at Randwick in Gloucestershire every May Day, when three large Gloucester cheeses were paraded around the village and then rolled around the church before being cut into pieces and distributed to parishioners. Unlike the Brockworth event, however, no chasing after the cheeses took place.

Sources and Reading:
Day, B., *A Chronicle of Folk Customs* (London: Hamlyn, 1988).
Hone, W., *The Every-Day Book* (London: Thomas Tegg, 1830).
Simpson, J. and Roud, S., *A Dictionary of English Folklore* (Oxford: Oxford University Press, 2000).

See also Egg Rolling, Orange Rolling

Tony Collins

Chester Races

Chester Races was one of the oldest horse-racing meetings in Britain. It was first recorded in 1511 when it was run for a prize of two bells on the site of what is now the modern Chester Racecourse. In 1540 the local Saddlers' Company provided silver bells as the first prize, and in 1610 the mayor and sheriff of the city commissioned three silver bells to be made as the prize for the winner. The race eventually became known as the City Plate, and was run until 1836.

Sources and Reading:
Hone, W., *The Every-Day Book* (London: Thomas Tegg, 1830).

See also Horseracing

Tony Collins

Chetham, James

James Chetham (1640–1692), writer on angling, was the author of *The Angler's Vade-Mecum*, which was published in 1681. This was an informative and influential account which, in some respects, was on a par with Izaak Walton's great work, *The Compleat Angler*. The text, in Diogenes's vein, was on occasions curt and caustic. While acknowledging the debt he owed to earlier writers, it provided an honest exposition of the author's views. The edition was issued under the designation 'Lover of Angling', noting in the preface that 'The author has forborne . . . to affix his name: not that he is ashamed to own it, but wishes the reader to regard things more than empty names'. Chetham's reputation might have been even greater had the text not been published in this way.

Some accounts have ascribed authorship to Chetham's nephew James (1682–1752), the eldest son of his younger brother. James was the eldest son of Edward and Alice Chetham of Smedley, near Manchester. Shortly before James's birth, Edward had

obtained the renewal of a lease his father-in-law had on Smedley. In 1653, following the death of his Uncle Humphrey Chetham, Edward had inherited the Ordall and Pendleton estates and, in 1659, had purchased a portion of the estates of the Chethams of Nuthurst. James was a student at St Edmund Hall, Oxford, following which he entered Gray's Inn. Shortly afterwards, his father became an invalid and James looked after the family estates and business, the bulk of which he inherited following his father's death in 1684.

Sources and Reading:
Martin, J., 'Chetham, James', in Harrison, B., *Oxford Dictionary of National Biography* (Oxford: Oxford University Press, 2004).

John Martin

Chifney Family

Samuel Chifney (1753–1807) and his two sons, William (1784–1862) and Samuel (1786–1854), were leading figures on the British turf. Sam the elder was both the greatest trainer and the greatest jockey of his era: at least that is what he proclaimed in his memoirs, conceitedly entitled *Genius Genuine*. His vanity was reflected in his dress, with its ruffs and frills and bundles of ribbons adorning his boots. He combined inherent horse sense with acquired tactical cunning to become an outstanding jockey. He began to ride in races in 1770, when attached to the stables of the Newmarket trainer Foxe. He had light hands and did not believe in hard pulling a horse. Only 5 feet 5 inches in height, he could go to the scales at 7 stones 12 pounds up to the end of his career. He won the Oaks, a Classic for fillies, four times, and in 1789 completed the Epsom double when he was also victorious in the Derby. Two years later he was banned from Newmarket over the inconsistent running of the Prince of Wales's horse Escape. Although the Prince stood by his jockey and promised to continue to pay his retainer, Sam sold the annuity for £1,260 and ended his days in Fleet Prison as a debtor.

Encouraged by their father, the sons also achieved fame on the turf, as trainer and jockey respectively. William, the more intelligent, was taught training and stable management, while young Sam, an even-tempered individual of few words who virtually lived in the saddle, was educated in all aspects of race riding, including the famous 'Chifney Rush' in which a waiting race was climaxed by a surge to the front in the last few strides. For several years the brothers prospered, especially after William trained and Sam rode the winners of the Derby in 1818 and 1820. Powerful rather than elegant in the saddle, Sam, like his father, also did well in the Oaks, winning that race five times. The brothers engineered several betting coups, the most rewarding of which occurred when William trained his own horse Priam to win the 1830 Derby. Unfortunately, the brothers tried to repeat the feat in 1834 when they plunged on Shilelagh, another animal from William's stables, which was narrowly beaten by Plenipotentiary. This loss forced them to sell their properties to meet the debts. William's old age was spent in poverty, but Sam was left a house and stables by a grateful Thomas Thornhill, owner of two of his Derby winners. Sam continued to ride till 1843 and in that year, aged 57, he won his last Classic, the One Thousand Guineas, on Extempore. However, for the later part of his career he increasingly picked his rides and wasted only if he really fancied a mount. His last visit to a racecourse was in 1853 to see his nephew, Frank Butler, win the Derby on West Australian.

Sources and Reading:
Mortimer, R., Onslow, R. and Willett, P., *Biographical Encyclopaedia of British Flat Racing* (London: Macdonald & Jane's, 1978).
Tanner, M. and Cranham, G., *Great Jockeys of the Flat* (London: Guinness, 1992).

Wray Vamplew

Chinnup

An old name for hockey.

See also Hockey, Shinnup, Jowls

Tony Collins

Chulle

A word that means to play football, which dates back to the fourteenth and fifteenth century and is closely related to the French words *choule* and *soule*.

Sources and Reading:
Birley, D., *Sport and the Making of Britain* (Manchester: Manchester University Press, 1993).
Goulstone, J., 'Shrovetide Football and Related Games', *British Society of Sports History Newsletter*, 5 (1996), 19–30, and 6 (1997), 23–4.

See also Football

Tony Collins

Church Ales

Church ales were community feasts held by local churches, primarily to raise money for the parish, at which eating, drinking and sports were the highlight. Usually taking place around May, they were sometimes also known as May games. Sports played at ales included football, stoolball, forms of cricket, bowls, fives, tug of war, cudgels, bull baiting and athletic events for both men and women. One can see a distant genteel relative of church ales in today's church or village fetes.

Church ales appear to have become popular around the fifteenth century and were common up until the end of the seventeenth century. However, from the sixteenth century, the growing influence of Puritanism meant that church ales were increasingly opposed because they were seen as promoting drunkenness, gluttony and licentiousness. The fact that games were often held in church grounds, and occasionally within the church itself, was seen as a form of Catholicism by Puritans, who sought to have them suppressed. Although there was a brief revival after the restoration of the monarchy in 1660, church ales eventually disappeared by the end of the century.

Many churches replaced the ales by rates as a way of raising money, although unsurprisingly this met with considerable opposition from parishioners. The end of church ales effectively ended the Church of England's widespread participation in the sports and leisure activities of the mass of the population. Ironically, the vacuum was filled by the pub, which became the unchallenged centre for the organisation of sports for the best part of the following two centuries.

Church ales were closely related to 'wakes', the regional name given to the holiday on which the local church's patron saint was celebrated. The name derives from the tradition of staying up all night to keep watch over the church before the day of revelry that followed. Originally, the wake consisted of a procession followed by sports, feasting and drinking, although due to Puritan pressure the licentiousness of the festival was toned down. Although some wakes eventually became fairs in their own right, most died out in the eighteenth and early nineteenth century as a result of the Church of England's withdrawal from popular festive activities. However, the tradition and name were carried over into nineteenth-century industrial Lancashire, with Wakes Week becoming the term used for the annual weekly holiday of textiles workers in Lancashire.

Sources and Reading:

Brailsford, D., *British Sport: A Social History* (Cambridge: Lutterworth Press, 1992).
Hutton, R., *The Rise and Fall of Merry England* (Oxford: Oxford University Press, 1994).
Hutton, R., *Stations of the Sun* (Oxford: Oxford University Press, 1996).
Malcolmson, R., *Popular Recreations in English Society 1700–1850* (Cambridge: Cambridge University Press, 1973).
Underdown, D., *Revel, Riot and Rebellion: Popular Politics and Culture in England 1603–1660* (Oxford: Clarendon, 1985).

See also Book of Sports, Pubs and Sport

Tony Collins

Clay Pigeon Shooting

Clay pigeon shooting is the art of shooting at flying clay targets, called clay pigeons. Originally, live pigeons, released into the air from a trap, were shot, but with the banning of live-pigeon shooting in 1921, shooting at clay targets became more popular. The actual clay target probably dates from 1880 when George Ligowoski observed boys skimming flat stones across a lake. This gave him the idea for aerodynamic saucer-shaped objects that could be launched into the air from a mechanical trap to provide challenging targets for the shooter. By the end of the nineteenth century these had evolved into disc-type clay targets made out of pitch and limestone, resembling an upside-down saucer approximately 4.5 inches in diameter.

In the twentieth century, clay pigeon shooting was radically transformed by the development of automatic clay traps, which can project targets in a variety of directions and imitating a multiplicity of quarry. Various disciplines have evolved, such as down the line, skeet and trap, each with its own special techniques, rules and regulations. Since the Second World War it has become a sophisticated type of target shooting. It attracts many game and rough shooters wishing to improve and develop their technical expertise, but a much greater number participate exclusively in the sport. Clay pigeon shooting is organised primarily by clubs operating their own permanent sites. It is an attractive sport, particularly for those shooters who do not wish to indulge in the killing of wild animals and birds.

The Inanimate Bird Shooting Association (IBSA) was formed in 1892 and held its first championship at Wimbledon Park in London in 1893. In 1900 and 1908 clay pigeon shooting appeared in the Olympic Games, Britain won the team competition on both occasions. Today, it is an established Olympic sport at which British teams are often successful. In 1903 the IBSA changed its name to the Clay Bird Shooting Association. A central body for the sport, the Amateur United Clay Pigeon Association of Great Britain was formed in 1928, and in 1929 this became the Clay Pigeon Shooting Association (CPSA), which is still the governing body of the sport today. The CPSA organises championships at county, regional and national level.

There are more than twenty different forms of regulated competitions, called disciplines, which can be divided into three main groups: trap, skeet and sporting. In the case of trap shooting, the targets are thrown as singles or doubles from one or more traps positioned 15 metres in front of the shooters. With skeet, the targets are thrown at set trajectories and speeds from two trap houses located some 40 metres apart at the opposite ends of a semicircle. Sporting, which is overwhelmingly the most popular, involves the targets being projected at a wide variety of trajectories, speeds, elevations and distances in order to simulate live shooting.

The terminology used by shooters can be traced back to the days of shooting live birds. A target is called a bird, a hit is a kill, and the machines that propel the targets are still called traps.

Sources and Reading:
Croft, P., *Clay Shooting* (London: Ward Lock, 1998).
Hammond, B., 'Glass Ball and Feathers', *Pull!* (1988).
Humphries, J., *Clay Pigeon Shooting* (London: Blandford, 1995).

See also Pigeon Shooting

John Martin

Closh

A skittles-type game that was played at least until the seventeenth century and which appears to have been very similar to ninepins. Also referred to as 'cloishe', 'claishe' and 'closhe', little is known about it other than that it was repeatedly banned by government order from 1477. Closh may have been an alternative name for kayles. It was sufficiently popular in the fifteenth century to have grounds specifically created for its playing, which were known as closh-banes. In the game played in Holland from the sixteenth century, the ball had to be driven through a hoop using a mallet shaped like a spade or chisel.

Sources and Reading:
Oxford English Dictionary (Second edition, on CD-Rom) (Oxford: Oxford University Press, 1993).

See also Bowls, Kayles, Ninepins, Skittles

Tony Collins

Club Ball

According to different authorities, club ball is either a generic name for bat-and-ball games played with a straight bat or a specific game that can be traced back to Saxon times. Others cast doubt on whether such a game ever existed: the *Oxford English Dictionary* could trace no use of the term 'club ball' prior to Joseph Strutt's *The Sports and Pastimes of the People of England* (1801).

Indeed, regardless of its existence, the importance of the game lies not so much in itself but in the status attached to it by those antiquarians seeking to establish a direct line of apostolic succession for cricket. This importance can be traced back to Strutt, who bestowed club ball with the title of parent to cricket. As is the case with many of his assertions, he adduced no written evidence to support his case, but only two illustrations, neither of which were dated. One shows a woman throwing a ball to a man holding a straight bat, with fielders of both sexes surrounding the batter. The other is even more vague, showing two men, one of whom holds both the bat and the ball while the other player waits to catch the ball. Other than the straight bat, which differentiates the game from those that used a curved bat (such as bandy), there is nothing to distinguish either illustration from any of the bat-and-ball games played at the time.

Joseph Strutt's assertions were followed, with qualifications, by John Nyren in his *The Cricketers of My Time* (1833). Nyren preferred to believe that the game could be traced back to Saxon times, but accepted Strutt's assertion that the term club ball was derived from the Welsh word *clwppa* and the Danish word *bol*. Somewhat in contradiction, he also described club ball as being similar to trap ball, a game that probably had more in common with baseball than with cricket.

The state of scholarship on the subject has advanced little further since. As with the football codes and baseball, it appears that the determination of cricket's early leaders and supporters to find a single line of evolution for their game persuaded them to ignore the multitude of roots that nourished the origins of their sport in favour of, at best, mistakenly singling out one source or, at worst, simply inventing it.

Sources and Reading:
Arlott, J. (ed.), *The Oxford Companion to Sports and Games* (Oxford: Oxford University Press, 1975).
Strutt, J., *The Sports and Pastimes of the People of England* (London: Bensley for White, 1801).

See also Baseball, Creag, Cricket, Trap Ball

Tony Collins

Cnapan

Cnapan describes a team game vaguely similar to modern rugby that was popular in Wales until the middle of the nineteenth century, particularly on Sundays and at seasonal festivals. Interparish contests took place on the sands or other large tracts of land and were open to men of all backgrounds. A round ball, roughly hand-size and usually made of wood such as box or yew, was used for play, and was made slippery to hold by being boiled in tallow. Known as the 'cnapan', the ball was thrown high into the air to begin a match, and whoever caught it then carried it, either on foot or on horseback, in the direction of their opponent's district. Play continued until the ball was taken so far by members of one team that it was impossible for the other side to run it back to the opposite parish that evening. Hurling and running with the ball formed the basis of the game and, there being no 'goals' as such, a ball was sometimes moved as far as two miles from the start of play.

A detailed account of *cnapan* is found in George Owen's *Description of Pembrokeshire*, published in 1603. According to Owen, the game had been extremely popular in Pembrokeshire since 'great antiquitie' and was used by the Ancient Britons as training for war as it improved their strength and stamina. Play usually began early in the afternoon and sometimes as many as 2,000 competitors took part. Save their light breeches, competitors discarded their clothes for fear of them being ripped to shreds during the match, for *cnapan* was notoriously riotous and savage. Rules were kept to a minimum and, owing to the lack of a referee, games often descended into chaos. The horsemen were armed with mighty cudgels, some eighteen inches long, and were permitted to strike any opponent on horseback who held the cnapan in an attempt to snatch it off him. Footmen used bare fists for the same reason, and also threw stones at the horsemen during the chase. Fighting ensued fairly regularly, with play itself being forsaken for the chance to assault one's opponents. Competitors often ended the game with multiple injuries, yet, if Owen is to be believed, they remained merry and joyful throughout and bore no long-term grudges toward the opposition.

Sources and Reading:
Bradley, A. G., 'A Welsh Game of the Tudor Period', *Badminton Magazine* (1898), 512–24.
Lloyd, H., 'Tri o Hen Chwaraeon Cymru', *Transactions of the Honourable Society of Cymmrodorion* (1960), 97–108.
Owen, G., *The Description of Penbrokshire*, (London: J. Clark, 1892).
Waddington, H. M., 'Games and Athletics in Bygone Wales', *Transactions of the Honourable Society of Cymmrodorion* (1953), 84–100.

Emma Lile

Coal Carrying

Not a traditional sport, although the destruction of the coal industry now gives the event a nostalgic air that it would probably prefer not to have, the World Coal Carrying Championship was established in 1963 and takes place at Gawthorpe near Wakefield in west Yorkshire every Easter Monday. The event's roots can be traced back to the local pub, the Beehive, where Amos Clapham challenged fellow miner Lewis Hartley to a race to prove who was the fitter. Sadly, it is rare today for a miner to compete in the championship.

The object is to carry 50 kilograms of coal over a mile course, which starts from the Royal Oak pub and runs up a steep hill to the village green, and unload the coal under the maypole. A top performer can achieve the feat in around four and a quarter minutes. It was originally a male-only event, but a women's race, in which slightly lighter coal bags are carried, now takes place before the men's race.

Sources and Reading:
Day, B., *A Chronicle of Folk Customs* (London: Hamlyn, 1988).

Financial Times (15 April 2000).

See also Invented Traditions

Tony Collins

Coarse Fishing

Coarse fishing involves the pursuit of a wide range of fish, but with the exception of game species. There are more than 30 different species of indigenous freshwater fish, but coarse fishing is dominated by the pursuit of barbel, bream, carp, chub, dace, eels, perch, pike, roach and tench. Coarse fishing also encompasses the pursuit of relatively recently introduced species, such as catfish and zander. Mixed bags of these fish are frequently caught by both match and pleasure anglers, although dedicated groups of enthusiasts specialise in the pursuit of particular species.

The sport is undertaken at a wide variety of venues, including reservoirs, ponds, lakes, canals and rivers. Each species of fish tends to be found in a particular type of water and so the selection of the method of fishing, tackle and type of bait differs from one to another. Historically, the most popular method was float fishing, where the bait, usually a worm or maggot, was attached to a hook and line suspended beneath a float. Since the Second World War, ledgering which uses a special rod tip as a bite indicator in place of a float, has become increasingly popular.

Fishing for the different species is very much determined by the seasons. The start of the open season in June traditionally heralded forays for tench, followed in the late summer and autumn by the pursuit of roach, chub, barbel and carp, with pike fishing taking place mainly in the autumn and winter. The number of leisure anglers declines rapidly during the colder winter period, when the fall in water temperatures leads to a reduction in the feeding activity of many species of coarse fish.

Roach used to be the main and most prestigious quarry. This status was confirmed in virtually every book on coarse fishing where, by tradition, the species was listed first, following the fashion established by John Bickerdyke in his nineteenth-century text *Book of the All-Round Angler* (1888). Catching a specimen roach of above two pounds was a lifelong ambition for most coarse fishermen.

The increased focus on the pursuit of carp since the 1950s can largely be attributed to the activities of a band of devoted members of the Carp Catchers Club, and to one man in particular, Richard Walker (1918–85). Walker, an engineer by trade, brought scientific methods to specimen hunting. In 1952 he landed the record 44 pound carp (Clarissa) and transferred it live to London Zoo. The publicity surrounding its capture helped to encourage many anglers to concentrate their efforts on specimen hunting. The boom in carp fishing led to many property developers, entrepreneurs and farmers creating artificial lakes and stocking them with specially bred large fish. Other groups of enthusiasts have devoted their efforts to pursuing other species of fish, such as barbel and bream.

The most significant long-term transformation has been the pursuit of pike, the largest of Britain's coarse fish. In the Victorian period the species was widely despised as vermin, not worthy of a respectable angler's attention. There were, however, a small number of fishermen who deliberately set out to catch the species, particularly in the lochs of Scotland and loughs of Ireland, by dead baiting, live baiting or, more occasionally, by spinning. By the 1960s, however, pike fishing had grown in popularity, a trend accompanied by a series of texts extolling improved and more productive ways of catching the species in general, and larger pike in particular.

Specimen fishing is regulated by its own internal organisation, the British Record Fish Committee. The Committee rejected all the freshwater records set up before 1957, except those where the body or cast of the fish was still available for inspection; this led to a furore, particularly in cases where the catch had been verified by independent witnesses. Specialist clubs have evolved for highly dedicated fishermen who use sophisticated rigs and pre-bait the swim. Increased use of high-protein artificial feed for ground baiting has caused the size of the fish to increase.

Match angling, where anglers compete either in teams or as individuals, has also experienced radical changes since its inception in the nineteenth century. Angling matches, which were originally organised by publicans and local clubs, have become increasingly competitive, with the development of a complex network of regional, national and international tournaments. Since the 1960s, tobacco firms, breweries, tackle manufacturers and dealers have increasingly provided sponsorship to ensure that teams, and even individuals, are seen to be endorsing their products. This has encouraged the emergence of a small number of professional and semi-professional anglers, although their rewards are considerably less than in other higher-profile spectator sports, which can attract a mass audience when shown on television.

Government controls over angling have changed since the 1990s. The Mundella Act of 1877 introduced close seasons from the middle of March to the middle of June, which allowed coarse fish to spawn undisturbed. In 1997 the close season was scrapped on lakes, and in 2001 this was extended to include canals. The rod-licensing system introduced in the 1960s for coarse fishing has also been amended. In most areas of the United Kingdom, a rod licence issued by the local water authority enabled the holder to use a rod in the area for which the licence was issued but did not necessarily grant permission to use particular waters. Following the establishment of the National Rivers Authority in 1989, when the old water authorities became regions of the new central authority, from 1992 single, all-species national licences were issued to cover English and Welsh waters.

Coarse fishing is the most popular type of angling and constitutes one of Britain's leading participation rural sports. It provides unprecedented opportunities for people of all ages to indulge in a relatively inexpensive activity in a variety of attractive venues in the countryside.

Sources and Reading:

Bailey, J., *Where to Coarse Fish in Britain and Ireland* (London: New Holland, 2002).

Miles, T. and Vaughan, B. (eds), *The Practical Guide to Coarse Fishing* (London: Southwater, 2000).

Pope, N. (ed.), Arbery, L. (Foreword), *Specimen Hunting* (London: Boxtree, 1993).

Websites

National Coarse Fishing Federation of Ireland: homepage.eircom.net/~ncffi/

See also Angling

Nicholas Goddard and John Martin

Cockfighting

Cockfighting, a direct and invariably bloody encounter between two or more birds in an enclosed space, was banned in Britain – not for the first time – more than 150 years ago, and yet manages to survive, albeit clandestinely.

Cockfighting is still a major national sport in Latin America, Pakistan, the Middle East and the Far East. It was known in ancient China and Persia, and later the Athenians and other Greeks made it part of their martial, political and social life, depicting it on their pottery and other artefacts. The Romans also fostered cockfighting, and almost certainly introduced it to Britain. But the first substantive account of the sport in this country did not occur until the writings of William Fitzstephen, who died in 1191. He described the Shrove Tuesday cockfighting rituals in London schools, for which privilege the pupils paid the schoolmaster one penny, the 'cock-penny'. Such customs became widespread in Britain over the succeeding centuries, when both the money, the dead birds and any unwanted survivors made a welcome addition to a teacher's stipend and diet. From the Middle Ages onwards, cockfighting was a regular feature at the many annual fairs in market towns and villages throughout the country.

Together with many other sports, cockfighting was banned by Edward III in 1366 in an attempt to encourage archery, and again suffered a similar fate under Henry VI. Although it was never totally suppressed, there was no serious revival until the reign of Henry VIII, who built the Royal Cockpit at Westminster. This survived until the early nineteenth century, and a number of other important pits were also built in the capital. James I of England was just as fond of cockfighting as of horseracing and hunting, and he may well have founded the cockpit in Newmarket (on the site of the present town hall) as he spent a great deal of time in the town. Certainly, this pit was in existence during the reign of Charles II, while the sport itself, like the theatre, had survived a ban under the Commonwealth. (The ban was imposed because cockfighting's devotees often profaned both the Sabbath and the local churchyard, rather than on any humanitarian grounds.) Cockfighting now resurfaced with renewed vigour, and the eighteenth and early nineteenth centuries saw the peak of its popularity as a socially acceptable, mainstream sporting activity. Cockfighting, like the race meetings with which it was often associated, united all levels of society, both in a shared pleasure and in an obsession – gambling.

Before continuing with the historical survey, it is appropriate here to review the breeding and training of the birds, the pits in which they fought, and the various contests in which they could become involved. Many breeds of fighting cocks were developed over the years, some known simply as black reds or gingers, or more specifically as duckwings, pollcats or Cheshire piles. There were local breeds, such as Brandling greys and Felton reds in the north-east, or Wednesbury greys in the Midlands. A well-known protagonist of cockfighting, the twelfth Earl of Derby (1752–1834) had his own black-breasted Knowsley reds, of which some 3,000 were bred annually on his Lancashire estates during his heyday. This may seem excessive, but in the 1780s it was estimated that during race week at Newcastle upon Tyne up to 1,000 cocks could die in the six main pits and untold other establishments.

The complexities of selection, feeding, training and delivering the birds in peak condition to the fight venue were the responsibility of the 'cocker' or 'feeder'. A top level feeder was a man of substance and well respected as a major breeder of cocks. Like a leading racehorse trainer, he was well-travelled in support of his charges, whose performance was a testament to his skill and experience, and he was at least as well-known as the cocks' owners, even if the latter were of exalted rank. Charles Cotton's *The Compleat Gamester* (1674) and its update *The School of Recreation; or, A Guide to the Most Ingenious Exercises* (1723) went into great detail on these activities, as did Macrie's *An Essay on the Royal Art and Recreation of Cocking* (1705), while *Hoyle's Games . . . with an Essay on Game Cocks*, in its revised edition (1820), ran to more than 30 pages.

Young birds required both space and exercise to develop stamina, so the provision of a 'walk' in a well-drained location, preferably with a stream and a supply of grass or other suitable green plants, was a prerequisite. Looking after the birds, or 'walking the cocks', could be an obligation for a tenant farmer, or a lucrative but arduous activity, as the walks might well be spread over a wide area in the neighbourhood of the owner's or major breeder's premises. Feeding cocks on the best available corn found general approval, but authorities were divided over the merits of raw meat or maggots when worms were not available in sufficient quantities.

But when a cock was judged to be ready for fight training, this comfortable life, where the company of other birds (except for the most belligerent) was not excluded, would come to a sudden end. Delabere P. Blain, in the third edition of his *An Encyclopaedia of Rural Sports* (1870), opted not to go into details, possibly because by then cockfighting was a proscribed

activity, but Cotton, some two centuries earlier, had no such inhibitions. From then on the bird was kept penned, it was purged of any residues of its earlier diet and fed on wheaten bread, moistened at times by human urine, which was found to be equally efficacious as an antiseptic and as a healing agent for birds injured in the fight. Each day, the bird was actively encouraged to spar with other cocks, although the spurs were sheathed in leather to avoid injury to each combatant. After exercise, the regime involved sweating in a closed bag filled with straw, coupled with the administering of various potions, the secret ingredients of which were jealously guarded. This routine was followed for up to six weeks, becoming more drastic a week or so before the fight, with stiff purges being administered right up to the time of the contest. The birds were then individually bagged for transport by coach or cart to the cockpit.

Most towns of any importance had several large cockpits and probably many less salubrious establishments, both of a permanent or temporary nature. The pit could be housed in a purpose-built structure, or incorporated into an existing building, usually a local inn, or in the assembly rooms, as at Ulverston. The octagonal stone pit at the George Hotel in Stamford, built about 1725 by the eighth Earl of Exeter, held 400 to 500 spectators, while the similarly shaped pit in Lowther Street in Carlisle was 40 feet in diameter. The sanded fighting area could be up to 20 feet in size and surrounded by a two-foot-high fence. Such pits had shuttered windows to admit air and light when required, with tiered galleries, so that spectators could get a good view of the action. Admission prices to such pits could range from sixpence to five shillings, depending on the fight programme and the viewing area selected. More modest pits, into which 50 to 100 spectators would crowd, generally had a central platform at least eight feet in diameter, which could be covered in turf (the sod or matting), and around which wooden sides were fitted for the fight. The various officials circulated in a shallow ditch between the ring and the spectators, who would sit or stand behind an outer fence, using benches or any other vantage point to gain a better view. Pits were also found in cellars, where the fighting area might well be sunken, and in special rooms or enclosed gardens in the town houses of the gentry. Even the attic, or 'cockloft', often used for the latter stages of fight training, could be pressed into use for a cockfight. In rural areas, pits were often out in the open and, as the sport was gradually forced underground, the basic earthworks were constructed in quite remote spots. These sites took advantage of the local terrain to provide spectators with a good view and to enable the lookouts to give early warning of the approaching constabulary. They would also facilitate concealment of any evidence of a cockfight, and provide a speedy escape route wherever possible.

Cocks were generally considered to be at their peak at around two years old, when they would be fighting at between three and five pounds in weight. (The rules of the Royal Cockpit at Westminster were more precise at 3 pounds 9 ounces to 4 pounds 10 ounces.) In fighting trim, the cocks would have had their comb and gills cut off, and both wings and tail feathers clipped. Two other categories of birds were regularly entered for contests: 'stags', which were under one year old, and 'blinkards', one-eyed or blind veterans. Losing an eye was a common wound, and plucky birds were nursed back to health and fighting trim by the feeders and their helpers with as much care and solicitude as if the bird were a household pet – hence the wide range of names given to favourite cocks.

The basic fight between a pair of cocks was staged in various ways. The simplest was the 'common main', in which a number of individual 'battles' – probably six to eight – were fought, with an agreed sum for the individual victor in a battle and a larger sum for the complete main. There was also the more strenuous and brutal 'Welsh main' – a knockout contest in which an initial eight or sixteen pairs of birds fought their individual battles, with the winners moving to the next round, until there was an undisputed champion. Generally only the winner and runner-up earned a prize in the Welsh main. If the organisers wanted to enliven the final stages of a Welsh main, they could create a 'battle royal' by putting all the last eight birds together to fight until only one survived. But perhaps the most popular approach for those individuals or groups of participants who had access to 40 or more birds was the 'long main'. This was a particular favourite during race weeks as it provided entertainment over a number of days, the eventual winner of the main being determined by the number of individual battles won by each side. Even this was not good enough for some enthusiasts, as a five-year main was fought at Huntingdon Races between 1817 and 1821.

As part of the build-up to the cockfight, the feeder would hand over his birds to the 'setter-to' who would handle them during the battle, just like the racehorse trainer hands over to the jockey for the race itself. The cocks were fitted with either steel or silver spurs, the latter generally being favoured for more upmarket contests as they tended to be less lethal and helped to prolong the excitement of the battle. Thereafter, the setter-to brought his bird to the scratch line and put it to fight, following the appropriate rules, until one bird was killed or maimed to such an extent that it was unable to continue the battle. Special rules applied when birds refused to fight for reasons other than as a result of injury, generally leading to the battle being declared a draw.

From the time of the Restoration onwards, major cockfights were widely advertised in London and provincial newspapers, and throughout the eighteenth century care was taken to avoid any clashes of dates, even over a wide area (such as that bounded by Edinburgh, Newcastle upon Tyne, Carlisle, York and Preston). Naturally, there were social gradations, particularly among the participants, and this was reflected in the level of prize money. At fights organised by the miners of the industrial north, ten shillings could be won in a single battle. This might seem quite modest in absolute terms, but it could be more than half a week's wages for some. The prize for the whole main, which could be £5 to £15, whether in cash or in kind (such as a cow or even a load of hay), could be a substantial boost to the family income, particularly in view of the expense of breeding and training the birds.

The cockfights associated with race meetings attracted the leading owners in the area, with average prizes of £10 to £20 for a battle and £100 to £200 for the whole of a main. Some towns such as Newcastle upon Tyne, also awarded gold cups or some other suitable trophy. Such prize money was well in excess of all but the most prestigious horse race. Small wonder, then, that cockfighting was so attractive. With battles lasting between 20 seconds and 20 minutes, there was plenty of suspense and excitement and, more importantly, ample opportunities for gambling. The total money changing hands at any cockfight was far in excess of the prize money. Fox, the Earl of Derby's biographer, recorded that the noble earl might wager as much as 5,000 guineas on a main, or even on a single battle, particularly at Newmarket, where many of the owners, subscribers or spectators were equally rich.

Matches were held between teams of owners, as for example between the gentlemen of Cambridgeshire and Hertfordshire at the Red Lion, Royston, during the Odsey Races in September 1764, or in the 1817 race week at Stamford between the gentlemen of Middlesex and Warwickshire. In 1835, a main was fought at Stockton between the gentlemen of Richmond and Guisborough, while for the ladies there was a footrace, although ladies had often attended cockfights in earlier years (and even trained their own birds). Details of many such contests can be found in the *Racing Calendar* right up to 1840, but those between individual owners are more interesting. The Earl of Derby had at least two long-term opponents in Thomas Legh and Henry Bold Hoghton, while in the northeast the leading lights were Sir Henry Vane Tempest and the Dukes of Cleveland and Northumberland, a descendant of the last being criticised in the 1930s for being a major supporter of the outlawed sport. A notable main took place in Durham in April 1751 between Captain Mark Milbank and a Dr Dunn with 31 birds a side, and there was the 11-day main between Bold Hoghton and the Earl of Derby in 1829. The more prestigious mains had prizes of 500 guineas, or even 1,000 guineas as in a 36-battle main at Preston in 1796, and at Edinburgh, Newcastle and York in the following decade. But the most valuable main for direct prize money was fought between the Earl of Derby and Joseph Gilliver at Lincoln in 1830. Although there were only seven birds a side, the stakes were 1,000 guineas a battle and 5,000 guineas for the main; Gilliver won the main prize with five victories. Gilliver was not well-known as an owner, but was probably the most celebrated feeder of all time, preparing birds for both George III and George IV, and generally figuring as the feeder for the Earl of Derby's leading opponents, the Earl favouring Potter to bring him success. Certainly, the reports of cockfights at the highest level were dominated by Gilliver and Potter, the ever-present feeders for some thirty years.

Despite its continuing acceptability at the highest level, the case against cockfighting had been gathering momentum, albeit slowly, over the previous 250 years. The rather puritanical Elizabethan activist Philip Stubbes had attacked cockfighting in his *Anatomie of Abuses* (1583), although he had to admit that it was a major pastime for all classes of the population. The seventeenth-century diarist Samuel Pepys thought it barbaric, while the caricaturist and painter William Hogarth in 1750 showed the sport bringing out man's baser instincts, driven by blood lust and gambling, which led both to violence and to misery for the families of the losing betters. But it took the poet George Crabbe to identify the savagery, cruelty and suffering caused to the birds in his long poem *The Parish Register* (1807), while ten years later Fancy, in his *General View of the Agriculture of Derbyshire*, deplored the breeding of large numbers of birds 'for the truly vile and disgraceful purpose of cocking'. In the early years of the nineteenth century, the humanitarian view gained many supporters, helped by more extensive religious pressure, particularly from non-conformist and evangelical groups. The formation of the Society for the Prevention of Cruelty to Animals (later the Royal Society for the Prevention of Cruelty to Animals) in 1824 was a major step forward, and some prosecutions were taken out against cockfighters, but these did not markedly increase until cockfighting became a misdemeanour under the 1835 Cruelty to Animals Act, which effectively also banned bear and bull baiting. Although some cock-pits closed and prosecutions increased, the general attitude was still ambivalent, as typified by the *Carlisle Journal* in the late 1830s, which carried advertisements for cockfights and then reported on the trials of their participants.

The *Racing Calendar* had stopped reporting cocking in 1840 but, when the Act for the Further Prevention of Cruelty to Animals came into force nine years later, there were still four major pits in both Liverpool and Manchester. Although cockfighting was now outlawed, its move underground was patchy and very gradual, depending very much on the attitude of local magistrates and the police, who were often supporters. Even in 1871, the *Day's Doing*, a disreputable London paper, had an engraving of a father with his young daughter at a cockfight. In the north-east of England particularly, business continued more or less as usual, with the last public pit at Gallowgate in Newcastle upon Tyne not being closed until a police raid in 1874. Even in the 1890s there was a South Cumberland and Furness Cockfighting Club, which had an organised league, using parish and county boundaries to foil police raids, just as the supporters of illegal prize-fights had done some years previously.

Little had changed by the time of the magazine *Cruel Sports* in the 1930s. Working men still continued their sport, both in the industrial north and all over rural England, enjoying pitting their wits against the police as much as the fights themselves. The gentry held cockfights in fashionable London locations and in the country and, when caught, seemed amazed

that they were committing a crime. They employed eminent QCs to argue their case, even though the Protection of Animals Act of 1911 had placed more stringent safe-guards on the statute book. The Duke of Northumberland openly attended a cock-fighting gala in Calais, although the sport was also banned in France. There were learned discussions on the merits of artificial spurs against the birds' natural weapons, and the *Daily Mail* advocated using rubber pads in the place of steel spurs to reduce injury.

But even today, despite increasing legis-lation, the sport still flourishes, particularly in the West Midlands and Yorkshire, where immigrants from countries in which cock-fighting is still legal have swelled the num-bers of supporters and participants. Videos of fights are now used to enhance the sale value of prize cocks, but although there are reputedly six cockfights each week in Birmingham alone, there were only 62 con-victions in the ten years after 1985 (although this was twice as many as for dog fighting).

There are numerous public houses whose names evoke memories of the sport, such as the Game Cock or the Cock and Bell. These may well have oil paintings or engravings of champion birds, or sporting relics such as sheaths, spurs or cocking bags. A decreasing number of street names still bear witness to their former association, as does the hamlet of Fighting Cocks, just to the east of Darlington.

Sources and Reading:
Blain, D. P., *An Encyclopaeadia of Rural Sports* (Third edition) (London: Longman, 1870).
Cudden, J. A., *The Macmillan Dictionary of Sports and Games* (London: Macmillan, 1980).
Derby Cox, M., *The Life and Times of the 12th Earl of Derby* (London: J. A. Allen, 1974).
Jewell, B., *Sports and Games: History and Origins* (Tunbridge Wells: Midas Books, 1977).
Jobey, G., 'Cockfighting in Northumberland and Durham during the Eighteenth and Nineteenth Centuries', *Archeologia Aeliana*, 5: XX (1992), 1–25.

Middleton, I. M., 'Cockfighting in Yorkshire During the Early Eighteenth Century', *Northern History*, XLL: I (2003), 131–46.

Peate, I. C., 'The Denbigh Cockpit and Cockfighting in Wales', *Denbighshire Historical Society Transactions*, 19 (1970), 125–32.

See also Cockfighting (Scotland), Cockfighting Charms

John Tolson

Cockfighting (Scotland)

Cockfighting was the one animal sport that was common in Scotland after the Protestant Reformation. Calvin's injunction that animals should be treated kindly was backed by the Kirk's will to enforce standards of behaviour, and the various forms of baiting were suppressed. Cockfighting continued, however, on one holiday, Fastern's E'en (Shrove Tuesday). It was held in the parish school under the supervision of the schoolmaster, who received the defeated birds as part of his salary. Each pupil was entitled to bring one bird. In the Western Isles, there was cockfighting on New Year's Day until it was put down in the Evangelical revival at the beginning of the nineteenth century.

Cockfighting was of little interest to adults in the Lowlands until the end of the eighteenth century, when in a few places men supplied trained birds for the Fastern's E'en matches and wagered on them. It had a limited popularity in Scotland between about 1780 and 1840. Cockfighting was never respectable for it was closely linked to gambling. William Brodie, an Edinburgh tradesman by day and thief by night, was an enthusiast for cockfighting; found guilty of burglary, he was executed in 1788. Matches between animals belonging to gentlemen from different counties were occasionally held, such as the Haddingtonshire v Lanarkshire main (in Edinburgh) in 1785. There had been a cockpit in Leith in the late seventeenth century, and another was built in Glasgow in the mid-1830s. Ordinary people held matches on holidays in the same period, particularly New Year's Day and Hansel Monday, the first Monday of the year. A court case in 1792 concerning an assault in one of the poorest parts of the town of Ayr suggests that cockfighting was an everyday occurrence there, and so it may have been more widespread than is generally recognised. Despite the disapproval of respectable people and the hostility of the law, cockfighting remained a clandestine sport, particularly in central Scotland, from the 1840s onwards.

Sources and Reading:
Burnett, J., *Riot, Revelry and Rout: Sport in Lowland Scotland before 1860* (East Linton: Tuckwell, 2000).

Close, R., 'Cock-fighting in Ayr', *Ayrshire Notes* (Spring 1996), 11–12.

John Burnett

Cockfighting Charms

Charms thought to protect and safeguard their wearer were sometimes used in cockfighting. These included biblical verses or cryptic words and signs written on pieces of paper small enough to be slotted into the spurs attached to the birds' legs. A verse commonly employed for this purpose was: Taking the shield of faith wherewith ye shall be able to quench all the fiery darts of the wicked.

An even stronger charm involved inserting a crumb from the consecrated bread left on the communion table following a religious service into the spur. For maximum power, this crumb should be removed from the church at midnight. Superstitious owners also believed that birds fed with soil acquired from under the church altar would become unbeatable, and capable of killing all opponents set against them. Such spells and charms were annulled, however, if the contest took place in the hallowed ground of a churchyard, where battles were fought honestly and could not be touched by any external forces.

Emma Lile

Cock Throwing

Cock throwing would usually take place annually on Shrove Tuesday. The mechanics of the game would vary according to the locality. In the Cornish version, the cock would be tied down and then weighted sticks thrown at it; the thrower who managed to knock the cock unconscious and take hold of it before it recovered was deemed the winner. The Sussex version saw the cock placed in a large earthenware pot, which was raised about 16 feet above the street. Participants paid two pence to have four throws at the pot with a heavy stone; the person who broke the pot won the cock. In some regional versions, cock throwing could also resemble bull baiting, with the cock being tethered to the ground with a rope of 4 to 5 feet long. Stones, sticks and other missiles were then thrown at it until it was stunned or (more likely) dead. A variant in Wales involved setting the bird in a pit and aiming at it with pieces of wood. Throwers were given three chances to knock the bird over and then catch it before it rose to its feet. The 'sport' was also known as shying at cocks, cock running, cock threshing, cock squailing (a squaile was a large stick) and, in Devon, as cock-kibbit.

It appears to have been widespread in the fifteenth and sixteenth centuries, and was played by all classes of society, including royalty. In 1409, the Corporation of London sought to stop schoolboys pestering passers-by for money to play the game. As with cockfighting, it was particularly popular with schoolboys at this time and was often played at Shrovetide, with the support of the boys' schoolmasters.

From the mid-eighteenth century, magistrates began to clamp down on the sport, usually by imposing fines for public-order offences on participants. Its association with the lower classes also helped to under-mine its popularity among the more well-to-do. It was also becoming associated with public disorder and unruly behaviour; for example, a thirteen-year-old boy was killed during cock throwing in Leeds in 1783.

For many sporting commentators, it was widely felt to be 'unmanly' and unsporting because the cock was tethered and so could not get away or defend itself. By 1797, the *Monthly Magazine* could claim, with some justification, that the sport 'is nearly extinct'. The last remaining survival of it appears to have been at Quainton in Buckinghamshire, where it was played until 1844.

Sources and Reading:
Hone, W., *The Every-Day Book* (London: Thomas Tegg, 1830).

Pegg, B., *Rites and Riots: Folk Customs of Britain and Europe* (Poole: Blandford, 1981).

Reeves, C., *Pleasures and Pastimes in Medieval England* (Stroud: Sutton, 1995).

Whitlock, R., *A Calendar of Country Customs* (London: Batsford, 1978).

See also Cockfighting, Cockfighting (Scotland), Thrashing the Hen

Tony Collins

The game of suspending a horse chestnut

Conkers

on a string and attempting to destroy an opponent's horse chestnut by hitting it would seem to be an old traditional game, yet the evidence for such an assertion is extremely thin. The first mention of the game is in Robert Southey's 1821 memoir of his childhood, although it appears a similar game was played with hazelnuts, cobnuts and snail shells in the seventeenth century. It is only from the 1850s that the use of horse chestnuts is regularly referred to, and even then the game is restricted to certain regions. The game's popularity appears to be a twentieth-century development.

Although it has traditionally been a schoolboys' game, adults (almost invariably male) also play the game. The world conker championships are held every October at Ashton in Northamptonshire. Walton-on-Trent in Derbyshire also hosts its own conker championships.

Sources and Reading:
Day, B., *A Chronicle of Folk Customs* (London: Hamlyn, 1988).
Simpson, J. and Roud, S., *A Dictionary of English Folklore* (Oxford: Oxford University Press, 2000).

See also Invented Traditions

Tony Collins

Copsole Pulling (*Tynnu Copstol*)

This sport was a test of physical strength. It involved two men sitting on the ground with their soles touching. A large piece of wood, of the type normally placed between two horses while ploughing, was set between them, and on a signal both men pulled it with all their might. Whoever lifted the other off the floor was victorious. In Scotland, the spat was called sweir-drauchts, sweir-erse or, most commonly, sweir-trees, and was often played without the piece of wood – merely by holding hands.

Sources and Reading:
Jones, W. R. ('Gwenieth Gwyn'). Papurau. Museum of Welsh Life, MS 1464.

Emma Lile

Coracle Racing

Coracles have been used since ancient times in rivers across Wales, and take the form of light, egg-shaped, one-man boats made of wood. Although their main purpose was fishing, they were also used for racing, as at Usk in 1856 to celebrate the opening of the town's railway.

Coracle challenges for wagers also took place. During the nineteenth century, a boatman on the river Wye successfully steered his coracle to the furthest extremity of the Bristol Channel, and despite great difficulties en route, returned safely to Wales after a fortnight.

Today, coracles can be seen on the rivers Teifi, Towy and Taf, and since 1950 coracle races have been held annually in Cilgerran, Pembrokeshire.

Sources and Reading:
Clark, J. H., *Usk, Past and Present* (Usk: County Observer, 1891).

Emma Lile

Cotswold Olympick Games

Held at Dover's Hill, Chipping Campden in Gloucestershire, the Cotswold Olympick Games began in 1612 and were initiated and organised by the Catholic Royalist lawyer Robert Dover (1582–1652). Apart from a break between 1622 and 1624, the games continued until 1643, when they became a casualty of the Civil War (1642–9), the overthrow of the monarchy and the establishment of Oliver Cromwell's Commonwealth (1649–60). In 1661, the games were revived by local innkeepers and called the 'Dover's Meeting'. The last of the Dover's Meetings was held in 1851 following an enclosure act that broke up the common land on which they were played. A campaign against the games had also been waged by a local clergyman, Canon Bourne. In 1963 the games were again revived, by the Robert Dover's Games Society, and are today held annually on the Friday after Late Spring Bank Holiday.

The games were based on the traditional Whitsun ales of Chipping Campden and Weston-sub-Edge, and were originally staged on Thursdays and Fridays at Whitsuntide. Sports played at the games included wrestling, leaping, skittles, football, pitching the bar, cudgels, throwing the iron hammer, handling the pike, leaping over the heads of kneeling men, hunting the hare, cockfighting, horseracing, backsword play, walking on hands, jumping in sacks and shin-kicking. Tug of war and climbing the greasy pole are still played today.

In organising the games, Dover had the explicitly political purpose of promoting traditional English sports and opposing the growing influence of Puritanism. In 1619, Cambridge students sought to organise their own Olympics, both in honour of him and to celebrate the first anniversary of the publication of James I's *Book of Sports*, the publication of which was seen as a victory over the forces of Puritanism.

Dover sought to include all classes of society in the games and designated particular sports for particular classes. Thus horse-racing, coursing and hunting by scent were provided for the gentry; wrestling, quintain and barriers for townspeople; balloon and shovelboard for the lesser ranks; and cudgel-play, shin-kicking, running, jumping, throwing the hammer, spurning the bar, tumbling and skittles for the rural population. Music was provided by a harpist dressed as Homer, to underline the Greek inspiration for the games. Dover himself paraded through the games on a white horse and used royal regalia (some old clothes belonging to James I were provided by a courtier, Endymion Porter, who was from the area) to underline where his political sympathies lay.

The games' popularity, at least among opponents of Puritanism, and fame led to the compilation in 1636 of what was probably the first anthology of sporting verse, *Annalia Dubrensia: Upon the Yeevely Celebration of Mr Robert Dover's Olympick Games upon Cotswold-Hills*. It featured celebratory poems by more than 30 contributors, including Ben Jonson and Michael Drayton, and was subsequently reprinted in 1736, 1814 and 1836. William Somerville's *Hobbinol* (1740) also commemorates the games.

Sources and Reading:
Brailsford, D., *British Sport: A Social History* (Cambridge: Lutterworth Press, 1992).
Burns, F., *Heigh for Cotswold! A History of Robert Dover's Olimpick Games* (Chipping Campden: Robert Dover's Games Society, 1981).
Clarke, S., 'Olympus in the Cotswolds: The Cotswold Games and Continuity in Popular Culture, 1612–1800', *International Journal of the History of Sport*, 14: 2 (1997).
Day, B., *A Chronicle of Folk Customs* (London: Hamlyn, 1988).
Whitfield, C., *A History of Chipping Campden and Captain Robert Dover's Olympick Games* (Eton: Shakespeare Head, 1958).

See also Book of Sports, Liverpool Olympics, Morpeth Olympic Games, Much Wenlock Games

Tony Collins

Countryside Alliance

The Countryside Alliance, formally established in March 1977, is an omnibus organisation with the aims of ensuring the promotion, protection and preservation of traditional country sports and related activities in a thriving countryside that is properly cared for. It is an amalgamation of the Countryside Movement, the Countryside Business Group and the British Field Sports Society (BFSS). The best known of these organisations was the BFSS, which was formed in 1930 to safeguard fox hunting by uniting all field sports under one banner. The group was instrumental in successfully mobilising opposition to a series of private members' bills to outlaw hunting. The BFSS made strenuous efforts to maintain the fragile unity that existed between the hunting and shooting factions of the Alliance.

The broad aims of the Alliance encompass the formulation of countryside initiatives to safeguard its vitality, viability and heritage. It operates as a pressure group, representing the interests of its members at all levels of government and in the media. Its 'Listen to Us' meeting on 10 July 1997 led to an estimated 120,000 people gathering in Hyde Park to draw public attention to the threatened way of life of country people. The Countryside March on 1 March 1988 brought nearly 300,000 people on to the streets of London in protest. An even larger 'Liberty and Livelihood' march, involving more than 400,000 people, took place on 18 September 2002 in an attempt to mobilise public support for the Alliance's concerns. The ruralists, protesting against government plans, walked through the streets of London to the sounds of Scottish bagpipes and hunting hounds. These concerns focused on the Government's proposals to ban hunting with hounds, perhaps precipitated by the Scottish Parliament's vote to ban hunting in February of that year, and also the parlous state of the farming industry. The Alliance's defence of field sports is based primarily on the concept of preserving civil liberties and ensuring the right to participate in traditional rural activities.

Sources and Reading:
Thomas, R. H., *The Politics of Hunting* (Aldershot: Gower, 1983).

Websites:
The Countryside Alliance: www.countryside-alliance.org

John Martin

Coursing

Hare coursing, or the chasing of live hares with specially bred greyhounds or lurchers, is one of the world's oldest field sports, out of which has evolved present-day greyhound racing using a mechanical hare. With live hare coursing, beaters drive hares one at a time onto the running ground, or alternatively participants flush the hares as they walk across the fields, as in rough shooting.

Coursing was first codified by the Duke of Norfolk in the 1560s, before being revised, according to popular legend, at the instruction of Queen Elizabeth I in 1591. The present variant of the sport can be traced back to the first public coursing club established at Swaffham in Norfolk in 1776. Its popularity increased rapidly during the latter stages of the Industrial Revolution. On the northern moors it was especially popular among farmers and colliers, who participated on an *ad hoc* basis. In the south it was undertaken on a much grander scale, with organised meetings at prestigious venues, such as Epsom, Leatherhead, Ashdown Park and Letcombe.

The vast majority of hare coursing takes place under National Coursing Club rules. These rules specify that the hare must be at least 80 yards in front of the two competing dogs. The dogs are held by the slipper, a trained official licensed by the club who is allowed to release, or slip, the hounds. The first phase consists of the run up to the hare. The second phase begins when the hounds try to catch the animal. The performance of the hounds is judged by a horse-mounted judge, suitably attired in hunting regalia, whose task is to adjudicate on the speed, stamina and agility of the dogs, rather than the actual killing of the hare. Indeed, as the hare is much more agile and has much more stamina, the pursuit is not invariably fatal.

All greyhounds participating in any of the events have to be registered in a studbook, which was first established by the National Coursing Club in 1882. Other coursing breeds are regulated by their own clubs and breed associations. At its peak in the 1880s, the National Coursing Club, founded in 1858, presided over the activities of more than 150 clubs, but today that number has been reduced to about 20. Nevertheless, despite constant parliamentary lobbying by animal rights' organisations, the sport survives.

Hare coursing is also undertaken on an informal basis using lurchers, which are crosses between greyhounds and other herding dogs. Illegal hare coursing remains a matter of concern in many rural areas.

Sources and Reading:
Cox, H., 'Coursing', in *Coursing and Falconry* (1892; Southampton: Ashford Press facsimile edition, 1986).
Grant-Rennick, R. (ed.), *Coursing* (London: Saul, 1977).

John Martin

Crabsow

A name used for hockey-type games in Lancashire.

Sources and Reading:
Gomme, A. B., *The Traditional Games of England, Scotland and Ireland* (London: Thames and Hudson facsimile edition, 1984).

See also Hockey

Tony Collins

Creag

A bat-and-ball game played in medieval times that is mentioned in Edward I's wardrobe account as one of the games played by his son. Despite little evidence of how the game was played, it is held by some to be the forerunner of cricket, largely on the basis of its name.

Sources and Reading:
Altham, H. S. and Swanton, E. W., *A History of Cricket* (London: Allen and Unwin, 1947).

See also Cricket

Tony Collins

Cribb, Tom

One of the most prominent prizefighters in the golden age of bare-knuckle boxing, Tom Cribb became the unofficial champion of the world in 1810 when he defeated the black American boxer Tom Molineaux. He held the title until he retired in May 1822. As a fighter, he was noted for his mastery of the skills of boxing and his gentlemanly conduct in the ring; the *Dictionary of National Biography* noted that 'as a professor of his art he was matchless and in his observance of fair play he was never excelled'.

Born one of seven children to Thomas and Hannah Cribb on 2 July 1871, he left his home village of Hanham in Gloucestershire for London when aged 13 to work as a bell-hanger. Eventually, he found work as a porter on the docks, where the constant lifting and carrying helped to develop his powerful physique. He made his public boxing debut in January 1805, when he defeated George Maddox at Wood Green. His talent was such that when he defeated Tom Blake the following month at Blackheath, he won a purse of 40 guineas (£42).

In February 1809 he defeated Jem Blecher for the second time and, on the retirement of the reigning champion John Gully that year, declared himself British champion. His defeat of Molineaux in 1810 was achieved in controversial circumstances; when he was knocked down in the 28th round by the former slave, his trainer argued with the referee to distract him from the count. When the fight resumed, Cribb was victorious thanks to a blow to Molineaux's throat. The result was greeted by many sections of the press as proof of the superiority of the white British race.

A rematch was arranged the following year, where Cribb won a hard-fought victory in front of 20,000 people at Thistleton Gap in Rutland. In December 1811, he was presented with the silver Champion's Cup at the Castle Tavern in Holborn. After holding the championship without challenge for ten years, Cribb was allowed to keep the title for the rest of his life.

Cribb's fame spread far beyond the confines of the English boxing scene. He gave sparring exhibitions for the Russian Tsar and the King of Prussia in 1814, and was a guard at the coronation of George IV in 1821. When he retired in May 1822 he was awarded a championship belt made of lion skin, a forerunner of today's Lonsdale Belt. Until 1839 he was the landlord of the Union Arms on Panton Street in Piccadilly, London. Today, the pub bears his name as a permanent reminder of the strength of his reputation. He died in 1848.

Sources and Reading:
Brailsford, D., *Bareknuckles: A Social History of Prize-Fighting* (Cambridge: Lutterworth Press, 1989).
Prestidge, D., *Tom Cribb at Thistleton Gap* (Cambridge: Brewhouse, 1971).

Tony Collins

Crick Ball

In Old English, a straight stick was known as a 'crick' and a curved stick as a 'bandy'. Crick ball dates from medieval times and may be a precursor to cricket.

Sources and Reading:
Reeves, C., *Pleasures and Pastimes in Medieval England* (Stroud: Sutton, 1995).

See also Bandy, Cricket

Tony Collins

Cricket

Cricket is a high-profile modern international sport which has become increasingly dynamic since the last quarter of the twentieth century. The sport has now spread throughout the world and the pattern of its development demonstrates its importance in England during the period of British imperial expansion. But cricket is perhaps unique amongst modern sports in also enjoying a long and celebrated history as a traditional sport, with rural origins in the south-eastern counties of England, which remained in evidence until the last quarter of the nineteenth century.

As the sport has gained prominence over the past 200 years, there has been much speculation about its origins. It is more than likely that the game that first came to be known as cricket was a variant of the numerous similar folk pastimes, such as stoolball, cat and dog, club ball, trap ball and tip cat, which were all based upon similar principles. Each of these traditional pastimes variously encompassed the basic tenets of cricket, and in common with other folk games they were played and spread informally, causing a degree of adaptation and reinterpretation between place and time. As a result, in the south-east of England cricket emerged as the derivative form of this generic game.

Many of the earliest historical references to cricket are closely linked to its status as a folk game of significant popularity in the sixteenth and seventeenth centuries. Until restrictions were relaxed following the Restoration in 1660, sabbatarianism and fear of civil and economic disorder resulted in the suppression of such pastimes. This has meant that prohibitive legislation and prosecutions provide sporadic early written references to the sport, which was centred around Kent, Surrey and Sussex, the counties encompassing the Downs and the Weald.

Although the earliest direct reference to the game comes from a dispute over a piece of land in Guildford in 1598, when John Derrick established that he had played cricket there as a schoolboy in the 1550s, prosecutions for playing the game on the Sabbath, such as that of several men at Boxgrove in 1622, were more frequent. Nevertheless, cricket was evidently seen as a fit pastime for children during this period, and also became tolerated in some parts, or played discreetly enough, to become an established game. Teams representing the Weald and Upland were able to meet at Chevening in 1610, and by 1677 venues such as 'the Dicker', an area of common land near Herstmonceux, were hosting matches which were attracting widespread local interest.

The basic premise of the sport has altered little since its early days. Matches were comprised of two innings per side and the batsmen attempted to outscore the opposition while avoiding dismissal by the ball breaking the wicket or by being caught or run out. But many of the techniques of play have altered significantly. In this early period, the ball was quite literally 'bowled' underarm, in a low skimming manner, at a wicket that was wider than it was high and consisted of two stumps with forked ends and one bail. In order to strike the ball effectively in this style of play, the 'bat', which before the 1720s was mainly referred to as a cricket 'staffe', 'stave' or 'stick', was long and curved, and shaped more like an ice-hockey stick. A description of the game in the poem *In Certamen Pilea*, written in 1706 by William Goldwin, also reveals that an over consisted of four balls and that to complete each run the batsman must touch his bat on a piece of wood, held by the umpire. Runs were recorded by scorers, who made cuts in a piece of wood; hence the term notches, which was used to describe runs well into the twentieth century. To run a batsman out, the ball had to be placed in a 'popping hole', which later became a 'popping crease'.

The eighteenth century saw cricket's first major stage of development. Through the interest of men such as Sir Horatio Mann, Lord John Sackville (third Duke of Dorset) and Charles Lennox (second Duke of Richmond), the sport became fashionable among the English social elite. These aristocratic patrons used cricket as a means of displaying their wealth and social position by staging 'great matches', upon which considerable stakes were commonly wagered.

Increasingly large numbers of spectators from all classes were attracted to matches as cricket became a popular entertainment, both as a form of social ritual and as part of a growing entertainment industry. In rural areas, matches were played at grounds built either on the country estates of the aristocratic enthusiasts, such as the Sackvilles at Knole in Kent, or in principal market towns.

Another common type of fixture was in London, where a commercial leisure industry had formed by the 1750s, with venues such as the Artillery Ground advertising fixtures, charging admission fees and selling refreshments. The Artillery Ground was the leading venue in London at this time. It was owned by George Smith, landlord of the Pyed Horse, which thus provides an early example of the publican-entrepreneur in cricket, a common feature throughout the country over the following two centuries.

The influence of cricket's roots in the folk game of rural south-east England remained a strong feature of the sport. The game was still largely confined to this region for most of the nineteenth century, and the competitive nature of major stake matches led to the engagement of leading players from the sport's rural heartland. These early professionals were either 'retained' men, who were employed on the estates of the patrons, or 'independent' players, who were available for hire per match. For example, the Duke of Richmond employed the noted cricketer Thomas Waymark on his estate at Goodwood in the 1720s and 1730s. Waymark no doubt featured in a match the duke arranged with a Mr Chambers at Richmond in Surrey in 1731, for 200 guineas a side, which attracted 'many thousands' to watch and a considerable number of side bets.

The independent professionals appeared mostly for teams that were assembled by a patron, or groups of patrons, to represent towns, villages and, occasionally, the south-eastern counties. These sides could also include leading gentleman players and the patrons themselves. The most notable early example of this type of professional was Richard Newland, who played for the village of Slindon in Sussex. Slindon was also backed by the Duke of Richmond and played in a number of matches at the Artillery Ground in the 1740s. Perhaps their most famous victory was against Surrey in 1741, which they won almost by an innings.

Gambling clearly played a vital role in the development of cricket during the Georgian era. This was reflected in the early development of written rules to prevent disputes in matches that carried often considerable wagers. In the earliest known instance, 'Articles of Agreement' were drawn up for two matches between the Duke of Richmond and Mr Alan Broderick in 1727. The 16 articles included the length of the pitch (23 yards), the jurisdiction of the umpires (from which the two gentlemen protagonists were naturally excluded) and rules for the qualification of players.

In 1752, the first attempt to standardise a set of regulations for the game was made when the 'Cricket Club', who played at the Artillery Ground, published the 'laws' by which they had been playing since 1744 in the *New Universal Magazine*. Further notable amendments were made in 1771, 1774 and 1788, by which time the no-ball, short run and the dismissals of hit-wicket and a prototype leg-before-wicket law, termed 'standing unfair to strike', had all been introduced, along with regulations for the size of the stumps, bails, ball and bat and the addition of a third stump.

The second half of the eighteenth century also saw the first major changes in the techniques that players used to play the game. This was largely due to the influence of the famous Hambledon club in Hampshire. Backed by a group of wealthy gentlemen, which included at various times the Reverend Charles Powlett, Sir Horace Mann, the Earls of Tankerville and Winchilsea and the Duke of Dorset, the club assembled a stable of professionals from an increasingly wide area.

Men such as Richard Nyren, the team's captain and proprietor of the Bat and Ball Inn, and John Small, the master bat and ball maker, were paid three shillings if they were on the losing side or four shillings if they were on the winning side – and that was just for practice matches. The constant practice and match play of many of the era's greatest players not only helped them to win considerable sums of money for their backers, but also enabled them to develop new techniques. So as Nyren and then David Harris perfected length bowling, which exploited the irregular bounce of uneven pitches, Small and then 'Silver' Billy

Beldham adopted the straight-bat approach, which encompassed forward play and playing down the line of the ball. Small's innovation was a literal one as he is credited with first changing the shape of the bat, from its original curved form to one similar to that which is used today.

The result of these developments was an increase in run scoring. Individual scores of over ten had been a rare achievement for most of the eighteenth century, but in 1769 John Minshull, who was employed as head gardener by the Duke of Dorset, scored the first recorded century when playing for the Duke's XI against Wrotham. Minshull was not a Hambledon player, nor a great practitioner of the new technique, unlike John Small, who had scored an unconfirmed 140 in 1768 (probably the total of both his scores in the match) and an unbeaten 80 in 1768. It was not until 1775 that Small scored his first century, 136 not out against Surrey, in a total of 357, which included 98 by Richard Nyren.

Hambledon was the climax of the great patrons' domination of cricket. The greatness of the club, and the level of gambling in the game at its highest level at this time, is reflected in the calculation, from surviving records, that between 1770 and 1790 Hambledon played for £32,527 in stake money, and won £22,497; however, it must also be noted that advertised stakes, which could top £1,000, were not always accurate. The success of the club also shows the immense popularity of cricket within the rural communities of south-eastern England, with estimated crowds of 20,000 being reported at a number of Hambledon's fixtures in the region.

The beginning of the nineteenth century saw the main focus of cricket move away from the centre of the folk game in the rural south-east. Social disharmony following the French Revolution and the early effects of both agricultural reform and the Industrial Revolution caused the aristocratic patrons to drift away from cricket. London became the main centre for major matches, with leadership of the game being assumed by Thomas Lord's cricket ground and the

Marylebone Cricket Club, both established in 1787.

Although Lord's and the MCC became synonymous with cricket during its next phase of development, through the Victorian era and beyond, the game still reflected many aspects of its traditional origins. As other bastions of Victorian cricket were inaugurated, such as the fixtures between Eton and Harrow (1805) and Gentleman and Players (1806), various forms of matches took place at the future headquarters of cricket. Lord's could also be hired for pedestrianism, pigeon shooting events and hopping contests, along with a number of divergent forms of cricket, until the second quarter of the nineteenth century.

Despite the early recognised laws of cricket, the informality that characterised traditional sports meant that agreed variations had always been accepted. The numbers of players per side was one such adaptation and was mostly linked with gambling. This could be through having any equal number of players on each side, by evening up the odds in matches by having a greater number of players on one side, or by players being 'given' to the weaker team. For instance, to make the early Gentleman v Players matches more equally contested, professional 'players' were sometimes given to the Gentlemen, and in 1829 Lillywhite and Broadridge took 19 of the 20 Players' wickets to fall in the Gentlemen's victory. Similarly, other alterations to the laws could be made to even out the contest, such as in the 1837 'Bar Door' match, when the Players were required to defend a wicket that was twice the normal size.

Single- and double-wicket matches were another example of these variations. Originally representing the common form of sporting contest, which was between individuals, they had been played since the 1700s. But a series of matches between rival gentlemen members of the MCC, such as Squire Osbalston and Lord Frederick Beauclerk, brought this form of the game to prominence in the early 1800s. By the 1820s, the popularity of the single-wicket contest had begun to spread northwards. Matches now began to resemble prizefights,

with leading players attracting groups of backers who sought challengers for big-money contests. These games were held as popular spectacles, and challenges were advertised in the press to attract interest. In 1828, the backers of Tom Marsden, from Sheffield, offered £10 travelling expenses to anyone in England willing to play their man for a £50 stake. The challenge was not taken up for five years, by which time Marsden was past his best. Finally, in 1833 Marsden met Fuller Pilch, the great Kent professional, in two contests, both of which he lost. The second of these, at Darnall near Sheffield in August 1833, was watched by an estimated crowd of 20,000. Despite the general reform of cricket after the 1830s, single-wicket matches for stake money continued to be played in the north and Midlands until the 1860s.

The growth of the game also saw its playing techniques developed further. The breakthrough was again in bowling, as a new round-arm style of delivery was pioneered by John Willes, from Kent, in the early nineteenth century and then taken up by the Sussex bowlers William Lillywhite and James Broadridge in the 1820s. At first it was disparagingly claimed that Willes had copied his sister's necessity to bowl in this fashion when she played wearing a hooped skirt. However, after much dispute, followed by three 'experimental matches' (organised by the MCC) in 1828 and a failed attempt to appease both sides by slightly altering the law in 1835, round-arm bowling was fully endorsed in 1845.

The Victorian era saw many aspects of cricket change. The new approach to sport initiated in the reformed public schools and the subsequent rise of amateurism began to take hold in the 1840s. Victorian predilections caused the suppression of many traditional forms of recreation. Most significantly for cricket, gambling was no longer universally seen as an acceptable part of the game, as the sport was given new meaning with the emergence of athleticism and the ideal of the 'amateur gentleman'.

Stake matches in the south-east were largely ended as new clubs based in the provincial towns of the region, such as the Town Malling Club (formed in 1827), became the chief organisers of major matches. Another of these, the West Kent Club (formed in 1812), was the basis of the great Kent XI in the 1830s, through the backing of cricket's last great patrons, the Earl of Thanet and Lord Sondes. The period also saw the first wave of county clubs being formed, such as Sussex (1839), Surrey (1845) and Nottinghamshire (1841). Also becoming popular among the new type of gentleman amateur cricketers were the alumni and wandering clubs, such as I Zingari (formed in 1845) and the Old Stagers (who were formed as part of the first Canterbury Cricket Week in 1842). All this meant that opportunities for professional cricketers to play in big matches were reduced and, although they were often employed by clubs, schools and universities as practice bowlers, their status began to decline.

The professionals reacted to these events by forming touring elevens which continued to play the traditional style of cricket match. Improving transport links meant that by the 1840s the leading players could stage matches away from the south-east, in regions where interest in cricket was increasing. So in 1846, William Clarke, a Nottingham professional and one-time proprietor of the Trent Bridge cricket ground, formed an All England XI, which was predominantly made up of professionals, and began to tour the country. Clarke's XI appeared in between 20 and 30 matches all over the British Isles, in places including Truro, Dublin and Glasgow, until 1879. The concept proved so successful that between 1850 and 1880 19 similar teams were formed, including the United All England XI, the United South of England XI and the United Midlands.

These teams mainly played odds matches, over two or three days, against local sides ranging from XIs to XXIIs. Clarke initially charged £65 for each appearance, which promoters recouped by attracting large crowds (demonstrating the considerable local interest) and providing them with refreshments and other entertainment. Some early matches were also played for

stakes and betting on the matches was also available, although this was not widely advertised. According to the *Leeds Times* of 5 September 1846, the first All England XI match in Sheffield was played for £200, while in the same year the *Leeds Intelligencer* of 12 September reported that betting for the match at Leeds was five-to-one in favour of the All England XI.

This progressive era of the professional cricketer saw the introduction of overseas tours. The first trip, for which the players received £50 plus expenses, was captained by George Parr and embarked for Canada and the United States in 1859. The inaugural tour to Australia was captained by H. H. Stephenson in 1861. Membership of these early overseas touring sides was by the invitation of the organisers, who saw them as profit-making ventures, and was predominantly professional. The first Australian tour was organised by Messrs Spies and Pond, a firm of tea exporters, who were said to have made around £11,000. The first tour of England by an overseas side was by the Australian Aboriginals in 1868.

This course of innovation also saw, in 1864, the final legislative development in bowling technique. Once again the change was controversial, and a famous incident at Lord's forced the MCC to take action. In the 1862 Surrey v All England match, Edgar Willsher of Kent was no-balled six consecutive times by Fred Lillywhite, son of William (the pioneer of round-arm bowling), for bowling with his elbow above his shoulder. As the new style of delivery was already being used by many professionals, and tolerated by most umpires, Willsher and his teammates (except for the two amateurs in the side) left the pitch in disgust. They did not return until the following morning, after Lillywhite had been replaced. Following this incident the new style of bowling effectively survived unchallenged until the law was changed two years later.

The manufacture and sale of cricket equipment also moved forward in the mid-nineteenth century. A triple-sewn ball made by Duke & Son (established in 1760) won a prize medal at the Great Exhibition in 1851. In 1853, after patenting cork pads twelve years earlier, Thomas Nixon revolutionised cricket bat design by using cane, a flexible wood, to make the already spliced handle. Protection for batsmen was also improved in 1848, when the kit manufacturer Robert Dark, who had been apprentice to John Small and was the brother of James Dark (the proprietor of Lord's), advertised batting gloves made with tubular Indian-rubber implants and improved leg-guards.

The commercial link between equipment sales and the star professionals was also established around the middle of the nineteenth century. William Lillywhite and John Wisden opened sports equipment stores in 1844 and 1850 respectively. Other opportunities were taken by the likes of William Dennison, James Lillywhite and Wisden, who began to produce popular cricket publications, with Wisden's first almanac appearing in 1864.

Although amateur cricketers largely played a secondary role throughout the middle years of the nineteenth century, a growing number still featured in the major matches away from Lord's. Clarke's initial All England XI had included Nicholas Wanostracht, commonly known as Felix, and Alfred Mynn. But the amateur profile began to rise after 1864, when W. G. Grace played his first major match, appearing for a Bristol and District XXII against the All England XI, when aged fifteen.

As well as playing for Gloucestershire, England, the MCC and the Gentlemen, Grace also appeared regularly for the United South of England touring XI as an amateur, although he received expenses and sometimes an appearance fee. Through a career that brought 54,896 runs, 126 centuries and 2,864 wickets, Grace became one of Victorian England's most recognisable figures. The importance of Grace to the fortunes of amateur cricket can be judged by his record in the Gentleman v Players fixtures, which before his debut in

1865 had been won 23 times by the Players in the 25 matches played. In the 20 years that followed, the Gentlemen won 27 matches and lost only 5.

The rise of Grace coincided with the formation of a second wave of county clubs in the 1860s, which included Yorkshire (1863), Lancashire (1864) and Middlesex (1864). An increase in intercounty fixtures then followed, from which the first declaration of a champion county, Surrey, came from the press in 1864. Although this was a far-from-satisfying conclusion, there being no rationalised fixtures list, it began the gradual move towards a recognisable county championship competition over the next half century.

The subsequent development of county cricket heralded the decline of professional dominance in the game and was essentially the end of cricket as a traditional sport. Through their growing schedule of first-class matches, which had also begun to attract public interest by the mid-1870s, the county clubs were beginning to rival the touring elevens as employers of players. This increase in fixtures resulted in a meeting of the counties in 1873, at which a series of new 'qualification' regulations, which severely limited the freedom of the professionals, was agreed. But the county circuit offered regular employment for professionals at a time when the one-sided odds matches were losing in popularity to competitive contests between county elevens of relatively equal strength. The emerging county cricket circuit therefore effectively saw the end of the touring elevens, along with the professional cricketer entrepreneurs and the style of cricket spectacle they had staged.

Sources and Reading:

Altham, H. S. and Swanton, E. W., *A History of Cricket* (Third edition) (London: Allen and Unwin Ltd, 1947).

Birley, D., *A Social History of English Cricket* (London: Aurum, 1999).

Brookes, C., *English Cricket: The Game and its Players through the Ages* (Exeter: Weidenfeld and Nicolson, 1978).

Underdown, D., *The Start of Play. Cricket and Culture in Eighteenth-Century England* (London: Penguin, 2000).

See also Cat and Dog, Club Ball, Creag, Stoolball, Trap Ball

Rob Light

Cricket (Wales)

The earliest reference to cricket in Wales appears to be that found in a song published in 1719 and known by its first line, 'Of noble race was Shinking'. The earliest pictures of bat-and-ball games depict female players, and this Welsh player follows the tradition:

> Her was the prettiest fellow,
> At foot-ball or at Cricket;
> At Hunting Chace, or nimble Race,
> Cots-plut her cou'd prick it.

While it is just possible that the game had reached Wales by this time, the above may be a piece of poetic licence. Although the Prince of Wales was patronising the game in Kent in the 1730s, the first record of a game played in the Principality was that at Pembroke in 1763 (albeit in an unconfirmed report), and the oldest printed instance of the Welsh word *cricced* dates only from 1772. The earliest match of which there are any details was played at Court Henry, near Llandeilo, for 50 guineas a side on 4 August 1783, between 'the Gentlemen of the East side of the Cothy [river] and those of the West'.

At the beginning of the eighteenth century, cricket was an unorganised folk game, usually played on any available open space rather than on a specially marked pitch. As the century progressed, the game became increasingly structured and several new clubs were formed, one of the first being the Swansea club, which was in existence in 1784. A club was formed in Cardiff in 1819, and there were others at Carmarthen, Overton and Hanmer by the 1820s, and Tenby, Merthyr, Aberystwyth and Aberdyfi by the 1830s. The first recorded county matches were played between Breconshire and Monmouthshire in 1825, and Welsh sides were taking on teams from England by the 1850s.

The coming of the railways to Wales during the 1840s and 1850s saw a further increase in the number of clubs, one of which was the Merthyr Early Cricket Club, formed in 1848, which practised three times a week for two hours, starting at 5.00 a.m. at the sound of a bugle. A more serious organisation was the South Wales Club (1859–86), the forerunner of the Glamorgan county side formed in 1888, which frequently included the great W. G. Grace himself, together with several other members of that renowned family. 'W. G.' often played in south Wales for various clubs, and was once famously out for 'a pair' against the Neath side, Cadoxton.

Although the game brought together all social classes, it was initially dominated by the gentry because of the high subscriptions required to join clubs. By the last quarter of the nineteenth century, however, it had spread to the working classes, though such players were probably not invited to participate in the occasional unconventional, light-hearted games, such as cricket on the ice at Powis Castle, near Welshpool, in 1879, and the Ladies v Gentlemen match at Aberystwyth in 1892, when the latter won despite batting with broomsticks and bowling left-handed.

Sources and Reading:

Buckley, G. B., *Fresh Light on Pre-Victorian Cricket* (Birmingham: Cotterell, 1937).

D'Urfey, T. (ed.), *Wit and Mirth; or, Pills to Purge Melancholy* (six volumes) (London, 1719–20).

Hignell, A., *A 'Favourit' Game: Cricket in South Wales before 1914* (Cardiff: University of Wales Press, 1992).

Waters, I., *Chepstow Miscellany* (Chepstow: Chepstow Society, 1958).

See also Cricket

Emma Lile

Cricklade Fair

Cricklade is a village in Wiltshire which traditionally held a fair on the first Sunday after 12 August. Linked with the opening of common lands for sheep-grazing, the fair was also a festival of sports, such as bull baiting, boxing, wrestling, cockfighting, cudgels and leg-kicking.

Sources and Reading:
Whitlock, R., *A Calendar of Country Customs* (London: Batsford, 1978).

Tony Collins

Croquet

Allegedly derived from Pall Mall, a game popular in London in the seventeenth century, modern croquet appears to have its roots in Ireland, from where it was imported to England in the early Victorian period.

Sports-goods manufacturer John Jaques first published a set of modern rules in 1857, and ten years later the first national championships were staged at Evesham. The All England Croquet and Lawn Tennis Club was formed in 1868, and in 1870 the championships were transferred to Wimbledon.

Unfortunately for its adherents, croquet's popularity among the suburban middle classes was eclipsed over the next 20 years by tennis. A new body, the Croquet Association, was founded in 1896 to oversee the sport, but today croquet largely remains a curiosity of the English upper-middle-class garden lawn.

Sources and Reading:
Arlott, J. (ed.), *The Oxford Companion to Sports and Games* (Oxford: Oxford University Press, 1975).
The Encyclopaedia of Sport (London: The Sportsman, 1912).

See also Pall Mall

Tony Collins

Crying the Mare

A Herefordshire game associated with harvesting. At the end of the harvest the final piece of standing corn was tied into sheaves and the men who had been harvesting would take turns to throw their sickles or scythes at it to cut it down. It is part of a tradition known as 'crying the neck', in which the cutting down of the last sheaf of corn would be acclaimed with shouting. The practice also took place in Wales, where the last sheaf was often known as '*y gaseg ben fedi*' (the end of reaping mare). This was an example of the ritual and superstition associated with harvest, the most crucial event in the farming calendar as it determined the amount of food people had to eat for the rest of the year. The activity might also be associated with the making of corn dollies which traditionally were made out of the last sheaf as a means of placating Ceres, the harvest god, in order to ensure a plentiful harvest the following year. The Church of England attempted to downplay the significance of these events by developing the harvest festival.

Sources and Reading:
Simpson, J. and Roud, S., *A Dictionary of English Folklore* (Oxford: Oxford University Press, 2000).

Tony Collins and John Martin

Cudgel

Not to be confused with cudgelling, this was a game usually played by boys. It is related to cricket, but instead of wickets, there are two small holes about ten feet apart, each with a ring (about a foot in diameter – larger than the hole) around them. A player with a stick stands at each hole and attempts to stop the bowler (of which there is one at each hole) from throwing a wooden puck, or cat, into the hole. If the cat is hit by a batsman, the players run between the holes, as in cricket. If the cat lands in the hole, both batsmen are out. If the cat lands in the ring, the bowlers pick it up and hide it on one of them. The batsmen have to decide which bowler has the cat and one runs to the hole of the bowler whom they believe has it. If they have guessed correctly, the first bowler has to throw the ball to the bowler at the other end for him to try and get the batsman out by putting the cat in the hole. If they are wrong, the bowler with the cat simply puts it in the hole and the batsmen are out; the bowlers then take their turn to bat.

Sources and Reading:
Gomme, A. B., *The Traditional Games of England, Scotland and Ireland* (London: Thames and Hudson facsimile edition, 1984).

See also Cricket, Lobber

Tony Collins

Cudgelling and Singlestick

Cudgelling and singlestick play were types of duelling with wooden weapons that grew out of sword practice. Cudgelling was initially the leading sport, but it was slowly overtaken in popularity by singlestick and was rarely seen after 1800. From Tudor times until the eighteenth century, the wooden staff and cudgel were employed to teach the long-sword and broadsword. During the Elizabethan period, those whose social status prohibited the wearing of the small sword, such as apprentices, carried wooden swords, and fighting with these 'wasters' became a common sport. After about 1540, up until the predominance of pugilism in the 1740s, swordsmen and instructors at London amphitheatres, including James Figg (1683–1734), popularised public prizefighting involving cudgelling, the quarterstaff and swords, especially the

backsword. The backsword was a metal sword with the cutting edge on the reverse; its use fulfilled the spectators' desire to see bloody – usually non-fatal – wounds inflicted. Backsword also became an alternative term for the singlestick, thus preserving an echo of the earlier stage-fighting era.

During the eighteenth century, at London gymnasia such as Angelo's Academy in St James Street, the singlestick had an important role in developing patience and attentiveness for gentlemen undergoing instruction in swordplay, especially the sabre. By the 1850s, such novices wore protective jackets and masks. The singlestick was also taught in private schools as a physical exercise.

Public competitions in cudgelling and singlestick are recorded with increasing frequency by regional newspapers after 1700, when they were becoming less popular in London. By the mid-eighteenth century, contests had become a common feature of parish wakes, revels, fairs and horserace meetings (including Ascot) in southern England, particularly in Somerset, Gloucestershire, Wiltshire and Berkshire, when they would be one of a number of attractions. Occasionally they were the only sport at events initiated and supported financially by the gentry, such as the cudgelling match involving 70 players held at Bristol in July 1753. Contests took place from 1725 at the annual Dover's Meetings, or Cotswold Olympick Games, held near Chipping Campden (Gloucestershire), and from at least 1755 at the scouring of the White Horse Hill figure near Uffington (Berkshire), undertaken every seven years, which up to 30,000 people attended. Other important singlestick contests were held at Hungerford Revels in Berkshire until 1824, at Botley (Hampshire) during the early eighteenth century and at Frome, when Somerset beat All England (actually Wiltshire) over two days in November 1808. There were sometimes separate events for young and old 'gamesters', therefore segregating contestants on the basis of experience. In 1824, Somerset youths fought Wiltshire youths at Calne.

For important bouts, a wooden stage was erected, perhaps 4 feet high with rope fencing, and umpires were used. Lots were drawn to determine the order of play, with the winner sometimes staying on the stage until beating all other challengers. Prizes included money, pieces of plate, gold rings, clothing, gloves or new hats, with the colour of the hat-lace or cockade denoting the placing of the player. Players travelled to events from surrounding counties. For example, the winner of the first day's backsword competition (and £8) at the White Horse in 1857 was James Bunn from Wedmore in Somerset, some 65 miles distant.

Rules were presumably formulated to prevent, for example, the seizing of an opponent's weapon, but seem to have varied over time and between regions. In the countryside, players removed their coats, rarely used padding and never wore masks, as the object was to 'break the head; that is, to win by cutting the skin on the head, face or neck above the lower jaw so that at least an inch of blood would run. When this happened the spectators would cry 'a head'. However, unlike fencing, strikes were usually allowed below the waist. Players stood within a yard of each other with straight legs, one foot forward and the body upright. In singlestick, the weapon was held out level to the forehead, angled towards the left shoulder. The positioning of the feet was critical and they were meant to be almost static. In cudgelling, nearly all the blows were aimed at the opponent's head, with a short cudgel and the left arm fending them off. Two sticks were used; the one for defence was about 2 feet long, made from a hard wood such as crab-tree, the one for attack was longer, with a wicker basket ('pot') to protect the hand. The longer weapon was probably the same as that used in singlestick, which was 36–40 inches long and made of a light wood (ash or willow), again with a wicker hilt. In Wiltshire, singlestick players loosely tied a belt or handkerchief around the left thigh, which was held by the left hand at chest-level, allowing the extended and raised elbow to reach the head and stop the adversary's blows. In Gloucestershire, the left hand was securely fastened to the thigh.

Fighting styles in singlestick varied. Players might resort to 'timbering' (quickly and wildly raining blows at the head), but the best gamesters exhibited great strength, speed and agility, perhaps fighting for 30 minutes without making any hit and for an hour before landing the winning blow. A player would shout 'hold' to halt the battle for a minute. Hits, guards and feints were employed, but no thrusts were allowed given the danger to the eyes. The main blows were delivered from the wrist in a whipping movement, aimed at the head and the ribs. Counter-attacking was done before the opponent's guard was restored, and the elbows, wrist or armpits were attacked to force the guard down.

Particular communities, such as Purton in Wiltshire, were renowned for producing good gamesters. John Shaw (1789–1815) from Wollaton in Nottinghamshire, a noted pugilist and swordsman who died at Waterloo, won the White Horse singlestick contest in 1808. Famous players from Berkshire included Tim Gibbons (*fl.*1755) of Lambourn, Harry Stanley (*fl.*1785) of Kingston Lisle and Joe Giles (*fl.*1843) of Shrivenham. Other leading players were John Edwards (*fl.*1753) from Wiltshire, Morris Pope from Liddington in Wiltshire in the 1820s, Simon Stone (*fl.*1843) from Somerset and several members of the Blackford family of Purton during the early nineteenth century. Often, these men were talented at other sports, such as wrestling.

The decline of patronage for rural sports generally, and the disappearance of specific events at which the sport was played, meant that the singlestick was not seen in public competition after 1860. Dover's Cotswold Olympick Games ended in 1852 with the enclosure of the fields adjacent to the site, and the last scouring of the Uffington White Horse, with the accompanying rural sports, took place in 1857. Singlestick competitions continued for members of the London gymnasia until the 1890s, but thereafter the popularity of the light Italian fencing sabre made the singlestick redundant. The singlestick was also used for training British solders and sailors in swordplay before the First World War.

Sources and Reading:

Allanson-Winn, R. G. and Phillipps-Wolley, C., *Broad-Sword and Single-Stick* (London: Bell, 1890).

Brand, J., *Observations on Popular Antiquities, with additions by Henry Ellis* (Revised edition) (London: F. C. & J. Rivington, 1813).

Bushaway, B., *By Rite: Custom, Ceremony and Community in England 1700–1880* (London: Junction Books, 1982).

Ditchfield, P. H., 'Cudgel Play and the Revels', in Ditchfield, P. H. and Page, W. (eds), *The Victoria History of the County of Berkshire* (Volume 2 of *The Victoria History of the Counties of England*) (London: Constable, 1907), 314–15.

Great Britain War Office, *Manual of Instruction for Single Stick Drill* (London: HMSO, 1886).

Hutton, A., *The Sword and the Centuries* (London: Grant Richards, 1901).

Malcolmson, R. W., *Popular Recreations in English Society 1700–1850* (Cambridge: Cambridge University Press, 1973).

Newton, A. J., *Boxing: with a Section on Single-Stick* (London: C. Pearson, 1904).

The Times (16 October 1805, 5; 12 September 1806, 2; 11 November 1808, 3).

Walker, D., *Defensive Exercises* (London: Hurst, 1840).

Mark Hathaway

Curling

Curling is a target sport played on ice. The target is the 'tee', a mark in the ice, which is at the centre of a group of concentric circles called the 'house'. The playing implements are 'stones', which are large, circular in plan and polished and have a handle fixed to the top surface. The maximum permitted weight for a stone is 44 pounds (19.96 kilograms). Games are played between teams, or 'rinks', of four curlers, each curler throwing two stones alternately with the opposite number from a platform, or 'hack', on the ice, 42 yards distant. At the conclusion of each section of the game, or 'end', when all 16 stones have been thrown to the house in one direction, points, or 'shots', are reckoned, one for every stone of one rink that is nearer the tee

than the opponents' nearest stone. The stones are then thrown to the house at the other end of the sheet of ice, and so on until a fixed time has passed or a fixed number of ends has been played.

From the earliest period of the game, brooms, or 'besoms', or 'brushes', have formed an integral part of the play. Originally their purpose was to clean the ice of any possible obstruction in the path of a running stone, but soon it was discovered that hard sweeping in front of a stone could cause it to run further than it would otherwise have done. So important did sweeping become that some early curling clubs enacted penalties for curlers who dared to appear on the ice without a broom.

The basic shot in the game is the 'draw', that is, the throwing of a stone with just enough weight to take it to a specified place in the house. Such a stone may be guarded by the placing of a stone directly in front of it so that an opposing stone cannot directly strike, or 'chap', it out. Sometimes the guard is laid first and then the task is to come around the guard to a safe position. This can be achieved because on delivery every stone is given either clockwise or anti-clockwise rotation, which causes the stone to deviate from a straight course in the direction of the rotation. The effect of the rotation becomes stronger as the stone slows down. Because hard sweeping slows down the rate of deceleration of a running stone, not only the distance but also the ultimate position of the stone in the house can be controlled. The third basic shot is the strike (chap), by which a stone lying in or about the house is struck out of play. Variations on each of these, such as the 'inwick', which occurs when a stone is deliberately played so as to rebound off a stone at an angle towards the tee, and the 'outwick' in which a lying stone is knocked teewards, give variety to the game.

The 'skip', or captain of the rink, determines the tactics and calls for particular shots. The two players who are not throwing follow the played stone up the ice, ready to sweep with vigour if the skip so directs. Every player in the rink, therefore, participates in every stone.

The game, which has been taken by the Scots to many of the colder parts of the world, such as Canada, the United States, Switzerland, Sweden and Norway, is undoubtedly Scottish, although there may have been some analogous sport in the Low Countries, as there still is in the form of *Eisstockschiessen* in Alpine Germany.

Curling is an ancient game for which evidence exists from the middle of the sixteenth century. That the Scots had no doubt of the Scottishness of their favourite game is evidenced in song and story. Curling was 'Scotland's ain game'. *Sic Scoti: alii non aeque felices* proclaimed the motto of the Duddingston curlers on their silver badges of 1802 – 'This is how the Scots enjoy themselves: the rest of mankind is not so lucky'.

Curlers have always been passionate about their sport. The thirteenth Earl of Eglinton, when he presided at the Grand Caledonian Curling Club's dinner after its annual general meeting in the town hall of Kilmarnock in October 1841, 'called for a bumper' and proposed the health of the club. He said:

Still there can be no doubt that there is no curler present who has sent his stone gliding through a port, which, at the distance of the rink, seemed almost impassable, or who has delicately cracked an egg on a stone . . . or who has, perhaps, performed a glorious in-wick . . . or who has planted his stone on the tee, the all-important stone upon which the success of his party depended, and who has enjoyed the rapturous applause with which such feats have been greeted by his fellow-players, there is not a person present I dare say, who has done and seen all this, who will not engage in the game with pleasure . . . Who that has passed the day at that game, or enjoyed the glories of in-wicking and out-wicking that does not rejoice that he was born a Scotsman; and [is not] glad to think that he is not like the poor

shivering wretches of other countries, who know not how to pass the frosty season of the year, and the tedious hours of winter!

In the year in which he spoke these words, the small town of Kilmarnock had no fewer than five curling clubs.

The nature of the stones is central to the development of the game. Until well into the seventeenth century the usual form of stone was the 'loofie', so-called from the loof or palm of the hand. Loofies were comparatively light, at about 20 pounds, and flat, and, being without a handle, were thrown by using a groove for the fingers in one side and a hole for the thumb on the other. By the early eighteenth century the 'channel' stone, which takes its name from being taken from the channel, or bed, of a river, had superseded the loofie. The insertion of an iron handle at the top enabled the curler to throw and control a stone of considerable weight, and many channel stones of over 60 pounds still survive. Such stones, of differing weights and shapes, must have meant a game where brute force preponderated.

By the second half of the eighteenth century it had come to be appreciated that circularity of the stones, and hence the ability to predict the angle at which one stone would rebound from another, would remove the element of luck, and add to the skill, and, therefore, the enjoyment afforded by the game. The Duddingston Curling Society, founded in 1795 in the village of Duddingston, about three miles from the centre of Edinburgh, was the first to commit its rules of play to paper, and by rule five it was provided: 'All Curling Stones to be of a circular shape'. By the third decade of the nineteenth century, the day of the channel stone was over. However, individuality was achieved by the choice of rock used and the degree of polish or other embellishment of the stone. Some curlers went to great lengths to choose a type of rock that was unusual and would look splendid on polishing; some spent very considerably on decoration.

The earliest circular stones generally had a handle of wood, iron or brass permanently fixed to the top surface. These were called 'single-soled'. A nineteenth-century development was the double-soled stone, in which a removable handle was screwed onto a bolt that ran through the centre of the stone. The two running surfaces, or soles, thus provided could be polished and configured differently so that each sole answered better to a keen or a dull ice surface. Moreover, the removable handle could be as expensive and extravagant as the curler wished; silver-mounted handles, smothered in engraved thistles, were not uncommon. A few were even cast from solid silver!

Early manufactured curling stones were generally made by local masons, although, of course, there were some who specialised in this sort of work. As the game increased in popularity throughout the nineteenth century, the large number of stones required were made by machinery in a small number of small factories. These stones were double-soled. Many were made of stone from the islet of Ailsa Craig, which lies in the Firth of Clyde, about ten miles off the mainland at Girvan in Ayrshire, but it is a misconception to think that all nineteenth-century stones were of Ailsa Craig origin: makers' price-lists named Burnock Waters, Tinkernhills, Blantyre Blacks, Carsphairn Reds, Crieff Serpentines and others.

On the rare occasions when natural stretches of water froze over, curlers made as great use of it as possible, on loch, river and inundated meadow. At least since the last quarter of the eighteenth century, curling has generally been played on artificial, very shallow ponds, usually of rectangular shape, which took fewer days to freeze sufficiently. The minute books of curling clubs show that the creation and maintenance of such ponds occupied the major part of the energies and finances of the clubs throughout the year, for the embankments had to be kept watertight during the season, and during the summer, after the water was let out in the spring, the grass had to be mown to prevent its marring the ice in the following winter.

In the 1820s, John Cairnie of Largs in Ayrshire had the idea of laying down an impermeable surface of clay, stone, or asphalt, and sprinkling water upon it as soon as the thermometer fell to 32 degrees Fahrenheit, so as to create a thin skin of ice. Such Cairnie rinks appeared all over Scotland, and it has been calculated that their introduction quadrupled the number of days on which curling could be enjoyed.

To John Cairnie also falls the honour of becoming the first president of the Grand Caledonian Curling Club, which was instituted in 1838 to organise Scotland's favourite game on a national basis. From its foundation in 1795, the Duddingston Curling Society had played for curling a role analogous to that of the Marylebone Cricket Club for cricket or the Jockey Club for racing. They had caused their rules to be printed in 1811 and saw them widely accepted. Curiously, they played no part in the formation of the Grand Club, nor did they participate in it subsequently, although a few of their members were active in the new national club. The presentation of a pair of curling stones to Prince Albert in 1842, when he and Queen Victoria were making their first visit to Scotland, secured royal patronage for the club and the game, which has been highly valued ever since.

The new Royal Caledonian Curling Club at once set about unifying the game. In 1838 there had been two main forms of the game: one in which rinks consisted of seven, eight or nine men, each throwing a single stone, and another, played in the Edinburgh area and elsewhere, in which rinks were composed of four men, each with a pair of stones. The Royal Club, by adopting the four-man form, eradicated the other by about 1861. Another way in which the game was fostered was by the provision of medals for competition between member clubs. This encouraged curlers to look a little further afield than merely the surrounding parishes when seeking opponents to conquer. The opening up of railways in this period assisted this 'nationalisation' of the game.

This also made possible the Royal Club's last great initiative, the Grand Match, in which curlers representing the north of Scotland played against those representing the south. A special pond of several acres was obtained in 1852 at the central location of Carsebreck at Blackford, between Stirling and Perth, close to the present-day Gleneagles. The railway companies cooperated by running special trains to the event from all over the country, and by building a special siding for the disembarkation of the thousands of curlers and their supporters and the unloading of the curling stones.

At the turn of the twentieth century, the size of the entry to the Grand Match mirrored the tremendous popularity of the game. There were 300 rinks in 1892, 348 in 1895, 494 in 1897, 452 in 1899, 442 in 1900, 480 in 1902, 572 in 1903 and 636 in 1909. In that last year, 1909, there were clubs from Braemar, Aberdeen, Durris, Insch and Upper Garioch in the north, and Minigaff and Castle Kennedy in the south.

In all, 30 matches were held in the first century of its institution. Twice, in 1880 and in 1886, two matches were played in the same calendar year, in January and in December. Both of the 1886 matches were won by New Monkland Curling Club, which was thus the first winner of the magnificent silver Grand Match trophy, which has at its base two silver curlers; one, who wears a kilt, represents the north, and the other, the south. The last Carsebreck Match, on 24 December 1935, was the largest, with 644 rinks. In these matches it was possible to see a whole nation at play.

These initiatives proved very successful. The numbers of clubs and curlers were far greater than, for example, those in golf throughout most of the nineteenth century: for example, in 1869 there were only 58 golf clubs in the whole of the United Kingdom, whereas there were 414 curling clubs – by far the majority of which were in Scotland – affiliated to the Royal Club, and untold numbers that never bothered to join the mother-club. Moreover, the geographical spread of curling within Scotland

was remarkable: by 1879 only four Scottish counties lacked an affiliated club. These were Banff, Caithness, Nairn and Sutherland – none of which were centres of population. Just ten years later, every county had at least one affiliated club.

The Royal Club has recorded the game faithfully in its annuals, which from 1839 have recorded all the member clubs (with lists of their members) and accounts of the game and its long history, together with the songs and poems composed in its honour. Since the game of curling depended on the chance of sufficient prolonged frost, the enthusiasm which it engendered was immense. All but the most informal of games were followed by the dinner of 'beef and greens [kale]' accompanied by whisky toddy and songs and recitations.

As early as 1847, curlers in Canada had begun to play the game in sheds, where although frost still provided and kept the ice, the roof and walls protected the curlers from the worst harshness of the climate. In the United Kingdom, the first indoor curling took place at Rusholme Ice Rink in Manchester in 1877, where the ice was made by machinery using Professor Gamgee's principle. Between 1877 and 1889, the Glaciarium at Southport afforded not only the only 'unnatural' ice in Britain but also regular competitions that were attended by Scottish curlers.

The first indoor rink in Scotland was at Crossmyloof in Glasgow (1907). Two rinks opened in Edinburgh in 1912, and one in Aberdeen in the same year. Only one had survived by 1917. A new rink opened in Glasgow in 1928 and nine more during the ice-hockey boom of the late 1930s. From the 1960s onwards there was a new boom in ice-rink building, and in 2003 Scotland had 29 rinks providing ice for the game.

The result of these developments in Canada and in Scotland is that nowadays almost all competitive curling now takes place indoors. The game that was played in the open, in biting cold and on very variable ice, has now, even in countries cold enough for natural ice to be guaranteed, moved indoors to specially prepared ice, kept at a steady temperature, and now uses matched sets of 16 identical stones, instead of varied pairs owned by the individual curlers. A curler still needs strength, particularly for sweeping, and dexterity, but the degree of delicate skill now required for success has grown immensely.

Sources and Reading:
Kerr, J., *History of Curling* (Edinburgh: Douglas, 1890).
Smith, D. B., *Curling: An Illustrated History* (Edinburgh: John Donald, 1981).
Smith, D. B., 'Curling', in Jarvie, G. and Burnett, J. (eds), *Sport: Scotland and the Scots* (East Linton: Tuckwell Press, 2000), 69–86.

John Burnett and
David B. Smith

Cwdwm Braich

Cwdwm braich was a type of wrestling which began by competitors grabbing each other by the arms. A fall was achieved when one wrestler succeeded in kicking his opponent and knocking him onto the floor. The contest was limited to three rounds, and whoever gained two falls was hailed the winner.

Sources and Reading:
Jones, W. R. ('Gwenith Gwyn'). Papurau. Museum of Welsh Life, MS 1464.
Williams, E., *The English Works of the late Eliezer Williams* (London: Cradock, 1840).

See also Cwdwm Cefn

Emma Lile

Cwdwm Cefn

The most common form of wrestling in Wales was the *cwdwm cefn*, known in England as the 'Cornish hug'. The intention was to pass one's right arm under the opponent's left and to clasp him around the waist. This would be followed by the fixing of knuckles against the opponent's chin and

abruptly wrenching him to the right, while simultaneously striking him under the left hamstring with the right knee. Such an attack was almost guaranteed to fell individuals, and through skill it was possible for smaller bodied men to triumph over heavier frames.

Sources and Reading:
Williams, E., *The English Works of the Late Eliezer Williams* (London: Cradock, 1840).

See also Cwdwm Braich

Emma Lile

Dab-an-Thicker

A version of knur and spell played in Holderness, in which the 'dab' is the wooden ball and the 'thicker' is the trigger that propels the dab into the air so that it can be hit by the striker.

Sources and Reading:
Gomme, A. B., *The Traditional Games of England, Scotland and Ireland* (London: Thames and Hudson facsimile edition, 1984).

See also Knur and Spell

Tony Collins

Daniel, William Barker

William Daniel (1754–1833), Church of England clergyman and writer, was best known for his two-volume text *Rural Sports*, first published in 1801. The advertisement for the text led one correspondent in the *Gentleman's Magazine* to suggest that 'I can not help thinking that he is fitter to act the character of Nimrod than that of a dignitary in the Church of England'. While this caustic comment was firmly rebuked by the editor in a note, the critique has been widely cited in subsequent biographical reviews of Daniel's career.

Rural Sports proved to be very popular among contemporary sportsmen, and even naturalists, with its detailed descriptions of hunting, coursing and fishing, interspersed with impressive plates and occasional references to Daniel's own exploits. It was reissued as a three-volume set in 1812, with a supplementary fourth volume being published the following year. It constituted the basis of many subsequent texts and was an early historical record of shooting before the introduction of breach-loading guns.

Daniel was educated at Cambridge, being ordained as a deacon at Lincoln in 1785 and priest at Gloucester in the following year, although he was never beneficed. In 1788 he secured an appointment as a private chaplain to the Prince Regent, a position he possibly retained until his retirement.

Sources and Reading:
Martin, J., 'Daniel, William Barker', in Harrison, B., *Oxford Dictionary of National Biography* (Oxford: Oxford University Press, 2004).

John Martin

Darts

Although darts is an ancient traditional English public-house game, the modern, standardised game is less than 100 years old.

Darts is a target sport involving two or more players, who throw three darts in turn. Originally dartboards were constructed from wood, normally elm or poplar, and these remained the most popular form of construction until the bristle (sisal) dartboards became readily available in the 1970s, although they were originally introduced in 1934. Other materials used in the past for dartboard construction include clay and compressed paper.

The earliest form of darts played in English public houses was 'puff and dart', a game in which small darts were puffed through a tube at a small concentric target, or at a circular or diamond-shaped target bearing numbers in a random order. These early dartboards were miniature forms of the archery target. The darts used in puff and dart, in their crudest form, comprised a piece of worsted and a pin. The game was thus potentially hazardous to any participant. By the mid-nineteenth century, puff and dart was becoming regarded by the medical profession as potentially life threatening (a good number of players had sucked instead of blown and died as a result of the dart being drawn into their lungs) or, at best, unsafe.

Fairgrounds, enjoying a renaissance during this period and always in search of original amusements for their customers, began to include darts stalls. Importing wooden darts from France (a form of darts had previously thrived in cafés in France, especially in the Nord Pas de Calais region), the showmen created large segmented targets and awarded prizes for punters scoring over or under particular numbers. This much safer variant of the game began to find its way into public houses, replacing the more dangerous puff and dart and introducing, by necessity, a much larger target. The wooden 'French dart' remained popular in public houses – usually loaned free of charge to players by the landlord – until the late 1920s when brass barrels with cane shafts and either feather or paper flights were introduced. An all-metal, chrome-plated dart was introduced in the late 1930s but, at two shillings and sixpence a set, were beyond the means of the working class. They were targeted instead at the middle and upper classes, who had recently taken to the game.

One of the larger targets introduced was the 'fives' board, a dartboard consisting of twelve segments (with scores of 5, 10, 15, 20, each repeated three times) and a bulls-eye (scoring 50 points) – similar scoring to that common in some archery targets. Improved skills demanded greater complexity of the target and, as a result, more-complicated numbering was introduced. The 'Grimsby Board' (*c*.1885) featured 28 segments; it also included hooks on the non-scoring surface, allowing the game of rings (indoor quoits) to be played on the same board. In Kent there existed a dartboard of 20 segments that covered its entire surface, the numbers having to be drawn on the wall around it. However, darts mythology insists that the modern dartboard design and numbering be accredited to a Lancastrian carpenter, Brian Gamlin from Bury, who came up with the devious system in 1898. The position of the numbers punish inaccuracy, the larger numbers having a smaller number either side so that the slightest error results in a significantly lower score. Despite extensive research, Gamlin's existence has yet to be confirmed, the task being made more difficult by the distinct possibility that Gamlin was a travelling showman.

In 1903, both puff and dart and the new emerging form of the game, dart and target, were defined as 'lawful games' in a publication produced by the Licensed Victuallers' Gazette Office. In both cases, the target was described as consisting of 'three or four concentric circles' with a bulls-eye, scores being made 'according to the nearness of the darts to the bulls-eye'. There is no mention of the segmented board.

However, by the outbreak of the First World War, puff and dart had practically disappeared and dart and target, now compressed simply to 'darts', was increasing in popularity in English public houses. The first signs of organisation began to emerge at this time. In the main, such organised matches took place either 'in-house', between regular customers of a public house, or were friendly matches between pubs that were in close proximity to each other. Only one brewery darts league has been traced to pre-1914. This was organised by Morland and Co. of Abingdon, Oxfordshire, who provided trophies and prizes for darts and other games. It is unlikely that this would have been the only example.

After the war, more brewery leagues appeared, especially in London and other expanding conurbations. Such was the growth of interest and participation in the game during the early 1920s that the brewers came under pressure from numerous clubs and pubs for regularisation of the rules of play. Eventually, in 1924 representatives of the brewers and the licensed trade met to discuss the establishment of a central darts control association. As a direct result of that meeting, the National Darts Association (NDA) was formed. The key objectives of the NDA were to 'protect the game of darts, as played in accordance with the association's rules, from the attacks of fanatics' and 'to further its interests by the legitimate means in its power'. In its previous form, darts, like the majority of pub games, had been associated with gaming – playing for money or money's worth. The NDA set out to promote itself as a self-policing agency of the brewers and 'the trade', suppressing all forms of gambling on the game and immediately suspending 'any club or player guilty of such an act'. The NDA also set itself up as a 'final court of appeal' for any disputes between any affiliated darts club and its competition management.

The rules of play were first standardised by the NDA in 1925 and disseminated by the Association's executive committee to its members. A number of alternative versions of the game were considered, and it is at this time that the decision was made that the 'clock' dartboard – and the rules that applied to that dartboard – be agreed as standard.

The clock dartboard – nowadays widely regarded as standard – consists of 20 segments (numbered 1 to 20, but situated apparently randomly around the board), an outer bulls-eye (value 25 points) and an inner bulls-eye (value 50 points). There is also an outer ring, scoring double the value of the segment, and an inner ring, between the double ring and the outer bulls-eye, scoring treble the value. The standard games played are 301, 501, or 1,001-up, starting either straight in or by first scoring a double. All standard games finish on a double. (The bulls-eye counts as double 25.)

Darts in this form is unique as a target sport in that the greatest number of points possible is not achieved by hitting the centre of the target. The maximum score possible in a single throw is 60 points. This is achieved by hitting the treble-20 segment, which is 4 inches distant from the bulls-eye (which scores 50 points).

The NDA set up the first major individual darts championship, the Licensees Cup, which was first contested in 1926. Initially, no provision was made for women to participate in this competition, but later it was agreed that a woman could compete if she was a licensee in her own right or the wife of a man who is eligible to play according to the rules. The following year, the NDA was approached by the *News of the World*, which offered to sponsor a competition, the proposal being that the NDA handled the organisational side and that it was played to NDA rules. In return, the newspaper would provide a silver trophy and promote the championship through its pages every Sunday. The *News of the World* Individual Darts Championship was first competed for in the metropolitan area of London in the 1927/8 season. The first winner of the trophy was Sammy Stone, a slater, a Boer War veteran and a father of nine, who played out of the New South-West Ham Club in West Ham.

Such was interest in darts as an expanding, increasingly popular leisure pursuit both in pubs and clubs and in the home, that by the 1930s it had become one of the most popular recreations in England. It was played by all classes too, although it never brought the classes together. Darts ousted existing pub games, such as skittles and rings, as more and more brewers saw the advantages of having dartboards in all of their pubs. However, this is not to say that 'standardised' darts was accepted without question. There were signs of resistance; for example, in parts of Manchester, where the smaller Manchester, or log-end, board was retained and still holds sway today. There is evidence also from the 1930s that isolated rural pubs were opposed to the imposition of standard play and preferred instead to adhere to local rules. Furthermore, landlords, whilst initially toeing the company line and installing dartboards, would soon take them down if they had an adverse impact on business.

During the 1930s the *News of the World* competition had expanded to cover most regions of England. The total number of entrants in the competition in 1938/9 was in excess of 280,000. Regional finals were being contested in London and the South, Lancashire and Cheshire, Yorkshire, the North of England, the Midland Counties and Wales, but there was no overall national champion. The competition ceased at the outbreak of war in 1939, and during the period of conflict the NDA folded. However, the rules of the game established by the NDA continue to be used today under other organisational banners with few amendments to those originally drawn up.

The *News of the World* Individual Darts Championship was revived in 1947/8, this time on a national basis, and earned a reputation for being the championship that every darts player wanted to win. This reputation lasted for another five decades, until darts became unfashionable in the late 1980s. With no interest from sponsors, falling numbers of entrants, a lack of volunteers to organise the area and regional events and a change in editorial policy, the *News of the World* Individual Darts Championship slipped off the darts calendar virtually unnoticed.

The People newspaper had introduced a National Team Championship that was first competed for in the 1938/9 season and was revived in 1946. With the NDA defunct, a number of attempts were made to introduce another national, controlling agency. Nothing firm was realised until 1954, when *The People* supported the setting-up of the National Darts Association of Great Britain (NDAGB).

Sources and Reading:
Chaplin, P., 'Target Archery and that Mr. Gamlin', *Darts World* (October 1990), 56.
Chaplin, P., 'You can take the darts out of the pub . . .', *Darts World* (May 1998), 34–5.
Croft-Cooke, R., *Darts* (London: Bles, 1936).

Licensed Victuallers' Gazette Office, *Lawful Games on Licensed Premises* (London: LVGO, 1903).

Taylor, A. R., *The Guinness Book of Traditional Pub Games* (Enfield: Guinness, 1992).

Turner, K., *Darts – The Complete Book of the Game* (Newton Abbot: David & Charles, 1980).

White, T. H., *England Have My Bones* (London: Collins, 1936).

Websites:

Patrick Chaplin, Darts Historian: www.patrickchaplin.com

See also Blow-Point

Patrick Chaplin

Davies, John

Welsh national champion during the 1840s and conqueror of many renowned English runners, professional pedestrian John Davies (1822–*c*.1909) was born in Llansanffraid-ym-Mechain in Powys, and was nicknamed *Y Cyw Cloff* ('The Lame Chick') on account of his distinctive running style. Davies's slight frame was ideal for distance events and his string of successes led to his immortalisation in various ballads, which marvelled at his remarkable speed and compared him with such animals as hares and deer. Davies competed until at least the late 1850s and is said to have died from pleurisy caught while bell-ringing in the freezing conditions of his local church.

Sources and Reading:

Lile, E., 'Professional Pedestrianism in South Wales during the Nineteenth Century', *Sports Historian*, 20 (2000), 94–105.

Emma Lile

Decline of Traditional Sports

That the coming of industry and the increasing urbanisation of British society from the beginnings of the nineteenth century led to a decline in traditional sports has become a widely accepted truism. However, the process is far more complex and sometimes more contradictory than is often assumed. Although many sports died out, some survived largely in their original form, while others were transformed by commercialism and technology.

By the early nineteenth century, it was clear to many commentators that industrial capitalism had begun to undermine the social basis for traditional sports. Enclosures of common land had already led in many areas to the end of football and other sports that needed large outdoor spaces, but it was urbanisation and industrialisation that destroyed old customs and imposed a new rhythm of daily life, geared to the needs of factory production. The old relations between the classes changed and became much more antagonistic, with class conflict and industrial strife commonplace. Under such changed circumstances, opportunities for sporting activities declined precipitously.

Whereas the agricultural economy demanded labour when necessary and allowed long periods of leisure, factory work was continuous, intensive and, up until the factory reforms that started with the 1847 Ten Hours Act, often took place 12 hours a day, 6 days a week. Public and communal holidays, so central to rural life, were slashed from 47 in 1761 to just four in 1834.

The demands for industrial efficiency and discipline led to concerted attempts to enforce not only new ways of working but also new attitudes to work itself, based on sobriety, order, thrift and hard work. The traditional values of the rural economy were seen as a hindrance to effective labour.

Large-scale sports such as football were viewed as interfering with business, which resulted in the banning of football on roads under the 1835 Highways Act. Practices such as 'Saint Monday', whereby workers would not go into work on a Monday, or at least worked at a much more leisurely pace than during the rest of the week, were also viewed as undermining productivity.

In order to impose a new set of values, which stressed the importance of hard work, numerous campaigns to bring 'morality' to the working classes began. These took the form of increased discipline inside and outside of work, the outlawing of sports seen as immoral or wasteful and, especially from the mid-nineteenth century, attempts to bring 'rational' recreations to the working class to prepare them for work and uplift morality.

Organised religion played a key role in this process. In general, the established church had withdrawn its support from popular recreation by the early eighteenth century. Church ales, traditionally a time to indulge in feasting, drinking and sporting activities, had almost completely died out. By 1800, evangelical Christianity had grown in strength and proved to be a vigorous campaigner against traditional sports. Methodists and other nonconformists opposed sports because, in their eyes, they led to licentiousness and vice. Much concern was expressed about the presence of young women at sporting and other festive events. In urban areas in particular, the nonconformists waged long, active and usually successful campaigns against a wide variety of sports.

A key struggle for the reformers was over the observance of the Sabbath. Sunday had long been the traditional day for sport, with football, cricket and many other sports being regularly played. Sabbatarianism, the demand to keep the Sabbath free of non-religious activity, dated back to Puritan demands of the sixteenth century. A Sunday Observance Act had been passed in 1625, although apart from under Cromwell this had remained a dead letter, but it was in the first decades of the nineteenth century that

the pressure began to make itself felt, most notably after the formation in 1831 of the Lord's Day Observance Society. The Society set its face against all sports, amusements, pastimes or recreations that were held on a Sunday, initiating legal actions and public campaigns which resulted in an almost complete absence of sporting activity on Sundays in Britain between the mid-nineteenth century and the latter decades of the twentieth.

Christian reformers also played a key role in the suppression of blood sports. From the mid-eighteenth century there had been a growing opposition to animal-baiting sports among the middle classes, partially based on newly emerging notions of fairness; the fact that in most blood sports the animals were tethered was seen as being 'unfair'. The early nineteenth century saw a number of attempts to outlaw animal baiting, culminating in the 1835 Cruelty to Animals Act and, the final triumph of the reformers, the banning of cockfighting in 1849.

Although there could be no doubting the concern of the reformers, their efforts were almost entirely directed against those blood sports practised by the working classes. One of the most often voiced criticisms of the Royal Society for the Prevention of Cruelty to Animals, founded in 1824, was that it did nothing to oppose upper-class sports such as hunting and shooting – indeed, many of the RSPCA's most prominent supporters were huntsmen. As with Sabbatarianism and campaigns for 'morality', the context, and often the explicit intent, of the campaign against animal cruelty was firmly based on a desire to reform working-class leisure and create a new moral framework suited to the needs of an industrial capitalist economy.

These attempts to suppress sport and earlier ways of working did not go unopposed. Despite troops being called out, popular support for bull running in Stamford meant that it took more than fifty years before it was finally abolished in 1840, and numerous attempts to stop Shrovetide football being played in Derby were foiled before it was extinguished in the 1850s. Cockfighting and dog fighting were driven underground following their banning. Nevertheless, it must also be noted that attitudes to traditional sports were also changing in sections of the working class; many Chartists opposed them and sought other forms of intellectual and physical improvement.

Despite the tremendous social changes of the nineteenth century, some traditional sports, such as knur and spell, did survive and their popularity increased during the early part of the twentieth century, especially in those areas where the economy remained predominantly agricultural or was based in rural areas, such as mining. The survival of others, such as bowls in the north of England, owed much to their close links with pubs.

However, most of those sports that survived changed their form and adopted modern structures, most obviously in the case of football and, in different ways, boxing, which was refashioned under the Marquis of Queensbury Rules of 1867. Some were radically transformed by modern technology, such as the development of coursing into greyhound racing.

These survivals, albeit in changed and often unexpected forms, demonstrate that although the immediate impact of the Industrial Revolution was to reduce the opportunities to organise sport, it remained deeply embedded within the culture of the working classes. The social upheaval of industrialisation changed the way in which sports were played and appreciated, but not their enduring appeal – as demonstrated by the explosion of mass spectator sport at the end of the nineteenth century.

Sources and Reading:

Bailey, P., *Leisure and Class in Victorian England* (Second edition) (London: Routledge, 1987).
Birley, D., *Sport and the Making of Britain* (Manchester: Manchester University Press, 1993).
Cunningham, H., *Leisure in the Industrial Revolution* (London: Croom Helm, 1980).
Holt, R., *Sport and the British* (Oxford: Oxford University Press, 1989).
Malcolmson, R., *Popular Recreations in English Society 1770–1850* (Cambridge: Cambridge University Press, 1975).
Reid, D. A., 'The Decline of Saint Monday', *Past & Present*, 71 (1976), 76–101.
Thompson, E. P., *Customs in Common* (London: Penguin, 1991).
Tranter, N., 'Popular Sports and the Industrial Revolution in Scotland: The Evidence of the Statistical Accounts', *International Journal of the History of Sport*, 4: 1 (1987), 21–38.

See also Book of Sports, Church Ales, Pubs and Sport

Tony Collins

Deer Hunting and Stalking

Deer hunting conducted on horseback entails the pursuit of red deer in the wild using hounds that hunt by scent. Historically, stag hunting was regarded as the noblest of sports, being reserved exclusively for the aristocracy and royalty, who retained large deer parks protected by foresters. The English followed the Norman tradition of hunting on horseback with scenting hounds, while the Scots coursed deer with specialist deerhounds. The so-called *tainchell* or deer drive was also used, where large numbers of beaters drove deer into gorges for the aristocracy to kill. This sport provided a diversion for the nobility whilst enabling their clansmen to be supplied with meat.

By the start of the eighteenth century, the shortage of deer had compelled hunters to switch to other types of prey, in particular the fox. Deer hunting was restricted almost exclusively to Devon and Somerset, but even in these localised areas the sport died out on several occasions before being revived for short periods, when it was but poorly supported. In some areas, carted stag hunting became popular in the early nineteenth century, when specially bred deer were released as quarry. Deer hunting in the south-west had mixed fortunes. It was not until 1855 that a pack of hounds was re-established, by which time the number of deer there had been reduced to about 75. The significance of deer hunting was recognised in 1917 by Lloyd George's government, which funded the re-establishment of red deer hunting on the Quantock Hills. This was partly intended to provide a means of enhancing wartime agricultural productivity by controlling the deer that were damaging farm crops.

In England, deer hunting is currently confined to the three packs based in the West Country, principally the Exmoor area. Like fox-hunting, deer hunting is conducted on horseback, although many members of the hunt follow the sport in cars or on motorbikes, armed with binoculars. The diversity of land ownership in the area and the large number of visitors means that stalking is not appropriate. Formal deer hunting takes place under legislation established by Parliament and a code of conduct specified by the sport's governing body, the Masters of Deerhounds Association. Before hunt meets, the harbourer, working in conjunction with local landowners, identifies the animals to be culled – a process known as harbouring. In autumn hunts, it is usually the old or weak animals that are destined to be killed. Occasionally, a stag in his prime or one that that been with the same group of hinds (females) for several years is selected for culling in order to prevent interbreeding. In contrast, stag hunting in the spring concentrates on the younger stags with inferior antlers. In the hind-hunting season, during the winter, the herd is chased until one of the animals breaks away from the rest.

Another popular method of hunting deer is by stalking and using long-range high-calibre rifles. Stalking deer is a highly developed craft because of deer's acute hearing and their sensitive scenting ability, which brings a constant stream of information on the breeze. In Scotland, professional gillies assist their clients to stalk the deer. Apart from controlling the population levels, shooting magnificent adult stags commands premium trophy fees from paying sportsmen guests. Following the Second World War, the stalking of roe deer in the Lowlands became fashionable among a small band of dedicated enthusiasts. The development of modern flat-trajectory rifles with telescopic sights has improved the accuracy of shooting in the poor light of early dawn and late dusk, when it was possible to get close to the deer.

It is important to differentiate between moorland and woodland deer stalking. The former is primarily, but not exclusively, a Scottish activity. There is only one deer-forest (in the accepted sense of the term) in England – at Martindale in Cumbria, where deer stalking is carried out as it is in the Highlands. Elsewhere in England where red deer are common, notably Exmoor, control of numbers by hunting only, or as in the Thetford Chase area of Norfolk by woodland techniques, is more akin to roe-stalking than Highland deer stalking. Stalking in woodlands is primarily an activity of the English lowlands, involving different techniques, with the hunter waiting in a secluded spot for the deer to come into view.

The Deer Act of 1963 forms the legislative, and in many respects philosophical, foundations of deer control and stalking, prescribing how the activity may be legally undertaken, and who is able to participate in the sport. Opposition to the sport led, in 1997, to the National Trust introducing a ban on deer hunting on its land, following an independent two-year scientific study. In Scotland, stalking with long-range, high-velocity rifles is the only lawful method of deer hunting.

Sources and Reading:

Beaver, D., 'The Great Deer Massacre: Animals, Honor, and Communication in Early Modern England', *Journal of British Studies* (1999), 187–217.

Carne, P., *Deer of Britain and Ireland: Their Origins and Distribution* (Shrewsbury: Swan Hill Press, 2000).

Coles, C., *Shooting and Stalking*, (London: Stanley Paul, 1988).

Parks, C. and Thornley, J., *Fair Game: The Law of Country Sports and the Protection of Wildlife* (London: Pelham, 1994).

Whitehead, G. K., *Hunting and Stalking Deer in Britain Throughout the Ages* (London: Batsford, 1980).

Website:
International Fund for Animal Welfare: www. ifaw.org/ifaw/dfiles/file_49.pdf

See also Field Sports

Nicholas Goddard and John Martin

Dobbers

An indoor game played mainly in public houses, the object of dobbers, a variation of quoits, is to throw four flat rings at a horizontal board. The dobbers board is around 50 centimetres deep and wide and has two concentric circles inside which lead down to a peg in the middle. A ring that lands over the peg is worth 5 points, the inner concentric circle is worth 2 points and the outer circle 1 point. The rings are black on one side and white on the other; a ring that lands white-side up does not score. The winner is the first to 61 points.

Sources and Reading:
Gorini, P., *Encyclopedia of Traditional Games* (Rome: Gremese International, 1994).

See also Quoits

Tony Collins

Doddart

An early north of England version of hockey or bandy, doddart is played by two teams on a large field. The 'doddart' is the curved stick used to propel a wooden ball called an 'orr' or 'coit'. The goals were hedges or other boundaries of the field.

Sources and Reading:
Gomme, A. B., *The Traditional Games of England, Scotland and Ireland* (London: Thames and Hudson facsimile edition, 1984).

See also Bandy, Hockey

Tony Collins

Dog Fighting

Dog fighting was witnessed by all social classes in Wales. The pitting together of two dogs for a bet was a frequent occurrence, such as at Bangor in Gwynedd in November 1830, when a large crowd of 'the lowest of the low' were joined by 'one or two individuals of rather higher rank in society'. Attitudes towards the activity were ambivalent, however, and by the end of the nineteenth century, dogs viciously attacking each other was widely condemned.

Sources and Reading:
The Cambrian (29 April 1887).
North Wales Chronicle (4 November 1830).

Emma Lile

Doggett's Coat and Badge Race

This sculling race takes place annually on 1 August on the river Thames, from the Old Swan pier at London Bridge to the site of the White Swan Inn at Chelsea Bridge, a distance of around 5 miles.

The race dates back to 1715 when the Irish actor-manager of the Haymarket and Drury Lane theatres, Thomas Doggett, offered an orange waterman's coat and a silver badge to be rowed for by six watermen who had completed their apprenticeship within the previous 12 months. A dedicated supporter of the Hanoverian succession, Doggett chose 1 August as the date of the race because it was the date on which George I ascended the throne.

Before he died in 1721, Doggett bequeathed a sum to buy the coat and badge annually to ensure that the race would continue. Historically, the race was organised by the Worshipful Company of Fishmongers, and the Company of Watermen and Lightermen run the event today. The race considerably predates now better-known events, such as the Thames and Henley regattas and looks back to a time when there were over 40,000 licensed watermen on the Thames and rowing as a sport was dominated by professional working oarsmen. One of the early winners of the race was Jack Broughton, who was to find rather greater renown as a champion prizefighter. In 1774, Charles Dibdin wrote an opera based on the race called *The Waterman, or The First of August*.

Since Doggett's day the race has changed in a number of ways. The six boatmen, originally chosen by lots, are now selected through qualifying heats. Originally, watermen were only allowed to row in one race, but the decline in the numbers taking part led to a relaxing of the rules; unsuccessful rowers are now allowed to enter the race a second time. The coat is now red and the timing of the race varies according to the tidal pattern of the Thames. Perhaps most welcome to those taking part, the race now takes place with the tide instead of against it.

Sources and Reading:
Day, B., *A Chronicle of Folk Customs* (London: Hamlyn, 1988).
Encyclopedia of Sports, Games and Pastimes (London: Fleetway, 1935).
Hone, W., *The Every-Day Book* (London: Thomas Tegg, 1830).

See also Rowing

Tony Collins

Dover, Robert

Captain Dover (1582–1652), as he was popularly known, was a Catholic lawyer and staunch Royalist. He was best known for pioneering the revival of athletic sports which had traditionally been held at Willesley and Chipping Campden in Gloucestershire. By the late sixteenth century, however, these annual activities had become more or less obsolete. His promotion of traditional English sports was a concerted attempt to oppose the growing influence of Puritanism.

By 1612, the growing interest in classical Greek and Roman studies had encouraged him to organise a cultural festival in conjunction with the sporting events. Dover entered with enthusiasm into the spirit of the events, which were probably held over two days with people of all classes taking part. In 1638, a detailed account of the custom was published with verses and a frontispiece illustrating some of the features of the programme, portraying Dover in a suit that had been given to him by James I. The King had also granted him permission to appropriate an open space for the games.

The events were interrupted by the Civil War but were subsequently revived. In the eighteenth century, the anniversary was celebrated at a point called Dover's Hill on Thursday in Whitsuntide week. Local authorities prevented the games continuing in 1852 because of the threat to public order, but in 1963 they were again revived by local people.

Sources and Reading:
Burns, F. D. A., *Robert Dover 1582–1652 and the Cotswold Olimpick Game* (Bristol: Stuart Press, 2000).
Whitfield, C., *A History of Chipping Campden and Captain Robert Dover's Olympick Games* (Eaton: Shakespeare Head, 1958).

See also Cotswold Olympick Games

John Martin

Drag Hunting

Drag hunting is a non-competitive cross-country equestrian sport, which frequently takes place using fox-hounds that are trained to follow a person who is dragging a particular scent. Another form of drag hunting, described as 'hunting the clean boot', uses blood hounds, which have an excellent scenting nose and are able to follow the natural scent of a human runner. Like other forms of mounted hunting, the sport takes place mainly in the autumn, winter and early spring. It is administrated and regulated by the Masters of Draghounds and Bloodhounds Association.

Drag hunting is organised on similar lines to fox-hunting, with riders and a pack of hounds, the main difference being that a prepared scent trial, laid by dragging material soaked in aniseed or another strong-smelling substance over the countryside, is followed. Its popularity can be traced back to the second half of the nineteenth century, when Oxford and Cambridge universities established separate packs. The Household Brigade become interested in the sport in 1863, and by 1870 the Royal Artillery in Woolwich and the Royal Military at Sandhurst had established their own packs. The motives for their establishment was that the sport provided the opportunity to ride at a good pace, where every fence was jumpable, and it was seen as an excellent preparation for beginners and those who were about to enter the cavalry divisions.

Other packs were established in the twentieth century, notably the Mid-Surrey Farmers Drag Hounds. All the packs are registered with the Master of Draghounds and Bloodhounds Association, which coordinates the sport. The drag hunting season usually starts in the middle of March. Opponents of blood sports argue that the sport provides a possible alternative to fox-hunting. However, the fox-hunting fraternity and supporters of drag hunting emphasise that they are two distinct equestrian activities.

A variant of the sport is hound trailing, popular among fell packs of fox-hounds, where the dogs follow a man-laid scent trail of up to 10 miles. The sport is a combination of hunting the drag and a form of steeplechasing, wherein the hounds take the place of horses, and is concentrated in the northern dales. It is widely believed to have originated from the challenges and wagers made by supporters of the local hunts over whose puppies possessed the better noses, tested by their ability to follow an artificial scent trail. The rapid rise in popularity of the sport led to the establishment of the Hound Trailing Association in 1906 to formalise rules and register the hounds.

Sources and Reading:
Kidd, J., *Drag Hunting* (London: J. A. Allen, 1978).
Strawson, J., *On Drag Hunting* (London: J. A. Allen, 1999).

Websites:
www.banbloodsports.com/Drag.htm
www.ifaw.org/ifaw/dfiles/file_56.pdf
www.countryside-alliance.net/edu/edu2-3-5drag.htm

See also Fox-Hunting, Hunting

Nicholas Goddard and
John Martin

Duck Baiting

It is generally forgotten nowadays that the popular pub name 'The Dog and Duck' did not usually refer to the hunting of ducks but to duck baiting, one of the more cruel manifestations of animal baiting in pre-industrial times. Duck baiting revolved around the use of dogs, usually spaniels, to catch a duck in a pond. The duck had its wings pinioned and so could not fly – its only means of escape was to dive to the bottom of the pond. Clearly its chances of survival in such circumstances were negligible.

The sport took place mainly in ponds that were owned by pub landlords and were adjacent to their pubs. The largest of these in London was the several acres of water kept by innkeeper Mr Ball, now remembered in the name Balls Pond Road. The last one to survive in the very heart of the city was within 50 yards of Bond Street, commemorated as Ducking Pond Mews. Like many such sports, its appeal reached right across the social spectrum and it was reputed to be one of the favoured sports of Charles II.

Sources and Reading:
Day, J. W., *Inns of Sport* (London: Naldrett, 1949).

See also Badger Baiting, Bear Baiting, Bull Baiting

Tony Collins

Dwile Flonking

A supposedly ancient Suffolk sport, which came to light in 1967 accompanied by widespread press interest, dwile flonking was actually invented by a local printer in 1966 to bring publicity to the annual Beccles village fete.

The inventor, or hoaxer, depending on one's point of view, successfully exploited well-known features of traditional sports to perpetrate the deception. A set of rules was drawn up and titled the *Waveney Rules of 1585* to suggest antiquarian authenticity, and terms redolent of 'merrie England' invented to describe the game. The game essentially consisted of one side dancing to music around a member of the opposing side who attempted to throw a beer-soaked cloth at them when the music stopped.

The fact that the game also involved drinking copious amounts of ale (renamed 'flonk') ensured that whatever critical faculties the participants may have possessed were soon extinguished.

Sources and Reading:
Cooper, Q. and Sullivan, P., *Maypoles, Martyrs and Mayhem* (London: Bloomsbury, 1994).

See also Invented Traditions

Tony Collins

Eating Challenges

Among the rather bizarre events sometimes witnessed on rural sportsdays were those involving eating at speed. From the devouring of a 'hot hasty pudding' at Llangyfelach in Swansea in 1780 for the prize of a silver table spoon, to the treacle-dipping challenges of the 1820 Oswestry wakes when contestants sought to be the quickest to consume sticky rolls hanging from a rope, contests featuring food seem to have appealed greatly to the Welsh population.

A weekly amusement at a village near Mydroilyn in Cardiganshire during the 1880s comprised one individual running a distance of around 600 yards, while another busily ate, in turn, biscuits, brown sugar and raw eggs against time. If the quarter pound of biscuits were not eaten before the runner finished, then the crowd was forced to pay for the food. The same procedure then took place with the half a pound of sugar and finally with a dozen raw eggs. While a successful eater earned a hero's applause from some quarters, other residents were annoyed at being kept awake by an event held between the hours of 10 p.m. and 2 a.m.

Sources and Reading:
Williams, G. J., 'Glamorgan Customs in the Eighteenth Century', *Gwerin*, 1 (1956–7), 99–108.

Emma Lile

Egg and Spoon Racing

Closely related to egg rolling, egg and spoon racing exists in two forms. In the most common, competitors have to race each other holding a spoon with an egg on it, while in the more difficult version, the spoon is held between the teeth. It is unclear whether the sport is a relatively recent invention, like pancake racing, or a genuine survival of an older tradition.

Sources and Reading:
Gorini, P., *Encyclopedia of Traditional Games* (Rome: Gremese, 1994).

See also Egg Rolling

Tony Collins

Egg Rolling

Common in many parts of the British Isles, egg rolling was a feature of Easter Monday (and occasionally Easter Sunday) celebrations. It consisted of competitors rolling hard-boiled eggs down grassy slopes, the object being either to keep the egg from cracking for as long as possible or to pass it through a goal, or possibly both.

Observers have sought to link the practice to pagan customs, such as the veneration of Flora, the goddess of spring, and the rebirth of life expressed in the egg, but there is no real evidence of this.

Such was its popularity that some towns set aside a designated area for rolling eggs, such as the Castle Moat at Penrith and Arthur's Seat in Edinburgh. The game can still be seen every Good Friday at Holcombe Hill near Bury in Lancashire, and every Easter Monday at Avenham Park in Preston and at Fountains Abbey near Ripon.

Sources and Reading:
Hutton, R., *Stations of the Sun* (Oxford: Oxford University Press, 1996).
Whitlock, R., *A Calendar of Country Customs* (London: Batsford, 1978).

See also Egg and Spoon Racing, Egg Shackling, Orange Rolling

Tony Collins

Egg Shackling

A game associated with Shrove Tuesday, egg shackling saw eggs marked with their owners' names and placed in a sieve. They would then be gently shaken until there was only one unbroken egg left, the owner of which would be declared the winner. The game continues to be played today at Sedgemoor in Somerset.

Jauping paste-eggs is a north-east variant of shackling, in which two players hold hard-boiled eggs in the fists and hit each other's hands until the eggs break.

Sources and Reading:
Day, B., *A Chronicle of Folk Customs* (London: Hamlyn, 1988).
Whitlock, R., *A Calendar of Country Customs* (London: Batsford, 1978).

See also Egg and Spoon Racing, Egg Rolling

Tony Collins

Egremont Crab Fair

Egremont is on the Cumbrian coast and holds a fair on the second or third Saturday in September. The fair is one of the oldest in Britain, having gained a charter in 1267, and sport has always played a central role in the festivities. Sports at the fair include wrestling, racing and hound trailing, and also climbing the greasy pole for a leg of lamb. Possibly more famously, the fair also stages the World Gurning (or face-pulling) Championship, where each gurner puts his or her head through a horse collar and pulls an ugly face.

Sources and Reading:
Day, B., *A Chronicle of Folk Customs* (London: Hamlyn, 1988).

See also Fell Running, Grasmere Sports

Tony Collins

Evans, Margaret

Margaret Evans, who lived during the eighteenth century in Llanberis in Caernarfonshire, was said to have been the best hunter, shooter and fisher of her generation. She owned many fine dogs, which allegedly killed more foxes in a year than the local hunting packs did in a decade. Her other sporting talents included rowing and wrestling, excelling at the latter against male competition, allegedly even at the ripe old age of 70.

Sources and Reading:
Sporting Magazine (April 1799).

Emma Lile

Falconry

Whilst the history of falconry is recorded much earlier in mainland Europe, it was probably introduced to the British Isles during AD 350–450. St Illtyd was fond of flying hawks in Wales around AD 520 and there is a carved falconer on the Bewcastle Cross in Cumberland, which is dated AD 670–700. By AD 800, falconry started to be mentioned in the chronicles and correspondence of the time. King Ethelbert (reigned AD 748–60) wrote to the Archbishop of Mayence, Boniface (died AD 755) to request a cast of falcons with which to fly cranes. Prior to this, Boniface had provided two falcons and a hawk for the King of Mercia.

So essential was falconry to the construction of rank and power in medieval Europe that hawks and falcons and their trainers accompanied armies on campaigns as a matter of course. The Bayeux Tapestry depicts the Saxon king Harold with a hawk, and certain Norman noblemen departing for the invasion of Britain under William the Conqueror are also shown with hawks and falcons. Richard I, The Lion Heart, halted one of his crusades to fly his falcons near Jaffa. Indeed, legend has it that Richard

sent an emissary to Melik el Aadile to request a supply of food for his hawks. That Richard and Melik had been involved in several long and bloody battles seems to have been unimportant in this respect.

Falconry became widely practised but it also became an indicator of social status. Certain species of raptor became associated with degrees of privilege and the *Boke of St Albans* provided a systematic assignment of species of birds of prey according to social rank. Whilst largely symbolic, this stood as indicative of the metaphorical importance of falconry, hence 'a gyrfalcon for a King . . . a falcon gentle [a male goshawk] for a poor man' and 'a kestrel for a knave'. The unfortunate knave or servant is allocated the Eurasian or common kestrel, which preys on mice, voles and beetles. This is illustrative of his social worthlessness in medieval social ranking.

When Edward III of England embarked on his military campaign of 1359 in France, he was accompanied by 30 mounted falconers with hawks. Apparently, the king hunted with hawks every morning during the martial excursion. The same English monarch introduced laws that compelled any of his citizens who found a lost hawk or falcon to take it to the sheriff of that county or be liable to pay a fine or face two years' imprisonment. Henry III was given gyrfalcons by the King of Norway, and the Bishop of Ely excommunicated the thief who stole his favourite hawk. In 1377 Richard II built the Royal Mews at Charing Cross in London. With the exception of his own falconry, Henry VII forbade all hunting in the Palace of Westminster, an area that encompassed what is now St Giles Fields, Islington, Hampstead and Highgate. He was also concerned with the supply of hawks and so laws were introduced to protect nesting hawks and falcons and make unauthorised taking of young a felony. Henry VIII was a keen and active falconer, and might have died in a bizarre accident when flying falcons at duck. Whilst he was leaping across a brook his vaulting pole broke and he pitched head first into the mud. A cadgeman (the lowest ranking servant of the hunt) saved the king by jumping in pulling him out. Hawking sky-larks with merlins was one of the few pleasures allowed to the imprisoned Mary, Queen of Scots. However, Elizabeth I removed this privilege on hearing of Mary's high spirits and fortitude during her captivity.

In Cromwell's Commonwealth (1649–60) falconry was curtailed by the Puritan rejection of frivolous earthly pleasures, especially those that had such close links with monarchy. On his restoration, Charles II rebuilt some of the sport's popularity but he was the last British monarch to actively participate in it. After Charles's death the sport lost its already diminished popularity in court society and with the landed nobility.

The tradition of falconry survived into the industrial age. A club for subscription-paying falconers, the Confederate Hawks of Great Britain, was started in 1772 under the management of a Colonel Thornton. It soon became known as the Falconer's Club and had its headquarters at Bourn Bridge in Cambridgeshire, where it met each March to fly at crows, rooks and kites.

There had long been a conflict between falconers and farmers, who increasingly objected to mounted spectators damaging crops or disturbing livestock. The tension had first been documented as long ago as AD 821, when King Kenulph of Mercia was petitioned by the monks of Abingdon to restrict falconers who were damaging their crops. The situation was not helped by falconers who often cried 'tradition' in the face of opposition, disregarding trespass or damage.

Ultimately, British falconers of the early nineteenth century were to take their sport abroad. The heath and downland of southern Holland were unfenced and ideal for flights at the then relatively plentiful herons. The Falconer's Club was renamed the Loo Hawking Club in 1839. It retained the element of subscription and employed professional staff. In an echo of days long past, the club was to receive royal patronage, from members of the Dutch royal family. Indeed, the name of the club was altered to the Royal Loo Club. Despite providing outstanding sport throughout the 1840s, the club was short-lived and, on having its royal patronage withdrawn, it was closed in 1853. The reason behind its failure was that the Dutch king habitually ate in the middle of the afternoon, and so, being part of the court, members of the club were obliged to do the same; unfortunately mid-afternoon is the most advantageous time to hawk for herons.

In 1864 the Old Hawking Club began with a membership of seven, the majority of whom were titled. The Old Hawking Club met in March and April on Salisbury Plain for rook hawking, in August in Perthshire or Caithness for grouse, and in Norfolk in October for partridges. The closing years of the nineteenth century were good ones for the members of the Old Hawking Club. They had recruited new members who were predominantly amateurs in the traditional sense: training and flying their hawks and falcons themselves. Many of the new members of the Old Hawking Club were army officers, and others came from the middle classes rather than the aristocracy.

If the practitioners were changing then so too was the sport, in order to accommodate the altered physical conditions found in the countryside. Rook hawking, which required a mounted field and vast open areas, was becoming less popular, whilst game hawking for partridge and pheasant, which could be undertaken in more enclosed country and on foot, was gaining advocates. Grouse hawking on the open heather moorland of Scotland, the north of England and Wales also became more popular among falconers.

All hawking was suspended during the First World War and the club's hawks were distributed among its members, with some going to Regent's Park Zoo. This break in continuity signalled the end of the Old Hawking Club. Many of its older members were too infirm to continue hawking after the war and many younger ones had been killed in the trenches. With a reduced membership, the club folded because it could not afford to rent good quality ground over which to hawk. However, on 11 November 1927 a falconers' feast was held in London. At this meeting of 12 falconers the British Falconers' Club was formed. The club now has over 1,200 members carrying on the tradition of organised falconry in Britain.

The twentieth century witnessed great changes in the nature and quality of the British countryside, and yet the sport of falconry saw a steady increase in popularity. With great steps forward in husbandry techniques, veterinary medicine and captive breeding, falconry was transformed in the latter years of the century. In the new millennium it is practised by a wide range of people from differing classes and backgrounds, from both town and country the length and breadth of the United Kingdom. Modern falconry is a flourishing field sport enabling the practitioner to encounter nature at an intimate and fundamental level. Having the credentials of sustainability and low impact, it thrives in a social climate that is largely hostile to other hunting activities.

Sources and Reading:
Blome, R., *Hawking; or, Faulconry* (*c*.1700, facsimile reprint; Maidenhead: Cresset Press, 1929).
Cummins, J., *The Hound and the Hawk* (London: Weidenfeld & Nicolson, 1988).
Oswald, A., *The History and Practice of Falconry* (Jersey: Spearman, 1982).
Upton, R., *A Bird in the Hand* (London: Debrett, 1980).

Gordon T. Mellor

Feat-Stone Throwing

Feat-stone throwing was a popular athletic pursuit in Wales from ancient times and was a benchmark of strength and power. It was included in the 24 ancient Welsh feats and several medieval poets alluded to the throwing skills of their patrons. Stones sometimes weighed over 100 pounds, and contestants proved their strength either by lifting them inches off the ground or, rather more testingly, raising them to shoulder height and hurling them backwards over the shoulder. Churchyards were the most common venues and champion throwers were widely admired. Llewelyn Thomas (died 1807), known as 'Llewelyn the Great', of Llanymawddwy in Montgomeryshire, was renowned for his power and for astonishing crowds by throwing 75-pound feat-stones up to 15 yards.

Sources and Reading:
Owen, E., *Old Stone Crosses of the Vale of Clwyd* (1886, facsimile reprint; Mold: Clwyd County Council Library and Information Services, 1995).
Waddington, H. M., 'Games and Athletics in Bygone Wales', *Transactions of the Honourable Society of Cymmrodorion* (1953), 84–100.

See also Stone Throwing, Stroud Throwing Contests

Emma Lile

Fell Running

Once popular throughout Cumberland, Westmorland and north-west Yorkshire, fell running was, along with Cumberland wrestling, the pre-eminent sport of the region. It was not, however, confined to the region and also took place among the more mountainous regions of Scotland and Wales. Today, it is a popular form of competitive endurance running and takes place throughout Britain.

The earliest recorded fell race appears to have taken place in 1064 up Creag Choinnich at Braemar. It was organised by King Malcolm Canmore to find a runner capable of delivering messages over the terrain. As the name suggests, races took place up and down the fells of the English Lake District and the surrounding areas, usually over a distance of around 3 miles, which would be covered by the best runners in around 20 minutes.

For the spectator, one of its most appealing features was the fact that, having started at the bottom of a fell, the runners' ascents and descents could be easily seen. The descents were especially spectacular as the runners covered the distance in about a third of the time that it took them to go up, leaping over walls, ditches and other natural features in the race to be first.

Despite the huge physical effort required, the runners traditionally have received small prizes, the biggest, and the most prestigious, being the £10 and silver cup awarded at the annual Grasmere Sports race. The sport was also included at Highland Games meetings. Although runners were traditionally semi-professional, the growing influence of the Amateur Athletic Association meant that the organisers of many events insisted that participants should be amateurs.

The sport underwent a renaissance in the 1960s, as did long-distance running in general. Today, races are run over distances that can be anything up to 40 miles, covering a number of fells, and the sport has much in common with orienteering in that maps and compasses can be used in some races. The Three Peaks race, run in north Yorkshire since 1954, is one of the best-known events and has assumed the mantle of the unofficial national championship.

Sources and Reading:

Arlott, J. (ed.), *The Oxford Companion to Sports and Games* (Oxford: Oxford University Press, 1975).

The Encyclopaedia of Sport (London: *The Sportsman*, 1912).

See also Egremont Crab Fair, Grasmere Sports, Wrestling (Cumberland)

Tony Collins

Fencing

Swords have probably been used for sport for as long as they have been used for combat. The earliest representations of the sport can be found in illustrations dating back to the time of the Egyptian Pharaoh Rameses III, around 1190 BC. Throughout history men, and occasionally women, have entertained themselves with variants of swordplay, using either real swords or wooden implements for the same purpose.

However, the history of fencing as a highly skilled form of swordplay in many ways owes its existence to the invention of gunpowder. The use of gunpowder removed the need for the large and heavy broadsword, which was instead replaced by lighter swords more useful for hand-to-hand combat. Fuelled by these changes, guilds and schools of swordsmanship, as the skill became known, grew up throughout Europe from the fifteenth and sixteenth centuries.

Initially, the art was dominated by Italian masters, who emphasised the use of the point of the sword, rather than the side of the blade. This style featured the lunge as the key attacking device and outlawed the wrestling and fighting that had previously been part of the swordfight. It was further enhanced by the development of the rapier sword, although this was soon displaced by a lighter sword more suited to recreational swordplay.

From the seventeenth century, and especially during the reign of Louis XIV, France became the focus for new developments in fencing. The light court sword replaced the rapier. In the late eighteenth century the mask was introduced to protect the eyes of fencers, damage to which was hitherto an occupational hazard for even the most experienced fencer. New rules were also introduced to reduce risk; for example, scoring hits could only be made on the right breast.

In England, fencing and its forerunners had a long history. In 1285, Edward I banned swordplay in London, seemingly because it had become disreputable due to the brawling and duelling which took place in the city. For similar reasons, fencing was banned at various times by the authorities at Cambridge University. The London ban lasted until 1540, when Henry VIII revoked it and gave the Corporation of Masters of Defence the right to teach fencing. This fencing was based on the European style rather than traditional, and less skilful, broadsword and buckler swordfighting, which had not been outlawed in 1285. The new style raised the levels of skill in fencing and increased its popularity as a recreational activity, not least because it did not allow the jostling and wrestling that was common in the more traditional forms. During the sixteenth century, professional fencing competitions were common in London.

Nevertheless, the demands of public entertainment saw punching and wrestling reintroduced into professional fencing in the mid-eighteenth century, most notably by the champion English prizefighter James Figg. Despite such associations with popular entertainment, fencing retained its popularity with the upper echelons of society, most notably through the work of Angelo Domenico, an Italian fencer who emigrated to England in 1754 and who became the fencing master to the royal family and founded the Academy of Arms. Fencing was also deemed to be sufficiently respectable to be taken up by upper-class women in the late 1700s.

The first British fencing club, the London Fencing Club, was formed as late as 1848, although similar establishments had existed as part of a fencing master's circle for the best part of the previous 100 years. A major boost to the sport's fortunes came, however, in 1861 when it was added to the curriculum of the Army School of Physical Training, adding to its status and making it available to many thousands of young officers. Inclusion in the 1896 Olympic Games helped to extend the sport's popularity, and the Amateur Fencing Association was founded in 1902.

Sources and Reading:
Cohen, R., *By the Sword* (London: Macmillan, 2003).
De Beaumont, C.-L., *Fencing. Ancient Art and Modern Sport* (Revised edition) (London: Kaye and Ward, 1978).

See also Broadsword, Cudgelling and Singlestick, Sword and Buckler

Tony Collins

Fennell, John Greville

Artist, angler and writer on fishing, Greville Fennell (1807–85) was a keen observer of the habits of waterside birds, a trait which he developed while on his regular fishing trips for he was an enthusiastic and excellent angling practitioner. He was especially fond of the river Thames and his writings helped to popularise coarse fishing there. He was a staff member of *The Field* from the commencement of that journal and, as 'Greville F.', wrote regularly on fishing subjects. He also wrote on angling and outdoor pursuits as 'Creel' for the *Fishing Gazette* and other sporting papers. In 1870 he authored *The Book of the Roach*, an exhaustive treatise on angling for that fish, and later wrote *The Rail and the Rod*, a guidebook to angling areas within 60 to 80 miles of London that could be reached by railway. He was a friend of Charles Dickens and actually wrote the angling portions of Dickens's *Dictionary of the Thames*. His epitaph, taken from Isaiah, was most appropriate: 'The fishers also shall mourn, and all they that cast angle into the brooks shall lament'.

Sources and Reading:
Vamplew, W., 'Fennell, John Greville', in Harrison, B., *New Dictionary of National Biography* (Oxford: Oxford University Press, 2004).

Wray Vamplew

Ferreting

Ferreting is the pursuit of rabbits by using ferrets, a breed of polecat, to flush the quarry out of their underground burrows and either to catch them in special purse nets set over their exit holes or to shoot them.

Rabbits were introduced into Britain at the time of the Norman Conquest and, until the eighteenth century, were never a serious menace to agriculture or forestry. For several centuries the rabbit was scarce enough to warrant protection by a close season and was bred for profit in enclosed warrens on sandy soil, being sold for food and fur. By the eighteenth century, the indigenous rabbit population had begun to increase, but it was not until the introduction of the Ground Game Act in the 1880s that agricultural tenants were given the right to kill rabbits on their holdings. Ferreting and other previously illegal methods of catching rabbits, such as snaring and trapping, now became permissible.

One of the main reasons for the proliferation of the rabbit population in the nineteenth century was the development of the saw-edged, spring-loaded gin trap, which was used to catch rabbits but which also contributed to reducing the rabbit's natural predators, such as the stoat, weasel, badger and polecat. The intensification of game management further decimated these species of predator, allowing the rabbit population to flourish, ensuring that ferreting was not only a commercial activity but also a sport undertaken by considerable numbers of mainly working-class rural male participants, who regarded it primarily as a relatively inexpensive means of catching rabbits to supplement their diet.

The outbreak of myxamatosis in the 1950s led to a dramatic decline in the rabbit population and the sudden loss of interest in rabbit meat practically exterminated the market for rabbits for several years. It also led to a loss of employment for the specialised professional rabbit trappers, who were reabsorbed into farming and to other rural industries.

Every year, thousands of ferreters help control the rabbit population during the October to March hunting season. It is practised by a number of professional pest controllers, but is mainly undertaken by amateur working-ferret enthusiasts.

The sport has been transformed by the increased use of albino ferrets, which are particularly popular because of their light coats, making them more conspicuous in dense vegetation. It has also been changed by technological improvements that have revolutionised the location of ferrets that fail to return to their handlers. The conventional way of locating a lost ferret was for the handler to press his ear to the ground in the hope of hearing the ferret fighting with a rabbit in its burrow so that it could then be dug out. A more efficient method developed in the late twentieth century employed the use of a small radio collar fitted around the ferret's neck, which allowed the ferret to be located using a special receiver.

Historically ferrets were owned mainly by rural people, who used them primarily for rabbiting, whereas by the late twentieth century the species had experienced a massive change in image to become more popular as a domestic pet. The demographics of ferret ownership shifted in favour of middle-class women, who are attracted to having the animals as pets because of their playfulness, intelligence, ease of care and, contrary to popular belief, because they do not bite or smell.

Sources and Reading:
McKay, J., *The Ferret and Ferreting Handbook* (Marlborough: Crowood Press, 1993).

Websites:
www.pakefieldferrets.co.uk
homepage.ntlworld.com/ferreter/f-sport.htm
www.countryside-alliance.net/edu/edu2-3-4.htm

See also Hunting

*Nicholas Goddard
and John Martin*

Field Sports

'Field sports' is the collective term to describe the rural activities involving the pursuit and killing of wild animals and birds. There are two main branches: the hunting of wild animals using dogs, and the use of firearms to shoot birds and animals.

Of the two, hunting has the longest history, its origins dating back to the pre-medieval period when wealthy lords indulged in deer hunting on horseback using specialist deerhounds. By the eighteenth century, the shortage of deer compelled huntsmen to pursue hares, and eventually foxes, which had been despised as vermin. The sport reached its heyday in the mid-nineteenth century in the Midland shires, when the prevailing system of pastoral farming enabled long chases over hedges to take place. Packs at this time were usually owned by a single landowner and meets were held early in the morning. By the latter part of the century, mid-morning meetings prevailed, while subscription packs funded by donations from their members had become commonplace. The agricultural depression of the late nineteenth century adversely affected, hunting not only by reducing the income of the hunts' patrons, the landed aristocracy, but also through the use of barbed wire for fencing, which made long chases more difficult. Hunting continued to play an important part in the rural economy in the twentieth century by creating employment for a multitude of occupations.

The other main branch of field sport involves the pursuit of animals and birds with firearms and takes a variety of forms. In the case of deer, this usually involves the stalking of the animals and the use of high-velocity rifles to kill them. Shotgun shooting encompasses covert shooting, where lines of beaters drive the quarry, game birds, to stationary guns, and rough shooting or walking-up, which entails the use of dogs to flush out a variety of species for the guns. Close seasons are enforced by legislation and shooters are encouraged to abide by a voluntary code of conduct.

All blood sports have historically been hotly debated. Supporters have consistently argued that they constitute an integral and functional part of rural life. To their opponents, blood sports should be prohibited because of the suffering they impose on defenceless animals. Opposition in the early twenty-first century has reached the stage where the Labour government has prohibited the hunting of all wild animals with dogs.

Sources and Reading:

Willock, C., *The ABC of Shooting* (London: Deutsch, 1975).

See also Deer Hunting and Stalking, Fox-Hunting, Game Shooting, Hunting, Shooting, Wildfowling

John Martin

Fishing (Wales)

With Wales's extensive coastline and numerous lakes, rivers and mountain streams, it is hardly surprising that fishing has long been well-established. A sixth-century nursery rhyme mentions a father hunting and fishing, at a time when such pursuits were essential life skills. Fishing was probably initially done by hand at the waterside, and then by means of nets and small wooden boats called 'coracles'. The prince and alleged explorer Madog ap Owain Gwynedd fished with nets during the twelfth century, while Owain Glyndŵr (*c*.1354–*c*.1416), last native Welsh prince of Wales, kept fishing nets in his Denbighshire home.

From roughly the start of the sixteenth century, fishing formed the livelihood of generations of coastal and riverside villagers, while as a leisure pursuit it was adopted by the Welsh gentry, probably inspired by Izaac Walton's *The Compleat Angler*, published in 1653. Fishing using rods and feathers was introduced around the seventeenth century and soon became a highly regarded, if difficult, technique.

Fishing for wagers sometimes took place in Wales. In May 1828, two members of the Dolgellau Fishing Club in Meirionethshire, who were both proficient anglers, placed money on the number of fish caught over a 6-hour period.

Sources and Reading:

Evans, E., *Traditional Fishing in Wales* (Llanrwst: Gwasg Carreg Gwalch, 1995).
Sporting Magazine (May 1828).

See also Angling

Emma Lile

Fives

Now virtually the preserve of public schools, fives was played as a popular sport in many areas of England up to the mid-nineteenth century, especially in Durham, London and the south-west. Players used a hand to hit a small ball against a wall or a three-walled court. A leather glove was eventually used, but the growth in the use of racquets undermined the appeal of the game in favour of squash.

It is probably safe to assume that the name 'fives' is derived from the five fingers of the hand that is used instead of a bat, although it has also been known as 'hand tennis'. It is a variant of the tennis family of games and a number of similar games are played in Europe. Its codified form seems to date back to the fourteenth century, the first recorded occasion on which a line, or cord, was drawn on a wall, above which the ball had to be hit.

The sport's history is closely entangled with that of the Church, especially in its heartland of south-west England. According to William Hone, writing in 1830, there is some evidence that fives was officially sanctioned to be played in churches during Easter, and that the ball itself became part of church ceremony. He also suggests that rules specifying the size of the ball were formulated in medieval times. The Synod of Exeter banned the game in 1287 because it was played against church walls. James Skeggs, a historian of Somerset, suggests that many churches planted trees in their grounds to prevent the game being played, which obviously led to long-term structural problems with church foundations. By the eighteenth century, many churches in the region had either been adapted to facilitate the playing of the game or taken measures to stop it. Special shutters were erected by some to stop church windows being broken, while others provided scoreboards or even smoothed the surface of walls to make playing easier. In 1813, a fives court was built at the base of the church tower at West Pennard in Somerset.

Fives was also popular across Wales throughout the year. Literary references to the game go back as far as the fifteenth century, when it was alluded to in a *cywydd* (a Welsh poetical metre) entitled *Y Bêl* ('The Ball'). Proficient players were widely revered, such as one Richard Edwards, who, during the eighteenth century, was said to be the champion at fives on every convenient church wall in Denbighshire from Llangollen to Llanrhaeadr-ym-Mochnant.

By the early nineteenth century, fives had also become a popular sport in pubs and many built fives courts to promote the game and, of course, bring in new customers to either play or watch. This commercial spirit also helped the sport to achieve a high profile in London in the early nineteenth century. Matches were played for high stakes before large crowds. Most prominent among the fives players of that time was an Irish-born Catholic, John Cavanagh, a house painter. Cavanagh played most of his matches at the court at Copenhagen House in Islington, one of the leading courts in London. When he played at the court at St Martin's Street, the owner charged two-shillings-and-sixpence admission and still sold out. On his death in 1819, his obituary was written by William Hazlitt, who claimed that he was 'the best fives player that perhaps ever lived'.

This was the high-water mark for popular fives. As with other sports that enjoyed a brief surge of popularity in London at that time, such as its close cousin rackets and also wrestling, fives went into decline and retreated largely back to its south-western roots, where it could still command crowds and reasonably high stakes. In 1855, two men from Bridport played two from Bath, who were described as the champions of England, at the Fives Court Inn in Bridport, at which £60 was taken in gate money.

Rather in the same way that the decline of folk football was paralleled by football's growing popularity in the public schools, fives too was taken up with enthusiasm by Eton, Winchester, Rugby and similar schools. Eton built its first courts in 1840, and by the end of the century fives had become an established game for public schools.

There are three variants of the public school fives: Eton, Rugby and Winchester. All the major public schools play one of these three forms. The games are very similar in that the ball has to hit the front wall, facing the players, above a certain line. The server and the returner must hit the ball against a side wall before it hits the front wall, after which striking the front wall will suffice. The Rugby game is played in an enclosed space with four walls, the Eton with three walls. There are various features peculiar to the Eton court, such as steps and buttresses against which the ball can be hit. In addition, the Eton ball is slightly larger and heavier. Winchester fives is a variant of Rugby fives, with a buttress running along the left-hand wall.

Despite its evolution away from its roots, it is probably true to say that fives as played today is one of the most unchanged of those sports that can trace their histories back over a number of centuries.

Sources and Reading:
The Encyclopaedia of Sport (London: The Sportsman, 1912).
Encyclopedia of Sports, Games and Pastimes (London: Fleetway, 1935).
Gillmeister, H., *Tennis. A Cultural History* (Leicester: Leicester University Press, 1997).
Hone, W., *The Every-Day Book* (London: Thomas Tegg, 1830).
Jones, T. V., 'Handball and Fives', *Medel*, 1 (1985).
Lloyd, H., 'Tri o Hen Chwaraeon Cymru', *Transactions of the Honourable Society of Cymmrodorion* (1960), 97–108.
Underdown, D., 'Regional Cultures?', in Harris, T. (ed.), *Popular Culture in England c.1550–1850* (Basingstoke: Macmillan, 1995).

See also Public School Sports, Rackets, Tennis

Tony Collins and Emma Lile

Football

'And life is itself but a game of football.' So wrote Sir Walter Scott in 1815 to mark the occasion of a match between teams from Ettrick and Yarrow in the Scottish Borders. The universality of this sentiment over time and place goes some way to explain football's popularity over the centuries, whatever the code of rules under which it has been played.

It is believed, although with little real evidence, that the first form of football played in Britain was the Roman game of harpastum. It is unlikely that the game survived into the Middle Ages, although the football games played at Chester and Kingston upon Thames were fancifully said to have begun with the kicking around of the head of a defeated Roman soldier. The reality is that the innate human urge to kick or throw spherical objects has had a place in most societies, whether as spectacle, ritual or simple recreation.

Football appears to have established itself as an important form of recreation in the eleventh and twelfth centuries. The first recorded description of the sport, by William Fitzstephen in 1174, chronicles its popularity in London:

> After dinner all the young men of the city go out into the fields to play at the well-known game of football. The scholars belonging to the several schools have each their ball; and the city tradesmen according to the respective crafts, have theirs. The more aged men, the fathers of the players, and the wealthy citizens, come on horseback to see the contests of the young men, with whom, after their manner, they participate, their natural heat seeming to be aroused by the sight of so much agility, and by their participation in the amusements of unrestrained youth.

Its popularity may have been connected with the growth of towns and trade during this period. Increased communications between communities intensified rivalry between, and within, towns and villages, so vital to the competitive nature of football. The fact that the word 'goal' seems to share some common etymological heritage with the word 'boundary', dating back to the sixteenth century, would tend to reinforce this view.

It is possible that the playing of folk football in rural towns and villages may also be linked in some way to a custom called 'beating the bounds', in which local people would ritually walk the boundaries of their parish to mark its exact bounds and to ensure that they were remembered in the future. Thus young boys were taken around the route to establish the bounds in the minds of new generations. This usually took place on or around Ascension Day, which falls 40 days after Easter Sunday.

The importance of football to national culture can also be seen by the references made to it in literature. The game was mentioned by many writers, including Shakespeare, Wordsworth, Gay, Nashe and Smollett. Indeed, the *Oxford English Dictionary* includes over 70 references to football and its variants dated between 1424 and 1850. Interestingly, given cricket's greater symbolism in English national identity, the *OED* lists more references in literature to football than to cricket in the 300 years up to 1750, roughly the point at which cricket became an organised sport.

Football was predominantly a rural game, played by young men in villages and market towns, and was closely linked to the festivals and holidays of the rural community. In particular, Shrove Tuesday was the main day for many of the renowned football matches across Britain. Christmas Day, New Year's Day and the Easter holidays, too, were popular dates for football. Easter Tuesday saw the annual game in Workington, and thousands would gather every Easter at Sancton, near Market Weighton in Yorkshire 'for the purpose of horse-racing, football, cudgel-playing, etc., which often ended in much fighting and bloodshed, each party contesting for the

honour of taking the ball home'. Football was also played in the summer, for example at West Haddon in Northamptonshire.

Participation in these games was often determined by the social categories of pre-industrial society, such as guild membership or occupation. At Corfe Castle in Dorset, football was used by the freemen marblers of the town as an apprentices' initiation ceremony. Colliers would take on sailors at Workington, while Whitehaven saw shipwrights do battle with quarrymen. At Sedgefield, tradesmen played countrymen. In London and other cities, football was particularly associated with apprentices.

In the main, however, most games were played on a territorial basis, between neighbouring villages or between areas within communities. Thus, the game at Alnwick was nominally played between the men of the parishes of St Paul's and St Michael's, while in Pudsey 'down-towners' played 'up-towners'. For the less well-established games, especially those played on an *ad hoc* basis, married men v bachelors was a popular dividing line for teams.

For these major encounters, football was primarily a game for large numbers. Derby often saw around 1,000 men involved in its annual game, while even the small town of Sedgefield saw 400 men playing on each side. Common to all games was the propelling of the ball towards goals, which were more often than not situated at prominent local landmarks. The goals were 3 miles apart for the Ashbourne game, at Workington they were set at Curwen's Hall at one end of the town and the harbour at the other, while Whitehaven's goals were set at the docks and a wall outside of the town.

Other than two sides and the propulsion of a ball to a target, the playing rules of the game could differ enormously from area to area, and even village to village. In some regions, the ball was driven primarily by foot. In others, the ball was carried or thrown. Often a mixture of the two was allowed; for example, at Sutton the ball was 'bunched' (kicked or carried) between villages. From a modern perspective, it is noticeable that there is no evidence to suggest that any form of folk football completely forbade the handling of the ball, as in modern soccer.

Football was also played outside of these well-known occasions, both formally and informally. David Underdown has described how in the seventeenth century football was commonly played on Sundays in Wiltshire villages. These matches were often played between much smaller teams; in 1735 the *Suffolk Mercury* published a challenge from '12 Norfolk men to play against 12 of any county or country whatever'. In East Anglia, camp ball, a more structured version of the game, was played. Cornish hurling was another highly organised variant of football

In some areas football was such a popular recreation that fields were especially set aside for the game; for example, the town of Hornsea on the east coast of Yorkshire had a 'football grene' as early as the 1680s. In the 1820s football was played every Sunday in Islington by teams from the local Irish community. By the 1840s, predating the formation of the Football Association and the Rugby Football Union, a number of clubs had been founded in England to play various forms of football. Informal and low-profile games, with varying degrees of organisation and rules, were clearly commonplace features of British social life for many centuries.

Although football was overwhelmingly a game for young males, women also participated on occasions. *Baily's Magazine* (April 1868) noted three references to women's involvement in football, including a married v unmarried women's game at Inverness.

In 1280 Henry de Ellington was accidentally killed during a game in Northumberland, probably becoming the game's first fatality. Numerous others followed, and between 1314 and 1496 there were 12 royal edicts forbidding football in England and four in Scotland between 1424 and 1491, together with numerous local bans. Although its

violence and disruption to public order were cited as reasons, football was also thought by many in authority to have no military or moral purpose. That football could be a very violent game is undoubtedly true. However, it must be noted that it would have been the more notorious events that were recorded by chroniclers, the courts or, later, newspapers, not to mention those who were simply opposed to the game. This gave reported cases of extreme violence a prominence that they perhaps did not deserve.

The fact that football was largely associated with the working classes, especially from the end of the Middle Ages, no doubt also caused some to associate it with violence. John Strype's 1720 edition of *Stow's Survey of London* spoke of football as something with which 'the lower classes divert themselves', in the Orkneys in 1787 it was noted that 'football is the principal diversion of the common people', and Joseph Strutt's *Sports and Pastimes of the People of England* (1801) describes football as 'formerly much in vogue among the common people of England'. During periods of social unrest football was also suspected, sometimes with justification, of being a cover for the organisation of protests or worse.

In general, however, major organised football matches were opportunities for social interaction between the classes. The patronage of the local gentry, landowners and, up to the seventeenth century at least, sympathetic clergy was necessary, not least because of the exigencies of closing roads and designating fields to enable the game to be played.

In certain areas, therefore, the game came to represent a vision of 'merrie England', in which social obligation at one pole was combined with rustic deference at the other. This was nostalgically captured by William Cail, a president of the Rugby Football Union in the 1890s, looking back on football in his grandfather's village in north Yorkshire:

> Each year my father invited the chief inhabitants from the vicars downwards,

of two neighbouring villages, and chief of the afternoon's entertainments was football; that was long before the days of either Rugby or Association, and all of one village kicked down a large field while those of the other kicked up; and if the ball hit the hedge at either end a goal was scored, and ample time for refreshment allowed.

By the first decades of the nineteenth century the growth of industrial capitalism had begun to undermine much of the traditional social basis for folk football. Enclosures of common land had already led to the ending of football in many areas, but urbanisation and the discipline of the factory system imposed a new rhythm of daily life, based on the needs of business, which led to folk football's decline.

In 1835, the Highways Act banned the playing of football on public highways, imposing a maximum penalty of 40 shillings. Religious objections to the playing of the game also grew during this period, especially from nonconformist denominations, which saw in football only debauchery and violence. The old relationships between the classes also no longer existed; gatherings of large numbers of working-class people for whatever purpose were viewed with some suspicion by the authorities.

But the decline and suppression of folk football was not without opposition. Nor was it totally successful. A long struggle took place in Derby during the 1840s against the outlawing of the Shrove Tuesday game, requiring troops to be called out in 1846. It took 69 years for the authorities to finally end the Kingston-upon-Thames game in 1868. Dorking's game was only banned in 1895. One Hull FC rugby player of the 1890s allegedly learnt the game playing traditional football in the East Riding village of Sutton. Those folk-football games that survive today are primarily in rural communities, where the straightjacket of time–work discipline was not so tight.

The codifications of modern football rules by bodies such as the Football Association

(formed in 1863) and the Rugby Football Union (1871) were in many ways attempts to establish football on a new moral basis, separate from the old ways of playing and strictly under the control of the Victorian middle classes. But football's transformation into a modern mass-spectator sport at the end of the nineteenth century was only possible because of the deep residual attachment of the British working classes to football down the ages.

Sources and Reading:

Alexander, M., 'Shrove Tuesday Football in Surrey', *Surrey Archaeological Collections*, 77 (1986).

Baily's Magazine, 14 (1868), 341.

Carter, J. M., *Sports and Pastimes of the Middle Ages* (Columbus: Brentwood University, 1984).

Day, B., *A Chronicle of Folk Customs* (London: Hamlyn, 1988).

Elias, N. and Dunning, E., *Quest for Excitement* (Oxford: Blackwell, 1986).

Goulstone, J., *Football's Secret History* (London: 3–2 Books, 2001).

Harvey, A., 'Football's Missing Link', in Mangan, J. A. (ed.), *Sport in Europe: Politics, Class, Gender* (London: Frank Cass, 1999).

Hole, C., *English Traditional Customs* (London: Batsford, 1975).

Magoun, F. P., *A History of British Football from the Beginnings to 1871* (Bochum-Langendveer: Poppinghüs, 1938).

Marshall, F. (ed.), *Football. The Rugby Union Game* (London: Cassell & Co., 1893).

Stonehenge [J. H. Walsh], *Manual of British Rural Sports* (London: Routledge, 1857).

Underdown, D., *Revel, Riot and Rebellion: Popular Politics and Culture in England 1603–1660* (Oxford: Clarendon, 1985).

See also Alnwick Football, Ashbourne Football, Atherstone Shrovetide Football, Camp Ball, Gaelic Football, Hallaton Bottle-Kicking, Hurling, Sedgefield Football

Tony Collins

Football (Scotland)

The medieval European game of mass football reached Scotland in the fifteenth century. It is first recorded when it was prohibited in 1424. In following centuries, football was played all over the Lowlands areas; in the south on Fastern's E'en (Shrove Tuesday), in the north-east at Yule (Christmas) and in a few places on New Year's Day. However, it did not displace shinty as the festival game in the Highlands and Islands. In some places, such as Westruther in Berwickshire, football was associated with the other sport of Fastern's E'en, cockfighting: the owner of the winning bird won the right to start the football game by throwing up the ball. From the north-east comes John Skinner's poem 'The Christmas Bawing [balling] of Monymusk' (1739), about a match in the Aberdeenshire parish in which Skinner was schoolmaster. It emphasised the brutality of the play:

> The hurry-burry now began,
> Was right weel worth the seeing,
> Wi' routs and raps frae man to man,
> Some getting, and some gieing [giving].

In the Borders, football was made safer by transforming it into handball, in which no kicking was allowed. This change seems to have taken place in the south by 1800, and at Kirkwall by about 1850, where the reason was the increasing number of players. Football was also discouraged because of the disorder that might follow it, as at Duns in Berwickshire in 1724 where after the game the players attempted to break into a house, to steal a drum with which to enliven the holiday, and broke a great deal of glass.

Matches were held between the two ends of a town, or one parish and the next, or the married and the single men, all reflecting the established structure of local society. At Inveresk in Midlothian the match was between married and unmarried fishwives; fishwives were one of the few female occupational groups who were largely free of male control. Women are also said to have joined in the men's game at Wandel in Lanarkshire.

There is early evidence of more-organised football which was not linked to the calendar. In a Latin textbook of 1636 the Aberdeen schoolmaster David Wedderburn gave his pupils a passage to translate which described a game with specific roles and tactics. In 1568 Mary Queen of Scots watched her courtiers play 'strongly, nimbly, skillfully', which indicates a different game from the one Skinner described.

By the nineteenth century the 'ba' game' (meaning either football or handball, but usually the latter) was in decline. It was, however, still played in widely-scattered places: most were small burghs which were, to some extent, backwaters, including Kirkwall in Orkney, Jedburgh in Roxburghshire and Wigtown. It was still played in a few country villages and one large town, Hawick. There were also instances of matches being played to celebrate particular events. The best-known was between Galashiels and Selkirk in 1815 in honour of the victory at Waterloo. It was recorded in verse by two enthusiasts for Border traditions, James Hogg and Walter Scott. At Innerleithen in Peebleshire, a ba' game was played in the 1820s and 1830s; it was one of the sports at the annual St Ronan's Games.

In Orkney, where much of the ground is flat, traditional football is recorded to have been played in no less than 26 places, and in nine locations in the Shetlands. These games were played on either Christmas Day or New Year's Day (or both), according to either the new Gregorian calendar, or the old Julian one, which in the nineteenth century meant 13 days later. Orcadian exiles played a match of some kind on Glasgow Green on New Year's Day in 1866. It is also possible that the game traditionally played on New Year's Day at Callander in Stirlingshire has a link with early football in Glasgow. The Irishmen who played football at Perth in 1850 were presumably playing the not yet codified Gaelic game.

The football game that was introduced from English public schools to their Scottish equivalents, starting with Edinburgh Academy in 1857, was neither modern rugby nor soccer, but an incompletely defined game which still had significant similarities to folk football in England.

The first known Scottish football club abroad is known from a manuscript membership list of 1863. It was formed almost entirely of the sons of two Ayrshire landed families, the Hunter Blairs and the Fairlies, who had gone to Spa in Belgium to live economically. The boys were educated respectively at Glenalmond and Harrow and must have played something closer to the Fastern's E'en game than to any modern sport.

In the 1860s, children at Newton Stewart in Kirkcudbright were supervised by older players in a traditional ba' game, indicating that formal organisation was being applied to the traditional game; the same kind of supervision mixed with teaching the game can still be seen at the Jedburgh ba'. There may be continuities between Borders ba' games and rugby, but they have yet to be uncovered. It is certain, however, that some folk football in the middle of the nineteenth century contained significant elements of organisation, though it is not clear whether these were traditional or of recent innovation. At the beginning of the century the teams included goalkeepers, and by the early 1860s the Callander game had defined roles for the players. On Whalsay in Shetland, teams of equal numbers included goalkeepers and free kicks were given. In 1835, workers from the Blairdrummond estate and the Deanston cotton mills (both near Callander) played against one another, and the matches at Innerleithen were between different villages. The early semi-organised football in public schools thus copied an existing popular tradition.

At the beginning of the twenty-first century, ba' games are still played at Kirkwall on Christmas Day, and at Jedburgh and a handful of other places in the Borders in the week of Shrove Tuesday.

Sources and Reading:

Burnett, J., *Riot, Revelry and Rout: Sport in Lowland Scotland before 1860* (East Linton: Tuckwell Press, 2000).

Hutton, R., *Stations of the Sun: A History of the Ritual Year in Britain* (Oxford: Oxford University Press, 1996).

Magoun, F. P., 'Scottish Popular Football 1424–1815', *American Historical Review*, 37 (1931), 1–13.

Robertson, J., *Uppies and Doonies: The Story of the Kirkwall Ba' Game* (Aberdeen: Aberdeen University Press, 1967).

See also Football

John Burnett and
Richard McBrearty

Football (Wales)

While primitive versions of the modern game of association football were doubtless enjoyed in Wales in antiquity, one forerunner of which there is a record is *cnapan*, played in Pembrokeshire in the sixteenth century. The earliest instance of the Welsh term *pêl-droed* ('football') dates from 1593 in a poem by William Middleton, while in 1629 Robert Lloyd, the vicar of Chirk, alluded to the nation's predilection for the game, regrettably even on Sundays. During the pre-industrial period, football was one of the most popular sports in the agricultural calendar and engendered a team spirit and sense of community worth, as well as interparish rivalry. Games were frequently played on parish saints' days and at rural seasonal festivals, which reached their heyday during the eighteenth and early nineteenth centuries, and were based around religious celebrations such as Shrove Tuesday, Christmas and the New Year.

Footballs were traditionally made from pigs' or bulls' bladders, or, occasionally, balls of wool or twine. Games could continue for many hours, not on a demarcated pitch, but across country, with landmarks, such as church spires, for goals. Scant regard was paid to the number of players in a team, or any semblance of rules, and, in the absence of referees, proceedings often descended into disarray. The reminiscences of one Rhys Cox, who observed the game at the turn of the eighteenth century, illustrate how far this zealousness could go:

As a youth, my whole object was to excel in the two chief games of that time – football and tennis. Scores of us assembled near Llandrygan [Anglesey] on a Sunday morning . . . and near the churchyard entrance, about the hour of service, down with the ball and away with it, everyone with his kick, taking it backwards and forwards, until sunset found the players sometimes on the Malltraeth Sands, sometimes on the Gader Point, from which it could be kicked into the sea in the direction of Gogarth Head or Bardsey Isle. Numbers of players would be left here and there on the road, some having limbs broken in the struggle, others severely injured, and some carried on biers to be buried in the churchyard nearest to where they had been mortally injured.

Almost as fearful was a game, again in Anglesey, mentioned in a diary entry by William Bulkeley in April 1734, which showed that violence left no hard feelings, the sides parting 'as good friends as they came, after they had spent half an hour together cherishing their spirits with a cup of ale . . . having finished Easter Holydays innocently and merrily'.

Football matches were common features of athletic sports meetings, to which spectators flocked in their hundreds. Most of the villagers of Llanwenog in south Cardiganshire, for example, turned out annually in the early nineteenth century for the boisterous Christmas Day game, known as *y bêl ddu* ('the black ball'), between the lads of the *Blaenau* and those of the *Bro* (the 'Hills' v the 'Vale'). Victory was so prized that a player 'would as soon lose a cow

from his cow-house, as the football from his portion of the parish'. Fighting was commonplace in such matches, and it was hardly surprising that from the mid-eighteenth century until the early twentieth century football was roundly condemned by nonconformist opinion which sought to rid the country of its supposedly sinful, or at least worthless, sporting pastimes. Widespread attacks from the pulpit on football matches led to their being supplanted by Sunday-school festivals, and in the 1830s the Llanwenog match, like several others, was stopped when 'a venerable nonconformist minister preached against it, and the people listened to him'.

Despite the continuing threat to football, both from the religious lobby and the process of industrialisation which so profoundly affected all aspects of social life, the game survived, and many of the traditional elements were transformed into the new, more structured 'association' football. The game, roughly as it is known now, first appeared in Wales in the 1860s, with its early stronghold in the north-east, around Wrexham and the border. A Wrexham club (forerunners of the 1872 club, the oldest of the Welsh clubs to have played in the Football League) played its last match of the season in May 1865, a week after the formation of Llandudno FC. In the south (though the game here may have more closely resembled rugby), Swansea Grammar School played Cilfái in February of the same year, and there was a town team by 1871. It was the north, however, that led the way, the Football Association of Wales being formed at Rhiwabon in 1876, and only one of the 19 teams that entered the first Welsh Cup in 1877 came from the south.

Sources and Reading:

Bulkeley, W., 'The Diary of William Bulkeley of Brynddu, Anglesey', *Anglesey Antiquarian Society and Field Club Transactions* (1931), 22–92.

Corrigan, P., *100 Years of Welsh Soccer* (Cardiff: Welsh Brewers, 1976).

Dent, A., *The Plaine Mans Path-way to Heaven* (London: Robert Dexter, 1601; translated and with introduction by Robert Lloyd as *Llwybr*

Hyffordd yn Cyfarwyddo yr Anghyfarwydd i'r Nefoedd, London: Georg Lathum [sic], 1630).

Evans, N. G., *Religion and Politics in Mid-eighteenth Century Anglesey* (Cardiff: University of Wales Press, 1953).

Lile, B. and Farmer, D., 'The Early Development of Association Football in South Wales, 1890–1906', *Transactions of the Honourable Society of Cymmrodorion* (1984), 193–215.

Owen, G., *The Description of Penbrokshire* (London: J. Clark, 1892).

See also Football

Emma Lile

Fox-Hunting

Fox-hunting, involving the pursuit of foxes with packs of dogs and mounted riders clad in scarlet, black or occasionally tweed jackets, is Britain's most popularly recognised field sport. For many of its supporters, the Boxing Day meet constitutes the highlight of the social calendar, although complementary activities such as puppy shows and summer balls ensure the continued involvement of the hunting fraternity with fox-hunting throughout the year.

Conventional wisdom suggests that the origins of fox-hunting can be traced back to the sixteenth century, when the decline in the numbers of deer in England led the aristocracy to turn increasingly to the hitherto despised fox as an appropriate quarry. More recent research, however, has suggested that foxes were hunted much more extensively than previously indicated in many historical accounts. The popularisation of the sport has traditionally been attributed to Squire Thomas Boothly, who in 1696, aged only 15, inherited the Tooley Pary Estate in Leicestershire. Two years later Boothly founded the Quorn Hunt, the first pack of foxhounds. He is widely credited as the person who revolutionised traditional hunting, formalised the sport and established the fox as the prime quarry (over the stag and the hare).

It was Hugo Meynell who, in 1753, appreciated the potential for fast riding around his new home in Leicestershire. He established a breeding programme over the next 47 years that was to produce what was widely accepted to be the fastest pack of foxhounds in England. As the popularity of this new approach to hunting spread, Leicestershire rapidly became a Mecca for fashionable London gentlemen who wished to participate in the sport. Melton Mowbray, being central to three Leicestershire hunts, became a leading venue. The sport was popularised by writers such as Charles James Apperley, who began to write enthralling articles under the pseudonym of 'Nimrod' for the *Sporting Magazine* in 1822, which contributed to the doubling of its circulation during the following two years. The fox became affectionately known as 'Charles James' by certain sections of the hunt fraternity in recognition of Apperley's role in encouraging more people to participate in the sport.

By 1839 fox-hunting was a very popular activity in virtually all rural counties of England, providing relaxation for the richer echelons of society, which included tenant farmers and sporting parsons. Meets included the occasional female rider who, social convention dictated, should ride side-saddle, and wear ankle-length, trailing skirts weighed down with lead shot in order to preserve decorum.

This highly sophisticated sport with its social conventions was associated with skilled huntsmen, highly bred hounds and fast, strong horses. It was the focal point of a minor economy providing employment for a multitude of trades, including farriers, blacksmiths and grooms, and was a spectator sport for foot-followers from the local villages, market towns and even industrial centres. Regional differences in the level of turnout and organisation were evident between the smart Midland packs from the historical heartland of the sport and their more provincial counterparts.

The sport reached its heyday in the mid-nineteenth century, when the prevailing system of pastoral farming enabled long chases over hedges to take place. The sport had a significant impact on the lowland landscape, with many wealthy estate owners planting a multitude of small coverts to attract the fox and maintaining their hedges and landscape to provide jumps and facilitate long chases. The sport also encouraged the emphasis on livestock and grassland farming because pasture provided a better scent than arable fields. The sport's rapid development was facilitated by the expansion of the railway network, which enabled wealthy urban dwellers to travel to the hunt in a morning and return home that evening.

Landowners used the hunt as a way of keeping in touch with the concerns of their tenants, creating goodwill within the local community. It was this inherent social mixing that historian and hunter Raymond Carr considered contributed to the lack of hatred between the rural population and the hunting fraternity and to a social cohesion which set the English aristocracy apart from that of the rest of Europe. This was borne out by the formation of the county yeomanry regiments after 1859, which were often run by fox-hunting officers with fox-hunting farmers as troopers.

The continued popularity of the sport led to a shortage of foxes in many counties, a problem which was partly solved by the use of bagged foxes. A thousand foxes a year were being sold annually from Leadenhall market, the principal centre for the sale of foxes, many of which were imported from the Continent.

The need for the organisation of the sport to be put on a more official footing was overcome by the establishment of an arbitrary body to adjudicate on disputes between neighbouring hunts. In 1856, the Masters of Foxhounds met at Boodle's, a county gentlemen's club in London, and successfully petitioned the club's manager to establish a committee for settling disputes over boundaries and access to coverts. In 1881, a more formal body was established at Tattersall's, which eventually became known as the Masters of Foxhounds

Association (MFHA). This organisation also became responsible for the publication of the *Kennel Stud Book*, which helped to improve the quality of foxhounds.

The onset of the agricultural depression in the 1870s undermined private packs, necessitating the shift to subscription packs. The introduction of barbed wire as an effective and cheap source of fencing material encouraged the decline in the well-kept brush hedges that were ideal for jumping, limiting opportunities for long-distance chases. Wire funds administered by committees consisting of hunt members enabled farmers to be paid a sum of money in return for taking wire down during the hunting season. Farmers were increasingly seeking compensation for the damage foxes did to poultry, which placed an additional burden on their finances.

One of the few serious historical studies of hunting, David C. Itzkowitz's *Peculiar Privilege* paints a much bleaker picture. In the latter decades of the nineteenth century, mid-morning meetings became commonplace, with subscriptions being funded by donations from members. By the end of the century, the cost of maintaining a hunt, with its plethora of grooms and hunt staff, combined with the cost of purchasing and managing coverts, resulted in many incurring serious financial losses which were beyond the ability of their Masters to sustain.

The subsequent collapse of landed society, as documented by the mass sale of estates in the aftermath of the First World War, coupled with creeping suburbanisation and the creation of new towns in prime hunting territory, changed the future of fox-hunting. The transformation was accompanied by the growing acceptability of women members of the hunt wearing breeches and using conventional saddles.

As in the First World War, fox-hunting was curtailed during the Second World War. All the recognised packs remained in existence, although with depleted numbers. By the 1950s, foxes had become such a pest that the Ministry of Agriculture, in conjunction with the Forestry Commission, encouraged the development of fox-destruction societies by providing bonus payments for each fox killed. In the late 1950s, the numbers killed in this way amounted on average to slightly more than 4,000 animals each year. In contrast, calculations by Vesey-Fitzgerald suggest that, at the same time, approximately 14,000 foxes were being killed each year by packs of hounds, the vast majority of the packs being affiliated to the MFHA.

Fox-hunting has been heavily subsidised through injections of cash from rich supporters who have been willing to serve as Masters of Foxhounds. Michael Clayton's authoritative study, published in 1987, considered that the Master of a four-day-a-week hunt was probably putting £10,000 a year into the pack.

There has been a great deal of debate in recent years about the place of fox-hunting in English society. Its supporters regard it as an essential and integral part of rural life. At the end of the twentieth century, fox hunting constituted the most-popular field sport, with estimates suggesting that in excess of 200,000 people hunted or followed hounds. The most incisive insight into the strange compulsion of the sport and its circumscribed world may be gleaned from Siegfried Sassoon's *Memoirs of a Foxhunting Man*. Whether it provides an efficient and cost-effective means of controlling the fox population or whether it is simply an opportunity for a ride and social prestige is a moot point. To its critics, fox-hunting is a cruel and barbaric blood sport which symbolises hunting in general.

Sources and Reading:
Carr, R., *English Foxhunting: A History* (London: Weidenfeld, 1976).
Clayton, M., *Foxhunting in Paradise* (London: J. Murray, 1993).
Itzkowitz, D. C., *Peculiar Privilege: A Social History of English Fox Hunting* (Hassocks: Harvester, 1977).
Sassoon, S., *Memoirs of a Foxhunting Man* (London: Faber, 1928).

See also Fox-Hunting: An Alternative History, Fox-Hunting (Wales), Hunting

Nicholas Goddard and
John Martin

Fox-Hunting: An Alternative History

The work of Iris Middleton has challenged conventional wisdom about the history of fox-hunting on two major counts, the timing of its adoption by the gentry and whether the modern style of hunting was devised by Hugo Meynell in the second half of the eighteenth century.

Both Carr and Itzkowitz, the accepted authorities on the history of fox-hunting, supported the idea that fox-hunting was only taken up by the gentry after the Restoration and that before then the fox was killed only as befitted vermin, by digging or forcing it out of its hole and killing it quickly with the aid of nets or terriers. Yet Middleton has shown that medieval art and literature both demonstrate that huntsmen of that time practised fox-hunting and employed similar techniques to those used today. She also provided many examples to illustrate that fox-hunting simply became more popular in the eighteenth century rather than being a newly developed sport.

Often called 'the father of modern hunting', Hugo Meynell is said to have bred a new and faster type of hound that allowed a later, more convenient starting time for hunting. He is also generally credited with making a huge change in the techniques used in fox-hunting. Middleton argued that the so-called innovations regularly attributed to Meynell did not originate with him, and that his reputation was created by a sycophantic nineteenth-century writer, Charles James Apperley ('Nimrod'), on whom subsequent writers have drawn. Despite claims to the contrary, Apperley neither knew nor hunted with Meynell and employed journalistic licence in eulogising the endeavours of the Meltonian huntsman.

There is no evidence that Meynell bred fast hounds on any scientific principles of selective breeding. He merely bred huge numbers of pups and used the best in his pack, later breeding from some of them. Moreover, his hounds do not appear to have been faster than any others. In any case, there is nothing to support the idea that the speed of hounds influenced hunt starting times. Meynell's reputation was made not by hunting methods nor the breeding of hounds, but by the social composition of the people who hunted with him.

Sources and Reading:

Carr, R., *English Foxhunting: A History* (London: Weidenfeld, 1976).

Itzkowitz, D. C., *Peculiar Privilege: A Social History of English Fox Hunting* (Hassocks: Harvester, 1977).

Middleton, I., 'Fox Hunting Traditions: Fact or Fantasy?', *Sport History Review*, 28 (1997), 19–32.

See also Fox-Hunting

Wray Vamplew

Fox-Hunting (Wales)

Fox-hunting was popular among all social classes in Wales from the mid-eighteenth century onwards, for although the presence of the game laws limited participation to the landed gentry, the lower orders were keen spectators. Dog and horse breeding was also extremely costly and could only be afforded by the wealthy, and fox-hunting was thus regarded as an important status symbol. In addition to the numerous small private packs kept by the local squires and landowners, regional hunts, which were maintained by gentry subscription, were held nationwide. Large estate owners, such as the influential Williams-Wynn family of Wynnstay in Denbighshire, could afford their own packs.

Among the oldest hunts in Wales were the Tivyside Hunt, Cardiganshire, formed

around 1736, and the Anglesey Hunt, formed in 1757, which soon developed into county institutions. The Holywell (Flintshire) Hunt was established in 1767 under the patronage of Earl Grosvenor, who was then, according to the *Sporting Magazine*, in the 'zenith of racing celebrity'. The Welsh terrain was evidently worth riding upon; those who have 'never experienced the delights of a hunt on the blue hills of Wales', claimed the *Caernarvon and Denbigh Herald* in 1838, have 'never enjoyed all the pleasures which bountiful nature has provided for her creatures'. Meets were generally considered incomplete without the lively social elements, and suppers and hunt balls were an integral part of the proceedings.

Sources and Reading:

Caernarvon and Denbigh Herald (3 November 1838).

Foxhunting in Wales (London: Field Sports Publications, 1960).

Howell, D. W., *Patriarchs and Parasites: The Gentry of Southwest Wales in the Eighteenth Century* (Cardiff: University of Wales Press, 1986).

Sporting Magazine (February 1824).

Emma Lile

Gaelic Athletic Association

British-inspired sporting movements in the nineteenth century were successful in re-packaging folk, traditional and customary games into rational, organised and disciplined modern sport formats. In erasing local peculiarities and adopting a standardised and nationally consistent form for many sports, political and cultural assumptions about sports and their models of organisation were made. Such a consensus was more easily achieved in Great Britain than in Ireland. In religious terms, for instance, sabbatarian attitudes precluded the playing of many games on Sunday, and while this was a barrier to sport in Britain it was a factor only for

Protestant communities in Ireland. The consequence of this simple religious and cultural difference was that any sport that was presented on a Sunday in Ireland was certain to attract support, but could not be aligned with any of the sports bodies that took their rules and lead from British bodies such as cricket's Marylebone Cricket Club (the MCC) or the football organisations.

Although there were contrasting religious outlooks in Great Britain and Ireland, nowhere were the different paths of both societies more apparent than in the areas of industrialisation and urbanisation. Britain became industrial and urban throughout the nineteenth century, whereas the predominant political issues in Ireland were land and agriculture. British sports movements were closely aligned with urban, industrial and commercial forces, while what became the Gaelic sports movement was aligned with agricultural and cultural forces and was more in tune with rural rhythms of life.

The growing cultural importance of sports in the late nineteenth century was signalled by the attachment to sport of cultural and political significances it did not possess in its pre-organised, localised and non-standard form. The playing of anthems, the development of national teams in rugby, football, cricket and shooting and the competition between nationally representative individuals in yachting, tennis and boxing all made assumptions about the definition of the nation. The first editorial (19 February 1870) of an Irish sports paper, the *Irish Sportsman and Farmer*, stated boldly that the story of a nation's sports presented 'the sunniest aspect of its history' and that 'there is a clear link between a country's history and its sports'. In Great Britain, history, sports and the nation were less contentious than in Ireland, where cultural entrepreneurs were increasingly forced to address the questions of the union between Great Britain and Ireland, Irish history and culture and Irish games.

One consequence of the association of games with national ties, emblems, sympathies and values was the addition of sport to

the list of culturally and politically sensitive issues. Increasingly, comparisons were made between the archetypal English game of cricket and the identifiably Irish game of hurling. The former was re-evaluated by many nationalists and was seen as effete, lacking vigour, aristocratic and foreign, while the latter was seen to epitomise the exact opposite of those qualities, being in its proponents' eyes masculine, vigorous, democratic and native. The outworking of such a process was the formation of the Gaelic Athletic Association for the Preservation and Cultivation of National Pastimes (GAA) in 1884 in the centre of Ireland's hurling heartland. The GAA was conceived as an avowedly political, cultural and sporting movement to counter the apparent 'Anglicisation' of Ireland through the medium of sports – emphasising the reactive nature of the movement. One historian has even described the GAA's stance as akin to a porcupine with its protective quills bristling.

The GAA was formed in November 1884 at Hayes's Hotel, Thurles, County Tipperary. Its early activity was in the area of athletics, but it soon transferred its attention to the increasingly more popular hurling and football. From the outset, control of the GAA was fought over between moderate and advanced nationalist forces. The GAA's appeal to young men made it attractive to radical nationalists eager to take their message to a wider audience. This political motive was checked by the reaction of the moderates, principally led by clerical figures. The struggle for control between the Fenian and clerical factions often led to the organisation of rival county boards to manage the development of the games and to run competitions. A nadir was reached during Parnell's travails over the divorce case of Captain and Kitty O'Shea. The Fenian school of the Gaelic sports movement sided with the under-pressure political maestro, while the clerical school stood back aghast. These political tensions hindered the GAA's ability to maximise its potential and made it even more repugnant to British-Ireland. By the mid-1890s an accommodation between both tendencies was reached and the games themselves became the GAA's number-one priority. This accommodation was assisted by the elevation of the local club to the status of icon in the Gaelic sports movement. The 'pride of the little village' was a totem around which all nationalists, radical and moderate, could gather with no diminution of their political fervour.

While the local rivalry upon which association football, rugby and other competitive team sports is based is important in British culture, localism in Gaelic sports has been developed to a much higher pitch. In contrast to the elevation of soccer players and teams to heroic status as promotional tools in British media, recent media campaigns for Gaelic sports emphasise the tribal loyalty of individuals to their club; the punch line of one advertisement notes that you do not choose a club, 'you inherit it'.

Gaelic games are now organised by county throughout the 32 counties of Ireland – emphasising its nationalist, political dimension. There are county boards in Great Britain and the United States, and representative teams from New York and London participate in the annual all-Ireland championships in hurling and football, while individuals participate in the GAA's handball competitions. In recent decades, clubs in Europe, Australia, the Middle East and Asia have affiliated to the GAA and their tournaments are often the focus of social and cultural events for the Irish communities in their host societies. The retention by many in the Irish diaspora of the Gaelic sports tradition is an example of the desire many emigrants feel in a new host culture to retain something of their own culture. Although patronage of Gaelic sports clubs does not preclude the possibility of assimilation into a new culture and society, it is an indicator of the desire to retain an identifiable and distinctive cultural heritage.

The GAA has a very democratic (some would say overly democratic) pyramidal structure. Clubs based on parish boundaries are the heart of the organisation. They are grouped into divisions (a subdivision of a county) for administrative and competition purposes. A number of divisions exist under the next layer of organisation, the county board level. County boards administer the game in an area defined by local government boundaries; this has proven to be an immense stumbling block to governmental attempts to alter some urban local-authority boundaries following changing urbanisation patterns in the late twentieth century. The city of Limerick, for instance, finds itself unable to expand beyond its nineteenth-century legal limits because its hinterland includes parts of County Clare, whose residents see their allegiance to that sporting entity as sufficient reason not to be subsumed into the neighbouring local authority. County boards are then grouped under provincial councils, which have responsibility for the games and competitions in areas that coincide with the ancient provinces of Ireland; Munster has six counties, Connacht has five, Leinster has twelve and Ulster has nine.

The identification by nationalist Ireland of the ancient nine-county province of Ulster through the structures of the GAA is obvious evidence of the GAA's nationalist mission. The dissonance between the cultural and sporting border as drawn by the GAA and the political and legal border as drawn by Unionist and British Ireland is of an entirely different order than arguments over local authority boundaries. The GAA's conception of 'Ulster' contributes greatly to the nationalist sense of the artificiality of the six-county state of Northern Ireland and explains to a large degree Unionist antipathy to the GAA.

The GAA Congress, to which counties send representatives, is the annual legislative assembly of the association; the Central Council is akin to the GAA's executive branch. Croke Park, in Dublin's north inner city, is the GAA's headquarters; it has been revamped in a grand project to become a modern stadium of 80,000 capacity that includes some terracing at the north end called 'Hill 16' – a label that recalls the Easter Rising of 1916, another pointer to the GAA's nationalist mission.

The GAA was the key agency of cultural nationalism at the beginning of the twentieth century and contributed immensely to political debates on the distinctiveness and separateness of Ireland from Great Britain. The sporting and cultural secession from British norms that the GAA symbolised was elevated to an almost religious intensity during the Irish Civil War when, in retaliation for the earlier assassination of British security agents, British soldiers shot at and killed supporters (and one player) at a Gaelic football match in Croke Park in 1921. The event was labelled 'Bloody Sunday' and was subsequently woven into nationalist lore as further evidence of both the complementarities of Gaelic sports and Irish nationalism and the association's antipathy to British political and cultural forms.

Although the coincidence of Irish nationalism and Gaelic sports emphasised the difference between Irish cultural forms and British models, the GAA performed a valuable role in ameliorating the worst effects of communal strife following the intensity of the Irish Civil War. After the civil war the GAA provided a forum for bringing ex-combatants together in a spirit of local patriotism, and though deep political divisions remained among GAA members, they could be suspended in the cause of local pride and the simple love of sport.

Early on, the GAA directed much of its energy towards athletics, but the more popular field games of hurling and football soon became the crowd-pullers and the real focus of the association. Another popular game – handball – also came under the aegis of the GAA. The first mission statement of the GAA to preserve and cultivate national pastimes was also reflected in the GAA's involvement in organising, for instance, non-military band competitions. This tradition of non-sporting output by the GAA has survived in the GAA's continued sponsorship of a nationwide talent and variety competition called, suitably, *Scór*.

The control of football and hurling by the same body, the GAA, had significant consequences for the development of the field layout for both games as the agreement of both sections of the association was necessary before any change in field layout and goal shape could be adopted. The provision of two major sporting codes within a single club was also an extension of the single sport club model popularised in Great Britain.

Sources and Reading:
Comerford, R. V., 'Patriotism as Pastime: The Appeal of Fenianism in the Mid-1860s', *Irish Historical Studies*, 22 (1981), 239–50.
Joyce, T., '"Ireland's Trained and Marshalled Manhood": The Fenians in the Mid 1860s', in Kelleher, M. and Murphy, J. H. (eds), *Gender Perspectives in Nineteenth Century Ireland: Public and Private Spheres* (Dublin: Irish Academic Press, 1997).
Mandle, W. F., *The Gaelic Athletic Association and Irish Nationist Politics 1884–1924* (Dublin: Gill & Macmillan, 1987).
Mullan, M., 'The Devolution of the Irish Economy in the Nineteenth Century and the Bifurcation of Irish Sport', *International Journal of the History of Sport*, 13: 2 (1996), 42–60.

Website:
Gaelic Athletic Association: www.gaa.ie

See also Gaelic Football, Hurling

Tom Hayes

Gaelic Football

Gaelic football is a field game played with a large round ball between two teams of 15 players. Teams line out with a goalkeeper, three full-backs (left-corner, full and right-corner), three half-backs (sometimes called wing-backs – left, centre and right), two midfield players, three half-forwards (left, centre and right) and three full-forwards (left-corner, full and right-corner). The length of the field is between 130 and 145 metres and the width can vary between 80 and 90 metres. The goalpost is the same H shape as found in rugby; goals are scored into the netted area under the crossbar and are worth three points, and a single point is awarded when the ball passes over the crossbar. The goalposts should be at least 7 metres high, while the netted goal area should be 6.5 metres wide by 2.5 metres high. The H-shaped goalposts have been used since 1910, but before that time two posts equidistant from a soccer-style goal area acted as point posts. These point posts were similar to the 'behind' posts in Australian Rules football. Though there is no offside rule, an attacking player should not arrive into the box in front of the goal area (called the small parallelogram) before the ball.

Games commence when the sole referee throws the ball into the air between the midfield contestants, and last for two halves of 30 minutes (except in the case of senior intercounty league and championship games when two halves of 35 minutes are played). Referees are assisted by two linesmen, and also by four umpires – one at the foot of each goalpost. Umpires signal to the referee and scorekeeper (and also the crowd) that a point has been scored by waving a white flag, and by waving a green flag to indicate a goal. In rare cases, an umpire will stand in the middle of the goal area and make an X with both flags to signal that a disputed score has been cancelled.

At first, games lasted for 80 minutes, but this was soon revised downwards to 60 minutes, which has remained the standard. Teams of 21-a-side were agreed, but this was subsequently reduced to 17 (1895) and then to the current 15 (1915). Initially, only goals counted, points were later counted to decide the winner where both teams scored the same number of goals. In 1895, the value of a goal was determined as being worth five points; this changed to three points in 1897.

Gaelic football is the largest participatory sport on the island of Ireland and its growing popularity is increasingly over-shadowing the game of hurling. Gaelic football also differs from hurling in that it is more competitive; more county teams enter the football championship with hopes of success than similarly enter the hurling championship.

Sources and Reading:
Lennon, J. F., *A Comparative Analysis of the Playing Rules of Football and Hurling 1884–1990* (Gormanstown: Northern Recreation Consultants, 1999).

See also Gaelic Athletic Association

Tom Hayes

Game Fishing

Game fishing involves the pursuit of a very select number of freshwater species. To the purist, the sport encompasses the pursuit of the Atlantic salmon, the brown trout and its migratory subtype the sea trout. Other anglers believe that the category 'game fish' includes not only these salmonid species but also the rainbow trout and its more distant cousins the grayling, char, pollen, vendace and powan (known locally as 'schelly' and 'gwyniad'). The distinguishing feature of all these species is that they are highly susceptible to pollution, historically being found in their natural state only in clear, relatively fast-running streams and rivers or cold-water lakes.

Game fishing was, in many respects, a product of the mid-Victorian period, being largely pursued by those members of the upper and middle classes who could afford the high costs incurred in leasing beats from riparian owners and who had the leisure time to indulge in the activity. The sport was primarily a male activity, entailing the use of ultra-long rods with brightly col-oured artificial flies (with graphic names such as 'Green Highlander' or 'Thunder and Lightening') to attract the fish. Spinning with lures (such as 'Devon minnows', 'phantoms' or 'wagtails') constructed from materials such as wood, metal or quill was also a popular way of fishing. In contrast, natural baits such as worms and prawns were also employed, although increasingly disapproved of and often banned on the most prestigious beats. Salmon fishermen were traditionally assisted by a 'gillie' (the term originally denoted the male attendants of a Highland chieftain, but in the late nineteenth century it had been broadened to encompass the paid professional attendants of sportsmen, usually fishermen).

The salmon is widely regarded as the king of all freshwater fish because of its size and because of the fight large specimens put up when caught on rod and line. Salmon hatch and develop in fresh water before migrating to the sea, returning as adults several years later for the sole purpose of breeding. It has been widely demonstrated that during this journey upstream they consume nothing, which raises the question as to why they should take an artificial fly or lure into their mouths. Many people believe that it is their curiosity about these objects coming into view that encourages them to take them to find out what they are and, on occasions, to become so irritated that they chase after them, grabbing them aggressively. The salmon was once widely distributed in most of Britain's rivers but overfishing with trawl nets at sea and the continuing decline in the quality of fresh water has heralded a long-term contraction in its numbers. As early as the 1870s, rod licences for game fish were introduced in order to preserve stocks of game fish from overfishing,

By the end of the twentieth century the most significant remaining strongholds of the salmon were the great river catchments on the east coast of Scotland, encompassing the Tweed, Tay, Tee and the Spey, and the countless smaller spate rivers in the west Highlands and the Isles. Populations of salmon can still be found in the chalk streams of the south of England and the spate rivers of the West Country, Wales and Ireland. The Wye, once widely acclaimed as England's most prolific salmon river, has also experienced a significant decline in recent years. In contrast, the Tyne has recovered from estuarial pollution to regain some of its earlier reputation as a salmon river. The numbers of salmon caught from rivers in England, Wales and Ireland are relatively minor in comparison with those from Scottish rivers. The size of salmon has also declined, with fish over 20 pounds (9 kilograms) in weight becoming an increasing rarity. This is graphically illustrated by the case of Miss Georgina Ballantine who,

on 7 October 1922, caught a 64 pound (29 kilogram) salmon when fishing in the River Tay, a record that has not been exceeded since. Earlier in the day, she had caught three other salmon, weighing 25, 21 and 17 pounds (11.3, 9.5 and 7.7 kilograms). Most salmon anglers of today would regard catching even one of her smaller fish as an outstanding and memorable achievement.

Opportunities to participate in salmon fishing were significantly enhanced from the late nineteenth century by the development of association water fishing, where beats were purchased by associations, or leased from estates. However, salmon fishing remains largely confined to those enthusiasts who can afford the high costs and the time involved in pursuing this prestigious and elusive quarry, and who are willing to accept a large number of blank days. Since the 1980s, salmon fishing has changed from a desire to capture and kill to a more conservationist approach, where the fisherman's skill and prowess is put to the test but with the emphasis on releasing the fish.

The sea trout has experienced a similar contraction in its population. It is now widely accepted as a migratory form of brown trout which is less well adapted than the salmon to life in the sea, and is more like the brown trout in that it feeds regularly in fresh water and will return from the sea without spawning. In the late nineteenth and early twentieth centuries, dedicated anglers set out, usually at dusk, specifically to catch sea trout by fly-fishing or by trolling special lures from boats, a technique which occasionally brought encounters with massive fish. By the end of the twentieth century, few anglers fished exclusively for sea trout, with most of those caught being a welcome bonus on an excursion for salmon or brown trout.

Brown-trout fishing is dispersed across Britain, with the species being found in clear, unpolluted water of burns, rivers and streams, most notably the Hampshire Test and Itchen, which have worldwide renown. On lakes and lochs it is more usually undertaken from small one- or two-person boats. It is a sport undertaken using lightweight rods casting a variety of small artificial flies or nymphs, which represent aquatic or terrestrial food items (mostly invertebrates but also small fish). These are deployed either 'dry' 'on the surface' or 'wet' below the surface. Dry-fly-fishing became highly stylised, particularly on the chalk streams, with a strict code of etiquette, epitomised by the rules of the Houghton Club (which continues to fish the Test below Stock-bridge, with the Grosvenor Hotel as their headquarters), and with emphasis on imitative fishing, using flies that imitate specific individual species, such as grannon, mayfly and stonefly, at different stages of the lifecycle, for example 'nymph', 'dun', or 'spinner'. Distinctive names are used for the different flies; they may refer to species, such as 'Mayfly', or they may denote the designer, such as 'Greenwell's Glory', or location, as in 'Houghton Ruby'.

Dry-fly purism, developed by highly articulate angling authors such as F. M. Halford, was responsible for the heightened early twentieth-century division between 'game' and 'coarse' angling. It was challenged by F. E. M. Skues, and later by Frank Sawyer (who was the River Keeper of the Services Dry Fly Fishing Association's water on the upper Avon in Wiltshire between 1928 and 1980) and his disciple Oliver Kite (one of the first to present the sport to a post-war television audience). They advocated the use of weighted imitative flies fished up-stream – 'nymphs' – as a logical alternative to the dry-fly under suitable conditions. Nevertheless, the dry-fly remains *de rigueur* on much of the finest chalk stream trout fishing, at least until the latter part of the season. Natural flies, such as 'Daddy Long Legs', are sometimes employed as bait on large lakes, a process known as 'dapping'.

The growing scarcity of indigenous game fish since the Second World War, coupled with improvements in artificial breeding programmes, has led to the popularisation of fishing for artificially reared rainbow trout, particularly in still waters and reservoirs, where the species' wandering instinct can be controlled. The rainbow trout has many advantages over the brown trout. Being a voracious feeder and better food converter, it transforms its fish-farm diet of nutrient pellets into flesh at a much faster rate than the brown trout. It also tolerates higher water temperatures than brown trout and continues to feed even on hot summer days, when brown trout sulk dourly in the cooler depths of rivers and lakes, becoming almost uncatchable. However, as the rainbow trout has not become naturalised, regular restocking with farmed fish is essential. After the Second World War, the expansion of reservoir building and construction of man-made lakes for recreational use provided an ideal opportunity for the rapid and sustained expansion of rainbow-trout fishing, and the emergence of a post-war generation of game fishermen who fish almost exclusively for this type of trout.

Game fish also include grayling and char. Fishing for grayling is a specialist activity pursued by a small number of enthusiasts, particularly during the winter. Grayling are found in the streams and rocky rivers of the uplands, and also in lowland chalk streams where they have been recently introduced and thrive. They are frequently caught at the same time as brown trout, during the summer months, when they are often considered a nuisance. In contrast, Arctic char are the relics following the retreat of the last ice age, being found in Scotland's deeper lochs and the lakes of northern England. Although they may be found in large shoals, few fishermen set out specifically to catch them in the small number of localities where they abound. More often they are caught during trout fishing on lochs, providing a varied and unexpected addition to the bag.

The unprecedented increase in living standards that has taken place in the twentieth century, particularly since the Second World War, has enabled many more anglers to legitimately pursue game fishing. Scottish and Welsh anglers have been more fortunate than their English counterparts because participation in the sport is more accessible, with streams and rivers containing indigenous populations of trout and salmon. However, it is the post-Second World War revolution in still-water reservoir fishing, coupled with the popularity of the rainbow trout, that has enabled game fishing to become affordable by larger numbers of the angling fraternity. This transformation had been accompanied by improved rods, tapered lines (which made casting less difficult) and mass-produced artificial flies and lures, which made it easier for beginners to participate in the sport.

Sources and Reading:

Miles, T., Ford, M. and Gathercole, P., *The Practical Fishing Encyclopaedia: A Comprehensive Guide to Coarse Fishing, Sea Angling and Game Fishing* (London: Lorenz Books, 1999).
Neale, I., *Shadows in the Stream: Seasonal Approaches to Game Fishing* (Shrewsbury: Swan Hill Press, 2002).
Orton, D. A., *The Good Fishing Guide: The Complete Angler's Directory for Coarse, Game and Sea Fishing in England, Scotland, Ireland and Wales* (London: Carlton Books, 2001).

Website:

International Game Fish Association: www.igfa.org

See also Angling, Coarse Fishing

*Nicholas Goddard
and John Martin*

Game Laws

Game laws are concerned with the legal rights and controls that exist with respect to a variety of animals. There is no overall definition of 'game'; rather, it has been defined for a number of Acts of Parliament. For example, the Game Act 1831 included hares, pheasants, partridges and grouse. Deer were added for the purposes of the Game Licences Act 1860, while the phrase 'ground game' refers to hares and rabbits. Wild animals are not considered to be goods or chattels and accordingly there are no absolute property rights in living wild animals. However a landowner or occupier has certain rights over game while it is alive on their land and absolute rights if it is dead.

Such rights are referred to as 'game rights'. Generally, such rights are bound with the ownership or possession of land and may be passed with occupation of the land or may be reserved even though there is a new occupier of the land. A landowner may therefore grant a lease to another person to occupy land while reserving the 'sporting rights'. If the sporting rights are not reserved they will pass on to the tenant.

Following the Ground Game Act of 1880 tenants were legally entitled to kill ground game (rabbits and hares), but the right to kill game birds (pheasants, partridges and grouse) was the right of the landowner. The rights to kill game birds could be determined by the agreement between the landlord and tenant, but will also be restricted by any of the protective legislation that applies to certain classes of wild animals.

Sources and Reading:

Howkins, A., 'Economic Crime and Class Law: Poaching and the Game Laws 1830–1880', in Burman, S. and Harrell Bond, B. (eds), *The Imposition of Law* (London: Academic Press, 1979).
Parkes, C. and Thornley, J., *Fair Game* (London: Pelham, 1994).

*Steve Greenfield
and Guy Osborn*

Game Shooting

For most people, the most esteemed and prestigious branch of shooting is game shooting, principally the pursuit of pheasants, partridges and grouse. Game also includes relatively localised species, such as capercaillie, ptarmigan and blackcock, as well as waders, woodcock and snipe. A salient feature of all these species is that they are protected by legally enforced close seasons and, since the 1970s, by a series of advisory codes drawn up by shooting and conservation organisations.

'Game' shooting is distinguished from more general 'rough' shooting not only by the type of quarry but also by the rules of the shoot. Organised game shooting is usually confined to predetermined species, with rabbits and other ground species being excluded in order to minimise the risk of accidentally injuring the other guns or the beaters when shooting at ground level. It has also been characterised by high levels of social etiquette, such as not shooting at birds going for a neighbouring gun and only firing at fast-flying high birds, which provide the most sporting shots. In contrast, rough shooting has not exhibited such rigid demarcations about the selection of quarry and the variety of shots, and the use of the shooters' own dogs to flush and retrieve is deemed much more permissible.

Most modern game shooters perceive driven grouse shooting in the uplands, where a small army of beaters drive the birds across heather towards the guns stationed in secluded butts, as the *crème de la crème* of sport. This style of shooting dates, however, from the late nineteenth century. Prior to that it was customary to use specially trained pointers or setters which, once they had scented the grouse, would stop dead, with head, body and tail aligned in the direction of the hidden cover. The guns took up position, one on each side of the pointing dog, which was then encouraged to move closer to the birds until they were flushed out for the guns. The decline of this type of shooting ('dogging') came about partly because of the intensification of moorland management, coupled with improvements in firearms technology, which enabled a move to driven shooting, particularly on the more favoured moors of northern England and Scotland where the careful management of the heather moorland habitat could maintain high densities of birds.

The golden age of driven grouse shooting lasted from about 1880 until the start of the Second World War. Its survival was dependent not only on suitable moors but also on the willingness of landowners and their paying guests to fund the costs of maintaining a suitable environment in which grouse could thrive. Record books reveal that one of the largest bags was achieved at Littledale and Abbeystead moors in Lancashire, where on the opening day of the grouse season on 12 August 1915, eight guns killed 2,929 grouse. Even during this golden age, population levels of grouse were subject to cyclical patterns, mainly due to the periodic flare-up of diseases such as strongylosis.

Since the end of the First World War, red grouse populations have experienced a long-term decline. Initially this contraction reflected the reduction in the number of gamekeepers and reductions in the level of expenditure on the management of moors. Grouse populations struggled to compete with the intensification of upland sheep farming, a process that has accelerated rapidly since the Second World War. This was often accompanied by forestation, which fragmented many existing moors and increased the number of the birds' natural predators. This decline in population densities led to a reduction in the more prestigious driven grouse shooting, for which wealthy shooters are willing to pay substantial premiums. On moors where bags are anticipated to be below 25 brace a day, providing insufficient birds for a party of shooters, it has been necessary to revert to dogging over pointers and setters and walking-up grouse with spaniels and retrievers.

Shooting driven grouse has attracted thousands of wealthy shooters, from both Britain and continental Europe, in late summer and early autumn and has made a valuable contribution to maintaining the viability of many upland areas by creating employment for a wide variety of service industries. The future of many of these upland areas has become precarious, balanced on the populations levels of grouse which are dependent on favourable seasons and are subject to cyclical patterns. Extensive research by the Game Conservancy Trust and other organisations has not yet managed to arrest the underlying long-term decline in their population levels.

In contrast, pheasants and partridges have dominated game shooting in the lowlands. For most of the nineteenth century, the grey partridge was the premier quarry in Britain and Ireland, a position it maintained up to the outbreak of the First World War, with many estates developing their conservation methods to a fine art. Driven partridge shooting with large numbers killed could only be undertaken on keepered shoots that were able to maintain a sufficiently high density of birds to warrant the deployment of large teams of beaters to drive the birds to the stationary guns. On specialist partridge manors, a highly sophisticated system of hedgerow keepering emerged, which involved finding and protecting nests. In some cases this even entailed replacing the eggs with pot substitutes, while incubating the real eggs under a broody hen until they were nearly ready to hatch before replacing them in the original nest. As with grouse shooting, the walking-up of partridges (using dogs to flush the birds) was frequently undertaken where the densities of birds were lower and also on smaller estates that could not justify the high costs of driven shooting.

English partridges were very difficult to breed in captivity, which encouraged the introduction to Britain of the larger red-legged partridges from France. When French partridges were shot using pointers or setters, the birds were reluctant to flush, instead creeping away and leaving behind a puzzled dog and a frustrated shooter. However, when driven they were more inclined to fly over the guns in ones and twos rather than as a covey, giving the sportsperson more opportunities for shots. In addition, the fact that they tended to fly straighter than grey partridges usually meant that the numbers of the imported species shot was out of proportion to its true numbers.

Since the First World War, partridge numbers have continued to decline, a process that accelerated rapidly in the latter decades of the twentieth century. In the 1920s, losses were sufficient to prompt Eley, Britain's largest shotgun cartridge manufacturer, to sponsor research into the causes of the decline. Subsequent studies undertaken by the Game Conservancy Trust in the 1970s confirmed that the decline could be attributed to a combination of three interrelated factors: increase in predation, the loss of habitat and reduction in food supplies (particularly insects for feeding young chicks in their crucial first few weeks of life). The revolution in farming practices since the Second World War markedly affected indigenous partridge stocks, a trend which shooting estate owners attempted to compensate for by the artificial rearing of partridges, particularly imported varieties. By 2000, however, commercial partridge shooting was confined to a number of specialised estates, with the vast majority of shooters having embraced the supremacy of the pheasant as Britain's most popular game bird.

As early as the late nineteenth century, pheasants began to supersede partridges as the shooter's main quarry since they were easier to rear artificially and large bags could be achieved more consistently. To the vast majority of shooters, pheasant shooting is associated with the 'battue' or 'covert' system, where organised teams of beaters drive the birds towards stationary guns. Driven shooting of this type reached its heyday in the early part of the twentieth century, when large estates vied with each other to achieve monumental bags, irrespective of the costs involved. On the 23,000-acre Elveden estate, for example, the Earl of Iveagh employed 70 men in the game department in order to maximise, with military precision, the shoot's achievements. On this estate in 1903, a party of eight guns, which included Edward VII, killed 3,948 pheasants in two days. In 1906 another party, which once again included the king, shot 4,310 pheasants in three days.

Pheasant shooting on this scale rapidly became an increasingly expensive activity, which could only be maintained by the wealthier and more dedicated landowner. The mass sale of estates, coupled with the decline in the number of gamekeepers during the First World War, marked a watershed for lavish expenditure of this kind. Reductions in the level of estate expenditure necessitated by the interwar depression and then the Second World War accentuated the long-term decline in this labour-intensive system of game preservation. This was accompanied by a shift to less-expensive methods of walking-up pheasants using dogs to flush the birds, which was essentially a more-refined variant of rough shooting.

Research by the Game Conservancy Trust shows that, since the 1960s, the number of pheasants shot per annum has continued to increase steadily, although the population levels of wild pheasants have declined. The increase in the size of the national bag reflects the rise in the artificial rearing of pheasant poults and their release in the autumn. Commercial game preservation has become concentrated in areas where shoots are sufficiently large to benefit from economies of scale and where full-time gamekeepers can be employed.

During the economic boom of the mid-1980s, the sport attracted the attention of weekend shooters and saw an increasing number of companies offering corporate hospitality to their clients and guests, many of whom were new to shooting. The quality of the sport was, in many cases, judged more in terms of the size of the bag rather than in the presentation of high-flying birds. The boom also led to a resurgence of game conservation, with many estates using it more as a revenue-generating activity. It encouraged the overintensification of rearing programmes, over-shooting, the neglect of sporting etiquette and inevitable criticism from both within and outside the shooting fraternity. Artificial rearing tended to increase faster than demand and, with the onset of economic depression in the late 1980s, there was a massive oversupply of pheasant poults and shoots.

One of the few advantages of the recession of the 1990s was that it undermined the demand for excessive bags of poor quality, immature birds, and led to attempts among the sport's representative bodies to place a greater emphasis on the presentation of the birds to the shooter. Intensive battue shooting has only been able to survive as a keepered activity where paying guns are willing to spend considerable sums of money on providing the necessary infrastructure to ensure sufficiently high densities of birds. Considerably lower densities of pheasants exist on unkeepered estates and farms, where shooters, including the farmers themselves, engage in pheasant shooting akin to rough shooting as an important and prestigious rural leisure activity.

Shooters occasionally pursue other species of game birds. One of the most geographically localised of these is the ptarmigan, a white variant of the grouse species that inhabits the subarctic Scottish Highlands, where the plant cover has become dwarfed because of the cold and wind and only mosses, bilberry, crowberry and tiny alpine plants survive among the scree and boulders. In the eastern Highlands the ptarmigan's range is usually above 800 metres, whereas in the western Highlands its range is above 600 metres, and on the storm-lashed Sutherland coast it descends down to about 200 metres.

Slightly smaller but otherwise similar in appearance to its better-known relative the red grouse, the ptarmigan differs in that it moults twice a year, in spring and in autumn. Its brown and grey summer plumage is transformed to an almost completely white plumage in winter, with only the tail remaining black. Pursuit of this game bird on the upper reaches of mountains takes the shooter to places they would not otherwise normally frequent. Unlike other types of game birds, ptarmigan population levels appear relatively static, amounting to a few thousand pairs, although the bird is no longer found as it once was in many of the uplands of Cumbria and the mountainous parts of Wales. Pressure from shooting is limited by the difficulty of accessibility and by the fact that the bird has limited appeal to the gourmet. Probably the best way for the modern enthusiast to record the bird is with a camera rather than as an entry in a game book.

The capercaillie is Scotland's most impressive game bird, a giant grouse that is confined to the ancient pinewoods. The species became extinct in Scotland in the nineteenth century but, following a successful reintroduction in about 1837, once more became established in localised pockets across the eastern and central Highlands. Population numbers have declined since the Second World War as a result of habitat loss, the increase in predation and the spread of wire deer fences into which the birds fly with fatal results. The capercaillie is occasionally shot on formal game drives, with a select number of estates organising special days in pursuit of this elusive and relatively rare bird.

Black grouse (or black game) is a species that survives on land in the margin between forest and moor. Once a widespread game bird, its range has contracted sharply since its heyday in the eighteenth century, now being confined to small, localised pockets. Black game are difficult to drive to guns and the birds occupy a fringe position for most upland shooters. The attractive lyre-shaped tail feathers of the male black game are a prized trophy for display in the cap badges of some Scottish regiments, making the bird a valuable asset on many estates. The continuing decline in black game populations has meant that those estates in south and north-east Scotland that were once fortunate enough to have annual black game days are now confined to seeing the bird only as a valuable addition to the bag on late-season grouse shoots. By the end of the twentieth century, a small number of dedicated shooters were still able to achieve a modest bag by dogging with pointers on the fringes of favoured moors.

Waders, such as woodcock and snipe, although not strictly game birds, are occasional but unpredictable visitors to most lowland shoots, where they may be shot as part of the normal day's activities. The woodcock is a highly prized species; its twirling flight pattern makes it a difficult target to hit. In the nineteenth century, in areas where the terrain was ideally suited to the migratory birds, specially organised shoots resulted in large bags of birds. In order to attract woodcock, many landowners planted large blocks of rhododendron bushes in their coverts, with open rides to encourage the birds. The popularity of woodcock shooting led to the breeding of the cocker spaniel specifically to flush the birds.

Agricultural intensification, coupled with afforestation, has led to a much wider dispersal of the resident woodcock population. Since the Second World War it has been virtually the only game bird to spread its range. At the end of the twentieth century, a few specialised woodcock shoots were still taking place in the Celtic fringes (western Scotland, west Wales, Ireland and Brittany), which are the traditional haunts of the overwintering population of European woodcock. In localised pockets, such as Bodmin Moor and the wilds of Pembrokeshire, sufficiently high densities occasionally exist to merit the employment of teams of beaters to drive the birds to stationary guns. The outcomes of these specialist woodcock forays are in stark contrast to driven pheasant shooting on well-organised estates, where the shooting days and the size of the bag can be closely predicted well in advance.

Like its relative the woodcock, the common snipe occupies a grey area in the laws on game. Neither species is technically classified as game and, as such, the open season for shooting and the close season for protection are not covered by the game laws, but rather by the Wildlife and Countryside Act of 1981. This legislation also gives total protection to the common snipe's diminutive and rather distant cousin, the jack snipe. Although they are regarded as wildfowl, a game licence is essential for shooting either woodcock or common snipe.

The snipe is a relatively common resident bird in Britain and Ireland, particularly in areas of bog. In the late nineteenth century, snipe were a favoured quarry of many shooters because of the testing targets they provided. Agricultural intensification, particularly improved drainage, which has taken place since the Second World War has severely curtailed the range of snipe, confining them increasingly to wetter areas, where they are pursued by a limited number of shooters.

Sources and Reading:
Brander, M., *A Concise Guide to Game Shooting* (London: Sportsman's Press, 1986).
McKelvie, C., *A Future for Game?* (London: Allen and Unwin, 1985).
Munsche, P. B., *Gentlemen and Poacher: The English Game Laws, 1671–1831* (Cambridge: Cambridge University Press, 1981).

See also Shooting, Shooting (Scotland)

*Nicholas Goddard and
John Martin*

Gimcrack Club

A horseracing club formed in 1767 and named after a famous racehorse of the time. Traditionally it held its annual dinner at York following the running of the Gimcrack Stakes in August of each year.

Sources and Reading:
Encyclopedia of Sports, Games and Pastimes (London: Fleetway, 1935).

See also Horseracing

Tony Collins

Golf

In looking for the origins of the game called 'golf', one has to establish the core features of the game: it is played over uneven terrain to a small target, namely a hole in the ground, by using a variety of clubs to make long initial shots followed by more precise shorter ones closer to the target. A number of such 'holes' comprise the complete game and the number of shots taken is counted. There is no race to the target, and the opponent's ball must not be interfered with.

In medieval times, golf probably emerged out of related European stick-and-ball games, which in turn can be traced back to hockey-like Greek sports. Support for the view that golf first originated in Scotland comes from a study of the closely related games in Europe. This shows they were not golf as defined above: Dutch 'colf' was a town sport favoured by children and played to a large target with a single club and large ball; 'chole' was a cross-country race that involved hitting a large ball using even larger implements. In addition, none of the European games survived over centuries with numerous societies and equipment production, as did golf in Scotland.

Early European games are illustrated in medieval *Books of Hours*, notably that of Jean duc de Berry, which shows a stick-and-ball game using a small ball and elegant long clubs as a noble pastime. A reasonable hypothesis is that interchanges between the royal and princely courts in Europe meant much copying of games, and the popularity of early golf with the Scottish monarchy and Stewart dynasty in particular is well known (even extending to a female player, Mary Queen of Scots). It is likely that in the interchanges golf emerged in Scotland as a stick-and-ball game appropriate to the county and moulded by local circumstance. An alternative is that the ancient Mediterranean hockey-like games that reached Ireland and changed into *camanachd* were brought by the Irish missionaries to the west of Scotland. However, the cost of the sophisticated early golf equipment makes it more likely that it was established as a noble courtly game first.

Winter was the time for early sports; summer had the cares of the harvest. Most European capital cities are inland and have a severe winter, with muddy parks and lasting snow and ice. Edinburgh, the capital of Scotland, has a relatively mild winter, largely ice- and snow-free, and at Leith on the coast nearby, the grassy links with tough, short grass were available for outdoor winter sport. The quality of turf had been greatly improved by the grazing of animals, notably sheep. St Andrews, the ecclesiastical capital of Scotland, had a similar opportunity, as did Aberdeen and many smaller coastal towns and villages. It is likely that well-off sportsmen used the extensive open links to develop a superior stick-and-ball game by encouraging construction of clubs and balls that would make shots travel as far as possible while retaining the need for finer shots closer to the hole. Such a winter game was not possible near the major towns elsewhere in Europe. The equipment became sophisticated and the existence of specialist artisans who made balls and clubs is known from royal purchases; the considerable expense involved shows the level of craftsmanship employed. These early clubs developed a hybrid construction, namely a head of hardwood joined firmly to an elastic softer shaft using methods familiar to bow-makers, giving maximum length of shot. The ball devised to travel furthest had a leather shell stuffed tightly with feathers.

This 'long' game of golf gave satisfaction, but played with expensive brittle equipment it was a costly sport. The many references to 'golf' as played by the humble are a puzzle, notably the encouragement in Acts of Parliament to ordinary soldiers to practise archery on Sundays after church rather than play golf. There were also many post-Reformation prosecutions of humble citizens and young men for playing golf on winter Sundays. These groups could not afford the expensive game, and their game must have been a cheaper imitation of the aristocratic long game that was seen on the links and watched with interest by the citizens. This other level of the game has been labelled as 'short' golf. This form of the game was often played in churchyards, and may have been similar to Dutch colf. Suitable cheap implements for the simpler short game were the home-made curved sticks and wooden balls known to be used in the hockey-like Scottish game of shinty. The two games may have been much more closely related in the Lowlands at this time than has previously been thought.

Short golf probably died out in the eighteenth century, leaving long golf to survive, perhaps the only surviving stick-and-ball game of this type in Europe with any substantial support. Some travellers noticed the game as a curious and unique feature of Scottish life. The vitality of the game is also evidenced by the emergence in Enlightenment Scotland of the world's first formal golfing societies, and to add to this there are traces of many cliques of aristocratic or professional men playing without written constitutional arrangements. Golf was played largely in winter as before, with evening conviviality at an inn being a routine addition to the outing. Betting was restrained, but drinking was not. The first written rules came in 1744 from the Edinburgh golfers playing at Leith, who included a large number of lawyers. It was the world's first golf club, namely an organisation with a membership, a captain, office bearers and rules for both play and membership. The routine style of play was person against person (match play) rather than counting scores for the whole round (stroke play); this is demonstrated by the absence of any rules governing stroke play incidents. Rapid match play was used within the cliques to determine the winner on important club days. A Masonic link has been proposed as a secret agenda of these early golf clubs, but since most Scottish gentlemen were openly Masons, and many gentlemen were also golfers, the finding that many golfers were Masons does not mean any conspiracy.

By the early nineteenth century there was a crisis in the game. There was war in Europe and the links close to the growing towns were now busier, with other activities making golf less comfortable. The Scottish golfing societies' memberships were shrinking, and even the pioneering Leith club folded following financial problems and fraud. Some players shared the decadence of the Regency period. Fortunes were made and lost on the gaming tables; there were also huge levels of betting in personal golf matches.

By 1850, society was more stable. Industrialisation meant the emergence of a new managerial cadre and better pay for the humble. The new urban society had summer leisure as holidays emerged, and the rural preoccupation with the summer harvest lost dominance over the sporting calendar. The spreading railway network, often taking the coastal routes through Scotland, beside the ancient golf links, meant new access to golf. An influx of day visitors and travellers from outside Scotland followed, notably to the healthy east-coast towns and villages which also had the golf links, sandy beaches and swimming. The growing need for wider availability of golf was met by the emergence of a new cheap golf ball made of gutta-percha (obtained in the Far East) and the use of tougher hickory wood (imported from Kentucky) for the shafts of golf clubs. The 'guttie' revolution was at first confined to Scotland, and is seen in the increase in the number of golf clubs in the 1860s and 1870s, and in the rise of golf in the west coast of Scotland, where equally good links and even milder winters existed. There was organisational pluralism in the new growth within Scotland. Larger numbers of players now played freely as before on the common land of many town links. Also playing on these open links were a growing number of small societies – 'clubs without courses' – from near and far, with minimal internal organisation and little written record. There were also many better-off golfing societies, also without courses but owning clubhouses at the edges of public links, of which the celebrated Royal and Ancient Golf Club of St Andrews is the best example. At this time, gambling and drinking became less obvious in society at large, and in the golf clubs in particular, and a new seriousness emerged as the vigorous temperance movements grew in strength.

An increasing number of makers of clubs and balls were supported by the Scottish growth of the game, and also at this time emerged the humble players who were the first golf professionals, players of skill outside the elite amateur clubs. Some of the gamblers' earlier energies were redirected from personal sport to support of challenge matches between rival professionals, and these noisy partisan occasions were to become a feature of golf for the rest of the century.

Growing numbers of English visitors now encountered the Scottish game and sought to set up clubs on returning home. At first these were set up on links land as in Scotland, but with the emergence of better earth-moving equipment and grass-cutting machinery, heathland was also found suitable. Other users of public land were hostile to the first experiments with this dangerous game outside Scotland, and the alternative necessarily meant purchase of land and construction of clubhouses. The result was membership from a limited moneyed social group; the game was often part of suburban snobbery and gained a middle-class label thereafter. The Scottish democratic game played on public space could not be replicated elsewhere.

In this rapid boom there was a demand for Scottish help with course design and staffing; after a club was formed it needed a greenkeeper to tend the course and a professional to teach the neophytes and supply and repair equipment. Unexportable, however, were the Scottish caddies, the free-spirited freelance men and boys who clustered round the links, and were famed for their knowledge of the game and their quick wit. There was deference to Scotland in matters of the rules and after any dispute the new non-Scottish clubs would turn to the Royal and Ancient Golf Club for guidance, a situation that remarkably still prevails today. Scotsmen also spread the game further afield; Scots employed by banks and industrial firms first took the game to Canada. Citizens from the United States, however, first encountered the game when they wintered in Europe on the aristocratic English winter circuit at the spas of Pau and Biarritz. Scottish golf, a game of the town's public land, was set on its way to be one of the world's most popular participation games, but in a subtly changed form.

Sources and Reading:

Gillmeister, H., 'Golf on the Rhine: On the Origin of Golf, with Sidelights on Polo', *International Journal of the History of Sport*, 19: 1 (2002), 1–30.

Hamilton, D., *Golf: Scotland's Game* (Kilmacolm: Partick Press, 1998).

Stirk, D., *Golf: History and Tradition 1500–1945* (Ludlow: Excellent Press, 1998).

David Hamilton

Grand Wardmote (of the Woodmen of Arden)

The Grand Wardmote is an archery competition played during August at Meriden in the West Midlands. The Woodmen of Arden archery society was founded in 1785 and membership is restricted to 80, drawn from the upper echelons of society. Each member wears the time-honoured dress of green hat and coat, buff waistcoat and white trousers. Their traditional longbows are made of yew, and the main prize is an old bugle.

Sources and Reading:
Day, B., *A Chronicle of Folk Customs* (London: Hamlyn, 1988).

See also Archery

Tony Collins

Grasmere Sports

A festival of traditional Cumberland sports – Cumberland wrestling, fell racing, pole-leaping and hound trails – which is held annually on the Thursday nearest to 20 August.

Founded in 1865 (although its supporters claim that it is descended from Viking and Saxon competitions), it built on the traditions of sports at fairs and festivals, in particular the town's September sheep fair. In 1870 it was moved to August to attract a bigger crowd. From the 1870s the event was supported by the local gentry, especially the Sandys and Machell families, as well as the Earl of Lonsdale.

The Grasmere Sports became a social occasion for sections of the aristocracy, and the event was moved from Saturday to Thursday to accommodate them. By 1890

the prize money available to competitors at the various events totalled £250, thanks to the patronage of the gentry. Guides' racing, foot races based on the routes used by tourist guides, was also initiated and introduced at the end of the nineteenth century.

The Grasmere Sports were also important in establishing hound-trailing, which involved hounds following an aniseed trail over the fell, as a replacement for hunting and cockfighting.

Sources and Reading:
Day, D., *A Chronicle of Folk Customs* (London: Hamlyn, 1988).
Martin, L., 'Sport in Cumbria, c1870–1939', *British Society of Sports History Bulletin*, 9 (1989), 51–62.

See also Egremont Crab Fair, Fell Running, Wrestling (Cumberland)

Tony Collins

Grouse Shooting (Wales)

Grouse shooting was common among the upper classes in nineteenth-century Wales and, despite the objective being purely to kill the birds, was described in the *North Wales Gazette* in September 1823 as 'a noble exercise, not only for the body, but for the mind'.

The shooting season traditionally began on 12 August and, in the Ebbw Vale area in Gwent, until around 1910 the Duke of Beaufort brought house-parties to shoot grouse on Llangynidr mountain. Following their arrival at the Rhyd-y-blew Inn, the groups were taken by horse-drawn trams to the nearby Trefil quarries, where they proceeded to the moorland butts to prepare themselves. The grouse were then driven overhead by beaters and subsequently shot down. In between shots, the gentry enjoyed sumptuous refreshments near the mountain spring.

Sources and Reading:
Gray-Jones, A., *A History of Ebbw Vale* (Ebbw Vale: Urban District Council, 1971).

See also Game Shooting

Emma Lile

Gun Dog Trials

These are formally organised competitions where working gun dogs are assessed in field conditions, using unhandled game that is shot for the purpose of the trials. In this respect the trials differ from the more open and informal systems that exist in America, where the judges think up a trial and engineer it with bird throwers and shooters.

Formal competitions are limited to gun dog clubs and societies that are registered with The Kennel Club and have been issued with a separate licence for the field trial. The performance of the dogs is evaluated by qualified panel judges who are appointed by the secretary of the organising club or society. The dogs are required to work a number of times under differing conditions. The Kennel Club's regulations specify the manner in which exercises are conducted for each breed.

In Britain, an application to enter a dog for a field trial does not ensure that it will be able to run; the number of entrants is strictly limited, with lots being drawn. Preference in the draw is given to dogs owned by members of the organising club and to dogs that have won previous awards. Gun dog trials of this kind were designed to improve the quality of the dogs by evaluating their working ability.

The origins of formal trials can be traced back to the development of specialised breeds of gun dogs during the transformation of shooting that took place in the late nineteenth century. Formal trials are confined to a small minority of gun dog owners. The majority of gun dog owners, many of whom are also shooters, work their dogs without joining one of the many breed societies or clubs and without entering their dogs in formal trials. Nevertheless, in the shooting field there is a deeply established tradition of judging each other's performance and that of their dogs on an informal basis. Societies also run dog shows where dogs compete against each other on the basis of their show points rather than working abilities.

Website:
The Kennel Club: www.the-kennel-club.org.uk

See also Shooting

John Martin

Guto Nyth Brân

– *see* **Morgan, Griffith**

Half-Bowl

Also known as 'roly-poly', the aim of half-bowl was to use a ball resembling half a cricket ball to knock over as many ninepins as possible. Seven of the pins are arranged in a circle, with another in the centre, known as the 'king'. Another pin is also placed about a foot outside of the circle, and is known as the 'jack'. The pin between the king and the jack is known as the 'queen'. Hitting the king scores 3 points, the queen 2 points and all the rest, except the jack, 1 point. If the jack is knocked over, the player who does so incurs a penalty of a deduction of all the points scored in that round before hitting the jack. For unknown reasons, the game was prohibited by Edward IV.

The game has similarities with kayles, with which it often seems to have been confused, although in kayles the pins seem to have been arranged in a straight line and a stick thrown to knock them down. Apart from the unusual shape of the ball, the game would appear to be a forerunner of ninepins.

Sources and Reading:
Gomme, A. B., *The Traditional Games of England, Scotland and Ireland* (London: Thames and Hudson facsimile edition, 1984).

See also Bowls, Kayles, Ninepins, Skittles

Tony Collins

Hallaton Bottle-Kicking

A variant of folk football but without a football, this is customarily played on Easter Monday at Hallaton in Leicestershire between men of the village and those of neighbouring Medbourne, although members of the latter side can be from any locality. The age and origins of the game are unknown.

The 'bottle' is small wooden cask filled with ale, of the type used by farm labourers when going to work, and the aim of the game is to score two goals. The game is played by propelling the bottle over a brook that divides the two parishes towards the appropriate goal, which is a hedge at one end and a stream at the other. Needless to say, the game rapidly develops into a mass scrum.

When a goal is scored, a second bottle is brought out, also filled with ale, and the game continues until a second goal is scored. If the second goal turns the game into a draw, a third bottle is brought out until the deciding goal is scored, although this bottle is not filled with ale.

The game is part of a wider Easter Monday custom that begins with a church service which blesses a locally made hare pie, although the pie is actually made of beef. Half of the pie is divided between churchgoers and the rest taken on a procession, with the three bottles, to Hare Pie Bank in the village, where it is cut into pieces and thrown to the crowd, after which the game begins.

Sources and Reading:
Morison, J. and Daisley, P., *Hallaton Hare Pie Scrambling and Bottle Kicking* (Hallaton: Hallaton Museum Press, 2000).
Whitlock, R., *A Calendar of Country Customs* (London: Batsford, 1978).

See also Football

Tony Collins

Hand Ba'

A variation of football, hand ba' is still played at five places in the Scottish Borders, the most celebrated of which is Jedburgh, where it takes place on the first Tuesday after the first new moon after Candlemas (in February). The game claims to date back to 1549, following the defeat of the English army at Ferniehurst Castle. It is played between those who live north of the town's market cross, the 'uppies', and those who live south of it, the 'doonies'. A boys' game starts at noon, and the main match begins at 2 p.m. Teams can be of any number, but the ball must be played by hand and cannot be kicked. The uppies' aim is to get the ball over the gates of the Castle, whereas the doonies must get it to the Jed Water at the town's foot. Banned in 1704 because of its violence, it was revived and, in 1849, survived another attempt to ban it when the High Court in Edinburgh upheld the footballers' appeal.

Sources and Reading:
Cooper, Q. and Sullivan, P., *Maypoles, Martyrs and Mayhem* (London: Bloomsbury, 1994).
Gorini, P., *Encyclopedia of Traditional Games* (Rome: Gremese International, 1994).

See also Football, Kirkwall Ba' Game

Tony Collins

Handball

A generic name originally applied to any game that involved a ball being propelled by the hand between two people, against a wall or between teams. Today, handball refers to two distinct games: the more traditional 'fives'-type game, especially Irish and Welsh handball, and the modern team sport that resembles soccer played with the hands.

As can be expected, the simplicity of hitting a ball with the hand means that handball has a long genealogy. The ancient Greeks had a handball game called *urania*, and various other forms can be seen at different times throughout the world. In 1926, a tombstone carving of what appeared to be handball players was excavated in Athens and dated to around 600 BC.

In England, handball games were sufficiently popular among the mass of the population to be banned in 1369 by Edward III and again in 1388 by Richard II. As can be seen with fives, a more organised version of the sport, handball was closely associated with pubs and churches, the walls of which providing the ideal surface against which to hit the ball. As well as fives, other variants of handball included 'pat ball', also known as 'balloon', which involved two people batting a hollow ball back and forth between each other, and has been identified as being a game played by girls and young women as far back as the fourteenth century.

Traditionally, Irish handball involved players striking a small hard ball, made from tightly bound leather and cloth, with the palm of the hand or a closed fist against a front wall, with the aim of serving or returning the ball so the opponent is unable to keep the ball in play. In Ireland the sport can be traced back as far as the sixteenth century, when the Town Statutes of Galway of 1527 forbade the playing of ball games against the walls of the town. Throughout the eighteenth century, handball became increasingly popular among both the aristocracy and peasant classes alike. The best handballer of his day was Fr John Murphy of Wexford, one of the chief leaders of the 1798 rebellion. Fr Murphy and his followers frequently held rebel meetings at his local handball alley. One of the catalysts of

this rebellion was the massacre of 40 suspected members of the United Irishmen on 1 June 1798, who were gunned down by loyalist forces in the handball court at Carnew in County Wicklow.

Irish migrants moving to England in the early nineteenth century introduced the 'one-walled' game to the English, and it is generally accepted that the returning Irishmen took back a revised version of the sport (which had the added feature of side walls).

Organised handball became a feature of the mid-nineteenth century, with the first professional tour taking place in 1850, when players such as Martin Butler of Kilkenny travelled across Ireland playing for money against local champions. It was during this period that Catholic teaching orders, such as the Christian Brothers, started promoting the sport within schools, both in Ireland and also abroad through their missionaries in South Africa, America and Australia.

The title of 'Champion of Ireland' was first contested in 1885, which was followed shortly by the contest between John Lawlor, the Irish champion, and American Phil Casey for the world title and a purse of $1,000, which Casey won. At this time interest and publicity for the sport were widespread, but organisation of the sport was chaotic and it was at this point that the Gaelic Athletic Association stepped in and attempted to rationalise it through codification of the rules and the organised promotion of tournaments.

In 1924 the Irish Handball Council was established under the auspices of the Gaelic Athletic Association and was allowed to govern the game independently, although to this day it remains part of the overall structure of the association. In the same year, the Irish Amateur Handball Association was established and its amateur status placed it in direct competition with the semi-professional Irish Handball Council; however, most players quickly transferred allegiance to the new association. The onset of the 1930s saw top players such as Soye, Perry and O'Neill become national celebrities and many were featured on sports cards similar to the baseball cards in America and other advertising media. However, this was the peak of the game's popularity.

Currently, there are three codes of Irish handball: the traditional game of hardball, played on a 60-foot by 30-foot court; softball, which is played with a lighter rubber ball; and the international game, which is played on smaller 40-foot by 20-foot courts.

Welsh handball, known in Welsh as *pêl-law*, is also a variant of the original handball game and has been played in Wales since at least the seventeenth century. It developed from the churchyard game of fives to one having its own purpose-built courts, often connected to public houses. Courts of varying dimensions were erected during the nineteenth century, especially in south Wales, and were either one- or three-walled. Singles and doubles matches were both customary, and were controlled by a referee and an official marker. Games were similar to squash minus the rackets, and although the exact rules differed between localities, play continued until a competitor failed to return the ball. It was only possible to score on service and the players' points were usually marked on the front wall in full view of everyone present. Matches generated great interest and large bets were often placed on their outcomes. In the 1870s, for example, Dr Ifor Ajax-Lewis of Llantrisant and Richard Andrews of Nelson challenged all-comers for a purse of £1,000. Handball matches are still held at Nelson in mid-Glamorgan, which boasts the last playable handball-court in Wales, dating from 1860. Handball underwent a revival in the 1980s with the formation of the Welsh Handball Association, founded in 1987 to protect traditional three-wall play, and in 1997 Lee Davies became the first world handball champion to hail from Wales.

The modern team sport of handball was developed in the 1880s and 1890s by Konrad Koch and Karl Schelenz, who adapted soccer rules for it. The basic principles are that it is a non-contact sport and that the ball cannot be kicked other than by the goalkeeper in the goal circles, which other players must not enter. It grew tremendously in popularity after the First World War and today the indoor seven-a-side variant is the most played version of the sport.

Sources and Reading:

Day, B., *A Chronicle of Folk Customs* (London: Hamlyn, 1988).

Dicks, K., 'The Most Famous Handball Court in South Wales', in Bacchetta, A. and Rudd, G. (eds), *Porth and Rhondda Fach* (Chalford: Chalford, 1998).

Jones, T. V., 'Handball and Fives', *Medel*, 1 (1985), 22–7.

Reeves, C., *Pleasures and Pastimes in Medieval England* (Stroud: Sutton, 1995).

Websites

United States Handball Association: www.ushandball.org/entertain/completehistory.html
Handball Ireland: www.handball.ie

See also Balloon, Fives

Tony Collins, Emma Lile and Annette Walsh

Hare Hunting

The pursuit of the brown hare with dogs predates fox-hunting as a leisure activity of the English aristocracy. Medieval and early modern writers gave pride of place to the hare. The celebrated treatise *The Master of Game*, written by Edward, Duke of York, about 1406, acclaims the hare 'as the king of all venery. For certain it is the most marvelous beast that is.' In a similar vein, Dame Juliana Berners, author of *The Book of St Albans* (1496), the first printed book on field sports in the English language, denotes the hare as 'Kyng of venery . . . the marvellest beast that is in any londe'. By the seventeenth and eighteenth centuries, the hunting of hares with small packs of beagles owned by private individuals of relatively modest means, such as the minor gentry and clergy, prevailed.

In the eighteenth and nineteenth century, increasingly specialised branches of the sport evolved, each with their own rules and different breeds of dogs suited for a different form of chase. Hares were either pursued on foot with packs of beagles or basset hounds, or on horseback using harriers. Basset hounds, while lacking the speed of the other breeds, are renowned for the excellent scenting ability and impressive voice.

As with fox-hunting, each pack of hounds has a master who is responsible for organising activities and the control of the hounds when hunting. Although hares are not formally protected with a close season, hunting starts in September and ends in March. The sport's governing bodies, the Association of Masters of Harriers and Beagles and the Masters of Basset Hounds Association, regulate hunting and enforce a code of conduct.

Opposition to hare hunting (and coursing) on humanitarian grounds has continued to intensify throughout the twentieth century, with constant parliamentary lobbying for the prohibition of the sports. In December 2003, hare hunting of all types was banned in Northern Ireland. The decline in this particular type of hunting throughout Britain has reflected not only social changes, but also the sharp falls in the population levels of hares as a result of the intensification of agricultural practices that has taken place since the Second World War.

Sources and Reading:
Hewitt, W. L., *Hare Hunting* (London: Seeley, 1975).
Plummer, D. B., *Lurcher and Long Dog Training* (London: Robinson, 1993).
Pye-Smith, C., *Hare-hunting: The Forgotten Field Sport* (Oakham: Wildlife Network, 1998).

Websites:
www.countryside-alliance.org/news/03/031217
　press.htm
www.ifaw.org/ifaw/dfiles/file_50.pdf

See also Coursing

Nicholas Goddard and
John Martin

Hawkey

This was a West Sussex version of bandy in which neither team can cross into its opponent's half of the pitch. The aim was to hit the ball so that it touched the boundary at the back of the opposing side's half. The first side to do so nine times won the game.

Sources and Reading:
Gomme, A. B., *The Traditional Games of England, Scotland and Ireland* (London: Thames and Hudson facsimile edition, 1984).

See also Bandy

Tony Collins

Haxey Hood

An 1836 witness to the Twelfth Night custom of 'Throwing the Hood' in Haxey in Lincolnshire was happy to report that the crowd attending was much smaller than usual. The 'coarse amusement' seemed to be 'losing much of its celebrity', although several hundred people joined in the game. In 1896 another visitor to Haxey on Hood Day observed much the same. Mr C. C. Bell believed that the custom would 'soon have to be numbered among the bygone amusements of English country life'. The number of key members of the custom's cast of players had dwindled from twelve to only four or five, and the quality of their performance was also in decline. The speech with which the Fool opened the proceedings, for example, was 'a very tame affair' compared with what it had been formerly: 'a great feature . . . the occasion of a good deal of topical wit and satire'.

The 'Hood', one of those wide-ranging mass 'football' games that were once common throughout the land but many of which disappeared during the nineteenth century, has proven far more resilient than either its Georgian critics or Victorian folklorists judged. At the opening of the twenty-first century it is firmly fixed in Haxey's annual calendar and is a core element of the village's history and culture. Indeed, since the 1920s when local people made the reinvigoration of their 'ancient custom' central to Haxey's process of mourning, memorialising and healing after the Great War, the hood may well never have been more secure.

The Hood is played on Twelfth Night, 6 January, after almost a week of associated rituals. These begin on New Year's Eve when the Hood's band of officers – the Lord, the Fool, the Chief Boggin and ten other Boggins – collect the 'sway hood' from the place of honour in which it has been displayed since the previous Twelfth Night, behind the bar of one of Haxey's pubs. The 'hood', the object over which participants in the game contest, is a leather cylinder some 24 inches in length and 3 inches in diameter, and the players' aim is to secure it and carry it off to their 'local'. In the week between New Year's Eve and Twelfth Night, the Hood band travels to pubs and private homes throughout Haxey and neighbouring parishes. They are treated to beer and rum, lead the assembly in singing three folk songs, and collect donations for local charitable and philanthropic causes. On the eve of the game they make their final preparations and tour Haxey's pubs, finishing up in the one that holds the hood. At midday on Twelfth Night they repeat this round and at about 2.30 p.m. assemble on a small green near the church. Standing on an old mounting stone, the Fool makes a speech inviting all to play and leads them in the Hood rallying cry:

> Hoose agen hoose
> Toon agen Toon
> If a man meets a man
> Knock 'im doon
> But doan't 'ot 'im'

The crowd then moves to a nearby ploughed field on Haxey Hill, the boundary with neighbouring Westwoodside, which is where the game proper begins.

There the Boggins form a cordon around the field and the Lord throws up the first of twelve sack hoods for the children's Running Hood game. Individual players try to capture a hood and make off with it to the nearest pub, where they receive a small cash prize. The Boggins try to prevent this. If they tackle and recover or even touch a hood before it is carried off the field, the cry 'Boggined!' goes up, the hood is then 'dead' and is returned to the Lord who throws it up for a fresh game. Once all twelve sack hoods have been carried off, the Sway Hood begins.

The Sway is the heart of the Hood, the core action. It is not for the faint hearted or the frail. It is a rough, sweaty, muddy trial of a tough, gritty kind of masculinity. Locked into a heaving, sprawling battle that can last hours, upwards of several hundred men scrummage for possession of the sway (leather) hood and try to move it through collective force to their goal. As daylight fades and one or other side gains momentum, the Sway picks up pace. At the entrance of the pub the landlord, making sure to keep one foot on his doorstep, reaches out to grasp the hood from the Sway and at that moment the game is won.

Antiquarians and folklorists have offered various explanations of the Hood's origins. In the nineteenth and early twentieth centuries scholars suggested that the custom was a residual of pagan sun and fertility rituals that might have included human or animal sacrifice. More recently the game has been associated with resistance to mid-seventeenth-century transformations in land rights and usage that accompanied the advent of agricultural capitalism in the area. But the most popular explanation of how the custom came in to being is the Lady de Mowbray legend. According to this, a medieval lady of the manor of Haxey was riding across Haxey Hill one Twelfth Night when a gust of wind caught hold of her hood and carried it away across the fields. Thirteen peasants working nearby saw what happened and chased after the headpiece. The one who retrieved the hood was too shy to return it to its owner and handed it to his friend to do so. Lady de Mowbray, delighted by the spectacle of the chase and the peasants' gallantry, promised every man a measure of land on Haxey Hill if they would re-enact the incident each year on Twelfth Night. To the one who first caught the hood her ladyship gave the name 'The Fool', his bolder friend she named 'The Lord', and the rest were 'Boggins'.

The documentary record of the Hood's history is not extensive and the earliest known reference is in W. Peck's *A Topographical Account of the Isle of Axholme* (1815). Other accounts appeared sporadically in the periodical press and folklore journals thereafter until the mid to late twentieth century when the custom became annual fodder for the local and regional media, and every now and then caught the national eye. Yet very many sources on the custom contain some version of the de Mowbray story, something that is probably very telling about the meanings that have accrued to it over the past two hundred or so years. The legend firmly anchors the Hood and therefore Haxey in the past, and thus asserts a dynamic link between the contemporary place, its people and their history. It speaks eloquently of Haxey's rural and agrarian roots and the people's historic relationship with the land; and it casts Haxey as a unique place, with a unique history out of which the unique custom of the Hood has – almost organically, it seems – sprung. In all these ways the Lady de Mowbray legend and the game of which it tells can be read as speaking volumes; in all these ways the Haxey Hood can be said to be much more than just a game.

Sources and Reading:
Colbeck, M., *The Calendar Year* (Leeds: EP Publishing, 1983).
Cooper, Q. and Sullivan, P., *Maypoles, Martyrs and Mayhem* (London: Bloomsbury, 1994).
Hole, C., *English Traditional Customs* (London: Batsford, 1975).
Simpson, J. and Roud, S., *A Dictionary of English Folklore* (Oxford: Oxford University Press, 2000).

Catriona M. Parratt

Hedge-Laying

Division of fields and properties by hedges was a significant feature of English agriculture as the enclosure movement took hold. Hedge-laying was widely promoted by Welsh agricultural societies formed from the mid-eighteenth century onwards, and competitions were frequently held to determine the most competent at the art. Between 1756 and 1763, Brecknockshire Agricultural Society awarded premiums for the re-laying of badly overgrown hedges, while at the end of the eighteenth century Anglesey Druidical Society offered five guineas to the person who exhibited the best quick-set hedge consisting of three rows of twenty roods or over. Hedging competitions were also encouraged by individuals. In 1869 the Reverend Roger Williams of Llanedi in Carmarthenshire was behind a hedging-match at which his farm-bailiff earned first prize for an exemplary hundred yards of stake fencing, banking and ditching.

Styles of hedge-laying varied across the regions of Britain. In the Midland shires, for example, where the majority of hedges were hawthorn, a specialised style of laying was practised. It was in this area too that cash prizes were frequently provided by members of hunts for hedgecutting competitions to encourage farmers to practise the art and not rely on barbed wire to strengthen their fences.

Emma Lile and
John Martin

High Diving (Wales)

Of the high diving events that took place in Wales, one of the most notable featured an American named Scott, who, in June 1838, leapt from the Menai Bridge in Caernarfonshire into the straits below. Scott's career came to an end the following

October, when he died during an attempt to jump into a canal in Stroud in Gloucestershire. In 1897, dock labourer and former Welsh champion swimmer Michael Kane high-dived off a ship in Swansea docks, seeking to beat a fatal 100-foot dive at Rhyl previously made by one Tommy Burn. Kane's dive, however, measured only 82 feet.

Sources and Reading:
The Cambrian (2 August 1897).
North Wales Chronicle (5 June 1838).

Emma Lile

Highland Games

Highland Games are an annual celebration in many rural and urban communities, both within Scotland and internationally. They include not only athletic events but also piping and dancing competitions, and they place a distinctive emphasis on feats of strength – the 'heavy' events of putting the shot, throwing the hammer, throwing a weight (for distance or height) and tossing the caber.

Highland Games have several origins, some of which date back to the eleventh century. They come partly from the informal practice of feats of agility, speed and strength, and, in their semi-formal expression, from the contests that were set up on the spur of the moment at weddings, funerals and *kirns* (harvest festivals). The apparatus of the heavy events consisted of everyday objects: throwing the blacksmith's heaviest hammer, putting a stone from the river bed, and tossing the *caber* (a tree trunk). The last of these is traditionally believed to have originated in the raising of the heavy timbers of a cruck-framed roof, the 'couples'. There is a modern flavour in some of this, however, because heavy hammers did not become common until industrially produced iron became much cheaper in the second half of the eighteenth century, at the time when smiths themselves became much more numerous in the Scottish countryside. Events were not standardised between different games: late in the nineteenth century putting the stone was done with a smooth stone at Inverness, but with a rough-surfaced iron ball at Luss and a lead ball with finger holes at Aboyne. Hammers differed in weight and length of the handle, and at some games the throwers were required to remain with their feet in one position.

Highland Games are also an example of the deliberate invention of tradition, both by landlords and by the people, though the gentry soon took over the management. The Games' emphasis on strength relates to the redefinition of the 'highlander' in the second half of the eighteenth century: having been a Jacobite rebel in 1745–6, he had become a valuable recruit for the British Army, making the Celt both picturesque and useful. The music of the bagpipe, a central part of Gaelic culture, was made up chiefly of laments and 'gatherings' (calls to arms). Piping competitions were held in the Lowlands from the early 1780s and later became subsumed within Highland Games. Sir Walter Scott picked up this enthusiasm for the Highlands and highland life: through his poems, starting with *The Lay of the Last Minstrel* (1805), and his novels, from *Waverley* (1815) onwards, Scott converted enthusiasm into mania. This was a major factor in, first, increasing the number of Highland games in the 1820s and 1830s, and later in maintaining the emphasis on traditional events and dress and in giving a leading place to local landowners in the ritual of the games day.

The first modern Highland Games were held at St Fillans in Perthshire in 1819. They were started by Peter Burrell, Lord Gwydir, an Englishman with a Welsh title who had married a Scots heiress, the only child of the Earl of Perth. St Fillans Games emphasised the value of Celtic traditions: solo piping, dress, language and games. Lairds started the games at Glenfinnan on the centenary of the raising of the Jacobite standard in 1745: the *Glasgow Herald* described how the 'the peasantry' watched from the distance.

Other early games stemmed from friendly societies, as at Strathdon, where the Lonach

Gathering starts with the march of the clans, emphasising community spirit. The rules of the Lonach Society (1825) gave its objectives as 'the preservation of the Highland Garb; and, as far as possible, the Celtic language; the support of loyal, peaceable, upright, and manly conduct; and the promotion of sociable and friendly feelings' – very much the same as at St Fillans. At Braemar, a 'wright's [joiner's] march' was first held in 1803, on the model of Lowland friendly society processions, and games were added to it in 1832. Queen Victoria first attended the Braemar Gathering in 1848, and it soon became closely associated with royalty. By the last quarter of the nineteenth century, the gentry controlled most games in the Highlands, but most of the competitors were (and remain) local people. Queen Victoria's patronage of the Braemar Gathering, and the Queen's enthusiasm for romance and tartanry, meant that the larger Highland Games emphasised these characteristics.

The Highland Games soon reached the Lowlands. There had been individual athletic events in a number of places, such as the foot races for a pair of red hose at Carnwath in Lanarkshire and on Fastern's E'en (Shrove Tuesday) at Kilmarnock. The small burghs up the Irvine Valley copied the latter. At the time of George IV's visit to Scotland in 1822, widely publicised Highland Games were held at Bannockburn in Stirlingshire. Six years later the sword of Prince Charles Edward Stewart was displayed at a gathering on the island of Inchcolm in the middle of the Firth of Forth. The only significant building on Inchcolm is the abbey which Alexander I had founded in the twelfth century: history was deliberately used to make games seem older than they really were.

In the late 1840s, following the development of the railway network, men emerged who could make their living from winning money at Highland Games. The first generally accepted national champion was Allister McHardie (1849): it might be argued that only the golfer Allan Robertson was recognised as a Scottish champion (at his sport) at an earlier date. McHardie was followed by the brothers John and William

Tait. They came from Glendorch, a remote sheep farm on a shoulder of the Lowther Hills: prizes at Highland Games were sufficient to attract men from the southern uplands.

Donald Dinnie (1837–1916), a mason from near Aboyne, was Scottish champion from 1856 to 1876 (with the exception of one year, when he was in America at the invitation of Caledonian clubs over there). As well as being immensely strong, he was a successful wrestler, high jumper and dancer. From 1903 until the First World War, the great figure was A. A. Cameron. Bill Anderson of Bucksburn was champion eight times between 1959 and 1973, challenged repeatedly from 1961 by Arthur Rowe, a Barnsley blacksmith and the first Englishman to be a major force on the Highland Games circuit. As an amateur, he had won the gold medal at the shot put in the 1958 British Empire Games, and in the 1970s prizes were large enough to attract Geoff Capes from Lincolnshire, a Commonwealth Games gold medallist in the shot put. The events themselves have changed little since the time of McHardie.

As well as the heavy events, there are also 'light' events: sprinting, distance running, and often the long jump and the pole vault. It is said that a hill race was held at Braemar in 1040, and nineteenth-century gatherings adopted the tradition where there was a suitable hill. Probably the earliest modern one was at Innerleithen in 1826, which set the pattern of shepherds being the leading competitors. Other events were Victorian standards, including fencing, rifle shooting and singlestick. The first tug o' war at a Highland gathering was at Braemar in 1871. The hop, step and jump (or leap) may be Scots in origin, for it appeared in various games in the middle of the nineteenth century. Prizes were almost always money, and as well as creating a professional 'circuit' they were sufficient to reward the local men who came second or third in major events or who won the minor ones needed to make up a full programme. In the 1940s it was still possible for a student to earn a healthy supplement to his scholarship money by picking up prizes at the dozens of minor games across the north-east.

In the 1840s there were perhaps two dozen Highland Games in Scotland, but by the end of the century the figure was in the region of a hundred. Highland Games, as they developed in the nineteenth century and as they exist today, form a heterogeneous group. Some are distinctly urban, such as Murrayfield (Edinburgh) and Airdrie, and many are local, with limited prize money; others are national events, such as Braemar and Luss. They can emphasise the heavy events, the light events, piping or dancing, and some are more important for sociability than for competition.

The Cowal Gathering at Dunoon was started in 1894. In 1906 a pipe-band competition was started there, which soon became the most important competition of the year, attended today by well over a hundred bands. The athletic events there are less important. In 1910, there was a crowd of 51,000 at the Cowal because the people of the industrial west of Scotland could reach Dunoon by steamer. Cowal thus has an ambiguous identity, the traditions within the games park being Highland, but the activities in the bars and streets are Glaswegian. The demand for summer games was such that other events were started by football clubs, the only existing sporting organisations which had professional management. These games were, in general, less explicitly Scottish, for they lacked tartan and bagpipes, though they often included the heavy events. By the 1890s they were more willing than traditional gatherings to adopt novelties such as cycling. Most Lowland games also included quoiting, which, although popular with working men, was a gambling sport and so unacceptable to games run in the Highland Games ethos.

In the 1930s, some of the Highland Games in the Lowlands attracted crowds of tens of thousands, not always in the most obvious places. The games at Alva, a textile-weaving town east of Stirling, were noted for their high attendance. At Thornton in Fife, a village with excellent rail connections to Glasgow, Edinburgh, Dundee and the Fife

mining towns, but in fact not much more than a railway junction, the crowd is said to have reached 70,000 just before the Second World War. The largest shinty crowd ever is said to have been the one at the Murrayfield (Edinburgh) Highland Games in 1947, at which Kingussie and Newtonmore played an exhibition match. The other events were for money prizes, but shinty was strictly amateur, so Newtonmore, the winners, were given sets of aluminium cooking pots, then in short supply. It became known as 'the pots and pans match'.

The first Scottish Border Games were at Innerleithen in the Tweed valley. They were started by the poet James Hogg (1770–1835) in 1826, and named the St Ronan's Games because Walter Scott's novel *St Ronan's Well* (1824) had been set in Innerleithen and Hogg admired the way in which Scott valued the ordinary people of Scotland. Hogg, a farmer himself, believed that the lives of ordinary people had been made poorer by the Napoleonic Wars. Farmers had made huge profits in wartime, and instead of dining with their workers they now set themselves apart. Increasing numbers of people were being forced to labour in textile mills. Hogg saw summer games as a way of celebrating their lives, and he assembled a programme which included many traditional events, including hill running and football. While Hogg lived, his fame attracted wide attention to the games, and after his death they continued, although in a less conspicuous way.

The St Ronan's Games were copied by other towns. At Border Games, wrestling and jumping events were particularly important. The latter included the 'hitch-and-kick' in which a tambourine was suspended in the air and the winner was the competitor who kicked it at the greatest height (the term was later transferred to a technique used in the long jump). Games, however, could take many forms and be held for a variety of reasons. In the 1850s the Earl of Galloway held the House o' Hill Games in a remote place in the Galloway hills as a way of thanking shepherds for their help in preserving game; the sports were followed by a dinner.

Although most games were held in summer, a few were on holidays at other times. At Cullen on the Banffshire coast, football, foot races, bowling games and throwing events were held on the sands on Hallowe'en. It was a community event: the young people walked to the beach behind a piper and in the evening there was a dance at which the best competitor wore a bonnet decorated with ribbons which had been made by the women of the village.

The Victorian period also gave rise to emigration overseas and from this exodus numerous Caledonian societies, in the United States, Australia, Canada, New Zealand and many other places, incorporated Highland Games into the festivities of *émigré* communities. Traditional games in Scotland have become associated with modern tourism. Cultural celebrities such as Billy Connolly and Robin Williams regularly attend the Lonach Highland Gathering, while the *Mission Impossible* and *Enigma* star, Dougray Scott, was chieftain to the 2003 Markinch Highland Games in Fife. The actor Ewan McGregor has similarly been chieftain to the Crieff Highland Games, which date back to 1819. The professional Highland Games circuit is run under the auspices of the Scottish Games Association. More international than global, the Scottish Highland Games continue to play an important role in local communities, from Airdrie to Arkansas, Braemar to Boston, and Skye to San Francisco.

Sources and Reading:
Jarvie, G., *Highland Games: The Making of the Myth* (Edinburgh: Edinburgh University Press, 1991).
Jarvie, G., 'Highland Games', in Jarvie, G. and Burnett, J. (eds), *Sport, Scotland and the Scots* (East Linton: Tuckwell Press, 2000), 128–42.
Jarvie, G., 'Highland Games, Ancient Sporting Traditions and Social Capital in Modern International Communities', *Studies in Physical Culture and Tourism*, 10: 1 (2003), 27–37.
Lonach Highland and Friendly Society, *Rules and Regulations* (Aberdeen: Chalmers, 1825).
Ray, C., *Highland Heritage: Scottish Americans in the American South* (London: University of North Carolina Press, 2001).
Webster, D., *Scottish Highland Games* (Edinburgh: Reprographia, 1973).

Website:
The American-Scottish Foundation: www.asgf. org

*John Burnett and
Grant Jarvie*

Hockey

Hockey is the modern form of the various games in which a ball is propelled by a stick, most obviously bandy, hurling and shinty. The name is possibly derived from the old French word for a shepherd's crook: *hoquet*. The first recorded use of the word refers not to a sport but to the stick – in 1527 it was noted in Galway that 'hockie stickes' were used for 'horling'. No other mention of the word can be found until 1785, when William Cowper cites it in one of his letters as the name of a game played in Olney.

Modern hockey traces it lineage from the rules drawn up at Eton College in 1868. As with the various codes of football, a number of public schools, such as Marlborough and Winchester, played their own version of the sport, as did a number of clubs such as Blackheath, formed in 1861, the first hockey club. The first set of modern rules was drawn up by London clubs in 1875 and the Hockey Association was formed in 1886.

Sources and Reading:
The Encyclopaedia of Sport (London: *The Sportsman*, 1912).
Miroy, N., *The History of Hockey* (Hemel: Chiltern, 1989).

See also Bandy, Camogie, Hurling, Shinty

Tony Collins

Hop, Skip and Jump

The direct precursor of the modern triple jump, 'hop, skip and jump' was popular in Ireland, Scotland and the north of England, where it was sometimes called 'hop, stride and loop'.

Sources and Reading:
The Encyclopaedia of Sport (London: *The Sportsman*, 1912).

See also Highland Games

Tony Collins

Horse Events (Wales)

Having existed at an informal level since the medieval period, organised horseracing developed in Wales during the seventeenth century under the patronage of leading gentry families. Although the sport was initially confined exclusively to the social elite, with meetings tending toward family events rather than public occasions, by the eighteenth century it had started to acquire a wider appeal. From the 1720s onwards one of the centres of racing in Wales was Haverfordwest in Pembrokeshire, where the town's annual races, usually spread over four days, attracted large crowds. Other recognised eighteenth-century Welsh flat races included those at Cowbridge, in the south, and Holywell, in the north. By the early nineteenth century, courses were so numerous nationwide that competitors were not required to travel far to race. In 1830, the *Racing Calendar* listed 125 Welsh courses at which flat racing took place. Up until the 1870s, local race meetings relied heavily on the financial support of the landed classes, who regarded their donations as a means of demonstrating their social status.

Trotting matches were held during the nineteenth century and were particularly popular with farmers and tradesmen. They often took place in conjunction with horse races and athletic sports, though separate trotting contests for wagers were also known. In 1829, a trotting match for 100 sovereigns between Mr Bonner's Glamorgan pony and Mr Perry's Flintshire pony was reported in the *Monmouthshire Merlin*, the animals trotting in harness over a course of 10 miles in front of a large crowd of spectators. Several trotting events against the clock were recorded, such as the attempts by Mr Platt of Bangor in Gwynedd in 1833 to trot a mile in 3 minutes, and by Mr Bagnell of Llanfoist in Gwent in 1838 to trot 2 miles in 8 minutes; both were unsuccessful.

The first point-to-point steeplechase held in Wales was that run by Cardiff and County Club horsemen in April 1887, when jockeys in hunting costume competed across a 4-mile course. Point-to-point was so popular in Cardiff by 1890 that it had succeeded in eclipsing the professional form, and when the sport arrived in west Wales in 1892 it engendered great excitement among the local sporting gentry.

As elsewhere in Britain, carthorse races took place across Wales during the nineteenth century, and prizes, such as bridles, were awarded to the winners. Yet not all horse races involved only equine competitors. According to legend, one of the impressive achievements of the champion eighteenth-century runner Guto Nyth Brân was to outrun a horse. Since 1980, a marathon event of 22 miles has been held at Llanwrtyd Wells in Powys in memory of Guto's win, yet despite a 15-minute head start for runners, none has yet been victorious.

Sources and Reading:
Lee, B., *The Races Came Off: The Story of Point-to-Point Racing in South and West Wales 1887–1985* (Cardiff: Welsh Sporting Publications, 1986).
Monmouthshire Beacon (29 September 1838).
Monmouthshire Merlin (27 June 1829).
Moore-Colyer, R. J., 'Gentlemen, Horses and the Turf in Nineteenth-Century Wales', *The Welsh History Review*, 16: 1 (1992), 47–62.
North Wales Chronicle (15 January 1833).

Thomas, W. ('Glanffrwd'), *Glanffrwd's History of Llanwynno* (Translated by Evans; Merthyr Tydfil: Southey, 1950).

Emma Lile

Horseracing

Informal horseracing has taken place throughout Britain wherever land and leisure have been available and owners have fancied their horse to beat a rival's. The Romans were said to have introduced the sport, although evidence suggests that horses had been domesticated, and possibly raced, as early as the Bronze Age. The Roman contests at York and perhaps other towns probably featured chariot racing in preference to bareback mounted horse races, the only option in an age before saddles were invented. There are references to racing horses from *Beowulf* in Anglo-Saxon times, to specialist 'running horses' from the ninth century onwards, and to horse sales and races at Smithfield in twelfth-century London. In Scotland there are claims of racing at Lanark in 1160 and an isolated record of races at Leith in 1503–4. The sport was probably more widespread in this early period but its informal nature has left little documentary evidence.

The sixteenth and early seventeenth centuries produced more-tangible proof of horseracing. Trophies were given by wealthy families or town councils – for example the tiny Carlisle Bells, dating from 1599 and the oldest still extant, which were intended to be fastened to the bridle of the winning horse. The wooden ball thought to have been presented at Chester races in 1511–12 had become a silver bell by 1540, the year in which the oldest surviving racecourse was laid out at the Roodee, just outside the town walls. There was racing in Scotland at Haddington, Peebles and Stirling before 1600, and the surviving Lanark Silver Bell dates from around 1608–10, although it is believed to have a history stretching back several hundred years earlier. A course was mapped out

on the Town Moor at Doncaster in 1595, and the earliest known rules of racing were drawn up at Kiplingcotes in Yorkshire in 1619. This county was to become the heartland of racing and breeding over the next 200 years, challenged and eventually eclipsed by only one other area – the vast expanses of Newmarket Heath.

The Stuart kings were responsible for the growth of Newmarket into the racing capital of Britain, a position it still holds today. Originally used as a hunting ground by James I, who is known to have attended a race there in 1619, it was further developed by his son Charles I, during whose reign the first course was laid out and a grandstand erected. But most of the folklore of the town attaches to Charles II, who made twice-yearly visits from the mid-1660s. He re-established the pattern begun by his father of spring and autumn race meetings, which still frame the Newmarket racing calendar over three centuries later, and also founded the oldest remaining horse race, the Newmarket Town Plate, which he is said to have ridden in and won in 1671.

Throughout Britain, the Restoration led to new race meetings and the revival of old ones. Racing became a fashionable pastime for the aristocracy and gentry, who engaged in match racing between two horses, on which large sums were wagered. Races also took place at local fairs dating back to pre-Reformation times. They were frequently held on public holidays and featured farmers' and tradesmen's horses, often competing for simple prizes such as a saddle or a pair of spurs. Others continued to be sponsored by the local burgh or magnate, whose trophy, once a simple bell, had now become a drinking cup or punch bowl, an early mark of racing's association with alcohol. Meanwhile, the monarchy maintained its support for elite racing. After the death of Charles II, both William III and Queen Anne, founder of Ascot racecourse, actively encouraged the sport, funding prizes, developing the Royal Stud at Hampton Court and appointing the first recognised trainer-manager, Tregonwell Frampton, to arrange matches at Newmarket.

The seventeenth and early eighteenth centuries also saw far-reaching developments in horse breeding with the importation of bloodstock from the Middle East. Tradition has it that the modern racing thoroughbred is descended from three stallions brought to England between 1690 and 1730 (the Byerley Turk, the Darley Arabian and the Godolphin Arabian). Recent research, however, has drawn attention to the significance of other Eastern horses and emphasised the contribution of mares to the genetic make-up of the breed. What is not disputed is the importance of Yorkshire as a location for the studs that supplied most racehorses. The Darley Arabian spent his life there, as did his son Bartlet's Childers, the progenitor of a strong thoroughbred dynasty. These horses and their offspring were much smaller than the average racehorse of the twenty-first century, often measuring little more than 15 hands (150 centimetres to the shoulder). The pattern of their race careers was also different: few were raced till they were five or six years old and the best were seldom tested on the racecourse. Flying Childers, another son of the Darley Arabian and reputed to be the best of his day, had his first race in 1721 aged six and his second, and last, the following year.

Early racing had an informality wholly lacking today. The course was marked out with occasional posts, spectators on horseback frequently followed, and sometimes overtook, the runners and several judges were appointed in an effort to identify the winners. The races themselves were long – 4 miles (6.4 kilometres) was a common distance – and many were run in heats, the winner being the horse to reach the finishing post first on two occasions. Horses carried heavy weights of 10–14 stone (64–90 kilograms), and some were ridden by their owners. There were no official races in the winter, with the season following the pattern of the present turf flat racing calendar, roughly mid-March to early November. The most popular race days, then as now, took place in the summer, but unlike today very few were held at weekends as Saturdays were market days and Sunday was the holy day of the Christian church. A race meeting might last an entire week, timed to coincide with an important regional event such as county assizes when society mixed business with pleasure at theatres and balls, or it might last only one afternoon, taking place on a local fair day or traditional holiday.

Wherever it was held, racing was always associated with having a good time – an occasion at which large crowds gathered to spend money on food and drink, and to gamble on horses and sideshows. John Cheny's first *Racing Calendar* (published in 1727, listing all the races valued at £10 or more that had taken place in England during the year) showed that meetings were held at 112 courses, but there would have been many other courses too insignificant to feature. So popular had horseracing become in the eighteenth century that in 1740 Parliament attempted to suppress the least valuable meetings that had sprung up at small towns and villages throughout the country, allegedly to the moral and financial detriment of the local population. To prevent 'the excessive increase of Horse-races' and 'excessive and deceitful Gaming', an Act was passed to raise the minimum value of any race prize to £50. The Act dealt a fatal blow to the smallest events, but although racing was concentrated on fewer courses in the short term the number of courses began to recover in the second half of the century after the Act's repeal in 1750. When James Weatherby published his first *Racing Calendar* in 1773, continuing the work of Cheny and others, there were 97 racecourses listed: 50 years later there were 125, not including those considered too paltry to be mentioned.

It was during the latter half of the eighteenth century that racing began to adopt more familiar aspects. Grandstands were built at major racecourses to accommodate wealthier patrons with substantial buildings erected at York, Doncaster and Richmond (Yorkshire) before 1780. Races for three-year-olds, first tried out in the 1730s, increased in popularity and three of the Classics – the St Leger, the Oaks and the Derby – were inaugurated, the first at Doncaster in 1776, the other two at Epsom in 1779 and 1780 respectively. Less-mature animals had to be raced over shorter distances and under smaller weights, leading to contests of 1–2 miles (1.5–3 kilometres) and the use of artificially light professional jockeys. Sprints were introduced featuring yearlings – though these were later banned – and two-year-olds. By the 1820s, nearly half of all recorded races were for animals under the age of four, while traditional heats and match races went into decline. Other developments included the birth around 1752 of the Jockey Club (at Newmarket). Destined to become the governing body of horseracing a century later, it was at this stage simply a racing club that organised meetings for the benefit of its members. Weatherbys, eventually the administrative arm of the sport, was founded in the 1770s by James Weatherby, the Keeper of the Match Book at Newmarket, who not only undertook the publication of the *Racing Calendar* but also, in 1791, the first *General Stud Book*. There were handicappers and bookmakers operating before 1800, and the specialist public trainer, in addition to those employed privately by major owners, could now be found, particularly at Newmarket. The cult of the personality also started to develop in an embryonic way. Sam Chifney and Frank Buckle became well-known jockeys, with Buckle's record of 27 Classic wins only surpassed in recent times. Robert Robson trained 33 Classic winners between 1793 and 1828. Eclipse was the champion horse of the late eighteenth century, never beaten in 18 races and an outstanding sire until his death in 1789.

However, the changes in horseracing have to be viewed alongside the many continuities. Traditional locations in the countryside, and especially on the edge of market towns, were still the norm. Courses were unenclosed and spectating remained free, unless the wealthier racegoer chose the segregation of a grandstand. The elite end of the sport continued to be dominated by wealthy, aristocratic owners, many of whom acted as stewards, patrons and donators of prizes. Parish races attracted crowds for which a race day was often the entertainment highlight of the year. Meetings in Wales, Scotland and the more-remote English counties still proudly advertised contests restricted to locally bred horses. Throughout Britain, races were organised by a local committee with local rules. In 1800, the age of standardisation and central control was not yet on the horizon.

Sources and Reading:

Birley, D., *Sport and the Making of Britain* (Manchester: Manchester University Press, 1993).

Burnett, J., *Riot, Revelry and Rout: Sport in Lowland Scotland before 1860* (East Linton: Tuckwell, 2000).

Middleton, I. and Vamplew, W., 'Horse-Racing and the Yorkshire Leisure Calendar in the Early Eighteenth Century', *Northern History*, 40: 2 (2003), 259–76.

Vamplew, W. and Kay, J., *Encyclopedia of British Horseracing* (London: Frank Cass, 2005).

Joyce Kay

Horseracing (Scotland)

Horseracing was from the sixteenth to the middle of the nineteenth century the most important spectator sport in Scotland. It existed in four forms, which can be labelled as: elite, traditional, ordinary country and draught-horse racing.

Elite racing, in which noblemen and the landed gentry owned the horses, was organised chiefly by the burghs before the second half of the eighteenth century. The premier venue was Leith sands, three miles from Edinburgh. The course was entirely on the sands, and the horses raced two miles out to a *stoup*, a post driven into the sand, then back past another post a quarter of a mile from the finish, and so to the winning post. The time of day at which the races were held depended on the tide. Other towns had their racecourses at a similar distance, including the English burgh of Berwick-upon-Tweed whose course on Lamberton Moor was in Scotland. Scottish meetings tended to be smaller than English ones, and the quality of the racing was often poor. At Leith, the supply of horses was often so limited in the eighteenth century that there was only one race each day, run in heats.

There was significantly more activity after 1750. Kelso races started in 1760. At Ayr the burgh put up a gold bell as a trophy in 1609 and there is evidence for later races on the sands, but in 1770 a formal course was laid out on the Town Moor through the backing of the gentry of the county. Safely distant from the cities and their crowds, Ayr became the most fashionable Scottish race meeting, and its premier race, the Ayr Gold Cup, dates from 1804. Around 1800, Leith races attracted massive crowds, particularly on the Saturday of race week, when racing was followed by a free fight among the spectators.

In this period Scottish racing was, however, generally conservative and of lower quality than in the south. In England there was an increasing move towards short races with younger horses, producing more-even fields and more interesting gambling. At Kelso in 1803, however, four horses appeared to race in four races, one in each race, and each won by walking the course. Leith races were last held in 1815. Their replacement by an event at Musselburgh, further from Edinburgh, where the course was on the links, led to better behaviour, smaller crowds and (in popular estimation) a great loss of status. The old emphasis on strong horses, which had the stamina for four miles of heavy going, was replaced by opportunities for faster animals. Scottish racing remained parochial: owners from the west of Scotland won the Ayr Gold Cup every year from 1804 to 1835, and English winners did not become common until the first decade of the twentieth century.

The Royal Caledonian Hunt Club was founded in 1777. Its role was to patronise race meetings with the aim of increasing their quality. The racing was accompanied by other activities: sometimes hunting in the morning, and in the evening dinners, balls and theatrical performances. The Hunt Club meetings were like the larger 'county' race meetings in England, but, with Scotland's lesser agricultural wealth and smaller aristocracy, they had to move around the country rather than being based in one town.

As elsewhere in Britain, the number of race venues in Scotland has declined steadily since the 1820s. The influence of the evangelical wing of the Kirk, which separated in 1843 from the Established Church to form the Free Church of Scotland, was a factor in the demise of the meetings at Cupar (last held in 1841), Dumfries (1847) and Stirling (1854). The Free Church was particularly hostile to gambling. In 1870 there were still nine courses in Scotland but by 1914 only four: Kelso, Ayr, Musselburgh and Scone (Perth). Racing was resumed at Hamilton in 1926.

In the nineteenth century, Glasgow people had to go some distance for their racing. The most popular venue was Ayr, whose crowd had ceased to be exclusive. Steamboats were sailing to the races in the 1830s and the Glasgow and Ayr Railway opened in 1840. Ayr had several two- or three-day meetings and its status was recognised by the suffragettes, who burnt down the grandstand in 1912. Racing was held at Bogside, near Irvine, from 1808 to 1965, with some gaps. The course was owned by the Earls of Eglinton until 1924 and was sometimes known as Eglinton Park. Steeplechasing is said to have been introduced to Scotland at Bogside, though races had been held across open country a few years earlier. Bogside was the venue of the Scottish Grand National from 1867 to 1965.

There were also fixtures at Stirling (to 1854), Airdrie (1853–70) and Paisley (to 1907), which were all accessible by train from Glasgow. For short periods, meetings were held closer to the city at Pollok (1838–9) and Maryhill (1869). The latter was a commercial speculation and was the first attempt in Scotland to charge for entrance to a race meeting; however, policing was inadequate, the crowd charged down the fencing, and the stewards reluctantly allowed the races to be held, fearing a riot if they were not. The course at Hamilton Park, 9 miles from Glasgow, opened in 1888, when the first meeting was held in the week of Glasgow Fair; the capital for the course came from the whisky trade.

During the nineteenth century, Scottish racing slowly became integrated with sport south of the border. When Kelso, with heavy investment from the Duke of Roxburgh, grew in status between 1780 and 1830, it began to attract racegoers from the north of England. The power of the Newmarket-based Jockey Club grew and its insistence on races having prizes over £50 for each flat race ended the meeting at Airdrie and discouraged others. The Jockey Club also withdrew the licence to race at Paisley on the grounds that the course did not comply with its requirements.

Since the eighteenth century, however, Scottish lairds had been involved with the English turf. They raced their horses in England, where the standards and prizes were much higher. For example, the Earl of Eglinton owned Flying Dutchman, which won the Derby in 1849 and a famous match against Voltigeur at York in 1851. The Duke of Portland, who had large estates near Kilmarnock, won the Derby in 1888 with Ayrshire. The horse had been trained at Malton, though its name indicated a major source of the duke's income. James Merry, the Motherwell ironmaster, had several Classic successes and employed as one of his trainers Matt Dawson, who had begun at Gullane on the East Lothian coast but had moved south. In 1891, training at Gullane ended when Muirfield golf course was laid out on the gallops.

Race meetings were sometimes the occasions for other sporting activities, though far less so than in England. Cockfighting and pugilism were rare. Kelso, closest to England, was the one meeting where miscellaneous events were likely to crop up, as in 1822 when there was a wrestling competition and a blind man walked 90 miles in 24 hours for a wager. In some places there were also foot races and jumping competitions. Occasionally, as at the Northern Meeting at Inverness in 1821, horseracing has been held at Highland Games.

Traditional racing was held in the Western Isles on Michaelmas (29 September), a much more important holiday there than in the Lowlands. The racing was not, however, particularly competitive. Before the race, young women gave the men a fertility symbol, usually a wild carrot. At the start, a young man and woman shared the horse; it was said to be lucky if she fell off. These races ended when the Evangelical revival spread through Scottish Gaeldom in the first half of the nineteenth century. The last race of this kind was held in North Uist in 1866.

In lowland Scotland the 'broose', a race from the church or place where the marriage had been held to the bride's house, was held after a wedding. It was named after the original prize, a dish of *broses* (rich broth), but the prize later became a drink of ale or whisky or a handkerchief. Originally it was a contest for good luck, but the winner also achieved local celebrity: the practice seems to have been at its peak in the decades around 1800. In 'The Auld Farmer's New-Year Salutation to his Auld Mare, Maggie' (1786), Robert Burns praised the plough horse's former prowess: 'At brooses thou had ne'er a fellow / For pith [stamina] and speed'. The broose survived until just before the First World War.

It is easier to provide illustrations of ordinary country racing than it is to make confident generalisations about it. The country meeting was the venue for farmers and minor lairds to race their horses. The mock-heroic 'Lament for Habbie Simpson, Piper of Kilbarchan' (*c*.1660) by Robert Sempill of Beltrees remembered that Habbie played 'at horse races, many a day' around Renfrewshire – pointing to the fact that music and sociability were as important as the racing itself. In the eighteenth century, these meetings were more densely scattered in the west and south-west of Scotland than elsewhere. Some were events started purely as races, others were old local holidays to which a race had been added, and a few were started by innkeepers who sought to increase their trade. At least one, at Whitletts near Ayr in 1820, was intended to boost a new cattle show: it failed.

Farmers also raced their horses in informal wagers on the high road. The loose scatter of newspaper references available suggests that when in the last quarter of the eighteenth century Scotland changed from being a poor country to being a comparatively wealthy one, farmers acquired horses to ride rather than to set to the plough or the cart. Whether a race was decided upon on the spur of the moment or over dinner or a dram, the new turnpike roads were an ideal venue.

The first record of draught-horse races in Scotland occurs at Dumfries in 1660 – presumably part of the Restoration enthusiasm for all forms of horseracing and gambling. In the eighteenth century, races are known at Sanquhar, and also in Dumfriesshire and at Kelso; they may not have existed for more than a few years. At Newton-on-Ayr, the little burgh facing Ayr on the north side of the river, in 1746 the carters started to race their horses – perhaps as a gesture of loyalty to the Hanoverian monarchy. The carters' staple trade was the carriage inland of smoked salmon, and their Kipper Fair was celebrated on the first Friday after the end of the salmon-fishing season (12 August). On the evening before, the carters paraded at the house of their captain, who served cheese and whisky. On the morning of the fair, the streets were cleaned for the only time in the year, and until 1879 the carters marched in procession through the principal streets. They called their event the 'Northern Meeting' to distinguish it from the Ayr Races, otherwise known as the 'Western Meeting', which were held about a mile to the south. The races were on the sands; horses might run into the sea (or the crowd) with excitement, and many refused to obey instructions to start, stop or turn. Often there were arguments (for there were no written rules) and sometimes fights. After several horse races, the blind wheel-barrow race, and the 'old wife's race for a pound of tea', the carters spent the night at a ball at which whisky circulated in pails. It ended at dawn. The extension of Ayr harbour reduced the size of the sands and the unregulated running of the horses began to cause concern. The few remaining carters carried not salmon but coal. The races were moved to a safer site inland, but expired in 1900.

Most carters' 'plays' (races) were in the Edinburgh region: 18 sites have been identified. Copying Leith Races, carters and ploughmen raced their horses after the meeting of their friendly society; in most cases, the societies pre-dated the races. Racing was common between 1820 and 1870, and the event survived at Gilmerton, on the outskirts of Edinburgh, until shortly before the First World War. As at Leith, the prize, typically a cart saddle, was carried in procession to the race ground on the top of a pole. The venue was usually the high road: the opposition of the county council was a major factor in the plays' demise.

The feast of the Assumption of the Virgin has been celebrated in the coastal burgh of Irvine in Ayrshire since the Middle Ages. In the seventeenth century, a horse race was added to its diversions. Under the patronage of both the burgh and the local landowner, the Earl of Eglinton, Marymas races nearly achieved elite status in the first half of the nineteenth century, but the Earl laid out his own course at Bogside, two miles further north, and the Marymas, which included cart-horse races, became less known for sport than for hard drinking. Marymas was reformed in 1870, when the sale of drink on the Town Moor was banned, and again in 1927, when it was reshaped round a historical pageant for schoolchildren (which spuriously linked the festival's name with Mary, Queen of Scots) – the races are still held.

Sources and Reading:

Burnett, J., 'The Kipper Fair and the Carters' Races at Newton-on-Ayr', *Review of Scottish Culture*, 9 (1995/6), 35–45.

Burnett, J., *Riot, Revelry and Rout: Sport in Lowland Scotland before 1860* (East Linton: Tuckwell Press, 2000).

Fairfax-Blakeborough, J., *The History of Horse Racing in Scotland* (Whitby: J. Fairfax-Blakeborough, 1973).

Kay, J., 'From Coarse to Course: the First Fifty Years of the Royal Caledonian Hunt, 1777–1826', *Review of Scottish Culture*, 13 (2000–1), 30–9.

Kay, J. and Vamplew, W., 'Horse Racing', in Jarvie, G. and Burnett, J., *Sport, Scotland and the Scots* (East Linton: Tuckwell Press, 2000), 159–73.

See also Horseracing

John Burnett

Hummie

An alternative name for shinty.

Sources and Reading:
Gomme, A. B., *The Traditional Games of England, Scotland and Ireland* (London: Thames and Hudson facsimile edition, 1984).

See also Bandy, Hockey, Shinty

Tony Collins

Hunt Clubs

Hunt clubs provided an important link, both social and financial, between horseracing and the sports from which they derived their names and interests. The eighteenth-century clubs were invariably aristocratic and exclusive – certainly as far as wealth and both social and sporting acceptability were concerned – with strict rules and rituals, both for wearing their distinctive uniforms and for attendance at dinners and other convivial activities.

Pre-eminent among these, and in many ways unique, was the Caledonian (Royal Caledonian from 1824) Hunt Club, founded in 1777 both to improve the standard of fox-hunting in Scotland (although it never had its own pack of hounds), and also to give worthwhile but selective support to race meetings north of the border. The club sponsored its first race at Kelso in 1789 but, after seven years there, moved its patronage to Ayr. Thus began the custom of rotating its annual fortnight of sporting activities to towns having both suitable packs of hounds and a racecourse, although after 1816 its outdoor activities were limited to a week dedicated to racing. In 1788, the club had been granted a 100 guinea Royal Plate for donation to the meetings in its itineraries, the first recipient being Dumfries, and this, together with its own increasing level of patronage, enabled support to be given to no less than ten Scottish race meetings over the years (even if Paisley was always considered beyond the pale and Lanark had to wait until 1880 for its first visit). This patronage still continues today although limited to flat racing at Ayr, Edinburgh and Hamilton Park as the other courses have either closed or, like Kelso and Perth, offer only National Hunt racing.

Although the Caledonian Hunt Club had the ability to transform a lowly one-day meeting into a prestigious four-day event, it never made any serious attempt to emulate the Jockey Club and seek to regulate horseracing north of the border. Conversely, the Jockey Club, certainly in the nineteenth century, rarely, if ever, gave its patronage to any races outside Newmarket, its own private fiefdom well before it succeeded in stamping its authority on flat racing in mainland Britain. It may have considered that the ever-growing number of Royal Plates provided a sufficient financial boost.

Two other important eighteenth-century hunt clubs, one in Cheshire and one just over the border in north Wales, are worthy of specific mention, even though their direct patronage was limited to the race meetings that they inaugurated. The Tarporley Hunt Club was formed in 1762 as a dining club for those interested in hare hunting. Initially limited to 20 members (later raised to 40) and with a £20 entrance fee, it did not get seriously involved in horseracing until 1775. By 1800, its annual meetings could produce five or six races for its members, and the strict rules of entry were gradually relaxed. Over the years, the races survived a number of changes of venue and, boosted by the introduction of hurdle races in 1848, the flat race meetings lasted until 1873. Steeplechase meetings were inaugurated two years later and the Tarporley Hunt meetings continued until the outbreak of the Second World War. Even now, their name lives on in a race at the nearby National Hunt meeting at Bangor-on-Dee.

In November 1767, the Holywell Hunt was founded mainly to organise an annual week devoted to convivial pursuits, including horse races, between its 25 members, raised to a total of 50 seven years later. The race meetings soon became the most fashionable in all Wales, attracting runners and visitors from all over Britain. There were also races for greyhounds, and the meeting survived for over 70 years with ever increasing prize money and a full three days of flat racing. Even as late as 1835 the Hunt still had 48 members and the attraction of its meetings seemed as great as ever, but after 1842 (apart from a brief revival in 1851 and 1852) the meetings ended abruptly. Although their demise has never been satisfactorily explained, it may be significant that the first autumn meeting at nearby Chester took place in October 1843, at the time normally occupied by the Holywell Hunt races, shortly after the Wrexham meeting, in accordance with the hunt rules.

Other Hunt Clubs such as the Pytchley at Northampton, the Yorkshire Union at York and the East Sussex at Lewes provided much needed support at difficult times or an extra day's racing. The Liverpool Hunt Club took over the faltering and relatively remote Hoylake meeting from 1849 and kept it going until 1876, when it succumbed to the aggressive local golf club.

The prime support given by all these clubs was to flat racing. But the Brocklesby Union Hunt Club founded in 1835, although adopting similar strict precepts on membership and uniform, was dedicated from the outset to supporting steeplechasing while this was still a minority sport and viewed with disapproval by the devotees of flat racing. Its members preferred to see 'hunters ridden by hunting men rather than

racehorses ridden by professional jockeys', and this attitude was preserved both in its National Hunt meetings, which survived until just before the Second World War, and in its current point-to-point races.

After the formation of the National Hunt Committee in 1866 and the Jockey Club's minimum prize money restrictions of the 1870s, numerous hunt and hunt club race meetings came into being; some transient, some long-lasting – but all dedicated to jump racing.

But no hunt club has equalled the Royal Caledonian Hunt Club's longevity, or the breadth of support it has given to flat racing over more than 200 years, although this was always confined to Scotland. Even the Bibury Club, a more ancient and exclusive club devoted solely to horseracing, cannot equal its support of a number of racecourses, as its venues of Bibury, Burford, Cheltenham, Stockbridge and Salisbury were merely the progression of a single meeting, driven either by club choice or outside circumstances.

Sources and Reading:

Fairfax-Blakeborough, J., *Northern Turf History* (Volume 4) (Whitby: J. Fairfax-Blakeborough, 1973).

Kay, J., 'From Coarse to Course: The First Fifty Years of the Royal Caledonian Hunt, 1777–1826', *Review of Scottish Culture*, 13 (2000/01), 30–9.

Latham, F. A. (ed.), *Tarporley* (Tarporley: Tarporley Local History Group, 1993).

Pitt, C. A., *Long Time Gone* (Halifax: Portway, 1996).

Vesey, A. G., 'The Holywell Hunt', *Clwyd Historian*, 37 (1996) 2–7.

See also Horseracing, Hunting

John Tolson

Hunting

In Britain, hunting is the general term used to denote the pursuit of a variety of wild animals, usually with dogs. This activity is as old as the human race, whose early ancestors hunted to feed themselves. As a specialised sport, its origins can be traced back to the medieval period, when deer hunting was undertaken by wealthy barons on horseback using bred hounds. It was the early monarchs, in particular King Canute and Malcolm II of Scotland, who framed the first laws to protect deer and salmon (salmon was also highly prized). The Norman Conquest brought to Britain a formal structure of legislation. The forest laws of William I, which were developed by his successors, enabled hunting to become an exclusive, royal and aristocratic pastime. The edibility of the quarry was less important than the pleasure provided by, and the skill involved in, the chase.

The growing popularity of deer hunting led to the creation of specialised deer forests, where 'warreners' were employed by the lord of the manor to protect the animals from illicit hunting. Forest laws imposed draconian punishments on those found guilty of poaching. In spite of the predilection of the Norman kings for deer hunting, hares were considered to be an equally prestigious quarry. In contrast, foxes were considered vermin to be destroyed.

By the latter part of the fifteenth century, hare hunting was no longer confined to the nobility but had become the principal sport of the vast majority of country squires owning a few couple of hounds. These packs hunted hares and foxes, and even deer in the winter months, and on some estates, otters provided sport in the summer. In 1390 a law was passed restricting the ownership of ferrets to those with an annual income of more than 40 shillings a year. The aim was to prevent the labouring masses from using ferrets to poach rabbits, which were then highly regarded for their meat and fur.

The indiscriminate pursuit of a variety of prey with dogs was gradually replaced by the hunting of individual species, each with its own rules, regulations and governing bodies. Yet there has been a tendency for supporters and opponents to lump individual sports together, so that the term

hunting encompasses the collective name for all such activities.

All forms of hunting have been marred by controversy about their merits and legitimacy.

Sources and Reading:
Wightman, A., Higgins, P., Jarvie, G. and Nicol, R., 'The Cultural Politics of Hunting: Sporting Estates and Recreational Land Use in the Highlands and Islands of Scotland', *Culture, Sport Society*, 5: 1 (2002), 53–70.

See also Deer Hunting and Stalking, Fox-Hunting, Hare Hunting, Otter Hunting

Nicholas Goddard
and John Martin

Hunting: The Case Against

The case against hunting is straightforward: it is morally wrong to pursue and kill an animal, causing it unnecessary suffering, purely for 'sport'. Hunting is a cruel and barbaric pastime – a civilised twenty-first-century society should not permit such cruelty to animals to continue. Many of the same arguments for retaining the now illegal 'sports' of cockfighting and bear baiting were advanced for retaining hunting with dogs, yet now no one argues that such 'sports' should be anything other than illegal. Just as cockfighting and bear baiting have been banned, so the equally cruel hunting with dogs has also been consigned to the history books.

Hunting with dogs is fundamentally cruel. The legal definition of cruelty to animals is 'an activity that causes unnecessary suffering'. It is clear that hunting with dogs causes suffering in the chased animal, both during the chase and during the kill. The report of the Burns Inquiry, commissioned by the Government to inquire into the practical aspects of hunting with dogs and a potential ban, concluded that the experience of being hunted 'seriously compromised' the welfare of all four quarry species (foxes, hares, mink and deer).

Is, then, this suffering unnecessary? The first point that stands out is that hounds are bred for stamina, rather than for speed, ensuring a lengthy chase to improve the 'sport' while causing the hunted animal to suffer for longer. This alone demonstrates that, at least to the extent that the chase is thus artificially lengthened, hunting is cruel.

If control of these species is necessary, there are methods available which cause less suffering. Deer and foxes are better controlled by shooting (in the case of foxes, shooting with a rifle at night using a spotlight), and mink by live trapping. The hare is on the Biodiversity Action List and thus arguably should not be culled at all. Again, this was the conclusion reached by the Burns Inquiry – that alternative culling methods cause less suffering to the animal.

The extent to which culling is necessary at all is robustly challenged. Pro-hunters claim that foxes in particular are a pest and that hunting is necessary to control them. However, this is flawed on several counts. Firstly, research by Dr Piran White of York University has demonstrated that foxes are a very minor cause of lamb loss – far fewer lambs are lost to foxes than to mismothering or exposure. This is confirmed by other studies that considered the impact of fox predation, which led the Burns report to conclude that 'only a small proportion of foxes kill lambs'. The most effective and efficient way of minimising lamb losses is to improve husbandry – for example, to keep ewes inside when they are due to lamb and for 24 hours afterwards.

Secondly, the Mammal Society commissioned research during the period of the foot-and-mouth disease outbreak in 2001 when hunting was banned for nearly a full year. The research (undertaken by Baker, Harris and Webbon) compared fox densities before and after the ban in both hunted and non-hunted areas. If hunting were controlling the population, fox numbers would have been expected to rise sharply in hunted areas during the period

of the ban. In fact, there was no significant difference in fox density changes between hunted and non-hunted areas. The study concluded 'These data show that the ban on hunting had no impact on fox numbers in Britain' – in other words, hunting does *not* control the fox population.

Finally, undercover investigation by the League Against Cruel Sports revealed that very many fox-hunts provide artificial earths in the areas in which they hunt, and even provide food for foxes, encouraging them to breed so as to produce more potential quarries for their 'sport'. Hunting is not about pest control; it is about causing suffering purely for 'sport'.

A further argument put forward by pro-hunters is that hunting is economically important, and that a ban would cause many job losses. However, again this is incorrect. A very small number of jobs are directly dependent on hunting – only 700 people are directly employed by hunts. The Burns Inquiry found that the short-term job loss would be 'limited', and that in the long term most, if not all, of the effects would be offset. Furthermore, even the small number of potential job losses could be reduced, or even eliminated altogether, if hunts were prepared to switch to drag hunting, which involves the following of an artificial scent trail. The claim that horse riding will shrink as an industry and thus that there will be a huge knock-on economic effect is also false. Horse riding is one of the fastest-growing leisure industries in the country, and the vast majority of this growth does not involve riding to hounds. Those who hunt because they enjoy to ride will simply find other ways in which to enjoy their riding – humane ways. Indeed, drag hunting might well attract some riders who have been put off by the cruelty of hunting.

Some hunt supporters will argue that hunting acts to conserve the population of the quarry species. Hunters often claim that they catch only old or ill foxes or deer. In the case of stags, this is clearly untrue – hunters will often pick out the most impressive stags to hunt. In the case of foxes, earths are blocked in advance so that the fox cannot follow its natural instinct and escape underground, and foxes that do manage to go to ground are dug out in a process that can take hours. Most unpleasantly, hounds are trained to kill a fox by 'cub hunting', which leads to the deaths of up to 6,000 cubs a year – hardly old and sick animals. Clearly, hunts do not restrict themselves to weak animals – they want a good chase. The idea of cruelty 'for the good of the species' is ridiculous. It is also notable that the claim by hunters to be conserving the fox population contradicts their simultaneous claim to be providing a pest control service.

The last-ditch argument by hunters is that a ban on hunting would infringe on their human rights. This is nonsense. A challenge on human rights grounds to the Protection of Wild Mammals (Scotland) Act 2002, which bans hunting with dogs in Scotland, failed. Rabinder Singh QC of Matrix Chambers commented that 'there is no right in that convention [the European Convention of Human Rights] to inflict cruelty upon animals'.

It is clear that there is no necessity to hunting – there is no reason to hunt other than for enjoyment. It is horrendous that in a modern society the idea of causing suffering simply for human pleasure, for 'sport', should be considered acceptable. If hunters wish to hunt, they can go drag hunting, which gives the enjoyment of riding together with the enjoyment of watching hounds follow a scent. The only difference is the lack of the kill.

It is therefore entirely appropriate that Parliament should have made legislation to ban this barbaric activity. After being consistently voted for by a majority in the House of Commons, the Hunting Act 2004 was made law. The Parliament Act enabled the legislation to reach the statute book after it became clear that the House of Lords would never agree to a total ban on hunting with dogs. After a three-month delay in implementation, the cruel 'sport' of hunting with dogs became illegal on 18 February 2005.

Sources and Reading:
Baker, P. J., Harris, S. and Webbon, C. C., 'Effect of British Hunting Ban on Fox Numbers', *Nature*, 419 (2002), 34.
Report of the Committee of Inquiry into Hunting With Dogs in England and Wales [Burns Inquiry] (London: The Stationery Office, 2000).
Unearthed: Canned Fox Hunting in the Heart of England. Available at: www.league.uk.com/investigations/index.htm.
White, P. C. L., Groves, H. L., Savery, J. R., Connington, J. and Hutchings, M. R., 'Fox Predation as a Cause of Lamb Mortality on Hill Farms', *Veterinary Record*, 147 (2000), 33–7.

Jess Barker

Hunting: The Case For

Since the first anti-hunting bill in 1893, which sought to ban the hunting, shooting or coursing of animals kept in confinement, there have been 48 bills that have aimed to ban or restrict one kind of hunting or another. In recent years the pace has increased, with 20 bills during the 1990s.

At the time of writing (February 2005), legislation banning hunting wild animals with dogs has come into force. Yet the situation is still not clear. An appeal that challenged the validity of the Parliament Act, which was used, quite inappropriately, to pass the Hunting Bill, failed. However, legal action under the European Convention on Human Rights has been commenced on the grounds that the Hunting Bill is an infringement of civil liberties and will cost the livelihood and possibly the homes of country sports workers.

The police have expressed serious concerns about the enforceability of the bill. It remains legal to dress up in pink coats, to ride horses across the countryside (with the landowner's permission), to exercise hounds, to follow a scent, to flush foxes from coverts with dogs and then to shoot them. No doubt the courts will interpret the law, but it currently appears that even if hounds pursue a fox and kill it, no offence may have been committed. It will be necessary to prove intent on the part not of the hounds, but of the hunt servants and followers.

The law may prove unworkable, as the corresponding bill in Scotland proved to be. And there are reports that the Welsh Assembly may exercise its right to opt out of the bill – an opportunity for country sports tourism in Wales.

The argument against hunting is simple and apparently watertight: that it is clearly painful for a fox to be killed by hounds, or a hare by greyhounds, and that hunting is therefore cruel. There has been much debate on the proposition that the hunted fox dies by 'a quick nip on the back of the neck', and therefore does not suffer. This is countered by studies purporting to show that foxes are disembowelled while still alive, or that coursed hares may be torn between two greyhounds for some seconds before being dispatched by a steward. Whether death is instantaneous or takes a few seconds, it is clear that the hunted animal dies quickly in a rush of adrenaline. Both soldiers and rugby players can testify that an injury sustained in the heat of the moment only starts to hurt later on. It is a reasonable supposition that the suffering of the hunted animal is similarly limited.

The anti-hunting case is based on a set of anthropomorphic assumptions – the 'Bambi fallacy' – often quite explicitly, as when Conservative politician Ann Widdecombe asked 'How would you like to be hunted and killed by a pack of hounds?' It also makes the implicit assumption that a fox or hare which is not hunted will have, by contrast, an easy and pleasant life and, eventually, an easy and pleasant death. But in reality a fox not hunted is likely to die either by another culling method, legal or illegal (shooting, trapping, snaring, poisoning or gas), through an accident, perhaps on the roads, of disease, or possibly of simple old age and starvation. All of these ways of dying carry a high risk of a slow, lingering and painful death, perhaps in agony from gangrene. A fox is not easy to shoot, and so may be simply wounded. There are no hospices for foxes. So there is a clear case that a quick death in the hunting field is actually more humane than any other likely outcome; and most hunted foxes get clean away, uninjured. Fox-hunting is the only culling method that preferentially takes old, weak or sick foxes, and thus contributes to the Darwinian fitness of the fox population. An anti once asked how foxhounds were supposed to tell the difference between fit and unfit foxes. The answer is: fit foxes run faster. As a result of hunting, the British fox population is the healthiest in Europe.

The anthropomorphic case against hunting also fails to recognise that virtually all animals are either predators or prey – and frequently both. Those who agonise over the hunting of foxes seem totally unconcerned that each fox, in its lifetime, will kill hundreds of birds, rabbits and other small mammals. As the bumper sticker puts it: 'Hunting is natural – 10,000 foxes can't be wrong'. Facing this argument, the antis will reply that the fox hunts naturally, by instinct, and for survival (ignoring the fact that a fox in a hen-house will kill 20 chickens and eat only one).

The problem, say the antis, is that *people take pleasure* from hunting. This is practically an admission that opposition to hunting is not, in fact, about animal welfare at all, but about attacking the behaviour of people. Opposition to hunting becomes a fig leaf allowing malcontents and obsessives to attack decent, law-abiding people. Again, the antis' views are based on a complete misconception. A headline in the *Lincolnshire Echo*, following the Waterloo Cup (the nation's premier hare coursing event) read 'Why do people travel hundreds of miles to see hares killed?' It would be as sensible to ask 'Why do rugby fans travel miles to see grown men break their collar bones?' Rugby fans go to see the game, not the injuries. Hunting and coursing supporters go for the chase, not the kill. Indeed, few hunt followers actually see the kill. And on the first day of the 2003 Waterloo Cup,

26 out of 32 coursed hares escaped unharmed. The objective of coursing is to test pairs of greyhounds against each other, not to kill hares.

There is a more general reason why hunting is essential for the maintenance of species such as the hare. The hare is finely adapted to escape predators by speed and agility. It is a well-established principle of evolutionary biology that extreme adaptations only survive if the evolutionary pressures that created them are maintained. This is evidenced, for example, by flightless birds on isolated islands, free of land-based predators, and by blind animals in caves. If the hare as a species were not hunted over many generations, it would lose its essential characteristics, and might end up more like an oversized gerbil. The very nature of the species depends upon it being hunted. Overall in Britain, the brown hare is in decline, and this is sometimes advanced as an argument against hare coursing. But there is overwhelming evidence that on coursing estates the land is managed in a hare-friendly way, and that numbers are stable or increasing. The threat to the survival of the hare is from modern agricultural methods, not from coursing.

Drag hunting is often proposed as a 'non-cruel' alternative to fox-hunting. But there are fundamental reasons why drag hunting cannot be a substitute for fox-hunting (as the Masters of Draghounds Association testified to the Burns Inquiry). Drag hunting is a much faster sport requiring higher standards of horsemanship, which would exclude many current hunt followers. Because it is faster, it covers more ground, but hunts are already threatened by limited availability of hunting country. There is simply no room for a major expansion of drag hunting. Landowners tolerate fox-hunting because it serves a pest-control function. There is no benefit to landowners from drag hunting: only damage.

The hunting tradition delivers enormous benefits for the countryside, landscape, conservation and biodiversity, as well as to rural communities, the rural economy and the fabric of rural life. One need only compare the English landscape in, say, Leicestershire with the prairie farms of East Anglia to see the difference. Hunting country is full of hedgerows, coverts, spinneys, small fields and detail, whereas much of East Anglia is given over to huge fields and wire fences. Hunting country offers a much better home for birds and small mammals. Since the Second World War, more acres of woodland have been planted in Britain by hunts than by any other organisation except the Forestry Commission.

While hunts themselves employ a limited number of staff, there is an extensive equestrian industry that is substantially dependent on hunting – such as tack shops, farriers and vets. Point-to-point races depend on hunting and would be unlikely to survive without it, and they in turn underpin National Hunt racing. Hunts provide an essential fallen-stock service to farmers, more vital than ever as the European Union seeks to ban on-farm burial, and in many rural areas the hunt is the essential matrix of social life.

Finally, as Anne Mallalieu has argued so often and so evocatively, there is an almost mystical link between hunting, the land, our national culture and indeed our evolutionary history. How many pubs are called the 'Fox and Hounds'? How many beer pumps are illustrated with hunting scenes? How many rural inns are hung with sporting prints?

We are descended from a hundred thousand generations of hunter-gatherers. We have enjoyed an almost symbiotic relationship with dogs for many thousands of years. Against this background, a century of misconceived, politically correct attempts to ban hunting count for little. Hunting may now be no more than a pale, ritualised shadow of our hunter-gatherer past, but it is a real and fundamental reflection of human nature, which we abandon at our peril.

Website:
www.rogerhelmer.com

Roger Helmer MEP

Hurling

Hurling is a stick-and-ball field game played between two teams of 15 players. The stick is called a *camán* and the ball a *sliotar*. A *camán* is made of ash wood and is shaped like a shinty stick except with a wider and flatter club end, called the *bas*. Goalkeepers usually use a *camán* with a large *bas* to defend the integrity of the goal, but this should not exceed 13 centimetres in width. There is great variety in the size of hurling sticks used. The size of the *bas* and the length of the *camán* handle can vary widely, depending on players' preferences. The *sliotar* has roughly the same dimension as a tennis or cricket ball, and is made of leather. However, unlike a cricket ball or baseball, the seams in the stitching are not flush with the surface of the ball, but are ridged. The ridged ball facilitates handling and catching and is particularly useful to players who wish to carry the ball on their stick while running at speed – a manoeuvre that excites crowds as the potential is there for it to be scooped away by an opponent. Some players elect to play with a helmet to lessen the potential for injury from a blow of the ball or stick. The original helmets used in hurling were ice hockey helmets and date from the 1960s and 1970s, but newer models more suited to hurling's particular needs (such as the inclusion of face visors) have since been developed. More recently, a glove that covers palm, wrist and much of the lower arm came into vogue among players in the 1990s. One glove only is worn – on the hand used for catching the ball; the possibility of hand injury is greatest in any contest between a player aiming to catch a ball and a rival aiming to strike it on the volley.

Handling of the ball is allowed in hurling. A player that is holding the ball may advance three paces, but must then place it on the *camán* or strike it, or else be penalised and lose possession. The ball must not be picked from the ground by hand, but must be lifted up by using the *camán*. A player may carry the ball on the *camán* indefinitely, but the risk of being dis-

possessed is great in this manoeuvre. The *sliotar* is propelled by the *camán* through the air or on the ground and there are no restrictions on the height a *camán* may be wielded.

Teams line out with a goalkeeper, three full-backs (left-corner, full and right-corner), three half-backs (sometimes called wing backs – left, centre and right), two midfield players, three half-forwards (left, centre and right), and three full-forwards (left-corner, full and right-corner). The length of the field is between 130 and 145 metres and the width can vary from 80 to 90 metres. The goal area is the same H shape as found in rugby; goals are scored into the netted area under the crossbar and are worth 3 points, a single point is awarded when the *sliotar* passes over the bar. The goal posts should be at least 7 metres high, while the netted goal area should be 6.5 metres wide by 2.5 metres high. Although there is no offside rule, an attacking player should not arrive into the box in front of the goal area (called the small parallelogram) before the *sliotar*.

Games commence when the sole referee throws the ball along the ground between the midfield contestants and last for two halves of 30 minutes (except in the case of senior intercounty league and championship games, when two halves of 35 minutes are played). Referees are assisted by two linesmen and by four umpires (one at the foot of each goal post). Umpires signal to the referee and the scorekeeper (and the crowd) that a point has been scored by waving a white flag and waving a green flag to indicate a goal. In rare cases an umpire stands in the middle of the goal area and makes an X with both flags, signalling that a disputed score has been cancelled.

Hurling is an ancient game and is celebrated in many Irish myths and legends. In one legend, the pre-eminent Gaelic superhero Cú Chulainn (whose boyhood name was Setanta) walked to the training camp of *Na Fianna* (an ancient Irish army) while propelling a *sliotar* through the air and running ahead to catch it as it fell. When in fear of his life he killed the hound (*cú*) of a man named Culann. He did this with the *sliotar*, struck with accuracy and ferocity by his *camán*. In recompense for his error, Setanta the boy adopted the title Cú Chulainn ('hound of Culann') and promised to protect the man as the hound once did. Another tale tells of Diarmuid, a great soldier of the *Fianna*, whose ability on the hurling field greatly captivated Gráinne, the daughter of the High King of Ireland. Diarmuid's subsequent difficulties, recounted in *Toraíocht Diarmuid agus Gráinne* ('The Pursuit of Diarmuid and Gráinne'), arose from the fact that Gráinne was the choice, for a wife, of Fionn MacCumhail, the chief of the *Fianna*, and at that time an old man. When Gráinne convinced Diarmuid to elope with her, Fionn was enraged and pursued the couple throughout Ireland – an early on-the-road tale of jealousy, love, betrayal, adventure, magic, tremendous athletic feats . . . and hurling.

Hurling developed into two principal premodern forms, *camán* and *iomáin*. *Camán* (or *camánacht*, anglicised as 'commons', is associated more with the north of Ireland and Scotland (where *camanachd*, or 'shinty', is the Scottish version of the game). *Camán* was played with a stick closer to the shinty stick in shape and disallowed handling. *Iomáin* was associated with the south of Ireland, utilised a stick with a *bas* and permitted handling. In the medieval period those areas where Norman and Gaelic cultures were most closely connected showed the greatest interest in *iomáin*, but the loss of political influence of that society in the seventeenth and early eighteenth centuries to Plantation and, later, Ascendancy society led to a decline in patronage for the game. Like cricket, folk-football and other games, the sport enjoyed renewed official patronage in the late eighteenth and early nineteenth centuries, but after the twin crises of Catholic emancipation (1829) and the disestablishment of the Church of Ireland (1867) the rift between the gentry and peasantry again opened up.

Following the famine of the late 1840s, emigration of the most vigorous and youthful cohorts of society dealt a severe blow to cultural enterprises, including sports. One 1871 proposal to allow hurling and football to be played at a proposed People's Park in Limerick city was even countered with the observation that the hurling and football classes had all emigrated. Complementing the negative impact of emigration on the game was the suspicion at official level that political elements sought to conceal their activities beneath apparently innocuous hurling gatherings.

Hurling survived as a local, customary, non-standardised and ad-hoc affair. Games were contested between variously sized teams over disparate terrain. Some games were contested on strands or beaches, but most were played over rough ground, with the goal areas often miles apart – usually two opposing parish landmarks. The variety in forms of the game is also indicated by the different names used in different parts of the country; *báire*, *iomáin*, *camán* and *scuaibín* were just some of the terms in the hurling family. The variety in nomenclature was complemented by variety in rules and methods of scoring. Some games involved bringing the ball back to one's own goal area, some involved the opposite manoeuvre. Other games concluded when one goal was scored, some allowed multiple scores.

Under the aegis of the Gaelic Athletic Association, standardised rules for hurling were adopted and promulgated; parish, county, and national layers of organisation were established and competitions at each level commenced. Reflecting the dominance of the southern game, the new national hurling code was, in essence, the *iomáin* handling game. At first, games lasted for 80 minutes; this was soon revised downwards to 60 minutes and field size and layout was decided. Teams of 21-a-side were agreed, but this was subsequently reduced to 17 (1895) and then to the current 15 (1915). Initially, only goals counted, later points counted if goals were equal. In 1895 the value of a goal was determined as being worth 5 points, this changed to 3 points in 1897. The H-shaped goalposts now in use were not introduced until 1910. Up until that time, two posts equidistant from a soccer-style goal area acted as point posts, similar to the 'behind' posts in Australian Rules football.

Hurling is most popular south of a line from Dublin to Galway and in two outposts in the northern counties of Down and Antrim. Three counties share almost 75 per cent of the total number of senior championship victories – Cork, Kilkenny and Tipperary. These are the game's principal heartlands, while counties Galway, Clare, Limerick, Waterford, Wexford, Laois and Offaly could be categorised as secondary powers in the game. The counties of Dublin, Antrim, Meath and the recently emergent counties of Tyrone and Derry occupy a position among hurling's equivalent of cricket's minor counties. The remaining counties are less significant in participation rates and exhibit less skill and quality; this is more often a result of their concentration on Gaelic football. Conversely, Gaelic football is weakest in County Kilkenny – one of the three traditional hurling powers. There are exceptions to the rule that strong hurling counties are weak football counties; Cork, Offaly and Galway are three that devote roughly equal attention to both codes and have the championship successes to show for it, but the fact that there are only three counties from 32 suggests that they are simply the exceptions that prove the rule.

Sources and Reading:
Ó Maolfabhail, A., *Camán: Two Thousand Years of Hurling in Ireland* (Dundalk: Dundalgan Press, 1973).
Whelan, K., 'A Geography of Hurling', *History Ireland*, 1: 1 (1993), 27–31.

See also Gaelic Athletic Association, Hurling (Cornwall), *Poc Fada*

Tom Hayes

Hurling (Cornwall)

It is claimed that the origins of rugby football lie in the ancient Cornish game of hurling. Indeed, contemporary written evidence from the seventeenth century shows that there are recognisable elements of the modern rugby and American gridiron football games in Cornish hurling. Legend has it that a circle of standing stones at Minions on Bodmin Moor dated to around 1500 BC were once men and women, turned to stone for playing the ancient game of hurling on a Sunday. A. K. Hamilton Jenkin has pointed out that the game has an association with *la soulle*, a type of hand football played in the Chouan district of Brittany.

Two kinds of hurling are described by Richard Carew in his 1602 *Survey of Cornwall*, hurling to goals and hurling to country. The former was more general in the eastern part of Cornwall, where the land was enclosed early, while the latter dominated in the west:

> For hurling to goales, there are 15, 20 or 30 players more or lesse, chosen out on each side, who strip themselves into their slightest apparel and then joyne hands in ranke one against another. Out of these ranks they match themselves by payres, one embracing another . . . every couple are to watch another during the play.
> After this, they pitch two bushes in the ground, some eight or ten foote asunder; and directly against them, ten or twelve score off, other twayne in like distance, which they terme their Goales. . . . There is assigned for their guard a couple of their best stopping Hurlers: the rest draw into the midst between both goales, where some indifferent person throweth up a ball the which whosoever can catch, and carry through his adversaries goale, hath wonne the game.

Carew continues to explain tactics of holding, butting and pushing, but points out that if a man cries 'hold' then the ball must be passed. There appears to have been a strict code of rules:

> [Hurlers] must hurle man to man, and not two set upon one man at once . . . he may not throw it [the ball] to any of his mates, standing nearer the goale than himself.

So within this evidence there are elements of the modern rules of rugby and American football. This version of the game was played at some weddings, where the guests took on all-comers. The other version, hurling to country, tended to be played on feast days:

> Some tow or more Gentleman doe commonly make this match, appointing that on such a holyday, they will to such an indifferent place, two, three or more parishes. . . . Their goales are either those Gentleman's houses, or some townes or villages, three or four miles asunder . . . a silver ball is cast up, and that company, which can catch, and carry it by force, or sleight, to their place assigned, gaineth the ball and victory.

The game was played with a so-called 'silver ball', a globe the size of a cricket ball made of cork, leather or wood, and covered with a thick casing of silver. When this required renewing, it was formerly the custom to collect the silver in the form of coins that were taken to the smith who beat them onto the ball. Many of the older hurling balls bore Cornish inscriptions, such as *Guare wheag yu guare teag* ('Fair play is good play').

Boase and Courtney, writing in the nineteenth century, used parish records to identify prominent players, such as a certain John Hockin, aged 19, who had such skill in the game that he carried the ball from Four Borrows to Camborne, a distance of ten miles, pursued 'by a vast number of horsemen and footmen'. It is possible that this John Hockin, who died in 1706, could have been one of those 'hundred Cornish

gentlemen' who in 1654 went up to London to give an exhibition of hurling in Hyde Park.

The *Moderate Intelligencer* of 4 May 1654 provides an account of the match:

> [There were] fifty Cornishmen on the one side and fifty on the other. One party played in red caps and the other in white. There was present His Highness the Lord Protector [Oliver Cromwell], many of the Privy Council and divers eminent gentlemen. . . . The ball they played withal was silver, and designed for that party which did win the ball.

There is also a report of a match between Cornish and Irish hurlers taking place in the same year in the presence of Cromwell (see Lennon, 1997). During the reign of Charles II another great display of Cornish hurling was staged in London and watched by many spectators. Daniel Defoe, writing in his *Tour Through the Whole Island of Great Britain, 1724–26*, noted rather disparagingly that hurling was 'a rude and violent play among the boors, or country people, brutish and furious'.

It was certainly no game for the faint-hearted, and pitted rival villages, towns and parishes against each other. Written in 1690, Durfey's *Collin's Walk Through London* described hurling as:

> . . . an ancient sport us'd to this day in the countys of Cornwall and Devon, when once a year the hardy young fellows of each county meet; and a cork ball thinly plated with silver being thrown up between 'em, they run, bustle, and fight for it, to the witty dislocating of many a shrew'd neck, or for the sport of telling how bravely their arms or legs came to be broke, when they got home.

Hamilton Jenkin has noted that the Camborne parish registers contain a 'William Trevarthen buried in Camborne Church, August 13, being disstroid to a hurling with Redruth men at the high downes the tenth day of August, AD 1705'.

In the interparish hurling matches of the past, the rivalry was intensified by the belief that good fortune went with the parish that won the game and thereby succeeded in retaining the ball throughout the ensuing year. In more recent times the claiming of the ball at the traditional St Columb hurling has given rise to a similar belief for the individual winner.

Along with many other similar recreations and activities, hurling declined in the mid-nineteenth century as more-regulated working hours, a reduction in the number of feast days, and the rise of rational sports combined to reduce the sport's appeal and the opportunities for its playing. However, hurling did continue into the early twentieth century, with games taking place at Helston, Newquay, St Merryn and Tregony. Today, the game is kept alive at St Ives and is played on the town's Feast Monday between 'goals' on the local beach.

The real spirit of hurling remains in its most popular form at St Columb. The teams are made up of players, who now also include women, living in the town who challenge those from the surrounding parish. The goals, which are shallow troughs, stand two miles apart. The game begins at 4.15 p.m. on Shrove Tuesday, with a return game the following Saturday. The ball is 'dealt', or thrown up in the air, in the Market Square by a local dignitary and the game commences. The rules follow a mixture of the two styles of hurling. The game often attracts up to 1,000 participants, and twice as many spectators. When the match is complete, either by a goal scored or by the ball being carried outside the parish, the players return to the Market Square for either 'twon ball' or 'country ball' to be declared, and the individual winner is carried off in triumph.

Sources and Reading:

Carew, R., *Survey of Cornwall 1602* (Redruth: Tamar Books, 2002).

Courtney, M. A., *Cornish Feasts and Folklore* (Penzance: Beare, 1886).

Deane, T. and Shaw, T., *The Folklore of Cornwall* (London: Batsford, 1975).

Jenkin, A. K. H., *Cornwall and its People* (London: Dent, 1945).

Lennon, J., 'The Playing Rules of Football and Hurling 1884–1995' (Volume 2 of *Towards a Philosophy for Legislation in Gaelic Games*) (Gormanston: Northern Recreation Consultants, 1997).

Rabey, I., *The Silver Ball: The Story of Hurling at St Columb* (St Columb: I. Rabey, 1991).

See also Hurling

Ian Clarke

Ice Skating

Skating on ice, an activity that is both a practical activity and a recreational sport, has a long history – skates made of animal bone have been excavated in London and York dating back about 2,000 years. Skating was probably derived from skiing.

Ice skating on the Moorfields outside London is described in the *Description of London*, written by William Fitzstephen between 1173 and 1174. He describes the method used by skilled skaters of the time:

> . . . for fitting to, and binding under feet the shinbones of some animal, and taking in their hands poles shod with iron, which at times they strike against the ice, they are carried along with a great rapidity as a bird flying or a bolt discharged from a cross-bow.

In the sixteenth and seventeenth centuries skating was used by people living in the Fens as a means of transport. On 1 December 1662 Samuel Pepys recorded watching an exhibition of skating on the Thames, noting that it was 'a very pretty art'. Injuries were not uncommon, and of course there was also the danger of falling through the ice: in 1899 in Ipswich archaeologists excavated the body of a woman wearing bone skates from what had been a river bed.

The first skating club was formed in Edinburgh, probably in the 1740s. In 1772,

Lieutenant R. Jones wrote *A Treatise on Skating* in which he described how to make a figure of eight and the shape of a heart. The first recorded skating race, a forerunner of modern speed skating, took place on the Fens in 1763. Such races were, inevitably, often accompanied by enthusiastic gambling.

Ice skating was popular in Wales in the winter months. During the mid to late nineteenth century it was frequently practised on frozen ponds, lakes and rivers, be they outside the towns and villages or in local parks. As well as individual skating for pleasure, team games were also sometimes played on ice. In January 1879, a novel and amusing nine-a-side cricket match was contested on skates in Powis Castle Park in Welshpool, while a similar event in Lymore Park, Montgomery a year later drew an eager crowd of spectators.

The pastime grew in popularity during the Victorian period, Prince Albert being known as a keen skater, and the London Skating Club was formed in 1842. The National Skating Association of Great Britain was established in 1879. Such was skating's popularity across all sections of society that by 1896 London had three indoor skating rinks. Many other towns also had rinks, such as Manchester which opened one in 1877.

Sources and Reading:
Carter, J. M., *Sports and Pastimes of the Middle Ages* (Columbus: Brentwood University, 1984).
Reeves, C., *Pleasures and Pastimes in Medieval England* (Stroud: Sutton, 1995).
Scott, M., 'The Edinburgh Skating Club', *Book of the Old Edinburgh Club*, I33 (1971).

Tony Collins
and Emma Lile

Invented Traditions

In the introduction to their book *The Invention of Tradition*, Eric Hobsbawm and Terence Ranger define an 'invented tradition' as being a set of practices 'which seek to inculcate certain values and norms of behaviour by repetition, which automatically implies continuity with the past'. Like politics and other cultural practices, sport is a field in which invented traditions and creation myths abound.

The most obvious forms of invented tradition are those so-called traditional sports which have been invented recently for commercial or nostalgic reasons. The most notable example of this being Dwile Flonking, an entirely fictitious 'sport' which hit the headlines in 1967. Cleverly exploiting the imagery of 'merrie England' and its mythology, it was invented as a publicity stunt to raise awareness of a local village fete in Suffolk. Maggot racing was similarly used for publicity purposes in 1989 by Scottish and Newcastle Breweries. The 1970s, a time in Britain when nostalgia was especially fashionable, also saw the revival of a number of traditional sports events, such as the Tetbury woolsack race. This was revived in 1973 as a focus for the revival of business and community in the town following the decline of the local wool industry.

The most interesting form of invented sporting tradition can be found in the accounts of the origins both of modern and pre-modern sports. Although it would perhaps be unfair in some cases to regard uncorroborated stories of the origins of sports as conscious inventions, many of them are based on the same appetite to legitimise a modern sport by establishing an historical authority for it. For example, there is almost no written evidence of club ball, however Strutt and Nyren (early historians of sport) held it to be the direct precursor of cricket. This must lead one to speculate that the desire to identify a single line of ancestry for cricket overrode critical examination of the sources.

There are also cases in which evidence has either been ignored or wilfully misinterpreted. The available English sources suggest that a stick-and-ball game called 'baseball' predates the game of rounders, yet historians of rounders have used these sources as if they refer to rounders and have further claimed that rounders predates baseball! A similar example can be seen for 'hockey', a term that appears as the name of a sport for the first time in 1785, yet because many stick-and-ball games date back at least to Roman times, the entry in *The Oxford Companion to Sports and Games* claims that 'hockey is thus the forerunner of all modern sports played with an implement'.

It seems that these invented traditions arise as part of an individual sport's process of organisational and ideological consolidation. Nyren's work sought to legitimize cricket as the quintessentially English game; rounders wanted to establish its superiority to the brash commerciality of American baseball; and hockey, a relatively new arrival in late-Victorian sport when compared with soccer, rugby and cricket, wished to demonstrate that it too had a deep-rooted heritage.

In contrast, the two most famous 'creation myths' of modern sport, William Webb Ellis in rugby and Abner Doubleday in baseball, are attempts to separate the histories of the two games from their origins in traditional sport. The Webb Ellis myth served to differentiate rugby union from working-class sports such as soccer and rugby league (although before the 1895 split in the game, rugby union originally sought to present itself as the contribution of folk football), while the Doubleday story helped to define baseball as a uniquely American institution.

It is not an accident that many of these sporting traditions saw the light of day in the Victorian era. The invention of the idea of 'merrie England' began in the early nineteenth century, in large part as a reaction to the Industrial Revolution, and was reflected in the works of writers such as Sir Walter Scott. The idea grew in popularity after the suppression of blood sports and disorderly sports, such as football, and helped the Victorians to discover an idealised past. Festivals such as the Fifth of November, which in parts of the country had been seen as a threat to public order,

were sanitised and re-emerged as expressions of communal solidarity.

Many other festivals and events were simply invented by the Victorians and passed off as traditional with little or no question. Pegg has pointed to the example of the Fire Ceremony, which takes place in Allendale in Northumberland on New Year's Eve. It was claimed that its origins lay variously with the Anglo-Saxons, Vikings and Phoenicians. In fact, it only began in 1883 and many of its distinctive features were added as recently as the 1940s.

This type of invented tradition is common throughout folklore and its customs, and is especially true of sport. For example, local football games are often said to have begun with a victory over an enemy or invader; the Derby football game was allegedly begun as a celebration of triumph over the Romans. Largesse by members of the aristocracy is another common origin story for sports, such as in the Haxey Hood game in Lincolnshire. Equally as common are games that researchers who follow J. G. Frazer's theory, expressed in his work *The Golden Bough* (1890), suggest can be linked to pagan or Celtic fertility rituals, despite the fact that there is no substantive evidence to support such ideas.

In a sense, the ubiquity of invented traditions in sport underlines sport's importance in the creation of value and belief systems. In popular culture, its use as a form of social glue linking the past to the present makes it one of the most potent informal means of creating and maintaining a sense of shared common heritage. Conversely, the need to give historical legitimisation to sport highlights the importance of tradition to the culture of sport. The traditions, invented or otherwise, of fairs, festivals and customs have been examined in great depth by historians. The traditions of sport deserve to be studied in the same serious way.

Sources and Reading:

Hobsbawm, E. and Ranger, T. (eds), *The Invention of Tradition* (Cambridge: Cambridge University Press, 1983).

Pegg, B., *Rites and Riots; Folk Customs of Britain and Europe* (Poole: Blandford, 1981).

Simpson, J. and Roud, S., *A Dictionary of English Folklore* (Oxford: Oxford University Press, 2000).

Thomas, K., *The Perception of the Past in Early Modern England* (London: University of London, 1983).

Tony Collins

Jingling

Jingling was a competitive activity usually played within a 40-yards square area enclosed with ropes. Twelve blindfolded women endeavoured to catch a person who had a small jingling bell, which they had to keep ringing while eluding their pursuers. Matches tended to be rather unequal in favour of the pursuers, as it became progressively more difficult for the jingler to avoid being caught. It provided an entertaining spectacle as the pursuers competed with each other to be the first to catch the jingler and secure a prize for their efforts. The sport was revived as an activity at the Much Wenlock Games, which were established in the mid-nineteenth century.

Sources and Reading:
Morsley, C., *Notes from the English Countryside* (1979).

John Martin

Jousting

'Joust' was originally the name given to single contests between knights as part of the events of the medieval tournament. Two mounted knights would ride at each other holding blunted lances, almost 4 metres long, the aim being to unseat or disarm the opponent, with a particular premium being placed on knocking off the opponent's helmet.

The dividing line between jousting for sport and for war was sometimes not entirely clear. 'Jousts of war', a form of tournament that was actually a military confrontation, were staged as part of military campaigns between England and the Scots and the French. For example, the English and the Scots organised jousts during the sieges of Cupar, Perth and Alnwick Castle. Even in ostensibly peaceful contests, lances were not always blunted. In the *joute à l'outrance*, standard combat weapons were used, making the joust a potentially deadly affair – Henry II of France was killed taking part in a joust. To avoid injury, and also to demonstrate the wealth of the knight, armour became more elaborate and heavier as the popularity of jousting increased. The Earl of Worcester's breast- and back-plates alone weighed almost 20 kilograms. Lances also had 'coronels', which tended to be made of softer wood, in place of the usual sharp steel ends to prevent injury.

From the early fifteenth century, rails, known as the 'tilt', were built between the two jousting lanes to separate the two horse riders. This was originally a rope but evolved into a wooden divide. The challenge of the knight to his opponent would specify the height of the barrier, which was sometimes almost 2 metres. By 1450 the lance-rest, which was attached to the jouster's breastplate to support the lance, had been introduced, making the use of longer and heavier lances more common. The 1466 rules drawn up by the Earl of Worcester allocated points to various achievements in the joust and disqualified jousters who knocked their opponents off their horses when their backs were turned.

Gradually, as the tournament declined in importance as a means of military training, jousting almost entirely replaced the other events of the tournament, partly because it was far more of a spectacle than were the other forms of combat, but also because its evolution meant that it had become less dangerous. Permanent sites for jousting were established at Westminster, Hampton Court and Greenwich.

Jousting became a common sight under Henry VIII, who revived the tournament in 1511. Jousts were held to celebrate the coronation of Elizabeth I and were subsequently held regularly as Ascension Day tilts. The last legal joust in England took place in 1571, but the tradition, albeit in a non-combatant mode, continued as the closely related 'tilting at the quintain'. Jousting also occasionally took place on the water; in 1573 Elizabeth I watched a boat joust at Sandwich.

Today jousting re-enactments can be seen in Britain, continental Europe and the United States during the summer months, often as part of country-house fairs and 'merrie England' revivals. The British Jousting Society was founded in 1969 and today the International Jousting Federation includes Britain, France, Germany, Sweden, Poland, Spain, Italy and Hungary.

Sources and Reading:
Barber, R. and Barker, J., *Tournaments: Jousts, Chivalry and Pageants in the Middle Ages* (Suffolk: Boydell, 1989).
Carter, J. M., *Sports and Pastimes of the Middle Ages* (Columbus: Brentwood University, 1984).
The Encyclopaedia of Sport (London: *The Sportsman*, 1912).
Reeves, C., *Pleasures and Pastimes in Medieval England* (Stroud: Sutton, 1995).

See also Round Table, Tilting at the Quintain, Tournaments

Tony Collins

Jowls

An old name used in the Cleveland region of north-east England for hockey.

Sources and Reading:
Gomme, A. B., *The Traditional Games of England, Scotland and Ireland* (London: Thames and Hudson facsimile edition, 1984).

See also Chinnup, Hockey, Shinnup

Tony Collins

Jumping

A popular pursuit with Welsh youths since ancient times. Through regular practice, jumpers excelled in leaping over roads and hedges and across fields. Difficult and dangerous feats were often intended to impress the womenfolk, as demonstrated by the poet prince Hywel ab Owain Gwynedd (*fl.*1140–70) who leapt 50 feet over the widest river in north Wales to win the hand of Einion ap Geraint's daughter. Medieval praise poetry is peppered with references to jumping long distances, and by the eighteenth and nineteenth centuries jumping contests were common features at local parish festivals. Exhibition leaping was also evident during this latter period. Despite the general supersession of traditional games by more organised sports toward the end of the nineteenth century, jumping competitions continued in the form of long jump, high jump and hop, step and jump.

See also Naid Berc, Naid Stond, Neidio Tair Naid

Emma Lile

Kayles

A form of skittles in which a stick rather than a ball was used to knock down pins, and which dates back at least as far as 1325. It was sufficiently popular in the fifteenth century for Edward IV to ban it along with closh, in an edict of 1477.

In some forms of the game it appears that the pins were arranged in a straight line, sometimes with a larger pin placed at the back, making it the most difficult to knock down. It may well also have been a generic name for skittles. According to Brailsford, the word 'skittles' was derived from the fact that the kayle pins became known as 'kettle' or 'kittle' pins which later became skittles. Antiquarians are divided over whether kayles was a forerunner of skittles or vice versa.

Sources and Reading:
Birley, D., *Sport and the Making of Britain* (Manchester: Manchester University Press, 1993).
Brailsford, D., *British Sport: A Social History* (Cambridge: Lutterworth Press, 1992).
Gomme, A. B., *The Traditional Games of England, Scotland and Ireland* (London: Thames and Hudson facsimile edition, 1984).

See also Aunt Sally, Bowls, Closh, Skittles

Tony Collins

Kibel and Nerspel

A version of knur and spell played at Stixwold in the early nineteenth century. The 'kibel' was the bat, the 'ner' the maple wood ball and 'spel' the trap that launched the ner into the air for the striker to hit with the kibel.

Sources and Reading:
Gomme, A. B., *The Traditional Games of England, Scotland and Ireland* (London: Thames and Hudson facsimile edition, 1984).

See also Knur and Spell

Tony Collins

Kick Shins (*Crimogiant*)

An activity first recorded in print in the late eighteenth century and practised by Pembrokeshire men wearing thick shoes with nails projecting from the sides. Such was their renown at the pursuit that the term *crimmogwr* (shin-kicker) was adopted as a nickname for the county's male inhabitants.

Sources and Reading:
B. H. G., 'The Game of Kick Shins', *Bye-Gones Relating to Wales and the Border Counties* (1902), 436.

See also Purring

Emma Lile

Kiplingcotes Derby

The oldest flat race in the English horse-racing calendar is the Kiplingcotes Derby, which takes place every third Thursday in March in the district of Market Weighton in east Yorkshire. Dating back to 1519, the race is open to men and women who weigh 65 kilograms (10 stone) or over. Those weighing less must carry stones to make up the weight. The race traverses around four miles of woods and countryside, starting at a stone post in the village of Etton and finishing at Londesborough Wold Farm.

The rules drawn up in 1618 define the derby as: 'a horse race to be observed and ridd yearly on the third Thursday in March; open to horses of all ages, to convey horsemen's weight, ten stones, exclusive of saddle, to enter the post before eleven o'clock on the morning of the race. The race to be run before two.'

The winner receives the interest accrued on the £365 fund set up for the winner by a local nobleman in 1619, but the second-placed rider receives the entry fees of the other riders, which often amounts to more than the winning prize.

Sources and Reading:
Ellerington, A., *The Kiplingcotes Derby – England's Oldest Horse Race* (Beverley: Highgate, 1990).
Smith, J., *Fairs, Feasts and Frolic: Customs and Traditions in Yorkshire* (Otley: Smith Settle, 1989).

See also Chester Races, Horseracing

Tony Collins

Kirkwall Ba' Game

The Kirkwall ba' game is a form of mass folk football which is played annually on Christmas Day and New Year's Day in Kirkwall, the capital of the Orkney Islands.

The ba' is a cork ball covered in hand-stitched leather about 28 inches in diameter. A new one is handmade for each game by local craftsmen. The ba' itself is also the trophy and is presented at the end of each game to a player on the winning side who has been a notable and respected contestant at that and previous matches.

The game is played by two teams: 'uppies' and 'doonies'. Uppies were traditionally men or boys born to the south of the town's St Magnus Cathedral and doonies were those born to the north. Today, however, family tradition plays the defining role and players take the side for which their forebears played. Each side normally has hundreds of players. The uppies' aim is to carry the ball to a wall at the south end of Kirkwall, while the doonies have to put the ball into the harbour at the opposite end of the town.

The game begins with the throwing out of the ball to the teams in front of the cathedral at 1 p.m. Play largely consists of a mass scrum, which is pushed and pulled to one or other of the goals through the streets of the town. There are no restrictions on the way in which the ball can be propelled – it was allegedly carried over the rooftops on one occasion – nor are there any rules governing the behaviour of the players, although injuries and foul play are relatively unusual.

The origins of the game are unknown. There are, of course, many stories that have developed to explain its beginnings. One has it that the game began by using the head of a particularly hated Scottish tyrant. Another account describes it as a survival of a pagan midwinter celebration marking the start of the New Year. Others hold that it is a form of fertility rite. Needless to say, there is no hard evidence to support any of these claims.

In fact, most of what is known about the game dates from the mid-seventeenth century, when it was played on the Ba' Lea in a different area of the town. It only moved into the centre of the town in 1800. Until the 1840s the ball was a more traditional inflated animal bladder. It also appears, unusually for a folk football game, that handling or carrying the ball was originally forbidden. The game was only played on New Year's Day until 1880, when the Christmas Day game was introduced.

There was also a short-lived women's ba' game, which took place on Christmas Day 1945 and New Year's Day 1946. The first game was interrupted when male players picked up the ba' and hid it in the cathedral graveyard. Both games were won by uppies.

Sources and Reading:
Brown, C. G., *Up-Helly-Aa: Custom, Culture and Community in Shetland* (Manchester: Manchester University Press, 1998).
Burns, N., 'First women's Ba' carried home by winner's sons', *The Orcadian* (31 August 2000).
Robertson, J., *Uppies and Doonies: The Story of the Kirkwall Ba' Game* (Aberdeen: Aberdeen University Press, 1967).

See also Football, Hand Ba'

Tony Collins

Knitting Competitions

Knitting stockings was customary in most areas of rural Wales during the eighteenth and nineteenth centuries and was practised by men, women and children. In the south-west of Wales during the early nineteenth century, people often met in each other's houses to take part in knitting assemblies. These sometimes included knitting competitions, designed to increase needle speed and dexterity. Among these contests was one involving the tying of two equal lengths of yarn together, with the winner being the first to knit up to the knot. Another contest was entitled *gweu gwryd* ('fathom knitting') and was, according to late nineteenth-century evidence from the Llanwrtyd area of Breconshire, usually contested by some half a dozen women. One fathom (6 feet) from each of the women's last point of knitting was marked with a knot. On the signal, competitors began knitting simultaneously; whoever completed the length first was victorious.

Sources and Reading:
Tibbott, S. M., 'Knitting Stockings in Wales: A Domestic Craft', *Folk Life*, 16 (1978), 61–73.

Emma Lile

Knur and Spell

'Knur and spell' is a game of indeterminate age played mainly in west and south Yorkshire and also in parts of Lancashire and Lincolnshire. In many ways it appears to the onlooker to be a variation of golf, in that the game is played by using a long-handled club to propel a small ball (the 'knur') over long distances. However, unlike golf, sheer distance alone is the aim of the contest.

Each player takes turns, known as 'rises', to hit their knur as far as possible, and a match can consist of anything from 15 to 40 rises. The distance is measured from the place of the strike to the eventual resting place of the knur and calculated in 'scores', units of 20 yards. Fractions of a score are not calculated and the winner is the player with the highest aggregate of scores over a match.

The game's origins most probably lie in the *nurspel* bat-and-ball game of northern Scandinavia. It has been played in Britain in an organised way since at least the middle of the eighteenth century, and Joseph Strutt's 1801 survey of English sports notes that the best practitioners of the time could

propel the ball around 16 scores (320 yards).

The game is essentially a working-class sport, highlighted by its nicknames of 'poor man's golf' or 'collier's golf' in the areas where it was strong. At the turn of the twentieth century *The Sportsman* noted that the game 'holds steady sway over the humble sporting masses of the crowded districts of the West Riding of Yorkshire and the adjoining Lancashire hives of industry'.

Knur and spell has also always been closely associated with playing for stake-money and gambling at matches. As early as 1826, contests were being held for significant stakes, such as one that took place on Leeds' Woodhouse Moor between Scott and Wheater for a stake of 40 guineas. The game is ideally suited to gambling, offering opportunities for betting on the result of each rise and on the game as a whole. It is also deeply linked to the public house, with pub landlords often being promoters and stakeholders, and land adjoining or near to a local pub being the site for many contests.

The production of the implements of competition was concentrated among participants, creating a minor cottage industry of small producers. Like the early golf professionals, leading players were often also the manufacturers of their own equipment. Other than sponsorship by pubs, and, in the latter half the twentieth century, breweries, the game was largely untouched by commercial interests.

Bats are made of alder, ash or hickory, and usually measure around four feet in length, although they could be up to six feet. The head of the bat, the 'pommel', is similar to a golf club's, with a curved back and flat striking surface and is made of compressed wood, such as hornbeam, maple or sycamore. The knur was originally made from lignum vitae or another hardwood, but by the end of the nineteenth century it was made of porcelain. A competition knur weighs half an ounce (approximately 16 grams). The 'spell', made of metal or wood, is a device that operates on the same principle as a mousetrap. A spring-loaded arm, which has a cup for the knur at one end, is pulled back and attached to a catch, which the player touches with his bat to launch the knur into the air.

The knur can also be launched from a 'pin', which resembles a small gallows from which the ball is suspended in mid-air from a loop of cord. The pin's ease of manufacture and the fact that the knur could be hit with greater precision from a pin meant that it gradually replaced the spell as the dominant form of launching the ball. The knur can also be hit out of the hand or, more unusually, by flicking it up after balancing it in a hole at the head of the bat.

The sport has almost no written literature and its history and traditions are passed down orally. Because of this, knur and spell is rich in linguistic and dialect variations: according to location, the player is a 'laiker' or a 'tipper' and the knur is commonly known as a 'pottie'. Even the sport itself goes under a variety of guises, including 'northern spell', 'knur laiking' and 'nor and spel'. There are also regional differences in the way in which it is played: in Barnsley, where 'nipsy' is the variation played, the bats are made from pickaxe handles.

Other than minor technological changes, such as the knur's change from wood to porcelain, the game appears to have changed little over the past two hundred years. The long distances recorded by Strutt at the turn of the eighteenth century were not substantially improved, although Fred Moore's distance of 18 scores at Halifax in 1899 with a wooden knur remains the record today, albeit being aided by a lucky bounce off a stone which allegedly improved the knur's initial distance. The record hit with a porcelain knur was 15 scores by Grinnersdale's Joe Machin at Barnsley in 1899.

Knur and spell reached the height of its popularity during the early decades of the twentieth century, when competitions organised by pubs became regular features of the Yorkshire weekend and matches could be attended by crowds of two to three thousand. Yet by the outbreak of the Second World War the game had fallen almost into terminal decline. In the 1960s and 1970s, helped by sponsorship mainly from local breweries, the game underwent something of a revival and a world championship, although drawing its contestants from the geographically unambitious areas of east Lancashire and west Yorkshire, was instituted. It was noted however that the championship's competitors could hit barely two-thirds of the distances recorded by the champions of the past.

Much of the game-play of knur and spell is almost ritualistic, with the players taking large amounts of time to measure the spring of the knur from the spell (if used), mark out the ground into scores and clear the ground of any obstacles. Weather conditions are also an important part of the game, with the best players maximising any advantage to be gained from the wind.

Today, knur and spell belongs largely to the realm of resurrected folk culture, similar to the staging of folk-football matches on Shrovetide Tuesday. However, it remains a symbol of English 'northern-ness', linking industrial towns and mining villages with the local countryside. Despite being viewed more as a contemporary curiosity than as serious sport, the depth of its traditions, and those of the northern culture of which it is a part, ensure that it continues to survive and is unlikely ever to be completely extinguished.

Sources and Reading:

The Encyclopaedia of Sport (London: *The Sportsman*, 1912).

Firth, G., *Victorian Yorkshire at Play* (Nelson: Hendon, 1989).

Gomme, A. B., *The Traditional Games of England, Scotland and Ireland* (London: Thames and Hudson facsimile edition, 1984).

Strutt, J., *The Sports and Pastimes of the People of England* (London: J. White, 1801).

Tomlinson, A., 'Shifting Patterns of Working Class Leisure: The Case of Knurr and Spell', *Sociology of Sport Journal*, 9: 2 (1992), 192–206.

See also Billeting, Dab-an-Thicker, Kibel and Nerspel, Trap Ball

Tony Collins

Kook

A type of quoits played in Cornwall in the eighteenth and nineteenth centuries. The object was either to throw the quoit farther than one's opponents or as near as possible to a target.

Sources and Reading:
Gomme, A. B., *The Traditional Games of England, Scotland and Ireland* (London: Thames and Hudson facsimile edition, 1984).

See also Quoits

Tony Collins

Lark Singing

A competition common in the Halifax area of Yorkshire before the First World War. Larks would be captured and trained to sing by enthusiasts known as 'lark men'. Contests would be held in pubs, with each lark being brought into the pub in a dark box. When the box was opened, the lark, thinking it was dawn, would sing. The larks would be judged on the quality and length of their song.

Sources and Reading:
Pegg, B., *Rites and Riots: Folk Customs of Britain and Europe* (Poole: Blandford, 1981).

Tony Collins

League Against Cruel Sports

The League Against Cruel Sports, established in 1924 by Henry Amos and Ernest Bell, pursues a dual approach to animal

protection that combines campaigning with conservation. It has ensured that the press, politicians and public are well informed of the cruelty involved in field sports. League investigators have made strenuous efforts to expose the reality behind the respectable facade of hunting. They remain vigilant and, if possible, bring to justice those involved in illegal blood sports including badger baiting, dog fighting and cockfighting. The organisation has been instrumental in promoting legal protection for the badger, including the protection of their setts. The League-sponsored Wild Mammals (Protection) Act introduced in 1996 provided basic protection for all wild mammals, although hunting remained legitimate. In the same year, the League joined forces with the RSPCA and the IFAW to promote the Campaign for the Protection of Hunted Animals. The League has successfully mobilised cross-party support in Parliament for the campaign to abolish both hunting with dogs and hare coursing.

Since 1959, the League has purchased land of special benefit to wildlife, mainly in Somerset and Devon, to which it organises educational visits. It has a small permanent group of staff based at its headquarters in London. Subscriptions provide the League's main source of funding, and members receive its *Wildlife Guardian* journal, outlining its work at national level, and have the opportunity to join one of the many local League support groups.

Sources and Reading:
Shipley, P., *The 'Guardian' Directory of Pressure Groups and Representative Associations* (London: Wilton House, 1976).
Wildlife Guardian

John Martin

Leaping Pole

The nineteenth-century forerunner of the pole-vault, the leaping pole was made of fir or bamboo and measured between two and five feet. Although it was used for leaping over high obstacles, such as gates and bars, its major use was for leaping lengths, such as ditches (in contrast to modern pole-vaulting) – the pole being placed in the centre of the ditch to propel the jumper forwards instead of upwards.

Sources and Reading:
Stonehenge [J. H. Walsh], *Manual of British Rural Sports* (London: Routledge, 1857).

See also Pedestrianism

Tony Collins

Liverpool Olympics

One of a number of events of the mid-nineteenth century that sought to revive in some way elements of the ancient Greek Olympic Games. In 1862, Charles Melly and John Hulley of the Liverpool Athletic Club staged a Grand Olympic Festival at the Mount Vernon Parade Ground in front of around 10,000 spectators. Twenty-two sports took place, including running, walking, boxing, Indian club exercises, sword fighting, pole-leaping, throwing a cricket ball and, somewhat out of kilter with the prevailing Olympism, essay writing. Gold, silver and bronze medals were awarded.

The following year, swimming and combat sports were added and a circular 440 yards-long track used for athletics. Two subsequent 'Olympics' were staged over the next two years, the fourth coinciding with the founding of the National Olympian Association. The 1866 games were held at Llandudno over four days and added aquatic sports to the events. The sixth and final games were held at three sites in Liverpool and Birkenhead in 1867.

The demise of the Liverpool Olympics seems to owe not a little to personal scandal surrounding Hulley, their driving force, who went bankrupt in 1871 and was rumoured to have eloped with the daughter of a wealthy Liverpool shipping magnate.

Sources and Reading:
Ruhl, J., 'Liverpool Olympics', in Cox, R., Jarvie, G. and Vamplew, W. (eds), *The Encyclopedia of British Sport* (Oxford: ABC-Clio, 2000).

See also Cotswold Olympicks, Morpeth Olympic Games, Much Wenlock Games

Tony Collins

Llandudno Grand Olympic Festival

A Grand Olympic Festival, organised by the Athletic Society of Great Britain, was held at Llandudno in Caernarfonshire between 25 and 28 June 1866. It was designed to promote athletic and manly exercises and was one of a series of six such festivals; the other five having taken place annually in Liverpool from 1861 to 1865 and again in 1867. The Llandudno event was situated in a field near the town centre and competitions were open to gentlemen amateurs. The festival included a diversity of sports, such as swimming, running, boxing, broadsword and Indian club exercises, as well as a sailing contest, from Liverpool to Llandudno, to end the proceedings. In total, 77 medals were awarded, with one special gold medal presented to the individual who had demonstrated the greatest athletic proficiency during the course of the four days.

Sources and Reading:
Anthony, D., *Minds, Bodies and Souls: An A to Z of the British Olympic Heritage Network* (London: British Olympic Association, 1995).
North Wales Chronicle (10 March 1866; 30 June 1866).

Emma Lile

Lobber

A version of cudgel in which a stick rather than a wooden puck was used.

Sources and Reading:
Gomme, A. B., *The Traditional Games of England, Scotland and Ireland* (London: Thames and Hudson facsimile edition, 1984).

See also Cudgel

Tony Collins

Loggats

Similar to quoits, loggats was a sport in which a stake was fixed to the ground and small logs, the 'loggats', thrown at it, the winner being the person who hits it or gets the nearest. Bones were reputedly used originally, both as targets and missiles. The game was allegedly banned by Henry VIII.

Sources and Reading:
Gomme, A. B., *The Traditional Games of England, Scotland and Ireland* (London: Thames and Hudson facsimile edition, 1984).

See also Quoits

Tony Collins

Long Alley

A version of skittles from the south-east of England, traditionally played outdoors on specially made alleys in pubs. A wooden disc known as a 'cheese' is thrown or rolled at nine skittles. Each player has three cheeses for each turn, and there are five turns in a game. In the team version of the game there are six to eight players per side and each player is matched against a specific member of the opposing team.

Sources and Reading:
Gorini, P., *Encyclopedia of Traditional Games* (Rome: Gremese, 1994).

See also Bowls, Skittles

Tony Collins

Long Bullets

An eighteenth-century form of skittles in which a lead ball was thrown at nine pins.

Sources and Reading:
Underdown, D., *Start of Play. Cricket and Culture in Eighteenth Century England* (Harmondsworth: Allen Lane, 2000).

See also Bowls, Skittles

Tony Collins

Lurchers

A 'lurcher' is any dog that is a cross between a greyhound and a herding dog (where the herding dog might typically be an Irish wolfhound, Bedlington or collie). The legends and folklore of the eighteenth century record accounts of amazing beasts that were brave, bold, cunning, loyal and adept at scent hunting. Lurchers and their owners were depicted as 'roguish' figures who were involved in illicit hunting. This popular view was encouraged by the belief that the word 'lurcher' originated from the Romany word 'lur', meaning 'thief'. Daytime sport involves the pursuit of hares (or even rabbits), when ferrets are used to persuade them to vacate their subterranean refuges, which the lurchers mark. Lurchers can also be used at night by using powerful lamps to spot the quarry, a practice known as 'lamping'. Lurcher owners are encouraged to become members of local clubs and to abide by a nationally agreed code of conduct, which involves a close season for their quarry.

John Martin

Marbles

Linked in its origins to bowls and claimed by some to be a miniature version of that game, marbles has a long, if somewhat unclear, history.

There are broadly four ways of playing the game: by rolling the marble into a hole, by using the marble to hit or knock down a target, by aiming the marbles at a number of targets on a board or other playing surface, or by using the marbles to hit others or force them outside a given area.

This last version is probably the most common today and is often known as 'ring taw' marbles. Forty-nine marbles are placed in a concrete circle 2 metres across and a 2-centimetre shooting marble, the 'tolley' or 'taw', is flicked at them using the thumb. The aim is to knock as many marbles as possible out of the ring while leaving the tolley inside. Ring taw is also known as 'pig ring'.

There are an almost infinite number of variations based on the basic principles of the game. 'Boss out', also known as 'boss and span', closely resembles modern bowls. The first player bowls a marble as far as they wish and the opponent then has to hit it. If the opponent's marble hits or gets to within a marble's width of the first ball, the opponent wins. If not, the opponent's marble becomes the target for the first player to hit, and so on until there is a winner. In 'long tawl', each player takes a turn to try to hit an opponent's marble; those that do so win the hit marble.

'Chock' is a version of marbles in which the aim is to get the marble into a hole, rather than hitting other marbles. It is also known as 'chock hole', 'dumps' and 'hoilakes'. 'Three holes' uses larger marbles, and the aim is to place three marbles in three holes in the ground consecutively. 'Cob' is essentially the same game but with the aim of getting four marbles into four holes.

The very earliest marbles were made of clay or stone. By the seventeenth century some marbles were actually made of marble, but alabaster, earthenware and porcelain were more common. Today's glass marbles were the products of advances in glass-making technology and appeared around the 1840s.

The marble-playing season traditionally began on Ash Wednesday, the first day of Lent. In Sussex, Good Friday marked the end of the marble-playing season, so much so that in some parts of the county the day was also known as Marble Day.

The self-proclaimed 'World Marbles Championship', dating from 1932, takes place every Good Friday at Tinsley Green near Crawley in West Sussex, using ring taw rules but with only 13 marbles in the circle. Legend has it that the event dates back to 1600, when two young men vied for the hand of a local woman by playing marbles for her. Len Smith and his team, The Terrible Toucans, dominated the championships in the period after the Second World War, winning 15 individual titles and 20 consecutive team titles.

Sources and Reading:
Day, B., *A Chronicle of Folk Customs* (London: Hamlyn, 1988).
Gomme, A. B., *The Traditional Games of England, Scotland and Ireland* (London: Thames and Hudson facsimile edition, 1984).
Gorini, P., *Encyclopedia of Traditional Games* (Rome: Gremese, 1994).
Whitlock, R., *A Calendar of Country Customs* (London: Batsford, 1978).

See also Bowls, Skittles, Spangie

Tony Collins

Material Culture

The 'material culture' of a sport includes the objects used in the play or pursuit of the sporting activity, as well as any special clothing, prizes or other things associated with sport.

Almost every game is defined by its implements. The possibilities of, and difficulties in, shooting are limited by the technology of the gun, and the use of a bias bowl shapes the strategy of bowling. Stick-and-ball games were often played with sheep's vertebrae or fishermen's cork floats; when the first hockey club was set up at Blackheath in 1861 it briefly followed this tradition by using a cubical 'ball' of India rubber: the introduction of a spherical ball changed the character of the play.

At first, the implements of play were largely made within the community in which players lived, by the players themselves or by craftsmen who had an appropriate skill. Thus skittles might be hewn by adze, worked on a pole-lathe on a farm, or turned by a joiner if one were available. In Ireland in the seventeenth and eighteenth centuries, hurling balls were made by rubbing cow hair between the hands to form a tough compact ball. These balls were superseded by ones covered with sewn leather.

As time passed, craftsmen played a larger part in producing sporting equipment. A bladder-filled football could be made only by a saddler or a cobbler. The football for the annual match at Chester, held until 1540, was provided by the city's Shoe-makers' Company. A notoriously unruly form of football called *y bêl ddu* (black ball) was played over the Christmas period in Cardiganshire during the early nineteenth century: the local shoemaker was paid to make the ball and deliver it to the field of play.

Curling demonstrates each stage in the progression from community to commercial manufacture. Early curling stones were collected from river beds by the players themselves. The earliest were quite small, with an impression large enough to enable the fingers to grip, but later the parish blacksmith would have been employed to let an iron handle into the stone. At the beginning of the nineteenth century circular stones were adopted, individually made by the local mason. In the 1850s, water-driven grinding and polishing machines were able to produce a standard, factory-made product, and the market was served by a handful of firms rather than by hundreds of masons.

Specialist craftsmen made equipment for the wealthy. Balls and rackets for royal tennis were very expensive: the costly hardware therefore limited play to those who could afford it. The point in Shakespeare's *Henry V* about the Dauphin's gift of tennis balls to the young king was that they were not warlike, not that they were cheap. Tennis also needed a specially built court, and courts were built only by royalty and the most wealthy (as at Petworth House in Sussex) or in the older universities. Occasionally equipment was made for a single event; in 1750 the Earls of March and of Eglinton won a wager of 1,000 guineas by having four horses pull a four-wheeled carriage 19 miles in one hour: the carriage was ingeniously made to be as light as possible. Technical change also affects sport. For example, falconry was killed off in the seventeenth century by improved firearms, and in the same period the replacement of bone skates by metal ones made ice skating more popular. The wealthy also bought equipment made at a distance: in the seventeenth and eighteenth centuries British archers got their arrows from fletchers in Ghent.

There were some specialist tradesmen, such as bowyers and fletchers, and makers of cricket bats and balls, and by the late eighteenth century a growing number of tailors and saddle makers concentrated on goods for huntsmen. In Ireland, balls for handball were made from easily available materials: the root of a briar as a core, wool or cow hair for the body of the ball, and sheep, goat or foal skin for the cover. The skill of crafting the balls was as much in the selection of the materials as in the packing and sewing. The best craftsmen are still remembered even though they worked nearly a century ago, such as Forde of Lucan and Keegan of Kells. Other craftsmen who worked at the highest level of skill gave their names to the things they made, such as Joe Manton (1766–1835) to his guns, Mantons.

In the nineteenth century the crucial materials for sporting implements were leather, catgut (for strings) and, from about 1830, rubber, which was newly available in quantity. In cricket, rubber provided protection for the fingers of batsmen and so played a part in the overarm revolution by allowing batsmen to play the ball with confidence. The golf ball made of gutta-percha (a kind of rubber) was introduced around 1848 and made the game much cheaper.

Specialist growers and manufacturers became associated with particular areas, such as growing cricket-bat willow in Suffolk or making cricket balls in various places in Kent. Several towns on the east coast of Scotland had golf ball and club makers. Gilbert's of Rugby specialised in rugby balls, and at the end of the nineteenth century Tomlinson's of Glasgow produced footballs. Rubber sports goods, however, were made in the cities where there were firms that already made other uses of rubber. One of them, the North British Rubber Company of Edinburgh, moved into making golf balls after the introduction of the rubber-cored ball and established its 'Clincher Cross' as a major seller.

In England, where patronage of sports was widespread, the typical prize was a piece of clothing: a smock for women's running or a beaver hat for men's wrestling. Sir Thomas Parkyns (died 1741) of Bunny in Nottinghamshire every year offered a gold-laced hat for wrestling. A song of 1686 from the north of England invites young women to 'loup' (leap) for a pair of slippers. The original prize (1860) for the Open golf tournament was a belt. Medals, which became a common minor prize towards the end of the eighteenth century, were intended to be worn on the chest or lapel like a military campaign medal. Animals, too, were given things to wear: at Dover's Cotswold Games the prize for hare coursing was a silver collar, and the oldest surviving prize in Britain is the Carlisle Bells for horseracing (1590). In Scotland, trophies based on the equipment of sport were common. Nineteen silver arrows made between around 1600 and 1838 survive. Other examples are the Edinburgh silver golf club (1744), its equivalent at St Andrews (1754) and the Edinburgh silver jack for bowling (1771). In the eighteenth century the cup became the standard prize for horseracing in England, and towards the end of the century it spread to other sports.

Ready-made sports clothing started to appear between 1860 and 1880. This was also the period of the rise of the entrepreneur Lillywhite, who might be remembered because he started the *Lillywhite's Cricketers' Almanac*, but who made far more money from a general sporting goods emporium that served the new mass market.

The material culture of sport also includes images, from the oils of George Stubbs (1724–1806) and John Fearnley, via sporting prints, which were particularly popular in the first half of the nineteenth century, to public art in the form of inn signs. One of the most popular subjects for sporting prints was the Earls' wager, mentioned above. There are also oddities, such as Parkyns's headstone, which shows him in the first position of the Cornish hug. In the MCC's museum is a handkerchief dating from the mid-1740s, an early example of the deliberate making of sporting souvenirs. Other examples of early souvenirs might be an engraved glass to commemorate a famous racehorse or a ceramic plate celebrating Dr Grace's hundredth century.

Finally, there are objects that are part of sporting history only because of the sudden impact of outside life on sport. There is no more poignant artefact than the pistol, now at the National Horseracing Museum at Newmarket, with which in 1886 the great Fred Archer shot himself after coming second in the Cambridgeshire Handicap.

Sources and Reading:

Burnett, J. and Griffiths, J., 'Early Protective Clothing in Cricket', *Costume*, 19 (1985), 100–20.

Lucas, A. T., 'Hair Hurling Balls', *Journal of the Cork Historical and Archaeological Society*, 57 (1952), 99–104.

Rice, T., *Treasures of Lord's* (London: Willow Books, 1989).

Sporting Glory: The Courage Exhibition of Sporting Trophies (London: Sporting Trophies Exhibitions, 1992).

John Burnett

Melton Carnegie Museum

This museum is the only institution in Britain dedicated primarily to addressing the history of hunting, not only as an aspect of Leicestershire history but also as a subject in its own right. The museum is located in Melton Mowbray, a town which in the eighteenth century became the Mecca for fox-hunting. As three of Britain's main fox-hunting packs had territory adjoining the town, it was possible for wealthy sportsmen to hunt every day of the week by spending two days with each pack. The region offered a favourable combination of hedges, fences, coverts and large areas of enclosed grazing land (which have the advantage of ensuring better scents than arable land). Easy access to the town following the development of the railways in the nineteenth century enhanced its popularity. At its peak in the nineteenth century, in excess of 500 stables were maintained in the town, including those of such luminaries as the Marquis of Waterford whose notorious exploits with a pot of red paint led to the rise of the expression 'painting the town red'. The museum houses an eclectic range of artefacts, from children's books to memorabilia, associated with hunting, including a collection of books. The exhibitions are intended to encourage visitors to form their own opinions and to share their views via a postbox system.

Websites:
www.leicestershire.gov.uk/index/community/
    museums/melton_carnegie.htm
www.aboutbritain.com/MeltonCarnegieMuseum
    .htm

John Martin

Mendoza, Daniel

One of the great bare-knuckle prizefighters of his, or any other, generation, Daniel Mendoza was born an orthodox Jew to a Sephardic family in east London's Aldgate in 1764. He left school at the age of 13 and found work with a tea dealer. He appears to have gained a reputation for being skilled in the use of his fists by standing up to anti-Semitism. By his late teens his prowess was recognised sufficiently that he was taken under the wing of the boxer Richard Humpreys, a fighter noted for fairness and respectability.

He won his first professional fight against 'Harry the Coal Heaver' and his defeat of Sam Martin, 'the Bath Butcher', in 1787 placed him in the top flight of fighters, competing for stakes as high as £1,000. The following year he fell out with his mentor, Humphreys, and fought him three times, losing the first in controversial circumstances – he slipped and injured himself – but winning the other two, the third in just fifteen minutes. The retirement in 1791 of the All England champion Ben Brain saw Mendoza claim the title. His ceaseless touring of Britain made him probably one of the most famous men in the country and it came as a great shock when in 1795 he was knocked out after nine rounds by John Jackson.

Mendoza retired and ran the Lord Nelson pub at Whitechapel. But like many boxers before and after, he found himself heavily in debt and returned to the ring in 1806, defeating Harry Lee over 53 rounds. He even boxed as late as 1820, although time was not on his side and he lost the match.

Standing around 1.7 metres (5 feet 7 inches) tall and weighing around 70 kilograms (11 stone), Mendoza owed his success as much to his approach to boxing as to his physical attributes. A keen student of technique, he published his thoughts on the 'noble art' in 1789 as *The Art of Boxing*, in which he outlined his belief that boxing strategy should be based on avoiding one's opponent's punches. Although this would appear to be based on common sense, it was a radical departure from the style of the time, which in large part consisted of swapping punches toe-to-toe until one man could take no more. The use of the guard, sidestepping and the straight left punch were innovations that, if not invented by Mendoza, were certainly popularised by him.

Many of his opponents explained his victories by reference to anti-Semitic stereotypes, such as the 'cunning Jew', yet his success helped him overcome much of the anti-Semitism of British society. He was granted an audience with the Prince of Wales, allegedly making him the first British Jew to meet royalty. More importantly, it was his prominence as a prizefighter, together with that of other Jewish boxers of the time, such as Sam Elias, Elisha Crabbe and Mendoza's cousins Angel Hyams and Aaron Mendoza, that helped to give Jews a new-found self-confidence. As the nineteenth-century radical Francis Place noted, Mendoza's triumphs meant that boxing 'soon spread among the young Jews and they became generally expert at it. The consequence was in a very few years seen and felt too. It was no longer safe to insult a Jew unless he was an old man and alone.'

Sources and Reading:
Brailsford, D., *Bareknuckles: A Social History of Prize Fighting* (Cambridge: Lutterworth Press, 1989).
Magriel, P. (ed.), *The Memoirs of the Life of Daniel Mendoza* (London: Batsford, 1951).
Roberts, J. B. and Skutt, A. G., *The Boxing Register* (New York: McBooks Press, 1999).

See also Prizefighting

Tony Collins

Mink Hunting

The prohibition of otter hunting in the 1970s led to many of the surviving otter packs switching to mink as an alternative quarry. Mink had originally been imported into England from the United States in 1920 to be bred on fur farms for their pelts. A number of escapees, coupled with mink that were released by animal liberation groups after the Second World War, established a self-sustaining feral population along the banks of the river Teign in Devon. This led

to the emergence of feral populations in other areas. As with otter hunting, the activity takes place in the summer months. As the mink is considerably smaller than the otter, the pursuit usually takes place over shorter distances and in a shorter period of time. Terriers usually accompany the hounds to locate and bolt the animals from their refuges. In 2003, there were 24 registered packs of mink hounds in Britain and two in Northern Ireland.

Sources and Reading:
Faler, R. E., *The Mink Trapper's Guide* (Beaver Pond Publishing, 1996).
Medwin, T., *The Angler in Wales, or, Days and Nights of Sportsmen* (Volume 2) (London: Richard Bentley, 1834).

Website:
League Against Cruel Sports: www.league.uk.com

Nicholas Goddard and John Martin

Model Yachting (Scotland)

Model yachting was enjoyed by adults in a wide range of places in the late nineteenth and early twentieth centuries. In some of the Clyde burghs it was a serious sport on specially built ponds in public parks. George Blake describes an event in Garvel near Greenock in the 1930s in his novel *The Piper's Tune* (1950), where:

model yachtsmen hastened round the banks of the reservoir in glistening thigh-boots, brandishing hooked poles and wading out to secure their charges, swiftly reset their sails and send them spinning on the next leg of the race.

Children's events on smaller ponds were less serious.

Near fishing villages on the Aberdeenshire and Moray Firth coasts models were raced on mill ponds, particularly on the afternoon of New Year's Day. In at least one place, Macduff in Banffshire, gambling was common. On the island of Stroma, between Caithness and Orkney, the men built a dam and so created a racing pond. A complicated system of handicapping was used; the results of a day's sailing were not known until they were announced in the village shop several hours after the last race.

John Burnett

Morgan, Griffith

A renowned eighteenth-century Welsh runner, Guto Nyth Brân (real name Griffith Morgan) was born at Llanwynno in south Glamorgan in 1700. Nicknamed after the farmhouse in which he lived, Guto frequently demonstrated his phenomenal fitness by catching hares, rounding up sheep and reportedly outpacing horses. He was said to have once covered seven miles on foot in the time it took for a kettle to boil.

Guto's racing successes were many, and following a pre-match sleep on a pile of warm manure so as to relax his limbs he was prepared to challenge any takers, especially over his favourite distance of 12 miles. His last victory was in 1737, over an Englishman named Prince; Guto was so confident of his ability that during the first few miles he stopped to talk to spectators en route. Despite such initial dawdling, Guto was said to have completed the course in an astonishing and rather incredible time of 53 minutes. His career was ended there and then, however, for the hearty congratulations and back-slapping heaped upon him by his sweetheart, Siân, proved too much for Guto's exhausted body and he collapsed and died on the spot. His gravestone in Llanwynno churchyard can still be seen today, along with a more recent one commemorating his life in a verse by Gwilym Glanffrwd:

Rhedegwr gorheinyf a gwrawl – cawr
Yn curo'n wastadawl,
Oedd Gruffudd, e fydd ei fawl
Wr iesin yn arhosawl

(He was a grand and courageous runner,
A giant who was always victorious;
May the praise for radiant Griffith's good name be eternal)

Sources and Reading:
Jones, T. V., 'Yr Hen Redwyr', *Llafar Gwlad*, 10 (1985–6), 8.
Thomas, W. ('Glanffrwd'), *Plwyf Llanwyno* (Pontypridd: D. J. Hopkin, 1888).

Emma Lile

Morpeth Olympic Games

Although not designated as Olympic Games until 1881, the Morpeth Games were established in 1873 by Edmund Dobson as the 'Wrestling and Athletics Games', with a strong emphasis placed on Cumberland and Westmorland wrestling. Held under the patronage of Lord Decies of Bolam, the games were an event for professional pedestrianism and included 120- and 440-yard races, 440-yard hurdles, the high jump and the pole leap. The core events did not change, but the gradual addition of more athletic events meant that by 1912 the games were held over two days. The games were extremely popular with both spectators and participants, with sprints often attracting over 250 competitors, but following the Second World War interest began to wane and the games were abandoned after 1958.

Sources and Reading:
Ruhl, J., 'Morpeth Olympic Games', in Cox, R., Jarvie, G. and Vamplew, W., *The Encyclopedia of British Sport* (Oxford: ABC-Clio, 2000).

See also Cotswold Olympick Games, Liverpool Olympics, Much Wenlock Games

Tony Collins

Morris Family

Between them, father and son golfers Tom Morris Senior (1821–1908) and Junior (1851–75) won the Open Championship eight times. 'Old Tom' played in every Open from its inauguration in 1860 until 1896 when he was 75. He won in 1867 when aged 46 years and 99 days, still the oldest player to have done so.

Son of a handloom weaver, in 1839 Old Tom was apprenticed as a featherie ball and club maker to Allan Robertson, indisputably the greatest player at St Andrews and, by implication, in the world. Twelve years later, in the year that 'Young Tom' was born, he had a dispute with his employer over his use of a gutta-percha ball, which Robertson (rightly) saw as a threat to the livelihood of the featherie ball makers. Morris left for Prestwick in Ayrshire, a foreign country so far as St Andreans were concerned, but was later reconciled with Robertson whom he later partnered in several high-stake challenge matches. In his years at Prestwick he made great improvements to the course, an experience that was to serve him well in his future work as a golf course designer in which he pioneered the idea of laying the links out in two loops of nine holes rather than simply going out and back. When Robertson died in 1864, Morris, by then twice Open winner, returned to St Andrews to succeed his former master as professional and Custodian of the Links (greenkeeper). He remained there some 44 years before his death following a fall down the clubhouse stairs. 'Old Tom' was one of the first percentage golfers, with the hallmark of his game being careful attention to playing the safe shot: he won games not so much by making brilliant strokes but by not playing bad ones.

In contrast, Young Tom was a flair player, willing and able to play superb shots at appropriate moments during a game. He had a great temperament for the game, with the ability to concentrate on the ball throughout his swing. He won his first competition against professionals at the age of 13 and only four years later he became Open champion (with a record low score). The next year he won it again, relegating his father into second place by virtue of a better inward half. His third successive win, for which he won the Championship belt outright, was by 12 strokes over the 36 holes. There was no Open in 1871 but when the silver claret jug became the championship trophy in 1872, Young Tom's was the first name to be engraved. Three years later his wife died in childbirth along with his baby son. He died three months later, a victim of depression and heavy drinking.

Sources and Reading:
Alliss, P. and Hobbs, M., *The Who's Who of Golf* (London: Rigby, 1983).
Stirk, D., *Golf History and Tradition 1500–1945* (Ludlow: Excellent, 1998).

See also Golf

Wray Vamplew

Mountaineering (Scotland)

The Scottish mountains were first noticed as a climbing destination in the period between 1836 and 1888. The romantic treatment of wild country by Scott, Wordsworth and others stimulated tourism in the Highlands in the early nineteenth century and prompted ascents of easy summits adjoining resorts. However, the first adventurous ascents were undertaken in Skye by two St Andrews professors, James Forbes and William Knight, and a Skye-born sheriff, Alexander Nicolson. Forbes climbed Sgurr nan Gillean in 1836, Bruach na Frithe in 1845 and produced a usable map of the Cuillins; Knight climbed the neighbouring impressive Knight's Peak in 1872; Nicolson climbed Sgurr Alasdair in 1873 and Sgurr Dubh in 1874. In the 1880s, members of the Alpine Club, notably the Pilkington brothers, explored other peaks in the range, including the so-called Inaccessible Pinnacle of Sgurr Dearg, and two climbers important in the next period – Norman Collie and William Naismith – made their first marks on Skye. City-based climbing groups (The Tramps, the Sandah Club, the Cairngorm Club) began to spring up.

Between 1889 and 1920, the Scottish peaks were subjected to systematic exploration. The Scottish Mountaineering Club (SMC) was formed in Glasgow in 1889 following correspondence initiated by Naismith. It rapidly acquired a large dispersed membership. A journal was founded in 1890 and a surprising 538 mountains of 3,000 feet or higher were soon tabulated by Hugh Munro. Description of these mountains continued for the next 20 years, resulting in the first (private) SMC guidebook series. The principal mountains in Munro's tables – the 283 'Munros' – were first traversed by Archibald Robertson in 1901, though it has become clear that he did not actually reach every summit. Climbing exploration of Arran, Arrochar, Glencoe, Ben Nevis and Skye began slowly but picked up pace in 1894, following the *tour de force* winter ascent of the Tower Ridge of Ben Nevis by Norman Collie's party. Outside these areas climbing was mostly confined to winter and spring, because of the large area of land preserved for shooting. The vast northern cliffs of Ben Nevis were comprehensively explored, particularly by William Inglis Clark (who wrote the first public guide to the mountain) and Harold Raeburn (who made several bold and difficult ascents in summer and winter). Activity on the peaks and crags of Skye was also intense and thorough, thanks to the efforts of SMC stalwarts Collie and Naismith and several visitors from England – Ashley and George Abraham, Archer Thomson, George Mallory and the Rucksack Club's Everard Steeple and Guy Barlow, authors of the first Skye guide (1923). The first integral traverse of the main Cuillin Ridge, a chain of some 25 peaks, was made by Leslie Shadbolt and Alistair McLaren in 1911. In Glencoe, inaccessible by public transport, exploration was more sporadic, but several fine ascents were made by Raeburn and others, including English 'raids' by the Abrahams, Noel Odell, Alfred Pigott and Morley Wood. In 1908, Jane Inglis Clark,

her daughter Mabel, and Lucy Smith formed the Ladies' Scottish Climbing Club, anticipating by a few years the formation of the Ladies' Alpine Club in London.

The Great War took a heavy toll, and climbing recovered slowly in the 1920s. A new geographically sectioned club, the Junior Mountaineering Club of Scotland (JMCS), was formed in 1925 and soon produced new blood. Jim Bell, Graham Macphee and the Glasgow JMCS group led by Bill Mackenzie and Bill Murray were the moving spirits in this revival, which still kept Glencoe, Ben Nevis and Skye as its focus. By the mid-1930s, these climbers had begun to find ways on impressively steep crags, such as the Orion Face of Ben Nevis. Mackenzie and Murray re-established the tradition of winter climbing, but as a virtuous rather than a necessary feature of Scottish climbing.

In the 1930s, several climbing groups un-affiliated to the SMC sprung up in the major cities, stimulated by outdoor movements and economic depression. Notable clubs of this type were: the Creagh Dhu, Lomond, Ptarmigan and Tricouni Clubs (Glasgow area); the Grampian and Corrie Clubs and a Creagh Dhu branch (Dundee); and the Etchachan and Moray Clubs (Aberdeen/ Elgin). In the same period, clubs were formed at all five universities. Two climbers from the loosely associated Glasgow groups, Hamish Hamilton and Jock Nimlin, made bold ascents in Arran, Arrochar and Glencoe. Hamilton's ascent of Agag's Groove on Rannoch Wall, Mackenzie and Murray's winter ascent of Garrick's Shelf, and Nimlin's ascent of Raven's Gully (all on Buachaille Etive) were the finest achievements of the period.

Scotland's first climbers' hut, the Clark Hut, was constructed on Ben Nevis below the northern cliffs in 1929, a few years after Helyg (north Wales) and the Robertson Lamb Hut (Lake District). The SMC's guidebook series now embraced seven volumes, covering all regions except the southern Highlands. The National Trust for Scotland, formed in 1931, soon acquired the Glencoe estates, thanks to the efforts of mountaineers, notably Percy Unna. These institutional developments marked a clear movement from the recreation of a few hundred enthusiasts to a popular sport.

The return of war in 1939 put an end to activity, except for the extraordinary anomaly of Brian Kellett, an English conscientious objector put to work in the Torlundy Forestry below Ben Nevis. Kellett made Ben Nevis his private battlefield during the war years, putting up many bold and difficult routes, often alone. His solo ascent of Gardyloo Buttress set a standard that stood for ten years or more. Ironically, he was killed on the easy Cousins' Buttress in 1945.

Following the Second World War, petrol rationing provoked the use of buses, promoting fellowship and strong club orientation. The publication of Bill Murray's inspirational books stimulated young climbers everywhere. Climbers in the Aberdeen area began to explore the Cairngorm crags, until now largely neglected. Bill Brooker and Tom Patey were leading lights of this group, which explored the impressive crags of Lochnagar, Creag an Dubh Loch and Coire Etchachan, in summer and winter. Patey enjoyed success in the Alps and Himalayas too, before dying in an abseil accident in 1970. Two Creagh Dhu climbers, John Cunningham and Pat Walsh, dominated Glencoe climbing, finding extremely difficult test-pieces on Buachaille's steeper walls.

In the early 1950s, in reaction to the formation of the British Mountaineering Council, an Association of Scottish Climbing Clubs was formed. More club huts were established too, at Derry Lodge in the Cairngorms, Lagangarbh in Glencoe and the Ling Hut in Torridon. Increasing participation led to the formation of volunteer mountain rescue teams in the important centres; technical advances were made by the Glencoe team under Hamish MacInnes and copied elsewhere. A national training centre was established at Glenmore Lodge near Aviemore. Rock- and ice-climbing guidebooks were produced by the SMC for the major centres. The National Trust for

Scotland added Ben Lawers, Kintail and Torridon to its mountain properties. Meanwhile, 'raids' from England continued, with visits from Joe Brown, Bob Downes and Don Whillans producing the best rock climbs on Ben Nevis: Sassenach, Centurion and Minus One Buttress. Downes, together with Cambridge friends Mike O'Hara and Eric Langmuir, also discovered the Trilleachan Slabs near Glencoe, soon rapidly developed by the Creagh Dhu, and Carnmore Crag in Letterewe Forest.

In the late 1950s and early 1960s, Edinburgh climbers came to the fore for the first time since the days of Raeburn. Jimmy Marshall, already a veteran, was joined by Robin Smith, Dougal Haston and others to form a very strong group, occasionally augmented by the Creagh Dhu's John McLean. Marshall put up fine new routes all over the country, even snatching the prizes of Parallel B Gully on Lochnagar and Mousetrap on the Dubh Loch from beneath the noses of the Cairngorm regulars. Along with Smith, he disposed of the remaining major unclimbed winter routes on Ben Nevis in a famous campaign in 1960. Smith, like Marshall, spread his huge talent far and wide: his routes, Shibboleth on Buachaille Etive, The Needle on the forbidding Shelter Stone Crag of Ben Macdhui and The Bat (with Haston) on Ben Nevis, are classics of the period and remain test-pieces even today. Smith died in the Pamirs in 1962, and Haston left Scotland for greater mountaineering in the Alps and beyond, eventually becoming not just the first Scot, but the first Briton to climb Mount Everest in 1975.

The 1970s was a period of consolidation and technical refinement. A more efficient method of ice-climbing using two short curved picks and eliminating step-cutting was developed by Hamish MacInnes, John Cunningham and Bill March. This ethically backward step, substituting aid for effort, was compensated by a puristic aid-free approach to rock-climbing championed by Dave Cuthbertson, Murray Hamilton and Kenny Spence. Institutional development proceeded apace, with rapid growth of clubs, climbers' huts and adopted bothies, the formation of a Mountaineering Council, and the completion to a high standard of the SMC guidebook programme. This was driven along by Graham Tiso, who also established a chain of climbing shops, soon to be jostling for business with competing chains.

In 1970, only 100 or so climbers had completed the 280-odd Munros. But the Munro 'curve' steepened markedly through the 1970s, and soared in the 1980s. Now, around 3,000 climbers have completed the Munros, wearing grooves up the mountains and producing parking chaos at their bases. This huge rise in participation has required costly management and provoked an uneasy response from landowners, but has also provided an all-season input to the Highland economy. While the problems of access and management have been assisted by the series of acquisitions by the National Trust for Scotland and the John Muir Trust, and also by legislation, the ramifications of what is essentially a change of use of land are likely to trouble us for many decades.

Other tendencies evident in the 1980s and 1990s were a downhill movement to low-level crags, quarries and sea-cliffs, and even to indoor climbing walls equipped with bolt-on holds. This movement is driven by various factors: technical advances have led to the search for steeper and less-eroded crags, warm winters have discouraged activists from visiting the high peaks, and the safety arrangements of indoor walls can be more easily emulated on small low-level crags. It is ironic that both new legislation providing access to mountains and a National Indoor Climbing Centre at Ratho Quarry were being planned at the same time.

Sources and Reading:

Bell, J. H. B., *A Progress in Mountaineering* (Edinburgh: Oliver & Boyd, 1950).

Borthwick, A., *Always a Little Further* (London: Faber, 1939).

Brooker, W. D., *A Century of Scottish Mountaineering* (Glasgow: Scottish Mountaineering Trust, 1989).

Campbell, R. N., *The Munroist's Companion* (Edinburgh: Scottish Mountaineering Trust, 1999).

Clark, R. W. and Pyatt, E. C., *Mountaineering in Britain* (London: Phoenix House, 1957).

Connor, J., *Creagh Dhu Climber* (London: Ernest Press, 1999).

Connor, J., *Dougal Haston: The Philosophy of Risk* (Edinburgh: Canongate, 2002).

Crocket, K., *Ben Nevis* (Edinburgh: Scottish Mountaineering Trust, 1986).

Haston, D., *In High Places* (London: Cassell, 1972).

Humble, B. H., *The Cuillin of Skye* (London: Robert Hale, 1952).

Mitchell, I., *Scotland's Mountains Before the Mountaineers* (Edinburgh: Luath Press, 1998).

Murray, W. H., *Mountaineering in Scotland* (London: Dent, 1947).

Murray, W. H., *Undiscovered Scotland* (London: Dent, 1951).

Patey, T. W., *One Man's Mountains* (London: Gollancz, 1971).

Thomson, I. D. S., *May the Fire Always be Lit: A Biography of Jock Nimlin* (London: Ernest Press, 1995).

Robin N. Campbell

Mountaineering (Wales)

Scaling the nation's peaks for pleasure began in Wales during the late eighteenth century and by the mid-nineteenth century had become extremely fashionable. With its dramatic and varied ranges, such as Snowdonia in the north and the Brecon Beacons and Black Mountains in the south, Wales attracted countless climbers. While many of the climbers were local, it was the English, who travelled over in hordes, that were largely responsible for developing the sports of mountaineering and rock-climbing. These included Alpine mountaineers, who sought winter practice in north Wales where there were good snow and ice conditions.

When the Climbers' Club was formed in 1898 to cater for those who climbed regularly in Wales, most of its members were drawn from England. Of the Welsh climbers, J. Archer Thomson (1863–1912) was one of the most eminent before the First World War, along with Owen Glynne Jones (1867–99), a Londoner by birth but with Welsh origins. Jones pioneered new rock-climbing techniques, until he lost his life at a young age in a climbing accident.

According to folk legend, if a person spends a night alone on either the peak of Snowdon or the peak of Cader Idris (the highest mountain in mid-Wales), the next morning they will either be found dead, mad or a gifted poet.

Sources and Reading:
Hankinson, A., *The Mountain Men: An Early History of Rock Climbing in North Wales* (London: Heinemann, 1977).
Jones, R. M., 'The Mountaineering of Wales, 1880–1925', *Welsh History Review*, 19: 1 (1998), 44–67.
Jones, T. and Milburn, G., *Welsh Rock* (Glossop: Pic, 1986).

Emma Lile

Mowing Matches (Wales)

Before the age of machinery, fields were often mown communally. This was the case at Ystradfellte in Powys, where, during the pre-industrial period, an event was held every August at the Waun Gron (round meadow) between the area's champion scythe-wielders.

The objective of the first Vale of Clwyd Mowing Competition, held at Denbigh in July 1883, was to demonstrate the best contemporary mowing implements to the local farmers. Competitors were each required to mow 1 acre of clover and 1 acre of rough meadow grass and the contest took place across two fields. The winning driver (whose machine had cut three-quarters of an acre in 33 minutes) received a prize of 10 shillings.

Mowing also took place for wagers, such as the £5 challenge undertaken by Mr Bagnell of Llanfoist in 1838 to mow 4 acres of barley between daybreak and late afternoon. He not only succeeded in completing the task, but then proceeded to mow a further 1½ acres. Some £50 to £60 changed hands overall, and among the large number of spectators were several members of the local elite.

Mowing matches were not, of course, confined to Wales but took place in most of the pastoral areas which predominated in the western areas of Britain.

Sources and Reading:
Cambria Daily Leader (29 July 1893).
Davies, D., *Brecknock Historian* (Brecon: D. G. and A. S. Evans, 1977).
Monmouthshire Beacon (29 September 1838).
North Wales Chronicle (14 July 1883).

Emma Lile

Much Wenlock Games

The Much Wenlock Games, named after the village in Shropshire in which they were held, were founded in 1850 by local doctor William Penny Brooks as part of his work to develop the physical, moral and intellectual qualities of the working classes of the area. In 1841 Brooks had founded the Wenlock Agricultural Reading Society as part of the same work of 'rational recreation'. He outlined the philosophy underlying his activities in a speech that closed the 1851 games. In it he noted that sports in the area had been associated with drunkenness and disorderly conduct, and that his aim was to bring 'properly conducted' sports to the working classes.

The games were first held on 22 and 23 October 1850 on the Much Wenlock racecourse amidst much pageantry, which included banners with Greek inscriptions and the presentation of laurel leaves to the winners. For the duration of the games the racecourse was renamed the 'Olympian Fields'. Although professional athletes were explicitly excluded from the games, cash prizes were originally awarded, but cups and medals soon became the method of rewarding the victors. In 1875 the winner of the tilting at the ring competition was presented with a silver goblet worth £10.

The games were staged 11 times until 1860 and included athletic, artistic and intellectual activities. Sporting activities were a mixture of the overtly Olympian athletic contests and rustic sports, such as football, cudgels and quoits. Singing, poetry, history, arithmetic, recitation, essay writing, knitting and sewing were among the artistic and intellectual activities, while the athletic events included foot racing, high and long jumps (standing and running), hopping, hurdling, hammer and stone throwing, together with more traditional activities such as tilting at the ring, prisoner's base, sack racing, pole climbing and archery. Football, cricket, quoits and shooting were also staged, although the programme of activities tended to vary from year to year. Events were staged for children, although most of the events for girls were traditionally 'feminine', such as sewing and knitting. Interestingly, however, a foot race was held for 'old women', a tradition which harked back to older sporting festivals such as the Hungerford Revel. This was in line with Brooks's vision of 'merrie England' and his endorsement in a speech of 1857 of 'those annual field sports and exercises which were in vogue when our country a long time ago . . . was really deserving of the title "Merrie England"'.

In 1860 Brooks initiated the Shropshire Olympian Society, which organised four annual 'Shropshire Olympian Games', two in Much Wenlock, one in Wellington (1861) and one in Shrewsbury (1864). The popularity of the games can be gauged by the fact that in 1861 they attracted a crowd of 5,000, which increased to 10,000 when Much Wenlock acquired a railway station later that decade.

Influenced heavily by Zappas's revival of the Greek Olympics in 1859, Brooks's games increasingly became marked by the use of Greek symbols, such as Greek inscriptions, laurel and olive wreaths and the awarding of medals. However, amateurism, viewed by most middle-class Victorian enthusiasts for sport as the most important of the Greek sporting ethics, was abandoned in 1868.

In 1865, Brooks established the National Olympian Association which staged the National Olympian Games in 1866 at Crystal Palace and in 1867 at Birmingham. Its 1868, 1874, 1877 and 1883 meetings were all held in Shropshire. However, its attempts to become an umbrella body for athletic sports in Britain brought it into conflict with the Amateur Athletic Club (later Association), which had been formed in 1866, and ultimately led to its demise.

Nevertheless, Brooks continued to be a committed supporter of attempts to propagate the Olympic idea. In 1877, he persuaded King George I of Greece to donate a silver cup for the winner of the pentathlon at the 1877 National Olympian Games, held at Shrewsbury. In 1880 he presaged Pierre de Coubertin's Games by attempting, unsuccessfully, to organise an 'International Olympian Festival' in Athens. Ten years later, the young Coubertin met Brooks on one of his visits to Britain to learn about British sport, and subsequently made him an honorary member of his Olympic Committee. Sadly, Brooks died just four months before the 1896 modern Olympics were staged in Athens.

The Much Wenlock Games did not survive the First World War; however, they were revived in 1950 and then again in 1977 and continue today.

Sources and Reading:

James, T., 'The Much Wenlock Olympian Games', *British Society of Sports History Bulletin*, 9 (1989), 38–50.

Mullins, S., *British Olympians: William Penny Brooks and the Wenlock Games* (London: British Olympic Association, 1986).

Ruhl, J., 'Much Wenlock Games', in Cox, R., Jarvie, G. and Vamplew, W., *The Encyclopedia of British Sport* (Oxford: ABC-Clio, 2000).

See also Cotswold Olympick Games, Liverpool Olympics, Morpeth Olympic Games

Tony Collins

Museum of Welsh Life

Opened in 1948, the Museum of Welsh Life, at St Fagans in Cardiff, is one of Europe's foremost open-air museums. Its aim is to convey Welsh traditional life and culture over the centuries, both through the re-erection of original houses and other holdings from across the country and by gallery displays.

Items relating to sports and games form an important component of the museum's collections and include a wide variety of artefacts, manuscripts and photographs. Rural sports items dating from the pre-industrial period include cockfighting memorabilia, archery equipment and papers relating to the Royal British Bowmen, and a nineteenth-century bando stick with associated ballad from Glamorgan. The museum's sound archive contains several recordings of speakers commenting on folk games and sports. A permanent sports exhibition is held in the Gallery of Material Culture.

Emma Lile

Nacks

A version of Aunt Sally played in Yorkshire in which wooden pegs are the target rather than a doll.

Sources and Reading:
Gomme, A. B., *The Traditional Games of England, Scotland and Ireland* (London: Thames and Hudson facsimile edition, 1984).

See also Aunt Sally, Skittles

Tony Collins

Naid Berc

Also known as *Naid Perc*, *Naid Perca*, *Neidio Perci*, the name of this sport can be translated as 'jumping over a stick'. It was a popular pastime with Glamorgan youth and involved jumping over three sticks, two of which were pushed into the ground with the other perched on top. Another form of the game involved jumping between two trees, with or without a stick to propel the individual across.

Sources and Reading:
Bevan, G. A. and Donovan, P. J. (eds), *Geiriadur Prifysgol Cymru / A Dictionary of the Welsh Language* (Volume 3) (Caerdydd [Cardiff]: Gwasg Prifysgol Cymru, 1950).

Emma Lile

Naid Stond

An activity describing one jump from a standing position. The competitor placed both feet on a mark and then leapt as far as possible, either with or without a stone in each hand.

Sources and Reading:
Jones, T., *Y Darian* (29 December 1927).

Emma Lile

Neidio Tair Naid

The sport of three consecutive jumps, as practised by the youth of the Rhondda in Glamorgan.

Sources and Reading:
Jones, T., *Y Darian* (29 December 1927).

Emma Lile

Nine Holes

One of the few games that can be played on a field or on a board, as its name suggests nine holes consists of trying to direct a ball into holes. There was also a version using twelve holes. In Suffolk and Norfolk the game was played by making nine holes in the ground in a square shape and players had to knock a ball into the holes from a certain distance. Other than being played on a board rather than a field, the board version is exactly the same and is an obvious relation of marbles.

Sources and Reading:
Gomme, A. B., *The Traditional Games of England, Scotland and Ireland* (London: Thames and Hudson facsimile edition, 1984).

See also Bowls, Marbles

Tony Collins

Nine Men's Morris

Also known as 'morettes' and 'merelles', or just simply 'morris', this is an old English game played either on a board or outdoors on the ground by two competitors. The game is played on a square made up of three concentric squares, connected by intersecting lines in the centre of each of the square's sides.

The players start with nine pieces, or 'men', each and take it in turn to place one man on the board with the intention of making a straight row of three of their own men. When this is achieved, one of the opponent's pieces is removed from the board. This continues until one player has been reduced to two pieces, when they forfeit the game. The game is believed to be an extension of the much simpler 'three men's morris' and was popular during the fourteenth century. The game is mentioned by Shakespeare in *A Midsummer Night's Dream* (Act 2, Scene 1), where he uses the phrase 'The Nine Men's Morris is filled up

with mud' to denote the way in which the rain had filled the holes made for the game on the village green.

John Martin

Ninepins

A form of skittles in which nine targets – 'pins' – have to be knocked over by a ball that is thrown or bowled at them. The earliest reference to the game is from 1580 and it is clear that by the late seventeenth and the eighteenth centuries the sport had become very popular. Numerous pubs had ninepin alleys and the game is referred to regularly by commentators of the time. As with all sports of the time, gambling was an integral part of its appeal. In all important aspects it is the forerunner of modern tenpin bowling.

Sources and Reading:
Arlott, J. (ed.), *The Oxford Companion to Sports and Games* (Oxford: Oxford University Press, 1975).

See also Aunt Sally, Bowls, Half-Bowl, Kayles, Marbles, Skittles

Tony Collins

Northumberland

If the history of traditional games in east Northumberland is typical, the demise of such pursuits has been exaggerated. In fact, at the outbreak of the First World War they were being participated in by more men than ever before and were, certainly, more popular than football. Of course, the question is what are 'traditional games'. Here they are considered to be those activities that were participated in by a very small group of miners at the beginning of the nineteenth century: potshare bowling, quoits, handball, rabbit coursing, dog racing, pigeon flying, pedestrianism, cockfighting and football. What happened to them during the course of the century provides insights into the strength of tradition and the conditions that precipitated them into decline or transformation into new forms. However, the history of each sport was different and, thus, reveals different aspects of the gradual decline of these games. The transition to the new was neither straightforward nor uncontested: tradition was an effective barrier to change.

All these games were characterised by certain common elements. They all involved challenge matches between individuals and money stakes, and provided opportunities for gambling. At the same time, the actual contest lay at the centre of a complex of social activities involving the players, their financial backers, their supporters and other hangers-on. Before a contest the rival groups would meet to discuss where it was to be held, the conditions of the contest, the referees and umpires and the stakeholder. They would meet several times before signing articles of agreement. These negotiations all took place in the pub, the centre of miners' social and sporting lives. The contest itself would take place on public ground – Newcastle Town Moor, Newbiggin Moor, the beaches, the public highways, disused waggonways or on land adjacent to the pub. As late as 1914 many of these games were still being organised and played in a way that would be familiar to their forefathers 100 years earlier. At the same time, significant changes had taken place. The histories of the games reveal the different elements that attacked the foundations of traditional sports.

One of the main elements attacking the foundations of traditional sports was action by the authorities. The attacks on blood sports in the first half of the century, which are well documented, effectively eliminated cockfighting at the seven Newcastle pits. Coal miners were recognised as among the strongest supporters of cockfighting: owning birds, acting as trainers and breeders and providing a substantial portion of spectators. Cockfighting in the north-east survived until the mid-1850s. In fact, it never totally disappeared, it simply moved underground. The authorities then turned their attention to pigeon shooting and

rabbit coursing. While rabbit coursing was successfully removed from the Town Moor, it maintained its popularity and simply moved within the coalfield. In fact, both rabbit coursing and pigeon shooting reached a peak of popularity in the 1890s. This revealed, clearly, the limitations on the power of the authorities.

There was another area in which the authorities had more success, the effects of which had a major impact upon traditional games: the gradual elimination of public space as a venue for these activities. The attack on pedestrianism contests on the roads started in 1844 and was ultimately successful in 1871. Potshare bowling was banned on the roads in the 1850s although the authorities were not successful in removing it from the Town Moor in 1881. The removal of games from public space precipitated one of the fundamental causes for the decline of traditional games: the construction of enclosed, commercial facilities for sport. This brings us back to the pub and publicans.

Prior to the 1850s, the pubs were used by miners as the focal point of all challenge matches and social activities. The publicans were, as far as can be ascertained, not involved in sponsoring the protagonists, in all probability because of the relatively small number of miners. This changed in the late 1860s and escalated during the 1870s: publicans started sponsoring handicaps and sweeps in all the traditional games. These attracted large numbers of competitors to the respective competitions. As the popularity of these contests increased and the authorities limited access to public space, publicans responded by opening, in the 1870s, commercial grounds for rabbit coursing, dog racing and pedestrianism. These became the sites for the challenge matches, but these matches were soon outnumbered by handicaps which attracted 32, 64 or 128 pedestrians or dogs. This process attacked the foundation of the traditional games: the involvement of miners in *all* aspects of the competition. Traditional games now entered the modern world, where sport became something to be bought and sold. Prior to this time the majority of competitions were held on public land and so no entrance fees were charged: the development of commercial grounds changed all that. After the authorities closed all commercial grounds in 1876, the centre of rabbit coursing and pedestrianism moved, in 1881, to the Bebside Recreation Ground, which was opened by Joseph Rutter, the proprietor of the Bebside Inn. It became the site of local challenge matches and handicaps in pedestrianism, rabbit coursing, dog racing, shooting and pigeon flying. Handicaps dominated the proceedings, for example the 120-yard handicap at the Morpeth Olympic Games attracted as many as 350 entries. This ground remained the centre for such sports until it closed in 1918: a victim of the First World War.

The implications of the commercialisation by publicans and entrepreneurs are seen, most clearly, in the most popular and prestigious of the traditional games, potshare bowling, played only by miners of Northumberland and Durham. At the highpoint of potshare bowling, the 1870s and 1880s, challenge matches dominated the offerings on the Town Moor. Handicaps promoted by publicans in the coalfield were infrequent. This all changed in 1905 when a group of Newcastle publicans made a concerted effort to commercialise the sport: they lowered entrance fees, promoted events on weekday evenings, and tried to attract different working-class groups. They were partially successful during the period 1905 to 1909: the Town Moor witnessed nightly events, new competitors and a proliferation of handicaps. By 1909, 40 per cent of the competitors were non-miners. The success was short-lived and by 1913 the number of handicaps had declined and challenge matches again dominated the calendar. Miners attempted to continue their old traditions by sponsoring competitions themselves.

The histories of the various games illustrate the different elements of the traditional games and the fragile nature of the conditions under which they thrived. Handball was played on courts in a few locations: Ashington and the villages around Seaton Delaval. It is probable that the game took root in these villages as a relatively large proportion of their miners had moved there from the Durham coalfield where handball was a major sport. In 1891, in Seaton Delaval and nine surrounding villages, where the game thrived, between 13 and 17 per cent of the miners had been born in Durham. This hypothesis of immigrants bringing their traditional games with them is supported by the existence of Cornish wrestling in the Cramlington area as a result of the importation of miners from Cornwall and Devon in 1875. As the natives of Cornwall and Devon died, the wrestling disappeared. Their sons were Northumbrians and played Northumbrian games. Pigeon flying demonstrates the predominantly local focus of traditional sport. Short-distance racing was the most popular form of racing practised in the coalfield. However, rarely did the owners fly their birds against individuals outside their own clubs. These sports were intensely local. Rabbit coursing and dog racing became the most commercialised sports of all. Once practised on the open moors, by 1914 they were confined to four grounds specifically designed for the sports. This was the beginning of the post-war transition to greyhound racing, which is still in existence today.

The most interesting example of all, and the one that reveals most about traditional games, was the very popular game of quoits, which held a special place in the culture of the mining villages. Quoits was played extensively in the 1860s and 1870s as individual challenge matches and a few handicaps, and at the annual village celebrations that became increasingly frequent in the 1870s. Celebrated by miner poets, it was *the* game. The process of commercialisation of quoits started in the 1880s when a number of publicans constructed covered quoit grounds with seating for up to 700 people! During the 1890s these commercial grounds became increasingly popular. By 1913, five of these grounds provided the focus for challenge matches and handicaps. The growth of commercial quoits was paralleled by an explosion of interest in the game, to such a degree that it became a nightly occurrence. However, the focus of these games was not the ubiquitous pubs but rather the miners' institutes and, after 1898, miner-owned and operated social clubs. By 1913 there were 53 institutes in the coalfield, all of which had quoit grounds that were used nightly. Quoits had become a mass sport. Within these institutes the focus was on internal competition. Even though two leagues were started, only one had any permanence. There was a clear rejection of league play.

The mixing of the old and the new is seen most clearly in running. Challenge matches were a regular occurrence throughout the century. The development of handicaps came with the opening of the Bedlington West End Running Grounds in 1873. Although there were some challenge matches, the majority of competitions were handicaps. And it was in the running handicaps that the process of standardisation was first observed. At first, handicaps were over a variety of distances: 100, 120, 130, 150 and 200 yards. By the early 1880s the 120-yard handicap had become the recognised championship distance. This development was paralleled by the disappearance of the traditional activities such as climbing the greasy pole and 'gorning' (gurning). The 120-yard handicap became the most popular event at the various annual village celebrations that proliferated in the 1880s. It was within the context of these events, in particular the flower shows, that a recognised circuit of athletic contests developed. By the mid-1890s there were seven flower shows held on different weekends throughout July, August and September. Athletic competition had gone from being a purely local event participated in once a year to a regular circuit in which individuals could compete regularly, and it was in these increasingly popular annual village celebrations that the symbiotic relationship between the old and the new is most evident. All the celebrations included at least one of the following: quoits, potshare bowling, athletic contests and pigeon flying. At the same time the dominant form of competition was the ubiquitous handicap. However, it was in football that the transition can best be seen. From the early 1850s many celebrations included football on their programme of events. This was local football where the rules varied and were passed on from generation to generation by word of mouth. This changed in the 1880s when association football became the game in the mining village. The new had come out of the old. Thus the village celebrations incorporated elements of both the old and the new.

The histories of these traditional games illustrate that at any given time the games contained elements of the past, present and future – traditions stubbornly endured. The gradual decline of traditional games depended very much on local conditions and on the traditions of that particular place. At the same time there were three factors that bubbled to the surface. First, there was the impact of the authorities in controlling the use of space. This was a causative factor in precipitating change, in particular the commercialisation of the games. The second factor was the role of the pubs and publicans in the commercialisation of the games. Finally, the development of education removed children from the predominant influence of their fathers. No longer did children go straight down the mine. They were subjected to outside influences for a longer period of time. As their horizons expanded, the dominance of local influences was undermined. At the outbreak of the First World War, traditional games were still being played but increasingly within the context of modern sport: leagues, handicaps and on a regular basis.

Sources and Reading:

Hill, J. and Williams, J. (eds), *Sport and Identity in the North of England* (Keele: Keele University Press, 1996).

Metcalfe, A., 'Organised Sport in the Mining Communities of South Northumberland, 1882–1914', *Victorian Studies*, 25: 4 (1982), 469–95.

Metcalfe, A., 'Resistance to Change: Folk Games in the Mining Communities of East Northumberland, 1800–1914', *Stadion*, 15 (1989), 143–9.

Metcalfe, A., 'Potshare Bowling in the Mining Communities of East Northumberland, 1800–1914', in Holt, R. (ed.), *Sport and the Working Class in Modern Britain*

(Manchester: Manchester University Press, 1990), 29–44.

Moffatt, F. C., *Turnpike Road to Tartan Track: The Story of Northern Foot Handicaps* (1979).

See also Morpeth Olympic Games

Alan Metcalfe

Not

A Gloucestershire version of bandy or hockey. The name derives from the fact that the ball was traditionally made from a knotty piece of wood.

Sources and Reading:

Gomme, A. B., *The Traditional Games of England, Scotland and Ireland* (London: Thames and Hudson facsimile edition, 1984).

See also Bandy, Hockey

Tony Collins

Novelty Events (Wales)

Novelty events, staged primarily for entertainment rather than as serious athletic contests, often took place in nineteenth-century rural Wales. Be they an accompaniment to professional pedestrianism matches, a feature of festivities held in honour of local or national luminaries, or merely part of seasonal parish sports days, competitions such as hopping and running backwards, or cycling with one's feet on the handle bars and hands on the pedals, were designed to provoke laughter and merriment.

At a sports day held in Abergavenny in Gwent in February 1840 to celebrate the Queen's recent marriage, the amusements included a boys' blindfold wheelbarrow race. Some of the boys fell into a ditch in the process, to the crowd's considerable hilarity, while the winner received five shillings for his troubles. Young lads were required to eat penny loaves covered in treacle, the difficulty being that their hands were tied together and that the loaves were suspended from a spring. Treacle-steeped roll competitions and wheelbarrow races were also included at a sports day in Beaumaris in Anglesey in January 1842 to honour the birth of the Prince of Wales. Taking place on the green, the event offered prizes for greasy-pole climbing (some boys filling their pockets with sand and chalk to rub over the pole, but to no avail), and for picking up with the mouth ten shillings placed in a tray of flour.

A mop contest formed part of an Aberystwyth artillery sports event in May 1895 and involved competitors mounting each other's shoulders and fighting with mops dipped in soot and flour, while a sports day held at the Vetch Field in Swansea in June 1884 included a wooden-leg race.

Among the unusual amusements at the bicycle gymkhana in Tywyn in Gwynedd in September 1899 were separate men's and women's riding competitions, which included: dropping three tennis balls into three flower-pots and, on the return, tilting at three rings placed at suitable distances apart with a billiard cue; steering between six bottles placed five feet apart without knocking them over, and then over a see-saw; and a 'bicycle tortoise race', in which the last to finish was victorious. The sexes even competed together in several events, such as the Gretna Green race, in which men and women rode to a table, dismounted to sign their names legibly, and then cycled back holding hands.

Sources and Reading:

Aberystwyth Observer (11 June 1896).

Cambrian News (31 May 1895; 25 August 1899).

Carnarvon and Denbigh Herald (1 January 1842).

Monmouthshire Beacon (15 February 1840).

Emma Lile

Onion Fayre

In praise of the adaptable pot-filling onion *Allium cepa*, the inhabitants of Newent in Gloucestershire celebrate an Onion Fayre every September. The fair, which is thought to be the largest British celebration of the common onion, dates back to the thirteenth century when Henry II granted Newent the right to hold a market and two annual fairs. One of these became known as the Onion Fayre because market gardeners from Evesham started to sell their onions to Welsh drovers who passed through Newent on their way to the celebrated Gloucester cattle market. The fairs also attracted people from the Forest of Dean. In the absence of trestle tables, cloths were laid over tombstones in the churchyard to make market stalls.

By the 1930s the fair had virtually disappeared, but it was revived in the mid-1990s. It features a highly competitive onion show, scores of onion-related stalls, an onion up-and-over contest for children, onion stringing lessons and a wide variety of food stands. A popular class in the onion show is the heaviest onion competition.

Sources and Reading:
Telegraph Weekend (9 September 2000).

John Martin

Orange Rolling

Similar to egg rolling, orange rolling today takes place every Good Friday at Pascombe Pit in Bedfordshire. Its origins appear to lie in the fact that in some egg rolling contests, the broken egg had to be eaten; oranges would help the contestants to avoid having egg stuck to their palettes.

Sources and Reading:
Day, B., *A Chronicle of Folk Customs* (London: Hamlyn, 1988).
Gorini, P., *Encyclopedia of Traditional Games* (Rome: Gremese, 1994).

See also Egg Rolling, Egg and Spoon Racing

Tony Collins

Osbaldeston, George

'Squire' George Osbaldeston (1786–1866) epitomised the rural sportsman, excelling as he did at hunting, shooting, angling, riding, royal tennis, rowing, boxing, cricket and coursing, usually with a wager attached. Such was his love of the chase that he often hunted five or six days a week, owning three packs of hounds for the purpose and buying foxes from a London dealer to ensure a day's sport. He did much to promote racing among the professional watermen on the Thames by making matches and offering purses. He was called on to referee prizefights, including the famous battle between Bendigo and Caunt at Newton Pagnell.

Generally, he was a man of integrity if sometimes alert to sharp but not illegal practice. On one occasion in 1835, however, he was challenged by Lord George Bentinck (later to become a driving force in turf reform), who felt that Osbaldeston had pulled his horse in a race so as to elicit larger bets next time out. The row led to a duel in which Osbaldeston, a good shot, deliberately did not wound his opponent. Some years on Osbaldeston agreed not to blackball Lord George's application to join the Bibury Club and a reconciliation was effected.

Although often in need of ready money, Osbaldeston wagered heavily on his sporting challenges. His view was that you should always back your opinion with a bet because losing money as well as the argument doubly annoyed your opponent. As a jockey capable of beating professional riders he backed himself for £500 in at least half a dozen steeplechase matches. Despite some successful coups, including riding 200 miles in nine hours (a feat achieved by the use of thoroughbred horses at four-mile intervals), his gambling eventually cost him his estates, which he sold in the 1840s.

Reputedly his losses on horseracing alone topped £200,000. However, it did not end his betting or his participation in sport. Age 68, he rode his own horse in the March Stakes at Goodwood and lost only by a neck, and even later he took a bet to sit 24 hours in a chair without moving.

Sources and Reading:
Cuming, E. D. (ed.), *Squire Osbaldeston: His Autobiography* (London: John Lane, 1926).

Wray Vamplew

Otter Hunting

Otter hunting using specially bred packs of hounds hunting by scent predates fox-hunting. In the Middle Ages, the otter was a much more esteemed quarry than the fox. However, otter hunting was always a minor activity in comparison with fox-hunting, being confined to a limited number of areas with suitable habitat for otters.

By 1842 there were five recognised packs of otter hounds. Fifty years later there were nine packs: one each in Scotland, Cumberland and Westmorland, three in the south-west of England and three in Wales and its borders, where otter hunting was a sport for the gentry, who killed the animals to protect local fish stocks. The sport's popularity rapidly increased so that by the outbreak of the First World War there were 22 registered packs, which accounted for, on average, slightly less than 500 otters each year. Unlike fox-hunting, the wartime curtailment of the sport encouraged a bout of further expansion in the 1920s. The formation of new packs in this period reflected the fact that the cost of hunting for both subscribers and followers was considerably less than for fox-hunting.

The post-Second World War intensification of agriculture, coupled with the widespread use of pesticides, resulted in a rapid decline in the otter population, with blank days becoming increasingly common. In an attempt to prevent further depletion of the otter population, legal protection of the species was granted in 1978. Although it remained legal to hunt otters, it became illegal to kill them. The surviving otter packs rapidly switched to hunting mink.

Sources and Reading:
Lloyd, J. I., *Come Hunting: Days in the Field and Some Thoughts About Hunting the Fox, Hare, Otter, Rabbit and Rat, Together with Other Sporting Adventures* (London: Vinton, 1952).
Medwin, T., *The Angler in Wales, or, Days and Nights of Sportsmen* (Volume 2) (London: Richard Bentley, 1834).
National Society for the Abolition of Cruel Sports, *Facts about Otter Hunting* (1968).

See also Hunting

John Martin and Emma Lile

Pall Mall

A mixture of golf and croquet, pall mall, derived from the French mallet and ball game of *paille maille*, was introduced to Britain in the first half of the seventeenth century. The favourite sport of Charles II, it achieved great popularity during the Restoration.

Mallets were used to hit wooden balls through two iron hoops on a course about 800 yards long. It appears to have been played near St James's Palace and gave its name to the famous London street that is now called Pall Mall.

It is claimed, without any real evidence, that pall mall is the progenitor of modern croquet, despite the fact that in many ways it is more closely related to golf.

Sources and Reading:
Encyclopedia of Sports, Games and Pastimes (London: Fleetway, 1935).

See also Croquet

Tony Collins

Pancake Racing

Pancake racing takes place on Shrove Tuesday in a number of towns and villages throughout England. The association between pancakes and Shrove Tuesday appears to have its origins in the fact that the pancakes used up food such as butter, eggs and fat that were prohibited during Lent, which begins the following day on Ash Wednesday. However, there is no evidence to suggest that pancake racing itself is anything but a twentieth-century invention.

Pancakes have been eaten on Shrove Tuesday since at least the sixteenth century. In some parishes it was the custom for the church bell to ring at noon as the signal for people to begin frying their pancakes. Traditionally football and cockfighting or cock throwing were the popular Shrove Tuesday sports.

At Olney in Buckinghamshire the annual pancake race allegedly dates back to 1445, although this is based on assertion rather than proof. Revived in 1948 after dying out during the First World War, it is open only to women and, as is the case in many other areas, competitors must be aged over 16 and wear headscarves and aprons. The pancakes must be tossed three times during the course of the race.

Today, pancake races can also be seen every Shrove Tuesday in Stone, near Dartford, Lincoln's Inn Fields in London and Whitby. In Thorpe Abbots in Norfolk the race takes place in fancy dress. At Winster near Matlock, which claims to have run a pancake race for centuries, there are separate races for men and women. The antiquity of these races is open to question, especially given the fact that few can trace their origins much further back than the 1960s.

In 1949, an annual pancake race was started in the American town of Liberal in Kansas, which subsequently challenged the women of Olney to an annual contest. This now takes place every year, the winner being decided by comparing the times of the winners of the two races, a similar arrangement to that which pertains in the Stroud Brick and Rolling Pin Throwing Contest.

Sources and Reading:
Colbeck, M., *The Calendar Year* (Leeds: EP Publishing, 1983).
Day, B., *A Chronicle of Folk Customs* (London: Hamlyn, 1988).
Hole, C., *English Traditional Customs* (London: Batsford, 1975).
Hulton, R., *Stations of the Sun* (Oxford: Oxford University Press, 1996).
Malcolmson, R., *Popular Recreations in English Society 1700–1850* (Cambridge: Cambridge University Press, 1973).

See also Public School Sports, Stroud Throwing Contests

Tony Collins

Parish Sports (Wales) (*Gwylmabsant*)

Gwylmabsant, or the annual commemoration of the local parish saint, constituted one of the most popular festivals in the traditional Welsh calendar. The earliest reference to it dates from the late fifteenth century and, although originally a religious celebration, it gradually developed into primarily a programme of sports and games enjoyed by men, women and children alike. Held until the mid-nineteenth century in and around the local churches, the *gwylmabsant* served as one of the highlights of the rural year and represented an opportunity to let off steam amid the monotony and drudgery of daily working lives.

A wide variety of athletic pursuits took place at the *gwylmabsant*; according to one observer, the churchyards became 'a kind of circus for every sport and exercise'. Cockfighting, bull baiting, throwing the bar and running races were among the commonplace games, while more unusual events, such as donkey races and treacle-dipping challenges (where contestants were required to consume sticky rolls hanging from a rope), were often also featured. Athletes and spectators alike were invariably fuelled by alcoholic drink, which usually heightened the general merriment and high spirits.

It was primarily the *gwylmabsant*'s association with alcohol and gambling, rather than the sports themselves, that led to its downfall. Although religious leaders, especially those of the Methodist Revival of the eighteenth century, were severely critical of supposedly time-wasting physical pursuits, it was the related raucousness that they mainly sought to end. As saints' days were increasingly denounced across Wales, censorious clerical attitudes undoubtedly played a major part in their disappearance, and few parishes were still holding the *gwylmabsant* after the 1860s.

Sources and Reading:

Suggett, R., 'Festivals and Social Structure in Early Modern Wales', *Past and Present*, 15 (1996), 79–112.

Emma Lile

Pat Ball

– *see* **Balloon, Handball**

Pedestrianism

'Pedestrianism' was originally a general term for all forms of foot-racing, probably at some point in the seventeenth century, but by the late 1700s was being used to describe professional race and distance walking.

Its origins reputedly lie in the races organised by noblemen between their footmen, servants who would walk or run beside a nobleman's carriage and were responsible for running ahead to deliver messages. The speed of the footmen became a source of pride for the nobility and, given the propensity of the aristocracy to gamble, contests between footmen quickly became a common form of wager. In August 1660 Samuel Pepys witnessed a race in Hyde Park between a footman and a professional runner.

As with all sports creation stories, this account probably contains a grain of truth, not least because races between footmen of well-known aristocrats would have attracted considerable interest, but foot races for wagers and stakes have undoubtedly existed since time immemorial. Falstaff, in Shakespeare's *Henry IV Part I*, challenges Ned Poins to a race for £1,000. By the eighteenth century, races for money were commonplace, both as public attractions for high stakes (especially in London) and at local fairs and festivals. Contests were staged over time and distance, and professionals would issue challenges to rivals in a similar way to prizefighters. Women were also keen runners and competed in 'smock races', so-called because the prize was often a dress of some sort. Needless to say, gambling was a major factor in these events.

However, the most popular form of pedestrianism came to prominence in the late 1700s when what is best described as endurance walking achieved great popularity. These feats involved walkers taking up a challenge to cover a specific distance within a specified time. The most notable of the period was Yorkshireman Foster Powell who in 1790 walked from York to London and back again in less than 5 days and 18 hours for a bet of 20 guineas. However, this was eclipsed in 1809 by the celebrated feat of Captain Robert Barclay, who walked 1,000 miles in 1,000 hours in 1809 on Newmarket Heath. Such was the popularity, and commercial attraction, of the sport that it became common for pedestrians from the United States (where the sport also attracted considerable public attention), and to a lesser extent Europe, to come to Britain to compete.

Perhaps most interesting was the fact that from the 1870s a significant number of women athletes started to compete in endurance events. In 1878 Barclay's record was broken by Ada Anderson, who completed 1,000 miles in less than 672 hours at King's Lynn. Her great rival, the French-born Exida La Chapelle, walked 3,000 miles in just 29 days in January and February the following year in the United States.

These endurance contests continued until the 1880s, but pedestrianism, which by now had come to encompass all professional racing on foot, was being eclipsed by amateur athletics. In 1880 the Amateur Athletic Association was founded. The propagandists of amateurism and also well-publicised accusations of race-fixing helped make pedestrianism become associated with sharp practices and cheating because of its close links to gambling. Its lack of centralised organisation and clear rules for events meant that it also appeared confused in the public eye. For example, unlike in amateur athletics, there was no recognised national professional sprint champion. Despite the success of events such as the Edinburgh Powderhall Sprint Championships, which began in 1870 and still continues, professional foot-racing had a marginalised existence throughout the twentieth century – until, of course, the amateur athletics authorities abandoned amateurism in the 1980s and embraced the same professionalism they had once claimed to despise.

Sources and Reading:

Goulstone, J., 'The Pioneering Years of International Athletics', *British Society of Sports History Newsletter*, 11 (2000), 25–34.

Jamieson, D. A., *Powderhall and Pedestrianism* (Edinburgh: W. & A. K. Johnston, 1943).

Lovesey, P., *The Official Centenary History of the AAA* (London: Guinness, 1979).

Thom, W., *Pedestrianism* (Aberdeen: Brown & Frost, 1813).

See also Athletics, Barclay, Captain Robert

Tony Collins

Pedestrianism (Wales)

Professional pedestrianism comprised an eclectic combination of running and walking events of varying types and distances, and peaked in popularity in Wales during the mid-nineteenth century. A precursor of modern amateur athletics, the sport had been practised since at least the late seventeenth century, when footmen were employed as messengers and competitive runners by the gentry. Athletic success led to increased social renown, and for working-class citizens not lucky enough to receive gentry patronage, pedestrianism offered a rare opportunity to achieve fame and possibly fortune, owing to the sums staked on race results. The sport was open to participants of all backgrounds who were willing, for the right price, to walk for several consecutive days, usually over fields or on turnpike roads. Gambling on the event's outcome was commonplace, and for those accustomed to poverty and hardship, victory could mean the difference between starvation and survival.

Pedestrian feats of an extremely demanding nature generated considerable monetary interest as well as large crowds. In September 1804, Bruce Knight completed an 86-mile return trip from Cardiff to Brecon in 33 hours, while in August 1825 John Townsend took six days to finish a 384-mile walk that began in Brecon and ended in Hay-on-Wye. For their efforts, talented athletes were lauded as local heroes, and none more so than John Davies (1822–*c*.1904), who, during the 1840s, became undisputed Welsh champion and conqueror of many celebrated English runners.

Although it was mainly men who took part, there was a small minority of women and children pedestrians. In March 1839, a seven-year-old boy ran the seven miles from Risca to Newport in 45 minutes for a sovereign wager, beating the Tredegar coach as he did so. Two men and a woman

(Mrs Rowlands) contested a pedestrian feat over a four-mile course between Cardiff and Penarth in August 1867. On nearing the finish, Mrs Rowlands put 'the spurt on' to win by 200 yards, and felt so fresh directly afterwards that she promptly challenged any spectator to race her over 24 miles. Other unusual events included trundling wheelbarrows, gathering potatoes, hopping and walking backwards. During the 1870s, William Richards of Denbigh described himself as the 'celebrated backward walker' and frequently adopted the 'retrograde movement' for his pedestrian challenges.

While pedestrianism undoubtedly boasted many dedicated athletes, it also attracted its fair share of dubious, untrustworthy characters, whose actions tarnished the sport. Swift-footed amateurs entering races under false names and race fixing dented its reputation, as did general unsportsman-like behaviour, such as that occurring during an event on the Swansea Sands in 1848, when Welshman Jackson, 'The Flying Tailor', achieved victory by pushing over his opponent Mr Knock 'by a clever dodge' halfway through the race. It was precisely this seamy side of pedestrianism, which engendered fierce attacks from ministers of religion and contrasted sharply with the emerging amateur sports and their empha-sis on fair play, that increasingly discredited the sport. The formation of the Amateur Athletic Club in 1866 and the codification of its official rules eventually sealed the fate of professional pedestrianism, for while it coexisted with athletics for a time, it was ultimately forced out of existence. By the 1890s, standardised athletics events were becoming ever more popular in Wales, while the fortunes of pedestrianism fell into sharp decline, leading to the sport's virtual disappearance by the turn of the twentieth century.

Sources and Reading:
Bridgend Chronicle (23 August 1867).
Lile, E., 'Professional Pedestrianism in South Wales during the Nineteenth Century', *The Sports Historian*, 20: 2 (2000), 94–105.
North Wales Chronicle (8 August 1874).

Emma Lile

Peg and Stick

A Yorkshire game in which a wooden peg is balanced on a ring on the ground and players take it in turns to hit it into the air with a short stout stick and then hit it again before it falls to the ground. The opposing player then estimates the number of leaps that the striker must make to reach the peg. If the striker reaches the peg in that number of leaps or less, the number of leaps is added to the striker's score. If not, the opponent has the opportunity to reach the peg in that number of leaps and, if successful, those leaps are added to his score.

Sources and Reading:
Gomme, A. B., *The Traditional Games of England, Scotland and Ireland* (London: Thames and Hudson facsimile edition, 1984).

See also Trap Ball

Tony Collins

Peg-Fiched

A game traditionally played in the south-west of England. Each player has a stick that is pointed at one end. One player pushes his stick into the ground and the others try to dislodge it by throwing their sticks at it.

Sources and Reading:
Gomme, A. B., *The Traditional Games of England, Scotland and Ireland* (London: Thames and Hudson facsimile edition, 1984).

Tony Collins

Penny Cast

A form of quoits played using round flat stones about six inches across. In Scotland it was called 'pennystane'.

Sources and Reading:
Gomme, A. B., *The Traditional Games of England, Scotland and Ireland* (London: Thames and Hudson facsimile edition, 1984).

See also Quoits

Tony Collins

Penny Prick

A game dating back to at least the sixteenth century in which small pieces of iron are thrown at a mark. It was originally a game in which a penny was placed on the top of a pole and the throwers would try to knock it off. In the fifteenth century the game was banned in Leicester by borough ordinances.

Sources and Reading:
Brailsford, D., *British Sport: A Social History* (Cambridge: Lutterworth Press, 1992).
Gomme, A. B., *The Traditional Games of England, Scotland and Ireland* (London: Thames and Hudson facsimile edition, 1984).

See also Quoits

Tony Collins

Pigeon Racing

The racing of rock doves, or homing pigeons, for recreational purposes is a relatively recent development. The ability of the pigeon to traverse hundreds, if not thousands, of miles has long been known. The Egyptians used the birds to send messages over 3,000 years ago and for centuries, until the widespread use of radio in the twentieth century, pigeons were an integral part of military communications, including during the Second World War.

Although there can be little doubt that pigeons would have been kept as pets, the first organisation to be formed to organise the sport was the Columbarian Society (called after the Latin name for the rock dove, *Columba livia*), founded in the late eighteenth century for London gentlemen who kept pigeons. The appeal of the sport was firmly based on gambling, with stakes of up to £40 being offered for matches. The fact that pigeons could fly from Newmarket to London in three hours was no doubt also part of their appeal. As Dennis Brailsford notes, this could give a gambler with a pigeon a distinct advantage over the bookmakers.

The most common form of racing at this time was over short distances. Taking place over flat terrain where the pigeon could see its owner, the bird would be released from a box and fly to its owner over a specific distance against the clock. However the sport was transformed by the advent of the railway and the telegraph. Whereas before that pigeons could only be transported a short distance, the railways meant that pigeons could now be carried virtually anywhere around the country. The telegraph meant that they could be timed accurately and news of the departures and arrivals easily communicated. The possibilities which were opened up by this technology were displayed in 1896 when the first officially recorded 500-mile flight home was made by G. P. Pointer's pigeon Motor.

The initial impetus to the widespread growth of the sport came from Belgium in the 1840s, and it soon began to enjoy broad popularity in Britain. Its respectability was ensured by the participation in the sport of two of Queen Victoria's sons, the Prince of Wales and the Duke of York, both of whom kept pigeon lofts at Sandringham. The Duke of York, who was also for a time a keen pigeon-shooter, continued to take part when he became Edward VII.

Despite this royal patronage, the sport had by the end of the nineteenth century effectively become a largely working-class pastime, especially among miners and weavers in the north of England. It combined both individual skill and a sporting community for its adherents; most local pigeon clubs met in pubs and the sport developed a thriving, largely oral, culture. On 28 March 1896 a number of pigeon owners met at the White Swan in Leeds to form the National Homing Union, which later added the word 'Royal' to its name as an indication of the extent of royal support for the sport.

Modern pigeon racing is largely a product of an urban industrial culture. James Mott notes that there is no evidence of it ever being practised in a rural setting. Yet, like other sports such as bowls, it also evokes a continuity with a rural past: the relationship between the pigeon and its keeper is reminiscent of that between humans and animals in pre-industrial times, and the delivery of the pigeon to the designated place for the start of the race often involves an escape to the countryside. Despite a somewhat unfashionable image at the present time, it has a far-reaching appeal, based on the high level of expertise (often self-taught) needed for success, the bond between bird and owner, and the invocation of the countryside for urban dwellers.

Sources and Reading:

Brailsford, D., *British Sport: A Social History* (Cambridge: Lutterworth Press, 1992).

Mott, J., 'Miners, Weavers and Pigeon Racing', in Smith, M. A., Parker, S. and Smith, C. S. (eds), *Leisure and Society in Britain* (London: Allen Lane, 1973), 86–96.

Osman, C., *Racing Pigeons: A Practical Guide to the Sport* (London: Faber, 1996).

Tony Collins

Pigeon Shooting

In the late nineteenth century, pigeon shooting, entailing the shooting of specially reared pigeons bred in captivity or captured wild birds, which were released from box traps, was a popular activity, with organised clubs regulating the sport. As the directions of the birds' flights were unpredictable, they challenged the shooters' skill.

Pigeon shooting of this type was confined primarily to a limited number of wealthy shooters who could afford to indulge in such activities. By the mid-nineteenth century it was a popular and internationally recognised pastime for the wealthier sections of the shooting fraternity. The leading centres of the sport were Monte Carlo, Cerle des Patineurs in Paris and Hurlingham (the latter under the jurisdiction of the London Gun Club). The organising bodies were responsible for ensuring the rules of fair play. At this time, the London Gun Club fulfilled the same role for its members as the Jockey Club did for the racing community. During the heyday of the officially organised side of the sport, elaborate sweepstake competitions were organised for wealthy patrons.

Concern for the welfare of the birds led to the sport being banned in Britain in 1921. Even prior to this, the increase in its popularity and shortages of live birds had led to substitutes for live pigeons being developed. In the initial phases, this took the form of shooting at glass balls (with specially designed ribs to prevent the shot glancing off them) which were projected by spring-loaded traps. Later, clay pigeon shooting took over.

In Britain, the wild wood pigeons were historically regarded as an occasional quarry that offered a shot when there was nothing better to shoot. Until the 1950s, there were few serious practitioners of this form of the sport, whereas in France the bird was considered to be a bird of *la chasse*.

The sport evolved into two distinct branches, which are regarded as specialised forms of rough shooting. Pigeon shooting is undertaken either by shooting the birds wild over decoys on their feeding grounds during the day (decoy shooting), or by shooting them at evening time, when they are preparing to roost (roost shooting).

In decoy shooting, pigeons are attracted to a specific area of their feeding ground by artificial decoys and then shot from a hide. Specially manufactured decoys are available, made out of rubber, plastic or cardboard. More sophisticated mechanical aids, such as 'flappers', which mimic the movements of the wild birds, have become available. Decoy shooting has become a specialist form of shooting and is generally undertaken during periods when the birds are feeding in specific areas, such as on oilseed rape fields in the winter months.

With roost shooting, the guns congregate in the evening around the roosting areas that the birds are currently using. In the aftermath of the Second World War, when pigeons were a serious agricultural pest, the government organised roost shoots on designated evenings in an effort to maximise the number of birds shot as they moved from one roost to another. With the decline of the pigeon population, organised roost shooting has been replaced by a more *ad hoc* system, which has often become an adjunct to rough shooting. As with duck flighting, rough or windy weather is best for this type of shooting as the birds are more likely to continue to fly into the roosts, being less disturbed by the gun shots.

Sources and Reading:
Murton, R. K., *The Wood Pigeon* (London: Collins, 1965).
Walsingham, T. and Payne, G. R., *Shooting: Field and Covert* (1900, reprinted; Southampton: Ashford Press, 1987).

See also Clay Pigeon Shooting, Shooting

John Martin

Pitch

Also known as 'pinch', 'pitch-halfpenny' and 'pitch and hustle', this is a game in which the aim is to toss, or 'pitch', a penny (or a similar disc) into a hole or mark in the ground from a particular distance.

Sources and Reading:
Gomme, A. B., *The Traditional Games of England, Scotland and Ireland* (London: Thames and Hudson facsimile edition, 1984).

Tony Collins

Pitch and Toss

A game that has much in common with both bowls and quoits, pitch and toss was played by two or more players who would take it in turns to throw their 'pitcher' at a mark some yards in front of them. The pitcher was a small circular piece of lead about half an inch thick and between one-and-a-half and two inches in diameter. An 'H' for heads would be carved on one side, with 'T' for tails on the opposite. The mark would be a stone, which would be thrown about seven or eight yards in front of the players.

The first player would throw his pitcher at the mark. If it was sufficiently near to the mark the player would let it 'lie'. If not, the player would pick it up and allow the second player to aim at the mark, who would again decide whether his pitcher would lie. The process would continue until one player decided that their pitcher would lie. Those players who had not let their pitcher lie before now had to throw again and let their pitcher lie, regardless of where they fell.

Once the throwing had finished, the player whose pitcher was nearest to the mark picked up all of the pitchers and threw them into the air. Those pitchers landing 'heads' up would go to him. Those that landed tails up would be given to the next nearest player, who would repeat the throwing into the air, keeping those that landed heads up. This was repeated through the players until all the pitchers were redistributed. The winner was the one who gained the most pitchers.

Much of the game's appeal was not merely related to its simplicity but also to the opportunities for gambling it afforded. Illegal games for money could be easily organised, and just as easily stopped if they appeared to be attracting the attention of the local law enforcement agencies.

The folk phrase 'You wouldn't let it lie', meaning that someone's dissatisfaction with a situation had led to worsened consequences (popularised as a catchphrase by the north-eastern comedian Vic Reeves in the late 1980s), may also have its origins in the game.

Sources and Reading:

Day, B., *A Chronicle of Folk Customs* (London: Hamlyn, 1988).

Gomme, A. B., *The Traditional Games of England, Scotland and Ireland* (London: Thames and Hudson facsimile edition, 1984).

See also Quoits, Bowls

Tony Collins

Pize Ball

A form of rounders or baseball in which two teams of equal number compete. Three or four marks, or 'tuts', are made in a field as bases and the fielding side bowls to the 'batting' side.

There are no bats however, instead the ball must be hit, or 'pized', with the hand. After pizing the ball, the batter runs to the next tut, but if the batter is touched by the ball before reaching the tut they are out, or 'burnt'.

Native to Derbyshire and Yorkshire, it is first recorded in 1796, and is also referred to, as 'piseball', in Richard Hoggart's 1957 study of working-class culture *The Uses of Literacy*.

Sources and Reading:

Gomme, A. B., *The Traditional Games of England, Scotland and Ireland* (London: Thames and Hudson facsimile edition, 1984).

See also Baseball, Club Ball, Rounders, Stoolball, Stowball, Trap Ball

Tony Collins

Places for Sport

Some sports and games were, and still are, associated with specific regions: skittles in pubs in south-west England, road bowls in counties Cork and Armagh, golf on the links of the east coast of Scotland, and different styles of wrestling in different places. Before the nineteenth century, cricket was largely confined to the south of England, with its heart in the area between Hampshire and Kent. Scotland has a stronger cricketing tradition than is generally realised, particularly in the north-east: almost every village in Aberdeenshire has a club. Hurling – folk football with a small ball – was Cornish, and the stick-and-ball game of hurling is purely Irish, although it is similar to shinty, whose home is in the Scottish Highlands.

Certain kinds of ground were particularly suitable for certain sports. The Highlands and Islands of Scotland are rugged: a beach of hard-packed sand was an ideal place for shinty, and certain places, such as Calgary Strand on the Isle of Mull, are remembered for great matches on New Year's Day. Similar hurling matches were played on the strand on Great Blasket Island, off the coast of County Kerry, on Christmas Day. Good-quality horseracing has been held on the sands at places such as Tramore (*Traigh Mor* – the great beach) in County Waterford, Redcar in Yorkshire and Leith near Edinburgh. The character of the natural environment made Leicestershire ideal for fox-hunting, the frozen expanses of the Norfolk Broads for speed skating and bandy, and the sheltered waters of the Solent, Belfast Lough and the Clyde for yachting.

Some sports were played on hill tops – dry open spaces – such as cricket on Broad Halfpenny Down near Hambledon, and later on nearby Windmill Down. Some racecourses, such as Hexham and Brighton, are on hills: Samuel Pepys went racing on Banstead Downs, and the name Racecourse Downs to the north of Bodmin commemorates a former venue. In the Scottish

Borders, towns such as Duns and Hawick had hill-top courses. James I of England chose Newmarket Heath for horseracing because of its dry, sound turf. Roads were also important for sport. In Ireland, road bowls started in the seventeenth century and survived police pressure in the nineteenth. Minor horse races were often on roads, and races for stagecoaches were inevitably run on the high road. The availability of suitable water and ice controlled the location of other activities. Rowing grew in the nineteenth century on rivers like the Thames and the Boyne (near Dublin).

Other places for country sport had established social functions into which leisure had to be fitted. The churchyard was the focal point of the community, both for religious reasons and as a meeting place, and so might be used for sport too. The village green could be thought of as the same space secularised, where cricket could be played or, as at Elsdon in Northumberland, where the cockpit could be sited.

The names of village pubs may commemorate sporting events and heroes, thus in a different way linking sport with a sociable place. The Derby winners of 1849 and 1850 gave their names to the 'Voltigeur' at Spennymoor in County Durham (named by a blacksmith who bought it with his winnings) and the 'Flying Dutchman' at Summerbridge near Harrogate. One of the bars at Ayr racecourse is called 'The Chancellor', after the first winner of the Ayr Gold Cup (1804). Hunting inns usually do not have hunting names, though there was the 'Hark to Bounty' at Slaidburn, named after a favourite hound, and the 'Bedale Hunt' at Howes, North Yorkshire.

Folk football tended to survive into the nineteenth century in what Hutton has called 'small, stable, conservative towns', such as Alnwick, Workington and a group of places around the border of Middlesex and Surrey – of which the last survivor in the face of police pressure was at Dorking (1909). Institutions, particularly schools, sometimes protected old sports – such as hailes (a form of shinty) at Edinburgh Academy, the Eton field and wall games, and Eton, Rugby and Winchester fives – and provided the distinctive spaces required. All Eton-fives courts are based on the north wall and buttresses of the chapel. The specific reasons for these schools being where they were thus affected the localities where sport was played.

Spectators came from a distance: Robert Fergusson's poem about Leith races (1773) mentions folk from Aberdeenshire, Thackeray in 1842 said that people walked 80 miles to Killarney races, and the anonymous song 'Galway Races' (*c.*1860) mentions not only Aran Islanders but also people from Cork. Other venues were chosen because they were easy to reach, such as Carno Moor in Montgomeryshire where men from five parishes met for cockfighting. Some sports have deliberately been held in places that were difficult to reach. During pugilism's illegal phase, matches were held on county boundaries so fighters could move quickly from one jurisdiction to another. After animal baiting became illegal, it retreated to secluded hollows or to fields behind woods.

In the eighteenth century country sports began to move towards the city: support for the Hambledon cricket club evaporated when the Marylebone Cricket Club was founded in 1787. Race meetings were set up near cities: Kempton Park and Aintree are examples. The premier curling club in Scotland was the Duddingston, three miles from Edinburgh. When Londoners took to hunting, W. S. Surtees's creation the city grocer Jorrocks and his like supported the easily accessible Surrey Hunt, and hare coursing events near cities were unusual among field sports in that they attracted significant numbers of spectators.

With improving communications, sportsmen were prepared to travel further. Better road transport affected sport in the 1820s and 1830s. For example, it made possible the cricket matches between Yorkshire and Nottinghamshire and various southern counties. Railways reshaped many aspects of social life from the 1840s onwards, but before the network was created huge crowds were reaching racecourses by road: over 100,000 at Doncaster around 1840 and 115,000 at Paisley in 1837. In the latter case, most of the spectators walked to the race, though some came by canal. Railway platforms were opened at venues such as Newbury racecourse and Banff golf course. The branch line to Epsom Downs, opened in 1865, handled tens of thousands of people going to the Derby. There was sufficient confidence in large crowds being regularly attracted to Epsom for a rival line to be opened to Tattenham Corner, nearer to the course, in 1901. Leopardstown racecourse near Dublin was laid out in 1888 with good access by rail. The Royal Caledonian Curling Club leased fields at Carsebreck, between Dunblane and Perth, which could be flooded to produce a large shallow pond for the Grand Match. The Caledonian Railway built a platform so that curlers and stones could be unloaded there.

As urban sport grew, artificial pieces of countryside were created in the town. Turf was brought to form bowling greens and cricket grounds. Artificial places were also made in the countryside, as when steeplechasing moved from open fields to a racecourse with jumps and water hazards. Curling rinks were made in the countryside in the form of shallow ponds, usually shaded by trees, and when refrigeration equipment was developed curlers moved into indoor rinks.

Simple though it is, the idea of making an urban space that is delimited by lines on grass (a kind of controlled piece of countryside) and then playing football, rugby or shinty on it is one of the most important developments in the history of sport. It meant that something approximating to a standard playing area could be reproduced wherever one was wanted – and standard rules could be developed.

Sources and Reading:

Bale, J., *Sport and Place: A Geography of Sport in England, Scotland and Wales* (London: Hurst, 1982).

Bale, J., *Sports Geography* (London: Spon, 1989).

Burnett, J., 'Traditional Sports and Their Structures and Sites in Scotland', *Scottish Local History Journal*, 38 (1996), 29–31.

Hutton, R., *Stations of the Sun: A History of the Ritual Year in Britain* (Oxford: Oxford University Press, 1996).

John Burnett

Ploughing Matches

Ploughing is a vital process in the agricultural cycle as adequate cultivation of the soil enables seeds to germinate efficiently and therefore good ploughmen were welcomed in the agricultural community. Ploughing contests enabled them to display their skill by ploughing a strip of ground according to a prescribed set of rules, each aspect of their work being judged by specified criteria. The origins of competitive ploughing can be traced back to the eighteenth century, when the ability to produce a straight, well-turned furrow was a means of demonstrating a ploughman's skill to both his employer and fellow workers. Matches were usually judged by experienced old hands, known in Wales as *hen gamsters*, who possessed years of farming experience.

The highest standards of tillage were to be found on the lighter soils of East Anglia. As Arthur Young noted in his *General View of the Agriculture of the County of Suffolk* (1813): 'a favourite amusement is ploughing such furrows, as prize for a hat, or a pair of breeches, given by alehouses keepers, or subscribed among themselves, as a prize for the straightest furrow'. This heralded the emergence of larger, more formal ploughing matches, where ploughmen could demonstrate their expertise in manipulating their plough, and plough teams, to produce straight, uniform furrows set up at the required angle, irrespective of the irregularities in the soil surface. They also provided an opportunity to illustrate the high quality of presentation of their plough teams, for which separate prizes were awarded.

In the mid-nineteenth century, ploughing matches were actively promoted by the newly established agricultural societies as a means of enhancing productivity and efficiency. These events allowed machinery manufacturers to demonstrate their improved iron ploughs, which were suitable for a wide range of soil types and topography. By 1875, Ransomes, Sims and Head, one of the leading plough manufacturers, claimed a total of 367 championship prizes at ploughing matches.

After the Second World War, ploughing matches were organised by local societies, most of which were affiliated to the British Ploughing Association. Financial difficulties led to its demise in 1971, after holding the World Ploughing Contest in Somerset. In the following year, the Society of Ploughmen was formed to enable the annual British National Ploughing Championships to take place. This organisation has a membership drawn from ploughmen and women from all over the world, and is an influential member of the World Ploughing Organization. By the year 2000 it comprised more than 250 affiliated local ploughing societies. The local societies organise ploughing matches, which are held mainly in the autumn months following the cereal harvest. One of the many benefits of affiliation is that a society may nominate one person to plough at the National Ploughing Championships, the high point of the British competitive ploughing season, which are held at a different venue every year. This prestigious event decides not only the supreme champion, but also those individuals who will represent England in the following year at the World Ploughing Contest, and at the European Reversible and Vintage Ploughing Contest.

Ploughing matches provide an opportunity for contestants to demonstrate their expertise in ploughing, and for spectators to marvel at the skill required to produce well-turned furrows, a task which has taken place since biblical times. Classes include not only the traditional oat-seed furrow using horses, but also semi-digger work, reversible ploughing, vintage and even horticultural tractors.

Historically closely associated with local taverns, ploughing contests were popular social events which attracted large crowds, and schoolchildren were sometimes given days off to attend. Today, these competitions provide an enjoyable day out, at which a wide variety of tractors and horses can be seen in action. They are often complemented by trade stands and other working demonstrations, which provide an enthralling mixture of rural trades and crafts for those interested in farming and the countryside.

Sources and Reading:
Garsed, J., *Records of the Glamorganshire Agricultural Society, from the Date of its Establishment in 1772 to the Year 1869* (Cardiff: The Society, 1890).
Jones, R. T., *Bedwellty Show: History of the Bedwellty Agricultural Society* (Newport: Starling Press, 1976).
Jones-Davies, J., *The Devynock Agricultural Society 1865–1965* (Brecon: The Brecon and Radnor Express and County Times, 1977).
Scourfield, E., *Astudiaeth o Ddiwylliant Lleol a Thraddodiadau Llafar Ardal Trelech*, MA dissertation, University of Wales, Swansea, 1969.
Sion yr Arddwr, *Llawlyfr yr Aradwr* (Llanelli: Swyddfar 'Guardian', 1890).

*John Martin and
Emma Lile*

Poaching

Poaching is trespassing on private property in order to take wildfowl, to fish or to hunt game using unlawful or 'unsportsmanlike' methods. Poaching is worthy of consideration in a sporting context because the poacher represented the antithesis of the values upheld by Georgian and Victorian sporting gentlemen, namely: poachers were not following a customary occupation or trade, they often operated at night and during the hunting close season, and they frequently sold their catch, which legally they did not own. As the artist and sportsman William Scrope (1772–1852) wrote, poachers were 'absolute thieves; for there can be no sport in taking a hare out of a wire, or shooting a pheasant on his perch by night'. The police were convinced that poachers were responsible for much other rural crime, and until about 1900 the game laws were a source of great conflict and resentment within rural society, as many, including tenant farmers, thought them inequitable.

In Britain, under Roman law wild animals were deemed *ferae naturae* ('in a state of nature') and regarded as communal property, but Norman forest law reserved the right to hunt for the crown and its assignees. In 1671, the introduction of a property qualification reiterated the legal exclusion of most of the population from hunting: legislation designed to help perpetuate a hierarchical, primarily rural society and improve the position of the gentry after the Restoration. During the eighteenth century hunting was transformed; hawking and netting declined while shooting and coursing became fashionable with the gentry. By about 1780 sportsmen expected easy access to large amounts of game, a demand satisfied by the breeding and preservation of game within country estates. Estate owners introduced legal barriers to maintain their control over game and regularly acted as magistrates in poaching cases. However, some landowners were more tolerant and allowed tenant farmers to kill the rabbits and hares eating their crops.

The legal definition of what constituted poaching changed between the eighteenth and nineteenth centuries. Until 1831 it encompassed the taking of partridges, grouse, hares and pheasants that were the property of the landowner. Foxes, badgers and otters were viewed as vermin and so were not protected. Legislation in 1770, 1816 and 1828 imposed severe penalties for night-time poaching, including transportation, although most poaching was carried out during the day. The Game Reform Act 1831 extinguished distinctions between different types of animals and for the first time the taking of deer and rabbits was prosecuted not as theft but as poaching. This act also introduced licences

for killing and trading game, and removed any property qualification. Nevertheless, lords of the manor, not freeholders or tenants, retained hunting rights over manorial lands and under tenancy agreements most tenants were still unable to shoot over the land they farmed. The county police had been operating since 1840, but not until the Poaching Prevention Act 1862 did they formally concern themselves with combating poaching. The Liberal government diluted the gentry's legal monopoly on game when its Ground Game Act 1880 conferred the right to kill game on both the occupiers and owners of land.

The naturalist Richard Jefferies (1848–87) emphasised that the vision of the poacher as a Robin Hood figure was fallacious. Poaching was normally an activity driven by economic motives, which to be carried out successfully required independence, intelligence, shrewdness, sobriety, stealth and 'a delicacy of touch which almost raises poaching to a fine art'. Poaching might also be undertaken as an act of protest ('social crime'), to gather food or, least commonly, for sport. Individuals who initially poached to appease hunger were sometimes habitually drawn back to it for the excitement. As the 'King of the Norfolk Poachers' explained to Lilas Rider Haggard: 'Poaching is something like drug taking – once begun no goen back, it get hold of you. . . . I loved the excitement of the Job. Beside you had the satafaction of knowen that you had got the keepers and police beat, and that went a long way towards recompence for the danger and risk run [*sic*].' The autobiographies of poachers also reveal that frequently the most articulate poachers were political radicals, sometimes engaged in poaching as a deliberate confrontational act with local game-preservers. James Hawker (1836–1921) from Oadby in Leicestershire began poaching as revenge for being imprisoned for stealing wood, and regarded all those who killed game as poachers.

Until the 1920s, poor rural families embraced poaching and other secondary economies, such as pig-keeping, gardening and laundering, together with multiple-occupations and kinship links, as part of their strategy against hardship. Such poverty was exacerbated by irregular and seasonal work, the parliamentary enclosures of common land after around 1790 and the administration of the poor law from 1834. In rural communities, the village poacher was not thought of as a criminal since he affirmed the generally held belief that hunting wild animals was a universal customary right. The Bible (Genesis 9:2 and 9:3) was often quoted to support this conviction: 'Every moving thing that liveth shall be meat for you; even as the green herb have I given you all things'. Thus, an entry for November 1874 in the diary of George Dew (1846–1928), a poor-law relieving officer from Oxfordshire, reads: 'Hares and rabbitts [*sic*] are wild animals & know no bounds in their settlement. This young man is gone to prison for three weeks with hard labour because he exercised a right which every man undoubtedly has . . . that of killing wild animals . . . in his native land.'

Most rural poaching resulted from the opportunistic activity of local men and it was always popular with miners from industrial villages. The few 'professional' village poachers, working alone or with one or two others, secured a modest living and were frequently able to pay the small fines that were the usual penalty for day-time poaching. Prosecutions for poaching in Norfolk between 1821 and 1861 reveal that although around 80 per cent of those convicted were male farm labourers, within their ranks were publicans, farmers, tradesmen, artisans and servants. Poaching was a seasonal activity with an explicit place in the rhythms of rural village life, where it was viewed as a craft, intensifying after the harvest in September when there was low employment. Bird catching was a winter activity, by March live birds would be caught, from April to June eggs taken, in June leverets became available and between July and August there were still plenty of rabbits to trap. Gamekeepers sometimes used poachers to help restock with live birds and eggs, usually poached from neighbouring estates.

The local poacher normally travelled no more than five miles from home and would take a wide variety of animals, including songbirds, hares, partridges, pheasants, salmon, trout, thrushes, lapwings, larks, grouse, blackbirds, plover, duck, snipe and woodcock. The use of guns – often collapsible – by village poachers was rare when compared with the use of traps, nets, snares, alcohol-soaked grain or sulphur to stupefy game, ferrets, dogs (whippets and lurchers), leisters (salmon spears), throwing sticks (similar to a boomerang) or stones and catapults. Poison and explosives were not used; doing so would have lost public sympathy. Reports of netting up to 90 rabbits in an evening are common, the catch often being limited only to what could be carried or hidden. The catch was sold to dealers and from door-to-door, or exchanged for beer or other goods in public houses. More generally, reliance was placed on a well-established network of receivers to get game to market, in which butchers, farmers, pedlars, innkeepers and grocers were all implicated.

After 1750, the demand for game from an expanding urban population made poaching attractive to gangs from towns and cities, which travelled up to 15 miles to invade country estates, as evidenced by convictions among Norwich artisans (1770s), Sheffield labourers (1820s) and the 40-strong Long Gang from Liverpool (1840s). Their unsubtle poaching methods (using firearms and violence to intimidate keepers, police and landowners) resulted from a lack of deference, working collectively and facing tough penalties for poaching at night and in a gang. The incidence of violent affrays involving poaching gangs declined with improving living standards after 1850, and gangs had disappeared by 1880. However, the general attractions of poaching continued to be widespread until after the First World War.

Sources and Reading:

Archer, J. E., '*By a Flash and a Scare*': *Incendiarism, Animal Maiming, and Poaching in East Anglia, 1815–1870* (Oxford: Oxford University Press, 1990).

Archer, J. E., 'A Reckless Spirit of Enterprise: Game-Preserving and Poaching in Nineteenth-Century Lancashire', in Howell, D. W. and Morgan, K. O. (eds), *Crime, Protest and Police in Modern British Society* (Oxford: Oxford University Press, 1990), 149–75.

Carter, M. J., *Peasants and Poachers: A Study in Rural Disorder in Norfolk* (Woodbridge: Boydell Press, 1980).

Christian, G. (ed.), *James Hawker's Journal: A Victorian Poacher* (Oxford: Oxford University Press, 1961).

Denwood, J. M., *Cumbrian Nights* (London: Jarrolds, 1932).

Eden, E. (ed.), *The Autobiography of a Working Man* (London: R. Bentley, 1862).

Haggard, L. Rider (ed.), *I Walked by Night: Being the Life and History of the King of the Norfolk Poachers* (London: Nicholson & Watson, 1935).

Hendry, C. C., *Scottish Poaching Equipment* (Edinburgh: HMSO, 1982).

Hopkins, H., *The Long Affray: The Poaching Wars in England, 1760–1914* (London: Secker & Warburg, 1985).

Horn, P. (ed.), *Oxfordshire Village Life: The Diaries of George James Dew (1846–1928), Relieving Officer* (Abingdon: Beacon, 1983).

Jones, D. J. V., 'The Poacher: A Study in Victorian Crime and Protest', *The Historical Journal*, XXII (1979), 825–60.

Munsche, P. B., *Gentleman and Poachers: The English Game Laws 1671–1831* (Cambridge: Cambridge University Press, 1981).

Samuel, R., '"Quarry Roughs": Life and Labour in Headington Quarry: An Essay in Oral History', in Samuel, R. (ed.), *Village Life and Labour* (London: Routledge & Kegan Paul, 1975), 139–263.

Walsh, E. G. (ed.), *The Poacher's Companion* (Woodbridge: Boydell Press, 1983).

Mark Hathaway

Poc Fada

Poc Fada is a hurling competition that celebrates the game's mythical Gaelic origins. The pre-eminent Gaelic superhero Cú Chulainn (whose boyhood name was Setanta) walked to the training camp of *Na Fianna* (an ancient Irish army) while propelling a *sliotar* (ball) through the air with his *camán* (stick) and running ahead to catch it as it fell. Setanta's journey from his home to Eamain Macha in County Armagh took him over the Cooley Mountains near Dundalk in neighbouring County Louth. To commemorate Setanta's feat with a *camán*, an annual competition, *Poc Fada* ('long puck or long strike'), has been held on his route, pitting the best strikers of a *sliotar* in the country against each other. Competitors traverse a mountain course, striking their ball ahead of them. The winner is the player who completes the route using the smallest number of strikes or pucks. Traditionally the winners of the contest have come from the country's cohort of top goalminders; these are the players whose role in hurling games is to restart the play following a score by striking the *sliotar* from the goal area as far as possible outfield.

Sources and Reading:
O' Maolfabhail, A., *Camán: Two Thousand Years of Hurling in Ireland* (Dundalk: Dundalgan Press, 1973).

See also Hurling

Tom Hayes

Prison Bars (Wales)

A game played in various parts of north Wales, which, in its simplest form, involved a contestant climbing on to a rock or mound of earth and defending his station from his opponents. The latter sought either to push him off or to drag him down. Prison bars continued among men and children until the early nineteenth century, when the rise of the Sunday school movement among the Calvinistic Methodists was believed to have gradually put an end to such entertainment.

Sources and Reading:
Jones, W. R. ('Gwenith Gwyn'), Papurau. Museum of Welsh Life, MS 1464.

Emma Lile

Prisoner's Bars

Prisoner's bars' heyday was in the seventeenth and eighteenth centuries. Although there were regional variations in the rules, the game essentially involved two teams lining up opposite each other. The members of one team linked hands while a member of the opposing team tried to cross to the other side of the playing area without being touched. Each team took it in turns for a member to try to cross over. Anyone who was touched joined the opposing team and the winning team was that which ended the game with the most members.

Its origins are claimed to lie in a medieval French street game called *aux barres*. According to the historian Joseph Strutt, the first written mention of the game in English is in a proclamation of Edward III, which banned its playing around the Palace of Westminster while Parliament was sitting. It is also known as 'prison bars' and 'prisoner's base', and is mentioned in Shakespeare's *Cymbeline* as 'country base'. According to a poem of 1764 by David Studley, the game was regularly played in Ellesmere between teams of married and single men.

In many respects the game resembled barley break and was often portrayed as a children's game, yet in the eighteenth century it became a popular spectator sport. In the 1740s public matches became common in London, with contests being held at Tothill Fields and at the Mitre pub in Highgate. There was even a pub named The Ten Prison Bars Players. As with wrestling and other sports of the time, teams from the provinces often travelled to London to provide crowd-pulling opposition. In 1744 a two-man team from Cheshire played a ten-strong Rest of England side, but the two northerners walked off in the middle of the game in a dispute over the rules. A rematch was only arranged after the Rest of England side had agreed to 'honourably play the right and accustomed way of playing'.

Its popularity was not confined to London: in 1764 Earl Gower staged a match between Cheshire and Staffordshire at his grounds at Trentham near Stoke in front of a large crowd, which included the Duke and Duchess of Bedford. As late as the second half of the nineteenth century the sport continued to be popular in areas of the West Midlands, eastern Wales and the Potteries, whose most famous writer Arnold Bennett described it as 'the Titanic sport of prison-bars'.

Sources and Reading:

Clark, P., *British Clubs and Societies 1580–1800: The Origins of an Associational World* (Oxford: Oxford University Press, 2000).

Day, B., *A Chronicle of Folk Customs* (London: Hamlyn, 1988).

Goulstone, J., 'English Folk Games and Sports', *British Society of Sports History Newsletter*, 10 (1999), 34–8.

Underdown, D., *Start of Play. Cricket and Culture in Eighteenth Century England* (Harmondsworth: Allen Lane, 2000).

See also Barley Break

Tony Collins

Prizefighting

Prizefighting, also known as bare-knuckle fighting or pugilism, played an important role in the development of modern sport. Its history exemplifies issues relating to the codification of rules, gambling, patronage, management, marketing, journalism, crowd control, chauvinism and legal regulation.

The first modern boxing match in England was in 1681, when the Duke of Albemarle organised a fight between his butler and his butcher. Prizefighting had been restricted to contests with sword, cudgel or quarter-staff until James Figg (1683–1734), the first recognised boxing champion of England, began exhibitions of fist-fighting at his London amphitheatre in about 1720. Jack Broughton (1705–89) continued with similar displays at George Taylor's amphitheatre in Oxford Street and after 1742 at his own booth nearby, enjoying royal patronage. In 1743 Broughton devised seven rules to regulate fights, which were subsequently adopted by other trainers. The rules attempted to standardise some practices and eliminate others. For example, they stipulated the functions of umpires, seconds and bottle-men; wrestling was allowed but hitting an opponent when he was down or pulling his hair were not. If a fighter was floored the 'round' was over and he had 30 seconds to 'square off' one yard from his opponent at the 'scratch', a line drawn in the middle of the ring, aided by his seconds if necessary; if he could not he had lost.

The sport flourished in London, where a growing number of pugilists appeared at indoor and outdoor venues. By 1760 fighting techniques were being perfected, matches systematically planned by managers and promoters, fighters becoming famous nationwide, gambling ubiquitous and patronage sought and given. The first match recorded outside London was in August 1758, when Faulkener beat Taylor at St Albans in Hertfordshire, and more followed after 1760. In the 1770s contests were taking place at racecourses such as Newmarket and being fostered at the local level by travelling fairs. The Bristol school of pugilism emerged in the later eighteenth century; of 112 leading British-born fighters active during the years 1780 to 1824, 36 were London-based and 26 were from the Bristol or Bath area.

While patronage, crowds, prize money and gambling grew during the 1790s, so did the concerns of authority in regard to crowd behaviour, since this implied an actual or feared lack of control. For example, in 1789 the theologian Edward Barry (1759–1822) protested that due to the number of fights 'the established order, and good decorum of society have been, of late, much disturbed, and nearly set at defiance'.

Prizefighting was illegal. From the end of the eighteenth century, magistrates instigated increasing numbers of prosecutions against spectators, competitors and managers for riot, affray, assault, unlawful assembly or breach of the peace. Fighters and their seconds were sometimes charged with manslaughter or murder if there was a fatality. Accordingly, after 1790 nearly all contests took place in the countryside, often near county boundaries, in order to frustrate the attempts of the magistracy to suppress them. Popular venues included Epping Forest in Essex and Coombe Warren, Coombe Wood and, from 1797, Mousley Hurst in Surrey. After the early 1820s matches encountered greater opposition. For example, in April 1837 the crowd and entourage for the Palmer v Luckett fight moved 35 miles from Banbury to Brickhill Heath, just inside Bedfordshire, to avoid magistrates who had authority to stop it taking place in Buckinghamshire, Northamptonshire, Oxfordshire and Warwickshire. By the mid-nineteenth century, trains and Thames steamers were taking spectators and contestants to venues beyond the reach of the authorities.

Prizefighting went through several periods of decline and revival. Throughout the Regency years (1810–20) it was very popular with wealthy supporters, collectively known as 'the Fancy', some of whom practised 'self-defence' with trainers in the London gymnasia. In concert with pedestrians and jockeys, prizefighters were the first professional sportsmen to enjoy national reputations. This development was greatly assisted by publications such as *Sporting Magazine* (established 1792), *Boxiana* (1812–18) by Pierce Egan (1772–1849), acknowledged as the first sports journalist, and *Bell's Life in London* (established 1822). Prize money could vary considerably. Bill Davis won 12½ guineas in July 1822 for beating Miller in 70 minutes at Woolwich, whereas Spring collected 500 guineas in June 1824 for defeating Langham over 108 minutes and 76 rounds near Chichester.

In 1824, John Badcock rated 80 leading fighters for weight, strength, activity, skill and 'bottom' (stamina). The top five were Tom Johnson (1750–97), Jem Belcher (1781–1811), John Gully (1783–1863), John Shaw (1789–1815) and Tom Spring (1795–1851). Johnson, who revived pugilism's fortunes during his championship years of 1784 to 1791, when his patrons included the Prince of Wales (George IV), and Belcher, champion from 1798 to 1803, were perhaps the two most outstanding fighters. The journal *Pugilistica* described Johnson's key attributes as his 'strength and science' and 'coolness and judgement'. Other leading personalities involved in the sport were Robert Barclay Allardice (1779–1854) and 'Gentleman' John Jackson (1769–1845). Allardice, otherwise known as Captain Barclay, was an athlete turned trainer who won £10,000 backing his protégé Tom Cribb (1781–1848) to beat the Afro-American Tom Molyneux in 1811, before a crowd of 20,000. Cribb retained the championship between 1808 and 1822. Jackson only fought professionally three times, his final bout being the defeat of the reigning champion Daniel Mendoza (1764–1836), a Jewish pugilist, by which he gained the championship which he held from 1795 to 1798. (The number of Romany, Jewish and black fighters at this time is noteworthy.)

By 1799 both Mendoza and Jackson had opened popular boxing-schools in London, which helped to promote pugilism among the Fancy and members of the aspirant middle and trading classes. Jackson was a central figure; he organised important fights and oversaw the security at George IV's coronation in 1821, perhaps pugilism's most respectable moment. Thereafter, support for prizefighting declined. Jackson's rooms in Bond Street closed in 1824 when an investor withdrew his support, as did the Mousley Hurst venue after Neale and Burns were prosecuted for fighting there. Additionally, efforts to set up pugilistic clubs outside London, for example in Norwich, failed. By 1830 the sport was considered by many to be disreputable and corrupt, given its attendant gambling, match-fixing, connections to criminals and its own illegality. It was also regulated by many different sets of rules. The *London Prize Ring Rules*, based on Broughton's rules, were introduced in 1838 (and revised by the Pugilistic Benevolent Association in 1853 and 1866) to help to restore prizefighting's fortunes. Under the London rules, contests were always fought in a roped-off ring, 24-foot square. As previously, the round finished when a fighter was knocked down, but he had to get up to scratch unaided within 8 seconds of the 30-second time-lapse and if he remained down for 10 seconds he lost the contest.

The last significant prizefight was in April 1860 before 12,000 spectators at Farnborough in Hampshire, when Tom Sayers (1826–65) from Brighton fought the American John Heenan for £200 and the World Championship. Amid crowd disorder, the fight ended in a draw after 2½ hours and 36 punishing rounds, during which Sayers broke his right arm. The Queensberry Rules of 1867 marked the demise of bare-knuckle fighting (although it continued into the 1890s), the increased use of gloves and the more effective regulation of both professional and amateur boxing. The Queensberry Rules helped to promote skill and dexterity above wrestling and brawn. They proscribed wrestling, hitting rivals on the ground and fights to the finish, and endeavoured to distance boxing from the prevalent mid-Victorian view of prizefighting as an uncultured and vicious scrap.

Sources and Reading:

Anderson, J., 'Pugilistic Prosecutions: Prize Fighting and the Courts in Nineteenth Century Britain', *The Sports Historian*, 21: 2 (2001), 35–53.

Bee, J. [John Badcock], *Fancy-Ana; or, A History of Pugilism* (Third edition) (London: J. Walker, 1824).

Brailsford, D., *Bareknuckles: A Social History of Prize-Fighting* (Cambridge: Lutterworth Press, 1988).

Dowling, F. L., *Fights for the Championship* (London: Bells' Life in London, 1855).

Dowling, F. L., *Fistiana, or, The Oracle of the Ring* (Fifth edition) (London: Bells' Life in London, 1868).

Ford, J., *Prizefighting: The Age of Regency Boximania* (Newton Abbot: David and Charles, 1971).

Henning, H., *Fights for the Championship* (London: Licensed Victuallers' Gazette, 1900).

Malcolmson, R. W., *Popular Recreations in English Society 1700–1850* (Cambridge: Cambridge University Press, 1973).

Reid, J. C., *Bucks and Bruisers: Pierce Egan and Regency England* (London: Routledge, 1971).

See also Broughton's Rules, Pugilism (Wales)

Mark Hathaway

Public School Sports

An abundance of free time for boarding pupils at Winchester College offered opportunities for the development of a range of sporting activities, and a mixture of activities, both noble and bucolic, were pursued by scholars and commoners at Winchester in the pre-modern period. These activities included archery, bat and ball, bowling, tennis, boxing, cricket, fives and football, even jousting, many of which had become regular features of life at Winchester as early as the late seventeenth century. In fact, some form of daily compulsory physical activity both within the college walls and on the adjacent St Catherine's Hill seems to have been part of Winchester life from the 1640s onwards.

The bifurcation of games into activities suited to a playground, ball-place or ball court within the walls (or using the walls) of schools, and those suited to an open sports field became increasingly a matter of numbers. As the numbers at Winchester (and at other public schools in the pre-modern period) grew, so there is increasing evidence of the need for larger areas for team games such as cricket and football. Meanwhile, tennis, fives and handball continued to be played singly or in pairs in spaces within the walls of these schools, formed, as often as not, by existing school buildings. Thus, just as forms of fives or handball were played in churchyards in areas of England as diffuse as Yorkshire and Dorset during this period, games were played using the architecture of the areas known as Little Dean's Yard at Westminster School or the Chapel Steps at Eton College.

Having been founded on lines similar to Winchester, Eton also provided opportunities for vigorous outdoor physical activity, although the evidence for magisterial encouragement for such activities at Winchester in the seventeenth and eighteenth centuries is clearer than at Eton. And while Westminster School, like Eton, enjoyed royal patronage and was well-regarded at this time, other schools, such as Rugby, Charterhouse, Shrewsbury, and even Harrow, had not yet become part of the group of institutions later known as the great public schools. Nevertheless, a number of the games and sports found at Winchester and Eton in the eighteenth century were also to be found at each of these other schools. In the pre-modern period, what differentiated the schools and their sports from each other, and thus made for unique forms of each of the games played, was, first and foremost, the context within which their games were played, and also, if to a lesser extent, the degree to which games were supported, ignored, or suppressed by masters and headmasters, and later by old boys.

The importance of context is best seen in the varying forms of football found in the schools. Field conditions, along with their size and shape, certainly influenced the style and form of football developed in each of these schools. Thus at Eton, there were two very different forms of the game, the wall game and the field game, dependent almost entirely on the surroundings in which they were played. The impact of one particular architectural feature, the 11-foot high wall built in 1717 to separate the Eton playing fields from the Slough Road, was critical to the development of one form of football, the Eton Wall Game. Possibly developed from the field game as the result of the building of this wall, the traditional contest is played between 'collegers' (scholars) and 'oppidans' (townsmen) on St Andrew's Day each year. The game is invariably low scoring. Originally 11-a-side, by 1914 the game had become 10-a-side and with a fair degree of specialisation of function among the players, played on an area 5 yards wide by 118 yards long. Eton's field game was similar to the field football played at each of the other schools, suggesting that there was perhaps a 'generic' form of the game which had formed the basis of the football played in each of the schools. However, the importance of context is again highlighted in the fact that there was originally a third form of the game at Eton, called Lower College, where goals were marked on trees. This game was discontinued in 1865, presumably in an effort to rationalise and unify Eton football and in response to the efforts of Etonians at Cambridge and elsewhere to proselytise their non-handling form of the game as Rugby's form of football gained in popularity from the 1850s onwards.

There were also two forms of football at Charterhouse and Westminster in the early years of the nineteenth century. One was played in the cloisters, the other was an open-field game played in an area called 'the Green'. Again, the physical surroundings, in this case the schools' cloisters, played a significant role in the rules, structure and style of play. The field games played in the Green at these two schools also show distinct aspects of modern association football, particularly the practice of limited offside. In both cases the playing area of the Green was substantial (unlike the game in cloisters or Eton's Wall Game) and allowed boys plenty of room to move. At Winchester by mid-century, football was something of a hybrid of these two forms, played on a field 27 yards by 80 yards with canvas (later netting) along the sides as a boundary. The canvas replaced the junior boys who were previously expected to line the field not only at Winchester but at Eton, Shrewsbury, Harrow, Rugby and elsewhere, as one of the traditional duties associated with 'fagging'. At Shrewsbury these boys were known by the Greek term *doulos* (slave), Shrewsbury's football being known as 'dowling'. In some cases these boys were even expected to defend the goal. In the early years of the nineteenth century the game at Shrewsbury did not receive magisterial support, being viewed by headmaster Butler as being 'a game fit only for farm boys and butcher boys', and therefore seems to have remained a more isolated form.

The biggest exception to the traditional forms of football played in the public

schools in the pre-modern period was to be found at Rugby, where running with the ball and 'hacking' were regular features of the game from the 1830s onwards. While catching the ball and being allowed three or four paces to generate momentum prior to kicking the ball out of hand ('punting') appears to have been allowed at all of the schools, only at Rugby was a player allowed to run with the ball and only at Rugby was the practice of 'hacking him down' sanctioned. It was these two features that eventually caused the rift in football rules that led to two different codes as football became increasingly rationalised as the modern sports of Association and Rugby Football.

The slow demise of most of the unique varieties of public school football in favour of one of the two widely accepted codes provides evidence for the modernisation of nineteenth-century sport. It also highlights to some degree the role of the public schools (and universities) in this process. Yet residual features of pre-modern era sport continued, both generally and in the public schools particularly, beyond the First World War. For example, at Shrewsbury an extraordinary and singular institution, the Royal Shrewsbury School Hunt, was tolerated by successive headmasters, Butler (1798–1836) and Kennedy (1836–66), and was still in operation, albeit in different guise, in the form of cross-country running in the 1950s. Modelled after the hunting that many of their fathers would have enjoyed with the Quorn and other hunts, the school hunt was organised by the boys into 'foxes', 'packs of hounds', 'whippers-in', 'gentlemen of the hunt' and a huntsman – all parts being played by the boys. The foxes originally carried 'scent', which was used in the same way that paper was used in paper chases. Scent bags were abandoned in the 1850s in favour of organised and planned courses in order to prevent continuing problems and community hostility caused by running 'out of bounds' – and perhaps also because Kennedy found that boys had torn up new copies of his famed Latin primer to fill the scent bags!

Like Eton and Westminster, Shrewsbury was located within easy reach of a river and rowing was a significant summer sporting activity at all three of these schools. Rowing offered an alternative to cricket. Affectionately known as 'wet-bobs', rowers had organised crews from as early as 1813 at Westminster. Boating clubs were officially recognised at Shrewsbury in 1835 and at Eton in 1840, although Etonians had been participating in rowing activities and events for many years prior to this date. The significance of rowing at Eton can be gauged by the fact that the school provided the majority of rowers in the Oxford and Cambridge boat race up until the First World War. Throughout this period, increasing competition, technological change, rationalisation and an emphasis on equality of competitive situation can be seen as important aspects in the development of rowing in the public schools. The increasingly ordered, organised, disciplined and controlled Victorians expected their public schoolmasters to provide training in moral values for their offspring, and the traditional sports of rowing, and more broadly football and cricket, became tools for this purpose as sport was pursued in these schools for its educational rather than merely its recreational value.

Technology also played a significant role in the development of sports. In rowing, the development of outriggers and the introduction of keel-less or 'shell' boats are but two examples of this. New methods of training to make boys 'fit', both for rowing and for the hunt, are in evidence at Shrewsbury from the 1870s onwards. A variety of technical and technological changes were impacting upon pre-modern sport in ways that would have significant long-term effects in these schools, as sport became increasingly not just a means but rather *the* 'means to virtue, nobleness of spirit, or even purity of body'. Technological changes also influenced the longest and most widely organised sport – cricket. They influenced equipment, costume, and pitch preparation in the sport and the public schools were certainly affected by, and even leaders in, such changes. And while such changes wrought further changes in the context within which sport was played in each of these schools, it was numbers that

continued to have the most significant impact on the growth and development of organised games and sports.

Increasing numbers of boys in each of the public schools, particularly from the 1850s onwards, meant that greater organisation and control were necessary in order to accommodate such growth. The growth of the middle classes and the increasing demand for a public school education also meant a growing push for comparison, contest and competition, both within and between the schools. Such status rivalry had as early as 1826 encouraged Eton, Winchester and Harrow to distance themselves from other schools by holding a triangular tournament later known as Public Schools Week at Lord's as a display of wealth and influence as the London season was coming to a close. These were important matches and garnered much coverage in the press. Other interschool matches, such as those between Westminster and Charterhouse, were also of long standing. But it was only at the end of the pre-modern period that a set of public school matches at Lord's, including those between Rugby and Marlborough, Cheltenham and Haileybury, and Tonbridge and Clifton, signified the arrival of *modern* public school sport. For, despite the ritual that surrounded the new extended Public Schools Week, this new set of organised schools matches was a display of secular, rational, quantified sport in which the record of wins and losses against opponents who were considered social and athletic equals exemplified the essence of modern public school sport.

Sources and Reading:

Bailey, S., 'Permission to Play: Education for Recreation and Distinction at Winchester College, 1382–1680', *International Journal of the History of Sport*, 12: 1 (1995), 1–17.

Curry, G., 'The Trinity Connection: An Analysis of the Role of Members of Cambridge University in the Development of Football in the Mid-Nineteenth Century', *The Sports Historian*, 22: 2 (2002), 46–73.

Malcolmson, R. W., *Popular Recreations in English Society, 1700–1850* (Cambridge: Cambridge University Press, 1973).

Money, T., *Manly and Muscular Diversions: Public Schools and the Nineteenth-Century Sporting Revival* (London: Duckworth, 1997).

Timothy J. L. Chandler

Pubs and Sport

It would be impossible to write a history of sport in any age without mention of the public house. For centuries the pub has been the initiator, the organiser and the promoter of sport of all types. This partly arose from the pivotal role that the pub played in rural, and later urban, life; it was simultaneously a place for socialising, meeting, doing business, finding work and, most important of all, drinking alcohol. The pub landlord was undoubtedly the earliest incarnation of the sporting entrepreneur by organising matches, providing prize money and taking bets.

By the sixteenth century at the latest, the pub had become the most important venue for sporting activities. With the decline of church ales in the seventeenth century, the pub often became the only stage for sport. Its rooms, yards and greens were used for skittles, quoits, bowls, boxing, wrestling, tennis, foot racing, cricket, animal baiting and many other sports. Its walls were used for playing rackets and fives.

Bowling or skittle alleys became common in pubs during the Elizabethan period. Indeed, more often than not it was the pub that brought the sport to a particular locality; for example, the first bowling green in Gloucester was opened in 1604 at the New Inn. The identification of pubs with their greens led to many adopting the name Bowling Green Inn (or some variant of it). In the north and Midlands of England, bowls was based almost entirely on the patronage of pub landlords.

Pubs were often the starting or finishing point for traditional folk football matches. The game played at Dorking uniquely allowed players to call a type of 'time-out', during which the game would stop while the participants went into a pub for a drink. The game would restart with the ball being thrown out of one of the pub's upstairs windows.

Quoits also had close associations with the pub. At least as early as 1830 teams representing Falkirk and Stirling played each other on grounds owned by pubs, and the popularity of the game can be gauged by the fact that in 1850 John Rennie of Alva and a Mr Heywood of Oldham played a match for a stake of £100 in a pub near Newcastle railway station. In the 1880s, 52 pubs in 33 villages in Northumberland had quoits grounds, a number of which had seating installed for spectators.

Pubs were not only associated with the labouring masses. Elite cricket teams and eighteenth-century coaching clubs often took their names from hostelries. Hunts and point-to-point races usually began or finished at inns. The pub also played a key role in horseracing; for example, Thomas Coleman, landlord of St Albans' Turf Hotel, organised the first modern steeplechase in 1830. Coursing's most famous trophy, the Waterloo Cup, is named after the pub that first initiated the tournament in 1836.

This relationships with sport that are seen in pub names and signs can be misleading – animals can represent the coats-of-arms of local nobility rather than sport. However, many of the animals in pub names do have a sporting connection, existing historically as advertisements of what might be provided by the landlord. Cockfighting was one of the most popular pub sports and animals were traditional sporting attractions at pubs. As well as dog fighting and rat catching, bull, bear and, occasionally, ape baiting were features of pubs large enough to have pits. Badgers and ducks were also often the target for dogs.

Aside from animal sports, no sport was more closely associated with pubs than prizefighting. Its semi-legal status made it reliant on the pub for its promotion, staging and administration, not to mention the gambling. This was not just in London.

Hundreds of pubs across Britain staged boxing matches; the George at Odiham in Hampshire hosted bouts for over 300 years from 1547, while the Ram Jam Inn at Stretton near Grantham hosted Tom Cribb's 1810 victory over America's Tom Molyneaux; and when they had retired from the ring, countless boxers became landlords. Sadly many ex-pugilists quickly became ex-publicans: for example, Jem Belcher's tenancy of the Jolly Brewer in Wardour Street was terminated by an alcohol-induced death aged just 30.

Cricket was also a child of the drinking house. The first known laws of the game, the 1755 *New Articles of the Game of Cricket*, were subtitled *Particularly That of the Star & Garter in Pall Mall*. John Nyren was the landlord of Hambledon's Bat and Ball Inn, which was also the village side's clubhouse. William Clarke, the force behind the professional All-England XI, married the landlady of the Trent Bridge Inn in Nottingham and opened a cricket ground there. Ex-professional cricketers often become pub landlords, many emulating their pugilist cousins by quickly becoming alcoholic or bankrupt ex-publicans.

The rise of modern mass spectator sport in the late nineteenth century was partially facilitated by the pub, which again provided the changing rooms and often the fields for soccer, rugby and cricket teams. But the pub also helped to sustain traditional sports too. Thanks to the patronage of the pub, knur and spell, rabbit coursing and pigeon shooting grew in strength in Yorkshire up until after the First World War. In other parts of Britain, traditional sports such as quoits, trap ball and skittles survived almost entirely due to pubs. In the 1960s and 1970s, traditional sports once again became regular sights in pubs as brewery marketing campaigns sought to revive old sports – not to mention some completely fictitious ones, such as maggot racing – in an attempt to bring more customers into pubs. There was even a TV show, 'Indoor League', which sought to bring pub sports to a wider audience. However, the decline of the pub as a social centre and its conversion into a mere retail outlet may mean that its days as an organising centre for modern and traditional sports are numbered.

Sources and Reading:

Clark, P., *The English Ale Houses: A Social History, 1200–1830* (London: Longman, 1983).

Collins, T. and Vamplew, W., *Mud, Sweat and Beers: A Cultural History of Sport and Alcohol* (Oxford: Berg, 2002).

Harrison, B., *Drink and the Victorians* (London: Faber, 1971).

Harrison, B., 'Pubs', in Dyos, H. J. and Wolff, M. (eds), *The Victorian City: Images and Realities* (Volume 1) (London: Routledge, 1973).

Harrison, B., 'Pubs', in Dyos, H. J. and Wolff, M. (eds), *The Victorian City: Images and Realities* (Volume 1) (London: Routledge, 1973).

Haydon, P., *The English Pub: A History* (London: Robert Hale, 1994).

Tony Collins

Puff and Dart

– see **Darts**

Pugilism

– see **Prizefighting**

Pugilism (Wales)

In Wales, pugilistic bouts were contested nationwide during the nineteenth century, initially supported by the gentry, who often donated prize money. Bare-knuckle fighting was an immensely popular spectator sport, with large crowds assembling to witness events. When Ned Turner, dubbed the 'pugilistic prince of Wales' by the *North Wales Gazette*, lost a bout to a bed maker called Inglis in 1823, the whole Vale of

Llangollen was said to have been distraught. In 1824 a fight in Monmouth was attended by some 4,000 spectators; the encounter was won by Parry, a quarryman, who beat his opponent, a fighter named Powell, for a prize of £60, over 103 rounds lasting almost two hours. The lack of a predetermined number of rounds led to lengthy and arduous fights; on Rhymney Hill, near Tredegar, in 1860 a match between Edwards and Stevens for £10-a-side went to 127 rounds.

Welsh bouts were held at a variety of venues, such as fields and sands, and at the local fairs, when the best fighter in the neighbourhood won the right to choose the prettiest young girl and escort her home. With the sport's gradual loss of credibility, secluded mountain tops (away from the eyes of the law) were often used for fights, and as the nineteenth century progressed, police officers were frequently called on to attend and make arrests for breach of the peace. Often promoted by innkeepers, matches were invariably savage and bloody affairs, for there were few actual rules and the rounds continued until one combatant was knocked to the ground. Fighting fatalities were not uncommon and newspaper accounts detail the plights of pugilists' widows, left with young children and totally dependent on the parish for financial support. The large prizes on offer undoubtedly appealed greatly to competitors, who, mostly drawn from the lower classes, were in desperate need of the money. With huge sums to be won, such as £2,000 for the winner of a Swansea fight in 1863, it was no wonder that enthusiasm for the sport endured.

By the 1860s, bare-knuckle and gloved fights were held simultaneously in Wales, only for the latter to eventually supersede the former by the end of the century. The withdrawal of gentry support, owing to the sport's increasingly unwholesome reputation, also contributed towards its disappearance.

Sources and Reading:
Bell's Life (22 January 1860).
Cambrian Daily Leader (1 April 1863).

Hereford Journal (4 August 1824).
North Wales Gazette (18 November 1823).

See also Prizefighting

Emma Lile

Purring

An informal game common until the late nineteenth century in Lancashire and the north-west of England in which men would kick at each other's shins until one admitted defeat. It was not the only game in which the ability to withstand hard kicks to the shins was important. Devonshire wrestling allowed kicking of the shins, a feature which made it unique among wrestling codes, until the late nineteenth century. Public school players of the rugby code of football also viewed 'hacking', as the practice was known, as the *sine qua non* of masculinity, with a number of adult clubs continuing to allow hacking in matches even after the Rugby Football Union outlawed it in 1871.

Sources and Reading:
Walton, J., *Lancashire: A Social History 1558–1939* (Manchester: Manchester University Press, 1987).

See also Football, Kick Shins, Wrestling

Tony Collins

Puw, Huw

An acclaimed Welsh jumper and thrower, who was born in 1663 at Cwmrhwyddfor in Meirionethshire and competed in Wales before attending Jesus College, Oxford, and then becoming a vicar. While Puw was still reportedly a fine athlete at the age of 60, one of his earliest exploits was to jump over his parents' heads on the way to church one Sunday, thereby shocking his mother so greatly that she collapsed and died. Puw's feats continued to amaze at university, where he excelled at jumping, wrestling and throwing. After his death in 1743 a memorial was erected in Oxford in respect of his sporting achievements and several literary odes were composed in his honour.

Emma Lile

Quarterstaff

The quarterstaff was a wooden pole approximately six to nine feet long with a circumference of between four and five inches, which for many centuries was used as a weapon. It was held in the middle and the skill of the holder was demonstrated by the speed with which the staff could be rotated. Its fame in English culture is probably due to the fact that Robin Hood was reputedly a master of the quarterstaff. One of his legendary contests, with Arthur a'Bland, lasted over two hours.

The quarterstaff was one of the weapons whose use was taught by the Maisters of the Noble Science of Defence, a body incorporated by Henry VIII in 1540. Like cudgelling, quarterstaff was popular at fairs and festivals up until the eighteenth century. There are also examples of contests between a combatant using a quarterstaff and another using a sword. As can be assumed, it seems that the greater length and weight of the quarterstaff would win against even the most skilled use of a sword.

Sources and Reading:
The Encyclopaedia of Sport (London: *The Sportsman*, 1912).
Malcolmson, R., *Popular Recreations in English Society 1700–1850* (Cambridge: Cambridge University Press, 1973).

See also Cudgelling and Singlestick

Tony Collins

Quoits

Dating back at least to medieval times, the aim of quoits is to throw the 'quoit', which can be a heavy circular metal ring or a horseshoe, over a peg, or 'hob', in the ground. Originally, the aim was to throw a heavy stone as near as possible to the peg. Also known as 'corts' in medieval times, its popularity can be gauged by the fact that it was banned in 1388 by Richard II, along with football, handball and a number of other sports, because of the enthusiasm for it among servants and labourers. By the mid-eighteenth century it was commonly played with a metal ring, weighing at least seven or eight pounds, which was thrown at a metal peg set in clay about 20 yards from the thrower's mark. Matches were decided on points, which were awarded for ringing the peg and for quoits that landed nearest the peg.

The sport experienced a tremendous growth in popularity in the 1820s and 1830s, possibly because the ease with which games could be organised and played fitted well with industrial life, which many working people now faced. It became especially popular in mining areas. It seems that quoits has always been associated with the working classes, particularly in England; for example, in 1829 George Oliver of Beverley in east Yorkshire noted that 'the lower classes of people have their quoits, their foot-ball, and their cricket'.

It was also closely associated with pubs, both in England and Scotland. As early as 1830, teams from Falkirk and Stirling played each other on grounds owned by pubs. Its success was such that it could support a level of semi-professionalism on both sides of the border. In 1850 Alva's John Rennie played Oldham's Mr Heywood in a pub near Newcastle railway station for a stake of £100. In 1875 Glasgow's D. Haddow played London's George Graham at the Abbey Arms at Plaistow for a prize of £100.

In Scotland, quoits was popular enough to have a number of playing areas devoted to the sport. For example, in 1890, when William Drysdale of Dalkeith beat Alva's Andrew Hunter for the quoits 'world championship at 18 yards', the match was held at Grangeham Quoiting Ground at Bo'ness.

In late nineteenth- and early twentieth-century Wales, the game was prevalent among miners in the south, and in the north, farmhands were known to play using horseshoes. Despite a decline in popularity during the mid-nineteenth century, owing to the game's alleged associations with vulgarity and intemperance, its fortunes turned by the 1880s as it began to attract female participants. Llanelli in Carmarthenshire was the home to a world champion quoiter in 1895, and the following year Wales competed internationally for the first time.

The first known written set of rules was published in 1881 by the Association of Amateur Quoits Clubs for the North of England. These rules became known as the 'northern game rules', and were differentiated from the rules under which the game was played in Scotland and Wales, which were known as 'long game rules'. These rules are still broadly played today.

In the northern game, the hobs are eleven yards apart set in squares of clay. The weight of the quoit has varied over time – with one allegedly weighing 23 pounds – but today the standard weight is about 5½ pounds with a diameter of 5½ inches. If a quoit lands on top of another, only the top quoit scores.

The long game was also known as the 'old game'. Its hobs are set 18 yards apart and, in contrast to the northern game, are flush to the ground. The quoits can weigh up to double that of the northern game and are 9 inches in diameter. Points are scored for each quoit that lands nearer to the hob than an opponent's. East Anglian quoits is a variant of the long game, although smaller quoits are used and there are differences in scoring. Internationals under long game rules were once played between Scotland and England, but eventually the differences between the Scottish game and that played in East Anglia became too great for meaningful contests to take place.

In England, quoits's working-class identity was probably stronger than in Scotland. It was especially popular among miners in

the north-east, Somerset, Kent and south Wales, and it was also played in Suffolk, Sussex and parts of the Midlands. In the 1880s, 52 pubs in 33 villages in Northumberland had quoits grounds, a number of which even had seating for spectators. The sport also acquired a reputation for violence, although whether this was justified or simply a reflection of the fact that it was viewed as a socially inferior sport by middle-class commentators (certainly when compared with the far more respectable bowls, for example) is debatable.

A police superintendent giving evidence to the 1929 Royal Commission on licensing laws went so far as to say that 'we used to say up north, if you want to be a good quoiter, you have to be a good fighter . . . Fighting and quoiting go together generally'. Even so, the standard guide for new pub landlords written in 1923 had no hesitation in recommending the formation of a quoits club as it was one of the most popular sports that a pub could promote. In Scotland, however, quoits was seen in some circles as providing an alternative to drinking in pubs.

By the 1920s the sport was in serious decline, partly due to the overwhelming popularity of soccer in working-class areas and also due to the long-term decline of the mining industry. The last world championship was staged in 1913 and despite attempts to organise international matches between England, Scotland and Wales, it appears that the view of Mass Observation's *The Pub and the People* (1943) that the game was dying out in Bolton pubs and being replaced by darts, was also true for quoits throughout Britain.

In the late 1970s and early 1980s, quoits underwent a mini-revival due to marketing campaigns by various breweries to revive traditional sports in order to attract customers back to pubs. The Welsh Quoiting Board was reformed in 1979, a number of local leagues were formed and in 1983 the world quoits championship was revived. International matches between Scotland and Wales were first organised in 1931 and still take place. The National Quoits Association was formed in 1986 to revivify the game under northern game rules and today quoits continues to enjoy a degree of popularity as a summer pub sport.

There are also other versions of the game – with self-explanatory names, such as lawn quoits (also known as sward quoits), deck quoits and rope quoits – which attest to the fact that whatever difficulties quoits as an organised sport may have, the basic game is one that has an enduring appeal.

Sources and Reading:

Baker, A. A., *The History of Quoits in Wales* (Abertillery: J. R. Davies, 1949).

Malcolmson, R., *Popular Recreations in English Society 1700–1850* (Cambridge: Cambridge University Press, 1973).

Metcalfe, A., 'Organised Sport in the Mining Communities of South Northumberland, 1880–1889', *Victorian Studies*, 25 (1982).

Museum of Welsh Life Tape no. 890.

Stonehenge [J. H. Walsh], *Manual of British Rural Sports* (London: Routledge, 1857).

Taylor, A., *The Guinness Book of Traditional Pub Games* (London: Guinness, 1992).

Tranter, N., 'Organised Sport and the Working Classes of Scotland, 1820–1900: The Neglected Sport of Quoiting', in Holt, R. (ed.), *Sport and the Working Class in Modern Britain* (Manchester: Manchester University Press, 1990).

Tranter, N., 'Quoits', in Jarvie, G. and Burnett, J. (eds), *Sport, Scotland and the Scots* (Edinburgh: Tuckwell, 1999).

See also Ringing the Bull, Stone Throwing

Tony Collins and
Emma Lile

Rackets

A form of fives played with a racket. It is similar to modern squash and a derivative of the tennis family of games. The racket is said to have developed from the cords and straps that were bound around the hands of players to give them more power and control over the ball as they hit it.

The game achieved great popularity in London in the late eighteenth and early nineteenth centuries. This appears to have been due to its being played in London's debtors' prisons – the King's Bench and the Fleet – because it required nothing more than a ball, something to hit it with and a wall to hit it against. It is mentioned in Howard's 1780 report on the state of prisons in England and Wales, and Dickens described it being played in the Fleet in *The Pickwick Papers*. It was reputed that every top player before the emergence of Sir William Hart-Dyke in the 1860s was either born in or had spent time in a debtors' prison.

The rackets court was substantially larger than a squash court, being 60 feet long at the sides and 30 feet wide at the front and back, with the walls being concrete, asphalt or, occasionally, marble. The racket was 2½ feet long and the ball made of tightly wound cloth covered in kid skin, making it much harder than the rubber squash ball.

As with fives, rackets was very popular in parts of Somerset and the south-west, with church walls commonly being used for the game, which, like fives, was either tacitly condoned or strenuously condemned depending on the moral fervour of the local clergy.

Outside prison, pubs were the favoured arena for the game. Initiated in 1820, when it was won by Robert Mackay, the national Open Court Championship was held at the Belvedere on Pentonville Road in 1838, and major matches also took place at the Eagle Tavern on the City Road, the White Bear in Kennington and the Rosemary Branch at Peckham.

Rackets enjoyed its great heyday in the early decades of the nineteenth century. In 1819, Hazlitt remarked that the best rackets player of the time was John Davies of London, commenting that 'he did not seem to follow the ball, but the ball seemed to follow him. Give him a foot of wall, and he was sure to make the ball.' He allegedly once beat four players playing against him simultaneously.

However, the sport's popularity among the lower classes did not find favour with its middle-class players. In 1832, Pierce Egan complained about London rackets courts:

> . . . the fault of these places is, that the company is not sufficiently select, and that the gentleman who is fond of the game (and all are fond of it who can play at all) are there compelled to join a miscellany of very respectable persons no doubt, but not of the highest grade in society.

It became the vogue for gentlemen's clubs to build their own courts, thus giving the game an exclusivity that ensured that from the mid-nineteenth century it became dominated by middle-class amateurs. Unlike most of the courts in prisons and pubs, where games were usually played against a single wall, these were enclosed and covered.

Many public schools which already played fives took up the sport. Harrow was the first public school to play rackets, beginning in the 1820s. The first Oxford v Cambridge varsity match was played in 1855, the Public Schools Championship was first held in 1868 and the first national amateur championship was staged at the Queen's Club in London in 1888. Rackets subsequently developed close links with real tennis and in 1907 the Tennis and Rackets Association was founded.

Although still played primarily by former public-school pupils today, rackets eventually lost its popularity to 'squash rackets' (as squash was originally called) because of the high costs involved in its playing. For squash, which had originated at Harrow school in 1850, courts could be quickly and easily assembled using wood for the walls, and the balls and rackets were also much cheaper. The ball was also softer and slower, making squash an easier game to play. Today, rackets must be counted among the most socially-exclusive of sports.

Sources and Reading:
Aberdare, Lord, *The Willis Faber Book of Tennis and Rackets* (London: Stanley Paul, 1980).

Egan, P., *Book of Sports* (London: Thomas Tegg, 1832).
The Encyclopaedia of Sport (London: *The Sportsman*, 1912).
Hone, W., *The Every-Day Book* (London: Thomas Tegg, 1830).

See also Fives, Squash, Tennis

Tony Collins

Ratting

Often associated with pubs, ratting competitions were organised as public spectacles in which specially trained terrier dogs killed as many rats as possible in the shortest possible time in specially constructed pits. It is probable that rats were sometimes doped in order to ensure a high kill rate. By the 1820s, this spectator activity was accompanied by heavy betting. As a formally organised activity that was associated with betting, it declined rapidly during the Victorian era. Ratting, however, continued on an informal basis, particularly at threshing time in the autumn and winter, when the ricks were cleared and the rats could easily be caught by dogs. Wagers were still placed on which dog could kill the most rats. Ferrets were also used to encourage rats to bolt so the dogs could catch them.

Rat hunting did not always use dogs. During the nineteenth century in Glangwili in Carmarthenshire, a popular pastime among the children was the killing of rats in the farmyard's cornricks. With the youngsters armed with sticks and with ferrets placed in the ricks, the rats stood little chance of surviving the subsequent attack. Although it was a rather barbaric activity, it was a practical way of saving grain and preventing damage.

Sources and Reading:
Billett, M., *A History of English Country Sports* (1994).
Vaughan, H. M., *The South Wales Squires* (London: Methuen, 1926; republished Carmarthen: Golden Grove, 1988).

John Martin and Emma Lile

Regattas (Wales)

Regattas, sporting events comprising a series of boat or yacht races, were a popular form of entertainment in Wales during the mid-nineteenth century. A great sense of occasion surrounded the regattas, with the attendance of bands and the decoration of bridges. Many regattas were dependent on gentry patronage, and the elite of society were staunch supporters.

While rowing racing took place in some areas at the beginning of the nineteenth century, contests were not advertised as 'regattas' until around the 1830s. By then, rowing and sculling races were common features of rural life, both for the sake of enjoyment and as a means for the watermen to parade their skill to potential ferry passengers. Competitions often attracted hefty wagers, which added to the overall excitement and encouraged widespread betting. Races were not confined to men, women occasionally took part in the rowing events.

One of the most highly regarded regattas of the mid-nineteenth century was that held in Swansea. It attracted some of the country's best yachtsmen, as well as thousands of spectators, who flocked to the bay to witness the various events. The vessels were adorned with flags and streamers and, in addition to the races, several pleasure booths were erected to enhance the general amusement. The scene was similar in north Wales, such as at Bala Lake in Gwynedd in 1869 when the town's first regatta took place to great success. Some 15,000 people attended, and a wooden stand was erected on one side of the lake to cater for the leading families of the neighbourhood. The races contested included those for pairs, canoes and coracles, and order was kept by an umpire in a miniature steamer.

Sources and Reading:
Cambria Daily Leader (11 August 1893).
Cambrian News (14 August 1869).

Cardiff and Merthyr Guardian (5 August 1848).

Emma Lile

Riding for Geese

A 'sport' practised in Wiltshire in the mid-eighteenth century in which a horseman would gallop towards a goose, which had usually been staked to the ground, and attempt to pull its head off as he went by. In Scotland, similar events were held at Haddington (East Lothian) and St Andrews (Fife), but here the goose was suspended above the rider.

Sources and Reading:
Underdown, D., *Start of Play: Cricket and Culture in Eighteenth Century England* (Harmondsworth: Allen Lane, 2000).

Tony Collins

Ringing the Bull

The object of the game, an indoor variation of quoits, is to throw a metal ring on to a hook on a wall. The hook is traditionally placed on the nose of a drawing of a bull's head. Occasionally, the targets are real bull's horns mounted on an oak plaque attached to the wall. The winner is the competitor who lands the ring on the target the most times in an allotted 21 throws.

Sources and Reading:
Gorini, P., *Encyclopedia of Traditional Games* (Rome: Gremese, 1994).

See also Quoits

Tony Collins

Road Bowls

Road bowls is a derivative of long bowls, a version of bowls in which a certain distance had to be bowled in the fewest number of throws. Although the simplicity of the game probably made it a common recreation, it was only in the eighteenth century that bowling for distance developed public popularity, no doubt because of the increased gambling and entrepreneurial opportunities for sport at the time. In August 1739 a farmer won 'a considerable wager' by bowling a bowl from Croydon to London Bridge in 445 throws, a distance of 11 miles, 55 throws less than the wager required.

In Northumberland the game had deep roots in the local mining communities and, although gambling was widespread, it was also seen as a communal experience. It was traditionally played on a course between 1,000 yards and 1 mile long, the aim being to bowl the ball along the course in as few throws as possible. The ball was traditionally made of stone or pottery and weighed anything between 3 and 50 ounces. Specially laid-out courses were constructed at Newcastle Town Moor and Blyth Links in the late nineteenth century.

In the Irish variation of the game, contestants take a long run and, throwing underarm, cast a 28 ounce solid iron ball along a length of road; subsequent throws are taken from the point where the ball stopped and the aim is again to complete a designated course in as few throws as possible. The length of courses may vary, however; 4 kilometres is typical. Contests are held between two individuals and though separate competitions exist for men and women the administration of the sport is not split on gender lines as in other sports.

The outstanding feature of the sport in Ireland is its confinement to two distinct regions, County Cork (with outposts in other nearby counties) and County Armagh (similarly with lesser centres in neighbouring counties). Road bowls has been practised customarily since the eighteenth century, but the sport was not rationalised until the formation of the All-Ireland Bowl Players Association, later An Bol Chumann Na hEireann, in 1954. The following decade witnessed a convergence of practices

and standards, which was consolidated by the amalgamation of northern and southern agencies for the sport in 1963, the year of the first official All-Ireland Men's Senior Championships. The women's championship followed in 1981. An Bol Chumann Na hEireann is the governing body of the sport, with two branches, Munster and Ulster, catering for the sport in those areas. Despite the sport's relative geographical isolation, from 1969 links were established and promoted between Irish bowls and the related yet different disciplines of Dutch 'moors bowls' and German 'lofting' through a quadrennial European Bowling Championships under the auspices of the International Bowl Playing Association.

The origins of the Irish form of bowls are unclear. One theory proposes a military genesis, involving soldiers holding contests of strength and skill using cannon balls. This has some validity as the game does seem to emerge coincidentally with the arrival, in late seventeenth-century Ireland, of Williamite forces from regions where, as has been noted, similar games are popular. More likely is the explanation that credits migrating northern England weavers with introducing the sport to Ireland. If this latter explanation is the right one, the pattern of Ireland adopting English sporting customs, such as road bowls and hare coursing, and retaining them after their popularity (and legality) disappeared in England represents an ironic tribute to sporting cultural exchanges between these islands. The survival of such early modern sports in Ireland after their 'best before date' has been reached in England is, simultaneously, a marker of the great cultural trade between these islands, and an indicator of the slightly differing trajectories of each island's cultures.

The Irish game is also an occasion for much gambling and involves the occupation of a public roadway for some considerable time. Bowls venues are long stretches of road, the use of which is now established in custom and remains, generally speaking, uncontroversial. Important contests can draw large crowds to rural roadsides, creating a scene not unlike those in the exciting high-mountain stages of the Tour de France as people await the arrival of the duellists, parting only to let the bowl pass then rejoining in the wake of the competitors' progress. The traditional image of the sport, a sturdy rustic casting a jacket to the grass verge between throws, is a durable one. However, as competitions become more intense, an increasingly serious approach to preparation and performance is becoming more discernible. This process has been aided by the necessity for the top bowlers, competing in international events, to prepare for the German and Dutch variations of the game, thereby allowing a cross-fertilisation of knowledge and practices to benefit technique, preparation, training and performance.

Sources and Reading:
The Encyclopaedia of Sport (London: *The Sportsman*, 1912).
Hone, W., *The Every-Day Book* (London: Thomas Tegg, 1830).
Piley, P., *The Story of Bowls, from Drake to Bryant* (London: Stanley Paul, 1987).
Stonehenge [J. H. Walsh], *Manual of British Rural Sports* (London: Routledge, 1857).
Toal, B., *Road Bowling in Ireland* (Armagh: B. Toal and Ulster Branch of Bol Chumann Na hEireann, 1996).

See also Bowls, Closh, Kayles, Marbles, Northumberland, Skittles, Troco

Tom Hayes and Tony Collins

Roberts, Huw

This thrower from north Wales, nicknamed 'Cymunod' after the road from Gwalchmai to Holyhead in Anglesey, outshone all the local strong men, for whereas they could hurl a heavy cannon ball over the shoulder after raising it with both hands, he could lift the object with just one. On one occasion, a visitor to the parish challenged Roberts to a fight; Roberts's pre-contest handshake was so strong that it brought tears to the challenger's eyes.

Sources and Reading:
Williams, D. W., 'Chwedlau am Huw Cymunod – Y Gwr Nerthol o Fodedern', *Môn*, 2: 8 (1964), 7–8.

Emma Lile

Rook Shooting

The shooting of young rooks in May, when they were nearly ready to fly from their nests, was a popular pastime in the Victorian era. It was particularly attractive for young, inexperienced shooters and for ladies wishing to develop their shooting skills. It was often undertaken with specially constructed smooth-bore rifles so that the birds would provide testing shoots. In the twentieth century, annual rook shooting events continued, but with an increasing tendency for the use of shotguns. Rook pie, made out of the breasts of the young birds, was a welcome addition to the diet for many poorer members of rural society.

Websites:
www.pest-rid.co.uk/Rook.html
hsa.enviroweb.org/features/shooting.html

See also Shooting, Rough Shooting

Nicholas Goddard and John Martin

Rope Splicing

Competitions offered at Welsh agricultural society events during the late nineteenth century, often intended for individuals not taking part in the ploughing contests.

Emma Lile

Rough Shooting

Rough shooting is usually perceived to be the polar opposite of organised driven game shooting as it is undertaken on a much more informal basis and the type of quarry is not restricted to a particular species. It is far more physically active than driven shooting and involves the walking-up of prey by small groups of guns over a variety of terrains and using dogs to flush the quarry.

The other main difference between game shooting and rough shooting is the degree to which the shooter is able to participate in the organisation of the sport. Most game shooters would simply pay a fixed sum of money for an agreed number of days shooting per year, with the day-to-day running of the shoot and the provision of beaters and dogs to retrieve the birds being the responsibility of a syndicate or landowner. In contrast, the majority of rough shooters would rent shooting rights for the season and have the opportunity to play a more active role in the running and organisation of the shoot. Rough shooters will tend to use their own dogs. While this difference is not always clear-cut in practice, with many shooters paying fees on a daily basis for the privilege of being able to go rough shooting, it is a less-expensive method of shooting and attracts larger numbers of participants.

The term 'rough shooting' is in many senses a misnomer as it can provide some of the most versatile and exciting shooting to be found in Britain. Many rough shooters are content to potter around their shoot, having the occasional potshot at a variety of prey, being very pleased if they bring back a rabbit or pigeon and delighted if the bag includes winged game. Rough shooting offers the joy and the disappointment of never quite being certain of the outcome the day's shooting will provide. Bags obtained from rough shooting will vary enormously in terms of size and composition but, on a red-letter day, may include grouse, pheasants, partridges, wildfowl, hares, snipe and even woodcock. In the lowlands, however, bags will almost invariably consist primarily of rabbits and pigeons, supplemented by a limited selection of winged game.

Sources and Reading:
Humphreys, J. and Bown, D., *Shooting Skills: Rough and Wild Shooting* (London: Cassell, 1995).

Swan, M., *Rough Shooting* (Shrewsbury: Swan Hill Press, 2000).

Website:
www.nationalreview.com/swan/swan051503. asp

See also Rook Shooting, Shooting

Nicholas Goddard and John Martin

Round Table

A variant of the medieval tournament, its name taken from the legends of King Arthur, the 'round table' was an event that included a number of different games, in particular jousting with blunted weapons. A royal order of 1232 forbade the holding of a round table, yet Matthew Paris mentions one being held at Walden in 1252. It may well be the case that the growing organisation and importance of tournaments removed the appeal of the less militaristic round table events.

Sources and Reading:
Reeves, C., *Pleasures and Pastimes in Medieval England* (Stroud: Sutton, 1995).

See also Jousting, Tournaments

Tony Collins

Rounders

A game played by two teams of nine players which closely resembles baseball. Since enjoying a resurgence in the late nineteenth century, it has become a staple of school summer physical education lessons.

Despite claims of its antiquity, with many sources stating it has been played since Tudor times, its prominence appears to be due to its popularity in educational circles and to the assertion that it is the progenitor of baseball as played in America. Writing in 1857, 'Stonehenge' noted that 'it was formerly a very favourite game in some of our English counties, but is now almost entirely displaced by cricket'. Yet, although it is undoubtedly one of the many versions of bat, ball and running games which are common in British history, documentary evidence of it is hard to find before the chapter in William Clarke's *Boys' Own Book* of 1828. The second edition of the *Oxford English Dictionary* contains no reference to the sport. Indeed, many of the examples to which histories of rounders refer, such as the 1744 *A Little Pretty Pocket Book* and Jane Austen's *Northanger Abbey*, are actually about baseball!

Interestingly, the first English rounders organisation was set up in 1889 in Liverpool, a city which has a strong baseball tradition. The Scottish Rounders Association was also established in the same year, yet it was not until 1943 that a countrywide National Rounders Association was set up. The first national rounders championship was held in 1976.

Sources and Reading:

Henderson, R. W., *Ball, Bat and Bishop: The Origin of Ball Games* (New York: Rockport, 1947).

Stonehenge [J. H. Walsh], *Manual of British Rural Sports* (London: Routledge, 1857).

See also Baseball, Club Ball, Cricket, Stoolball, Stowball

Tony Collins

Rowing

It is no accident that the rowing gallery at the River and Rowing Museum (in Henley on Thames) professes its theme to be 'the quest for speed' while beginning with displays on the Athenian trireme of 2,500 years ago and continuing with whaleboats, Cornish pilot gigs and Thames wherries. The first racing boats that the visitor sees date from 1812 and 1828, but the point being made is that, for centuries, rowing was a way of life. To cross the Thames or the Mediterranean, oars were essential.

Oar-powered ships built empires for Athenians and Venetians, fast gigs performed every kind of delivery and taxi service for the Isles of Scilly as well as bringing transatlantic business to Cornish ports, and the wherry, the original 'black cab', was king on the tidal Thames from Richmond to Gravesend before the coming of steam and the encroachment of bridges.

In ports, on lakes, on rivers and at sea, rowing enabled people to get about, and there can be no doubt that informal competition took place, either for wagers or simply from a desire to get there first. Doggett's Coat and Badge, a race from London Bridge to Chelsea for watermen in their first year of freedom, began in 1715. There was a regatta at Walton in 1768, Ranelagh in 1775, and an eight-oared race for the huge prize of 60 guineas from Westminster to Richmond-upon-Thames in 1778. The amateur sculling championship on the Thames started in 1830 and the professional championship a year later, the latter developing into a world championship. Around 5,000 professional sculling matches were recorded on the Thames between 1835 and 1851. Such activity was also evident on the Tyne and other rivers.

From the early nineteenth century rowing was being organised among amateurs, notably Eton and Westminster schools and Oxford and Cambridge universities. Professionals and amateurs alike competed for money prizes, and regattas at Chester (1733) and Durham (1816) pre-dated Henley, the one that was to put rowing on the world map before the century was out.

From the litany above it is evident that the Industrial Revolution, which changed Britain's landscape, society, wealth and leisure pursuits, merely washed over rowing. Urban growth brought a bigger market for boats of every kind, and races provided betting opportunities. As the nineteenth century progressed, the oar became increasingly sidelined in the commercial world, but it became more popular for sport and recreation.

Rowing was an activity that fitted perfectly with the ethos of the public school education system which served the expanding business and professional classes, an approach exported by its graduates to the truly public education system that they designed for the lower orders. Rowing was the ultimate team sport, requiring the discipline of putting common cause before self while throwing up leadership challenges. In the first half of the century it transformed itself from a traditional activity to a modern sport by codifying the rules of racing and attempting to define the status of who can take part.

Two institutions played a major role in this: the Oxford and Cambridge Boat Race and the Henley Royal Regatta. The first university boat race was in Henley in 1829, and the interest shown in it led to the first regatta in 1839. The boat race moved to London, became annual in 1856, and grew into a hugely popular event for Londoners. Henley was annual from its inception. The growth of rowing was dependent on two factors: the railways, to move people about and, for example, open the Thames valley to Londoners, and newspapers, to report sporting encounters in great detail.

In 1847, the first rules of racing were drawn up by representatives of Oxford and Cambridge universities and prominent London clubs, and adopted by the Henley regatta a year later. This was the very time that the whole of Europe except the British Isles was incandescent with revolution. The Home Countries engaged only in evolutionary social adjustment; they confined violent disruption to the British Empire.

By the time that the Amateur Rowing Association (ARA), begat by the Metropolitan Rowing Association (1879), came into being in 1882, defining the amateur had become a controversial muddle. Manual workers and men who worked in and about boats were barred as amateurs, and true professionals were often treated as a separate species by the 'gentlemen' amateurs, banned from coaching crews or entering amateur clubs.

Ironically, one of the aims of the new ARA was to produce representative crews to beat foreigners at Henley, while by the end of the century social exclusion was accompanied by an unsuccessful move among the Henley stewards to ban foreigners from their regatta. These disputes caused a breakaway National Amateur Rowing Association to be formed in 1890 to cater for amateurs who might soil their hands with work, and in the early twentieth century led to a steady stream of English professionals seeking work as coaches and boatmen in Europe and the United States. Victims of peculiar class divisions, their influence enhanced the spread of the British way of rowing to the five continents that was begun by colonialists, businessmen, muscular Christians and educators from the 1830s onwards. The ARA was not the first sports federation established in Britain, but it preceded the international rowing federation (FISA) – the world's first international federation – by ten years. Characteristically, it declined to be a founding member, and stayed away until 1948.

Beneath the razzmatazz and self-importance of the amateurs, the contribution of watermen, boatbuilders and those who worked Britain's rivers and ports was immense. Among them were champion oarsmen, brilliant teachers and innovative designers. The outrigger (1840s) and the 'shell' (smooth-bottomed racing boat) (1850s) came from the Tyne, and Tynesiders almost got to the sliding seat of the 1870s first. By the time of the creation of the ARA, the fixed-seat heavy inrigger of 1828 had become the smooth-bottomed sleek outrigger recognisable in the twenty-first century. A hundred years elapsed between the sliding seat and the next major innovation, the move to composite materials.

Sources and Reading:
Dodd, C., *The Story of World Rowing* (London: Stanley Paul, 1992).

See also Doggett's Coat and Badge

Christopher Dodd

Rowing (Scotland)

Rowing emerged as a sport in Scotland at the same time as yachting, about 1820. Regattas in the sea usually included both of these sports, and members of the professional crews of the yachts doubled as the oarsmen. Those on rivers and canals were confined to rowing, and were found over most of the Lowlands: on the Tweed at Sprouston and Coldstream in the 1840s, for example, and on the Clyde at Glasgow Green in the middle of the century. As other sports expanded in the last quarter of the nineteenth century, rowing became relatively less important, not least because Scottish schools and universities took only a limited interest in it.

Sources and Reading:
Wigglesworth, N., *A Social History of English Rowing* (London: Frank Cass, 1992).

John Burnett

Royal British Bowmen

The Society of the Royal British Bowmen was founded in 1787. Its membership was originally confined to the gentry families residing in Denbighshire, Flintshire and Montgomeryshire, before later being extended to those of Cheshire and Shropshire. Fortnightly meetings took place between April and October at various country estates in the Wrexham area, and until 1847 the society enjoyed royal patronage in the form of specially donated prizes. These included silver bows, arrows and bugles and a variety of medals. Both sexes shot together, and the Royal British Bowmen was notable for being the first society of its kind to admit lady members. A green and buff coloured uniform was worn on all occasions, with fines imposed should this regulation be violated. Proceedings were punctuated by refreshments served at lunchtime and teatime in a tent erected on site, while in the evening a grand ball was held. The latter was renowned for its musical entertainment, for it was customary for ballads to be specially composed in commemoration of the day's shoot.

Abandoned on account of the Napoleonic Wars between 1794 and 1818 (although it was revived temporarily in 1802–3), the society continued throughout most of the nineteenth century and was eventually dissolved in 1880.

Sources and Reading:
Lake, F., 'Royal British Bowmen 1787–1880', *British Archer*, 25: 3 (1973), 132–5.
Usher, G., 'The Society of Royal British Bowmen (1787)', *Denbighshire Historical Society Transactions*, 4 (1955), 85–90.

See also Archery

Emma Lile

Sack Racing

Sack races often took place during rustic sports days and were generally regarded as light-hearted and rather frivolous contests, as competitors jumped along, sometimes covered in the sacks' remaining flour. At the Mynydd y Pysgodlyn Sports at Llangyfelach in Swansea in 1780, the programme included a sack race for men for a first prize of a gold-laced hat, and also a sack race after a cock, to win the bird itself and a sack of flour. Rather worryingly, the Cardiganshire Sports of July 1814 featured a race between seven young men in sacks 'tied round their necks', while in 1875 the Aberystwyth-based newspaper the *Cambrian News* warned, in an editorial entitled 'The manufacture of wickedness', how 'the height of evil is clearly reached in the sack race'.

Sources and Reading:
Williams, G. J., 'Glamorgan Customs in the Eighteenth Century', *Gwerin*, 1 (1956–7), 99–108.

Emma Lile

Salter, Thomas Frederick

A writer on angling, Thomas Salter (*fl.* 1814–26) began fishing as a child, when he would accompany his father on angling expeditions, and until the age of 52 he used to fish wherever possible in the vicinity of London, remaining at favourite stations for weeks at a time. He retired from his Charing Cross hat business because of ill health and then proceeded to put into writing his observations on his chosen sport. His first book, *The Angler's Guide, or, Complete London Angler in the Thames, Lea, and Other Waters Twenty Miles around London*, was published in 1814 and went to nine editions, as did an abridged version first published in 1816.

Wray Vamplew

Scorton Silver Arrow

The Silver Arrow archery contest, which was first held in 1673, takes place annually during May or June at Scorton, near Richmond in Yorkshire. Archers compete for the original silver arrow, with a tail made of silver from the sixteenth century and the forepart from seventeenth-century silver.

The winner is the archer who is the first to strike the inner gold, measuring three inches across, on a target 100 yards away, for which he is acclaimed with the title of 'captain' and the responsibility for organising the following year's tournament. The Scorton archery club, The Society of Archers, claims to be the oldest sporting club in Britain. Women are not allowed to compete in the Silver Arrow, but a separate women's competition for the Ascham Arrow was established in the 1970s.

Sources and Reading:
Colbeck, M., *The Calendar Year* (Leeds: EP Publishing, 1983).

See also Archery

Tony Collins

Scotland

Scotland, lying north of England, has a cooler climate than its neighbour. It is also less fertile, and this, combined with a shorter growing season, meant that before 1750 it was a poorer country as well as a smaller one. The cold weather did, however, favour it for some winter sports.

One consequence of the poverty in Scotland is that very little written material survives from the Middle Ages. There is therefore insufficient evidence to say much about pre-Reformation sport; one certainty, though, is that as in the rest of Europe it was related closely to the farming and religious calendars. The Reformers were thorough in the suppression of the celebration of saints' days, and few of these holidays were enjoyed after 1600: one of the main foci for sport was thus removed. Neither was Easter or Yule (Christmas) held in Calvinist Scotland. In the Western Isles, far from central authority and with a significant Catholic population, some holidays and their associated sports survived. Shinty managed to survive the nineteenth century, but horseracing on Michaelmas and its associated fertility rites was suppressed during the evangelical revival around 1830. Yule continued to be celebrated in the northeast, where there was an Episcopalian minority.

From the middle of the eighteenth century, lowland Scotland became wealthier as a result of the growth of first the textile industry, and then mining and the iron and engineering industries. At the same time, agricultural improvement resulted in higher productivity and Scotland was thus able to feed its rapidly growing cities. By the 1820s, people had money and sufficient leisure to be able to indulge in sport, and its towns were large enough to act as centres for spectator sports. The history of Scottish sport before 1914 can therefore be divided into three periods: before 1820, when only a limited quantity of sport was played; 1820–70, when sport grew and changed in a variety of ways; and after 1870, when the quantity of sport continued to increase and it became as much a British phenomenon as a Scottish one. The following sections discuss these three periods in turn.

In terms of royal sport, Scotland was part of late medieval Europe. A tennis court was built at Falkland Palace in Fife in 1540–1 after King James V had visited Paris, and there was also one at the Palace of Holyroodhouse in Edinburgh. The game probably did not last beyond the end of the seventeenth century, though the court at Falkland was restored for the third Marquess of Bute in 1896. Until the end of the eighteenth century, field sports were also the province of Scots royalty, nobility and lairds: at that point Englishmen began to appear on Scottish rivers, moors and hills. The method for hunting deer was for men to drive them towards the hunters, who set dogs on the prey. In the Scots language this was a *tinchel* (in Gaelic *tainchell*), but the practice was European: a painting in the Prado shows the Emperor Charles V watching the sport. Falconry was practised by royalty and the nobility; James IV (1487–1513) was a notable enthusiast, his household accounts include payments to men who brought promising birds.

There were also European links in popular sports, such as cockfighting on Shrove Tuesday. Folk football, played in every Lowland parish, was a European tradition. Other sports were local: as a condition of holding their lands from the king, the Lockharts of Carnwath (Lanarkshire) were required to offer a pair of red stockings as a prize for a foot race to identify runners who could spread the alarm in the event of English invasion. It was certainly held around 1450, but may be several decades older. In 1832 the race was incorporated in a general games: still held today, the Red Hose Race is the oldest sporting event in Scotland.

For lairds and Edinburgh burghers, Leith emerged at the beginning of the sixteenth century as a sporting centre. Three miles from the capital, it was close to the city but also sufficiently distant to allow a sense of freedom. Horseracing was held on the sands by 1504 and major meetings are recorded between 1660 and 1690, and again after 1750. Golf was played on the links and golfing activity at Leith was more important for the development of the game before 1800 than that at St Andrews. A cockpit was built in 1683. Gentlemen swam in the sea, and when urban growth and the construction of docks threatened this pleasure, a little swimming bath was constructed in 1813. It survives as a pub.

The burghs were important for sport. At this time only Edinburgh was comparable in size with an English country town, so the sport was as much for people who lived near the town as for those in it. The burghs put up the prizes for horseracing in the sixteenth century and archery in the seventeenth. Edinburgh gave a purse for horseracing (the tounis prize) and presented trophies for annual competition at archery (a silver arrow, 1709), golf (silver club, 1744) and bowling (silver jack, 1771). Other burghs had similar trophies, such as the silver club at St Andrews (1754) and the silver guns at Dumfries and Kirkcudbright (both 1587). St Andrews University had three silver arrows in succession (1618, 1675 and 1704) and Aberdeen Grammar School an arrow in 1664.

After 1770 new patterns start to be seen. Curling began its growth towards becoming the most popular sport in Scotland. Cricket was first recorded in 1785. The following year, some Edinburgh medical men started an athletic society, the Gymnastic Club. Ploughing matches started to be held sporadically and became a central feature of Lowland country life. They link with the traditional 'love darg', the practice of neighbouring farmers giving a day's work to help a new tenant or, perhaps, a man who had fallen behind with his work because of illness.

The period between the 1820s and 1870s was a time of tremendous change for sports in Scotland, with a move away from its more traditional roots. The most important development in the 1820s was the introduction of general games days. Unlike England, Scotland had no tradition of parish ales with their attendant sports. Some Scots games grew from the addition of events to existing fairs; a horserace had been added to Marymas (the Feast of the Assumption of the Virgin) at Irvine early in the eighteenth century, and foot races were added early in the nineteenth century. Around 1820, there is more evidence for these events, such as the horse, foot and donkey races at Fykes Fair at Auchencairn (Kirkcudbright). At Straiton in Ayrshire, a long-established midsummer fair had by 1830 acquired foot and sack races, and a horserace for which two animals were entered: they ran three heats. Games were for working people: at Dalkeith they started at 8 a.m., and at Haddington an hour earlier, and in 1850 the Colinsburgh Games in Fife were said to be for 'the agricultural peasantry of the district'. Some games were held around midsummer, although others, such as the Tyneside Games (East Lothian), were held in October, after the harvest. The events at these sports were for men or boys: foot races for women, probably copied from English smock races, are sometimes found, but very rarely.

There were various mechanisms by which games started. Several Highland games were begun by friendly societies, whose sports followed their annual meeting to check accounts and elect office holders. Many events were established by landlords, such as the oldest Highland Games, at St Fillans in Perthshire (1819). But some were started by men who had made their money abroad. One example was Biggar Park Games in Lanarkshire, which included a race to the top of Tinto Hill (711 metres high) for a pocket knife, founded by George Gillespie, who had been a fur trader at Hudson's Bay. At Errol in Perthshire the innkeeper was seeking to increase his trade. In the Borders, Walter Scott and James Hogg encouraged sport. After a great football match to celebrate the victory at Waterloo, they both honoured the event with poems, and Hogg went on to start the annual St Ronan's Games at Innerleithen in 1826, at which he acted as master of ceremonies. He hated the new industrial society, which he saw as breaking the traditional loyalties of master and man to one another: his response was to try to restore some fun.

In this period, field sports start to be seen as a way of escaping from the city; hare coursing in particular because it could be held on a specific, predefined site, close to a centre of population. It attracted spectators; in 1840 the *Glasgow Herald* wrote of a coursing meeting evoking 'that bounding spirit of delight with which one who has been long immersed in the smoke, din, and harassing routine of city existence, flies for even a single day to the enjoyments of the green earth'. The same newspaper recorded that in the second round of the Cambuslang Stakes in 1840, 'Prince Albert beat Hero; Dreadnought beat Mars', indicating the pretension to classical learning and the military leanings of the owners of the dogs. Deer stalking was already growing before the railways reached the Highlands (Perth was connected to London in 1848). In social terms, it was a new kind of sport because many of the sportsmen were English. The railways soon brought larger numbers to the grouse moors, including some female shots, and the rivers of the Southern Uplands and Highlands were rich in fish, particularly salmon. The occasional 'shooting box' was replaced by shooting lodges and houses along the best rivers: lairds knew that sporting leases could easily be sold. At the same time, inns were built in remote places for sportsmen, particularly fishermen.

Curling grew rapidly in the Lowlands, particularly when local clubs followed the example of the Duddingston Curling Society and started to use circular stones rather than water-worn boulders. The game was suited to the climate because it could be played when work in the fields and crafts such as the masons' were impossible because of frost. Curling was the national passion until it was displaced by football at the end of the century.

As in England, horseracing drew large crowds: 115,000 were at the elite meeting at Paisley in 1837. Glasgow overtook Edinburgh in size in about 1800, and its burgeoning population went to race meetings at Paisley (to 1907), Airdrie (1853–70), Stirling (to 1854), Ayr and Bogside or Eglinton Park (1808–1964). There was less horseracing in Scotland than in England, and the Scots never matched the Irish passion for the horse. Nevertheless, it was the first major spectator sport in Scotland.

Scottish horseracing took place on several levels. Below the elite races with professional jockeys were Yeomanry Cavalry meetings. For example, in 1824 the cavalry raced on the sands at Kirkcaldy, and at Alloa the day ended with refreshment provided by Lady Abercrombie. Only horses that were owned by one of the corps and had been drilled for three days before the review were eligible. The gentry and larger tenant farmers organised most of the racing in Scotland and owned the horses. Steeplechasing appeared as 'a very novel spectacle' near Dundee in 1824, when a horse following the turnpike beat the ones that went across country: its rider was said to lack sporting spirit.

In a few places there was a tradition of foot racing on holidays, particularly in Kilmarnock and the little burghs along the Irvine Water to the east.

Cricket was the first summer team game to be widely popular. There are scattered references to it before 1820. Played both in country and town, it seems to have grown steadily for the rest of the century. The All England XI first came to Scotland in 1849, and they, or one of the other professional teams, visited Edinburgh seven times in 10 years, and made 19 appearances in Glasgow in 1851–72. They created interest and established cricket both as a game to play and to watch. Cricket suffered badly from the dislocation of the First World War, from which it emerged with less working-class support than before. At its highest level, Scotland could put out a team which was as strong as one of the weaker English counties.

A notable change during this period was the growth of rifle shooting. The volunteer movement grew rapidly after the threat of a French invasion in 1859. In England volunteers were mostly middle class, but in rural Scotland they were drawn more widely from society. Both the volunteers and the closely associated National Rifle Association (NRA) held shooting competitions at every level from the local to the national. The first national events were at Wimbledon in 1860: they may be the first sporting competitions of any kind that drew competitors from all over the British Islands. The Queen's Prize was won by a Scot living in England, Edward Ross. The prize was £250, which may not have been a significant sum to a comparatively wealthy man like Ross, but to Alexander Ferguson of the 1st Argyll Rifle Volunteers, a working mason from Campbeltown and Queen's Prizeman for 1880, it was several years' wages.

Ploughing matches spread to every arable area: they were encouraged by local agricultural societies. In 1860 an Aberdeenshire newspaper, the *Peterhead Sentinel*, said that there had once been a match in each district, but now there was one for every two or three farms. As the importance of the turnip for winter feed increased, hoeing competitions were started, particularly in Aberdeenshire. As in England, a range of other events was held from time to time, such as for digging drains.

In the last third of the nineteenth century, after about 1870, sport in Scotland was influenced by, and integrated with, sport in England. The Scottish Cup, first held in the 1873/4 season, copied the FA Cup (1871/2), and was in turn the model for dozens of local competitions, such as the Ayrshire Cup (1977/8) and Perthshire Cup (1884/5).

The Scottish public schools were in effect English schools sited in Scotland, and the Scottish universities copied sports from Cambridge and Oxford. Some schools took sport seriously. Under the headmastership of H. H. Almond, Loretto made a cult of it, and it is said that the school took the passing game from football and applied it to rugby and, when there were seven

Lorettians in the Oxford XV of 1894, took it to England too. Another school, Blairlodge, made a point of employing cricketers, including Herbert Pigg who had been a member of the undefeated Cambridge XI of 1878 and W. A. Bettesworth who played for Sussex and later wrote cricket books.

Many country sports moved into urban environments. To the football supporter, the countryside was an obstacle bridged by trains, but by 1890 there were dozens of football teams in country towns. Two areas took a different course. In the Borders, rugby, introduced by Yorkshire workers in the woollen mills, was the winter game; the Border League was set up in 1901. In the Highlands, shinty experienced a sudden revival, which included the formation of a national organisation, the Camanachd Association, in 1893. Golf remained in the country, served by trains which sometimes stopped at halts adjacent to the clubhouse. Special trains ran from Glasgow to the south coast of Fife, bringing golfers to the seaside links, and the Lothian Coast Express fulfilled a similar role on the opposite shore of the Forth.

Seaside resorts were important to sport because they almost always had golf courses and tennis courts, and sometimes bowling greens. The spa village of Moffat was central to the early growth of tennis in Scotland: the Scottish Lawn Tennis Championship was played there from 1895 to 1907. It was also the venue of the most important croquet competition in the country, the Moffat Mallet. Moffat was one of the places where middle- and upper-class women started to take an active part in sport. Spas, the more exclusive seaside resorts such as North Berwick, and country houses, were central to the development of women's sport between 1880 and 1914.

The Royal Northern Yacht Club was founded in 1822. Originally, the number of participants was limited, but by the 1850s yachts were coming from the south of England to race on the Clyde, and by the 1880s European and American yachts had appeared. From then until 1914 the Clyde was an international venue, and the 12-metre yacht races of the 1908 Olympic Games were held on the firth, the only time an Olympic event has been held in Scotland.

At the end of the century professional football clubs promoted games, often holding them on established holidays. Thus Ayr United FC held games at Glasgow Fair, which in 1899 drew a crowd of over 10,000. New Year was by far the most important single holiday in Scotland, and after 1890 dozens of sporting events were held on New Year's Day. Football was the most common sport, recorded in 1897 at Whithorn, Girvan, Kelso, Alyth, Granton-on-Spey and Wick. There were also widespread athletic sports, as at Dunoon, Rhu and Campbeltown on the Clyde estuary, and the old practice of playing shinty on New Year's Day was continued at Inverary. Golf continued to expand, and became Scotland's contribution first to British sport and then to world leisure. It was spread partly by Scots living in England, but more by English visitors who wanted a holiday in Scotland that was more varied than merely shooting grouse.

Scottish sport retained its own institutions in the late nineteenth and twentieth centuries. This may be ascribed partly to latent national identity, but a more important factor is geography: the Southern Uplands and northern Pennines, which separate the main centres of population from Northumberland, Lancashire and Yorkshire. The first international match between the two countries was at rifle shooting (1862); this was soon followed by rugby (1871) and football (1872). The NRA's close link with the volunteers meant that its members were more aware than most sportsmen of geography (for regiments were based on counties) and of issues of nationhood. It is ironic that the British patriotism of the volunteer riflemen led, via the national consciousness that is a part of international sport, to the re-establishment of the Scottish parliament in 1999.

Sources and Reading:
Burnett, J., *Riot, Revelry and Rout: Sport in Lowland Scotland before 1860* (East Linton: Tuckwell Press, 2000).
Fittis, R. S., *Sports and Pastimes of Scotland* (Paisley: Alexander Gardner, 1891).
Jarvie, G. and Burnett, J., *Sport, Scotland and the Scots* (East Linton: Tuckwell Press, 2000).

John Burnett

Scrush

A variant of hockey played in Dorset in which two sides use 'scrushes', sticks with curved ends, known elsewhere as 'bandies', to hit a round stone over their opponents' line.

Sources and Reading:
Gomme, A. B., *The Traditional Games of England, Scotland and Ireland* (London: Thames and Hudson facsimile edition, 1984).

See also Bandy, Hockey

Tony Collins

Sedgefield Football

A form of Shrove Tuesday mass football, the Sedgefield game consists of two teams of unlimited numbers, ostensibly divided between farmers and tradesmen, who try to propel a ball towards the goals (one of which is a duck pond and the other a stream) around 500 yards apart.

The game, which claims to date back to the twelfth century, starts with the ball being passed three times through a small ring on the village green, whereupon it is thrown to the assembled players, who have been known to number around 1,000.

Once a goal is scored, which, because the game resembles a somewhat immobile mass scrummage, often takes some time, the ball

is taken back to the green where it is again passed through the ring three times to signify the end of the game.

Sources and Reading:
Day, B., *A Chronicle of Folk Customs* (London: Hamlyn, 1988).
Hole, C., *English Traditional Customs* (London: Batsford, 1975).

See also Football

Tony Collins

Sheep Shearing (Wales)

Sheep shearing contests were usually organised by agricultural societies and took place across Wales long before the days of electrical shears. In 1883, a sheep shearing exhibition featured in an event hosted by the Llanboidy Farmers' Agricultural Society, in Carmarthenshire, in which three sheep were to be shorn by each competitor in the space of three hours. A £1 first prize was awarded to the winner.

The first annual Gower sheep shearing contest was held in 1892, and organised by the Gower Union District Ploughing Society. A row of sheep pens was set up near the Bishopston Hotel and competitors from Gower and further afield took part. The sheep to be sheared included a cart-load of 'Welsh language' sheep from Llandeilo in Carmarthenshire. Three sheep were placed in every pen; the rules being for each entrant to shear three sheep and tie up the fleeces in 90 minutes. The judges were then called in, who signified the victors by placing coloured stickers on their pens.

As elsewhere in Britain, Welsh sheep shearing competitions were transformed by the development of mechanical (power driven) shears. With hand shears the emphasis was on the quality and neatness of the work. The sheep were literally clipped, leaving about 1–2 centimetres of wool. The development of mechanical clippers, where the wool was cut much closer to the skin, placed greater emphasis on speed of operation, with competitions to see who could shear the most sheep in a given amount of time.

Sources and Reading:
Cambria Daily Leader (10 June 1892).
Frankenberg, R., *Communities in Britain* (1966), 53–4.
Picton Castle Museum of Welsh Life, MS 4824.

Emma Lile

Sheepdog Trials

Sheepdog trials consist of competitions designed to compare the skills of handlers of working dogs. Events take a variety of forms, including nursery trials for young dogs, and open trials where handlers are awarded points that permit entry to national trials.

Contestants in national trials direct their Border collie dogs to drive a group of, usually, five sheep through a 400-yard obstacle course, encompassing the standard elements of outrun, lift, drive, shed, pen and single. These movements are intended to simulate the conditions and work experienced in everyday shepherding. Judges evaluate a contestant's performance in controlling their dogs by awarding marks for each aspect of the trial. The 15 highest-placed competitors at these trials are eligible to compete at the international trials which, for the first two days of the event, evaluate the dogs using the same parameters. On the third and final day, the 15 highest-placed competitors use a 700-yard course with 20 sheep to determine the supreme champion.

The first recorded sheepdog trial was held at Bala in North Wales in 1873, and in October 1877 the Welsh national sheepdog trials were also held there. Described by the *Cambrian News* as being 'open to the whole world', they took place under the patronage of the Kennel Club and attracted a large crowd of spectators. With a champion cup on offer to the winner, the trials required each dog to round up three sheep, take them through gates and around flags to its master, before penning them close to the spectators. In 1906 the International Sheep Dog Society (ISDS) was established. Shortly afterwards the first international trials were held at Gullane in Scotland. This event has taken place every year since, except during the First and Second World Wars. The activities of local sheepdog trialling societies are coordinated by the ISDS, which organises major sheepdog trials in England, Scotland, Wales and Ireland. The society also produces a list of reputable breeders and regulates the registration of Border collies.

Traditionally, most of the sport's participants were commercial sheep farmers, many of whom bred and trained their own Border collies. However, since the 1960s, an increase in the numbers of competitors has been due to individuals who are not directly employed in livestock farming but who enjoy demonstrating the rapport they have developed with their dogs.

The sport has a few thousand actual participants, but a much greater number of watchers. Its enhanced popularity can, at least in part, be attributed to the cult BBC TV series 'One Man and His Dog', which brought the thrills of sheepdog trials to the living rooms of millions. At its peak in the early 1980s, as many as 8 million people tuned into the programme, spawning a new generation of dog lovers eager to take up the challenge of the sport. In September 2002, the ISDS hosted the first World Sheepdog Trial at Bala. The highly successful event involved 122 competitors from 13 nations and had 18,000 visitors.

Sources and Reading:
Cambrian News (12 October 1877).
Jones-Davies, J., *The Devynock Agricultural Society 1865–1965* (Brecon: Brecon and Radnor Express, 1965).

John Martin and Emma Lile

Shinney and Whipping

Played at Newark in Leicestershire as an early form of hockey, the sport takes its name from the practice at the end of a match when 'Whipping Toms' whipped the players' legs. Players were expected to stand their ground, those that did not were booed by the crowd, but the Toms were only allowed to whip below knee-level. The last recorded match took place in 1847.

Sources and Reading:
Day, B., *A Chronicle of Folk Customs* (London: Hamlyn, 1988).

See also Hockey

Tony Collins

Shinnup

An old name used in Holderness for hockey. In other parts of Yorkshire it was known as 'shinnop'.

Sources and Reading:
Gomme, A. B., *The Traditional Games of England, Scotland and Ireland* (London: Thames and Hudson facsimile edition, 1984).

See also Chinnup, Hockey

Tony Collins

Shinty

Shinty, which is also known in Gaelic as *iomáin* and *camanachd*, is one of the stick-and-ball games that have been played across Europe since the earliest of times. The word *shinty* is probably derived from the Gaelic *sinteag* meaning 'a leap or bound', and the game itself is closely related to hurling in Ireland. A lay observer of a shinty match will see elements of hockey, ice hockey, golf and many other sports in its play: indeed shinty may have been influential in the early development of some of these games.

Shinty is a 12-a-side team sport, where matches last for 90 minutes and are split, like association football, into two halves of 45 minutes. Scoring is achieved by using the *camán* (the shinty stick) to strike the ball past the goalkeeper and through the goalposts more times than the opposition. Unlike in hurling, only the goalkeeper is allowed to actually handle the ball during the course of the game.

Matches are normally played on grass pitches ideally measuring 160 yards in length and 80 yards wide. The goalposts are 12 feet apart and 10 feet high, there is a penalty spot 20 yards from each hail-line (*hail* being another word for goal). A penalty is awarded if a foul is committed within a 10-yard area in front of the goal.

While the game of shinty in Scotland can be traced back through 2,000 years to the time of St Columba and other Irish missionaries, the earliest written evidence of the game being played in Scotland is found in an edict of the Kirk session records of Glasgow in 1589. On this occasion the playing of shinty in the kirkyard was forbidden, and across the country for the next century there are Kirk censures banning the game from being played on the Sabbath. Although frequently thought of today as a Highland sport, shinty was almost certainly played all over Scotland until the seventeenth century. It was not until the nineteenth century that shinty retreated almost exclusively to the Highlands, being played in what were to become the traditional areas of the sport: Badenoch, Lochaber and Strathglass.

The principal games of shinty took place at the main winter holiday: New Year (1 January) or Old New Year (12–13 January). These games, which were frequently contested between neighbouring parishes, could last all day and the number of players on each side knew no limit. The last of these contests is said to have been played about 1910 on the side of Loch Ness.

The sport returned to the Lowlands during the second half of the nineteenth century, where it was played by the migrant Highlanders who had moved south for work. Whereas previously the game would have been played by Lowlander adult males, from 1860 matches normally involved exiled Highlanders or rowdy local youths.

But shinty and Scotland is not an exclusive association. While Jamieson's *Dictionary of the Scottish Language* helps uncover linguistic evidence of the game being played across Scotland in the first quarter of the nineteenth century, Wright's *English Dialect Dictionary* mentions, among others, 'shinham', 'shinny', 'shinty', 'shinnins' and 'shinnop' across the north of England, into Yorkshire and further south into Nottinghamshire and Lincolnshire. There is evidence that the game of shinty was being played in parts of England until as late as 1888. By the second half of the nineteenth century, the game in England, as in lowland Scotland, was being played mainly by exiled Highlanders. As in Scotland, organised clubs began to come into existence, the first being Manchester Camanachd Club in 1878. There soon followed similar clubs in locations as diverse as Birmingham, London, Bolton and Nottingham.

Although the earliest mention of an organised shinty club in Scotland comes in 1849, when the *Inverness Courier* reports a meeting of the North of Spey Shinty Club in Aberdeen, it is not until the last quarter of the nineteenth century that the sport of shinty in Scotland becomes formally organised and codified. In 1879 the Glasgow Celtic Society instituted a cup competition and established one set of playing rules. At the same time, Captain Chisholm of Glassburn was drawing up *The Constitution, Rules and Regulations of the Strathglass Shinty Club*, which were published in 1880. The Strathglass rules, revised in 1888, became the accepted form for northern clubs, although clubs in the south still adhered to the Celtic rules.

Challenge matches between northern and southern clubs illustrated that there was an obvious need for a Scotland-wide form of the rules to be laid down. A meeting on 10 October 1893 led to an establishment of one set of written rules and the formation of the Camanachd Association, with Simon, Lord Lovat as president. A national trophy, the Camanachd Cup, was instituted in 1895; the first final was contested at Inverness a year later, when Kingussie beat Glasgow Cowal by two hails to nil.

For the Scots Lowlander and for many people in England, the game of shinty remains something of a mystery: 'legalised mayhem' and 'hockey without the rules' are common but misplaced perceptions. The veil of mystery covering the sport is slowly being lifted and shinty has enjoyed something of a renaissance in recent years. The sport of shinty is gradually being introduced to a wider audience through schools, while teams are being established outside 'traditional' shinty areas, such as Edinburgh East Lothian Shinty Club. In 2001, the Camanachd Cup Final was held in Glasgow for the first time in nine years. With the emergence of a six-a-side and women's versions of the game, an annual 'shinty–hurling' international match against Ireland, increased television coverage and major sponsorship, the sport is now increasingly accessible and popular within Scotland.

While shinty is now better organised than ever before, with teams playing within formal league structures, the age-old passions and spirit of the game in Scotland among players, administrators and supporters remain as strong as ever. Local pride and local rivalry continue to play a massive part in the survival of this ancient game. On a national level, the all-conquering Kingussie Shinty Club is seen by many as the team to beat, while old rivalries, such as between the Oban clubs or within the Lochaber area, are as enduring and just as keen as ever. The social aspect of the sport is also a key element in understanding a game which plays a huge community role in many Highland towns and villages. Oban is just one shinty-playing town where the under-30s and the over-30s play an informal Christmas-time match against each other before retiring en masse to the local bar for the rest of the evening.

Sources and Reading:
MacLennan, H. D., *Shinty: 100 Years of the Camanachd Association* (Nairn: Balnain Books, 1993).
MacLennan, H. D., *Not an Orchid* (Inverness: Kessock, 1995).

Websites:
The official website of the Camanachd Association: www.shinty.com

Malcolm MacCallum

Shooting

In Britain, 'shooting' is the collective term used to denote the use of guns, usually shotguns, in the pursuit and killing of a variety of birds and mammals. Those who use guns are not denoted as 'hunters', but as 'shooters' or 'guns' (the word 'gun' can apply to the person as well as the weapon). Several variants of the sport have evolved, ranging from driven or battue shooting to rough shooting, and specialist branches such as wildfowling and pigeon shooting, all of which involve different techniques.

The origins of shooting can be traced back to the development of flintlock guns in the seventeenth century. Among the wealthier members of society, to whom the sport was restricted by draconian game laws, shooting rapidly began to supersede falconry as the premier sporting activity. The poor construction and capacity of the early flintlock guns meant that shooting at moving birds and animals was very difficult. Hence illustrations of early shooters show them taking aim at motionless objects.

The sport's popularity increased rapidly in the eighteenth century as a result of significant improvements in the speed of ignition and quickness of loading that came with the introduction of percussion ignition. It was not until the mid-nineteenth century that loading at the breech end of the barrels became both practicable and acceptable.

Even in 1851, when the first successful breech-loading shotgun was exhibited at the Great Exhibition, there were many people who considered that this new system was not going to be widely adopted. These improvements, coupled with the development of the choke bore (which concentrated the shot), made it possible to reload more quickly and also to kill more effectively. The new firearms enabled shooting at moving birds and animals which, in turn, encouraged a greater focus on game preservation in order to ensure a sufficiently high density of birds for the upper-class sportsperson.

Wild animals and birds are not considered to be goods or chattels and, as such, landowners have certain rights over the animals or birds on their property while they are alive and absolute rights when they are dead. These game rights were enshrined in a series of acts in the nineteenth century, favouring the owners of land. Such rights are generally bound with the ownership or possession of land and might be passed with fresh occupation of the land or might be reserved even though there was a new occupier of the land. Owners could grant a lease to another person to occupy the land but reserve the 'sporting rights' for themselves. Only if the sporting rights were not reserved in this way did they pass to the tenant.

Legislation controlling the pursuit of birds and animals has been determined by a series of Acts of Parliament. Under the Game Act of 1831, which is the legal basis of all modern British field sports, 'game' included pheasants, partridges and grouse, while deer were incorporated in 1860 for the purposes of the Game Licences Act. Hares and rabbits, while not specifically covered by this legislation, were commonly regarded as ground game under the jurisdiction of the landowner. Subsequent legislation has specified not only close seasons, the periods of the year when the pursuit of certain wild birds and animals is prohibited, but also who can legally participate in the sport and in what circumstances.

There is a long history of government controls over firearms. Modern firearms laws date back to 1920, since when they have been progressively tightened with the intention of keeping firearms out of the hands of criminals and terrorists. There were major reviews of the legislation in 1968, 1988 and 1997. In order to purchase, acquire or possess a shotgun, a person must hold a current shotgun certificate issued by the chief constable of the area within which the person normally resides. A chief constable has wide discretion over the grant or renewal of a certificate and is required to refuse the certificate if the applicant is perceived as a danger to the public or to the peace, or for any other reason is deemed unfit. Legislation allows young people access to firearms on a progressive basis as they develop in age, maturity and responsibility. Even more stringent regulations govern the use and acquisition of rifles.

The main organisation responsible for fostering and safeguarding shooting since the 1970s is the British Association for Shooting and Conservation (BASC). Funded by subscriptions from sportsmen, the association provides training and education. BASC's Proficiency Award Scheme has been designed to promote high standards of competence and responsibility to the environment, quarry and fellow shooters, with the result that the sport has a low incidence of accidental injuries compared with most other participation sports. One of the main functions of BASC is to monitor political activity at local, governmental and European levels. Its permanent advisory staff is responsible for reviewing legislation affecting land use, wildlife conservation and firearms. In addition, the organisation provides a multitude of advice services, covering all aspects of shooting and practical conservation, to both individuals and clubs. Work by its research staff includes investigations into the effects of harsh weather upon wildfowl, and joint projects with other organisations have centred on the effects on wildfowl of the ingestion of lead shot.

Shooting is a popular country activity run by private individuals and syndicates. Farmers and landowners manage 88 per cent of the British countryside, roughly half of which sustains some kind of shooting. Actively managed commercial shoots with professional gamekeepers and paying guests are confined primarily to the larger estates. On smaller estates it is more common for shoots to be run on a non-profit-making basis, where the shooters play a more direct role in the management of the shoot and game preservation. By 2001, nearly three-quarters of a million people participated in shooting with shotguns in some form or another and, according to the Countryside Alliance, it provides direct employment for over 39,000 and generates over £310 million per annum.

The future of shooting is threatened not only by groups who are hostile to the sport on humanitarian or political grounds, but also by agricultural change. Habitat loss and changing land use have compounded the general struggle to maintain viable population levels of quarry, a process that has become increasingly evident since the Second World War.

Sources and Reading:
Mitchell, A., *Goose Shooting* (Shrewsbury: Swan Hill Press, 1997).

Websites:
www.premier-pages.co.uk/sports/british.html
www.countryside-alliance.org
www.basc.org.uk

See also Game Shooting, Pigeon Shooting, Rough Shooting, Wildfowling

*Nicholas Goddard
and John Martin*

Shooting (Scotland)

The oldest sports trophies in Scotland are the 'siller' (silver) guns of the burghs of Dumfries and Kirkcudbright, both of which date from 1587–8. The latter, in the Stewarty Museum in Kirkcudbright survives unaltered, a miniature culverin 15 centimetres long. The Dumfries gun was damaged about 1810, and when it was repaired it was given a stock so that it looked like a contemporary firearm. Both were donated by King James VI for competition between the members of the incorporations (guilds) of each town. Both competitions have been shot at irregular intervals. Between 1720 and 1830, the Dumfries gun was shot about twenty times, the event of 1778 being recorded in delightful verse by John Mayne; his poem 'The Siller Gun' expanded until it had reached 1,650 lines by 1836. He describes the processions, formal dinner, hard drinking, seduction and, in quite a short passage, the shooting. Violence occurs at both the personal and general levels:

> Foul play or fair; kick, cuff and clout
> Right side, or wrang
> Friends feghting friends, rampag'd about
> A drucken [drunken] thrang!

The siller guns were thus used in social events first and sporting contests second. The Kirkcudbright gun was shot on occasions such as coronations or the marriage of the local laird (the Earl of Selkirk), placing it in wider social structures. It did, however, have a community element: when a new trophy was needed in 1838 for an apprentices' competition, a silver arrow was hammered out of three half-crown coins by the local clockmaker.

In the eighteenth and early nineteenth centuries, 'wad' (wager) shooting took place on winter holidays. Typically, a publican bought a bullock and offered its various parts as prizes: for a few pence entry money, men and boys shot with an old and inaccurate muzzle-loader at a door. In one or two places there were other kinds of prize, such as fishing rods at Auchterarder in Perthshire and waistcoats at Garlieston in Wigtownshire, where the competition was held on the beach. Wad shooting was in effect a lottery, and was accompanied by heavy drinking. When a boy was killed by a gun exploding at the Old Toll, east of Ayr, in 1855, the report in the *Ayr Advertiser* said that New Year shooting matches were held all over the county.

One Scot played an important part in initiating the development of better firearms. Alexander Forsyth (1768–1843), minister of Belhelvie on the Aberdeenshire coast, patented the percussion cap in 1807. He was an enthusiastic wildfowler who realised that birds learned to dive when they saw the flash of the powder in the firing pan, which preceded the discharge of the gun by a second or more. His ideas led to replacement of the inefficient flintlock by the percussion lock, which was more reliable and was easy to use in wet or windy weather. At the same time, the technology of the rifled barrel was being developed, and rifle-shooting competitions were held in the west of Scotland from the 1820s.

The sport of shooting was expanded greatly by the military volunteer movement, founded in 1859–60. Every volunteer was expected to subscribe towards his own uniform and rifle: this tended to restrict membership to the better off, particularly the urban middle classes. However, in Scotland there were lairds and employers who were willing to help men volunteer, and so the social pattern of membership was different from that in England.

The National Rifle Association, set up in 1860, was closely associated with the volunteer movement. Every village had its rifle range, and the venues of the larger competitions, such as the West of Scotland meeting at Gailes in Ayrshire, covered an extensive area. There were also volunteer artillery ranges. In Scotland, shooting had some particular features, such as local events on New Year's Day. Larger meetings were called *wapenschaws* (weapon-shows), giving them a spurious link with the Middle Ages.

The national meeting held at Wimbledon from 1860 (then at Bisley from 1890) linked Scottish sport to a British framework. Rifle shooting was a focus for patronage. At the highest level, Lord Elcho (later the Earl of Wemyss and March), president of the National Rifle Association in 1859–67 and 1869–70, gave the Elcho Shield for competition between Scotland and England. It was first shot for in 1862. The biggest individual competition of the year, the Queen's Prize at Wimbledon, was worth a staggering £250: Scots were unusually successful, winning it 15 times between 1860 and 1898. Reports of the various competitions at Wimbledon and Bisley were printed at length in local and national newspapers. When a winner of the Queen's Prize arrived back in Scotland he was met by crowds at the station, who carried him off, shoulder-high, in triumph, and the scene was repeated when he reached his suburb or village. Celebration dinners followed. In medium-sized competitions, such as county matches, the leading prizes were often rifles, to enable the winners to shoot even better. The prizes for local events were given by landowners (usually cash) and tradesmen who offered something from their own stock.

Sources and Reading:

Burnett, J., *Riot, Revelry and Rout: Sport in Lowland Scotland before 1860* (East Linton: Tuckwell Press, 2000).

Cornfield, S., *The Queen's Prize: The Story of the National Rifle Association* (London: Pelham, 1987).

Jackson, L., 'Patriotism or Pleasure? The Nineteenth-Century Volunteer Force as a Vehicle for Rural Working-Class Male Sport', *The Sport Historian*, 19: 1 (1999), 125–39.

John Burnett

Shrovetide

The holiday most associated with sports such as football, cockfighting and throwing at cocks, Shrovetide comprises the three days before Lent, the name of the holiday being derived from the word *shrive*, or 'confess'. Lent, which begins on Ash Wednesday and lasts until Easter, is the longest and most rigorous fast in the Christian calendar, and so Shrovetide became a time of indulgence, a 'feast before the famine'.

Shrove Tuesday is also synonymous with pancake making, and in many parts of the north of England is probably more commonly known as Pancake Day. This is due to the strict fasting regulations of Lent, which insisted on only one meal a day and forbade the use of meat, eggs and all dairy products. It is the need to use up these foodstuffs that explains the ubiquity of pancake making on Shrove Tuesday.

In many towns and villages, church bells would sound at 11 o'clock to signify the start of pancake making, and in many areas the ringing was known as 'the pancake bell'. The link between Shrovetide and pancakes was first recorded in 1586, although it clearly dates back to much earlier times. However, pancake racing appears to be a twentieth-century phenomenon.

Shrove Tuesday pancake traditions are not exclusive to the mass of the population. Pancake Greaze takes place at Westminster School every Shrove Tuesday and dates back at least to the mid-eighteenth century. A large pancake is tossed over the high bar (5 metres high) of the Old School Room into a crowd of boys, each representing a form in the school. The boy who comes up with the largest piece of whatever is left wins one guinea from the dean of the school. Today, the 'pancake' is made from a combination of Polyfilla and horsehair. A similar custom also exists at Eton.

As well as food, Shrovetide has always been closely associated with sports. As early as the twelfth century, William Fitzstephen noted in his *Description of the City of London* that on Shrove Tuesday schoolboys in London brought their fighting cocks to fight in schoolrooms and then played football in the afternoon. This custom lasted at least up until the 1790s in some parts of England.

Many folk football matches took place on Shrove Tuesday, as do those that survive today at Alnwick, Ashbourne, Atherstone and Sedgefield. Hurling matches also traditionally took place in Cornwall during Shrovetide. Football was often part of wider celebrations and local customs. For example, on Shrove Tuesday in Twickenham and Kingston it was the tradition to take the football door-to-door asking for money before the afternoon's football match.

By the nineteenth century, Shrove Tuesday was often a time of confrontation between the players of traditional football and the authorities. In Derby, there were repeated Shrove Tuesday confrontations between footballers and the police until the game was eventually suppressed. Successful demonstrations by players meant that it was not until 1895 that the Dorking Shrove Tuesday game was finally outlawed.

Other sports associated with Shrovetide are skipping, egg shackling, battledore and shuttlecock, and the tug of war at Ludlow, which was abandoned in 1851 due to widespread violence and disorder by spectators. Not all Shrovetide customs were harmless however. It should also be noted that during the Middle Ages and beyond, Shrove Tuesday 'celebrations' were traditionally times at which Jews in England were physically attacked.

Sources and Reading:
Goulstone, J., 'Shrovetide Football and Related Games', *British Society of Sports History Newsletter*, 5 (Winter 1996) and 6 (Winter 1997), 23–34.
Hone, W., *The Every-Day Book* (London: Thomas Tegg, 1830).
Hutton, R., *The Rise and Fall of Merry England* (Oxford: Oxford University Press, 1994).
Simpson, J. and Roud, S., *A Dictionary of English Folklore* (Oxford: Oxford University Press, 2000).

See also Cockfighting, Egg Shackling, Football, Pancake Racing, Public School Sports, Skipping, Tug of War

Tony Collins

Singlestick

– *see* **Cudgelling and Singlestick**

Skipping

Traditionally a sport played in spring, skipping was often associated with Good Friday. In Cambridge, families would gather at Parker's Piece with picnics and watch or take part in skipping all day long. Tradition has it that women would skip while men turned the skipping ropes, which were often long to allow as many women to skip as possible.

In the coastal towns and villages of Sussex, Good Friday skipping was associated with the local fishermen, as for example at Brighton. The closing of beaches during the Second World War appears to have ended the tradition, although it was in decline for some years before.

In Scarborough, skipping traditionally takes place on the foreshore on the afternoon of Shrove Tuesday. The earliest record of it dates back only to 1903, but custom has it that the ropes were originally stretched across the road on the seafront and turned by fishermen as they disentangled the ropes from their fishing boats. Nowadays the ropes are smaller and tend to be confined to groups of families and friends.

Joseph Strutt says that it was originally a boys' game, the aim being to jump as many times as possible without touching the rope. In the hop-picking season, a hop stem stripped of its leaves was used. The two basic forms of skipping are the short rope and long rope versions, the former being for one or perhaps two skippers, the latter being a more collective form.

Sources and Reading:
Gomme, A. B., *The Traditional Games of England, Scotland and Ireland* (London: Thames and Hudson facsimile edition, 1984).
Hole, C., *English Traditional Customs* (London: Batsford, 1975).
Opie, I. and Opie, P., *Children's Games with Things* (Oxford, Oxford University Press, 1997).
Whitlock, R., *A Calendar of Country Customs* (London: Batsford, 1978).

Tony Collins

Skittles

A generic term which is most often used to describe a derivative of bowls in which nine skittles, or 'pins', are placed in a diamond formation on a circular metal plate on a platform. The player has three 'cheeses', which are disks made of lignum vitae, to throw at the skittle. Points are awarded for each skittle knocked down and another turn is awarded if all are knocked down. Each set of throws is called a 'chalk', three of which make up a game.

Skittles has always been generally associated with the working classes and had a somewhat dubious image in the eyes of the middle classes. Writing in the mid-nineteenth century, Stonehenge commented that 'as far as London is concerned . . . a skittle player is generally considered to be everything that is bad'.

Sources and Reading:
Day, B., *A Chronicle of Folk Customs* (London: Hamlyn, 1988).
Stonehenge [J. H. Walsh], *Manual of British Rural Sports* (London: Routledge, 1857).

See also Aunt Sally, Bowls, Half-Bowl, Kayles, Marbles, Ninepins

Tony Collins

Spangie

An apparent derivative of pitch and toss, in which marbles or halfpennies are thrown at a wall. The second player attempts to throw a marble or coin as close as possible to that of the first player. If it hits it or is within the width of the first marble or coin, the second player wins. The game is also known as 'span counter' and 'span farthing'.

Sources and Reading:
Gomme, A. B., *The Traditional Games of England, Scotland and Ireland* (London: Thames and Hudson facsimile edition, 1984).

See also Pitch and Toss

Tony Collins

Stagging

A combat game for two in which each combatant has his ankles tied together and his wrists tied behind his back. Once tied, he has to try to knock his opponent down.

Sources and Reading:
Gomme, A. B., *The Traditional Games of England, Scotland and Ireland* (London: Thames and Hudson facsimile edition, 1984).

See also Wrestling

Tony Collins

Stone Drilling

These contests took place in Welsh limestone quarries, usually to determine the best worker amid each sledgehammer and wedge section. Participants were each provided with a wedge-holder, and the winner was the quarryman who hammered out the deepest hole within a specific time limit. Such tests were customary before the invention of boring machinery.

Sources and Reading:
Davies, D., *Brecknock Historian* (Brecon: D. G. and A. S. Evans, 1977).

Emma Lile

Stone Throwing

Also known as 'casting the stone', competitive stone throwing was a common sporting activity during medieval times, and was no doubt given credibility by the Bible story of David and Goliath. It is obviously related to modern shot-putting.

Throwing for distance, often using a slingshot, and throwing heavy stones were the two most important forms of the sport. The *Histoire de Guillaume le'Marechal* of *c*.1225 records that William Marshal, Earl of Pembroke, was a noted stone-thrower and was reputed to have a thrown a stone further than anyone else. The sport was banned in 1388 by Richard II as part of his clampdown on sports.

Sources and Reading:
Reeves, C., *Pleasures and Pastimes in Medieval England* (Stroud: Sutton, 1995).

See also Feat-Stone Throwing, Quoits, Stroud Throwing Contests

Tony Collins

Stoolball

First referred to in the *Domesday Book* and probably originating in the south of England, particularly in Sussex, stoolball consists of bowling underarm at a wicket-like target that is defended by a batter using the hand or a small bat. Historically, it appears that the 'stool' could refer to the target or the bat. The game should not be confused with stowball.

The game was allegedly originally played by milkmaids and their swains; the woman sitting on a stool trying to dodge balls thrown at her by the men. It was a social sport and the winners would receive prizes of cakes or kisses. This romantic story may well be mythic, however: the bittle-battle version of stoolball played in Sussex is clearly one in which the stool is a wicket that is defended with a bat. It has also been claimed that the sport was so named because it was played with a bat shaped like a milking stool, like a larger version of a table-tennis bat.

In the fifteenth century stoolball was commonly played in Surrey on Sundays. There are at least three references to the game in seventeenth-century literature, and there is evidence that it was also played in parts of Lancashire, Yorkshire and Wales. Most interestingly, given its future development,

it appears to have always been seen as a game that women and girls could play. As early as 1586 there is a reference to 'gyrles at stoolball playes', while Fletcher and Shakespeare's *The Two Noble Kinsmen* contains a reference to women playing the game.

By the late eighteenth century there appears to have been a number of variants of the game. According to Dr Johnson the ball was hit from stool to stool, which suggests it was similar to golf, while Joseph Strutt describes the game as being similar to 'goff' or bandy ball. In fact, Strutt, in his *The Sports and Pastimes of the People of England* (1801), also describes the game as being played 'in the northern parts of England' and that it:

> . . . consists in simply setting a stool upon the ground, and one of the players takes his place before it, while his antagonist, standing at a distance, tosses a ball with the intention of striking the stool; and this it is the business of the former to prevent by beating it away with the hand. If, on the contrary, it should be missed by the hand and touch the stool, the players change places: the conqueror at this game is he who strikes the ball most times before it touches the stool.

In 1797 a match was staged between Kent and Sussex.

In the 1840s, stoolball underwent rapid growth as a game for women and girls in East Sussex, especially among the middle classes. Village clubs were organised and regular matches took place throughout summer. The sport's modern rules were codified at Glynde in East Sussex in 1881, when the two slightly different sets of rules played in the east and west of Sussex were brought together. These rules were based on those of cricket, with, for example, teams being 11-a-side and having designated bowlers and wicketkeepers. The bats were wooden and the ball was a tennis ball which had to be bowled underarm without pitching on the ground. The wickets, which were 16 yards apart, were not stools but boards that were 1 foot square and mounted on sticks, 4 feet 9 inches from the ground.

Following the First World War, Major William W. Grantham emerged as an enthusiastic promoter of the sport, using it to advance his vision of 'merrie England' and as a recreation for soldiers recuperating from war wounds. He promoted it as a game for mixed teams, much to the chagrin of those who saw it exclusively as an all-female game. Such was its popularity that games were staged at Sussex County Cricket Ground, and in 1919 a match was staged at Lord's. Grantham's reincarnated stoolball drew heavily on an idealised image of rural England. His teams and their opponents often played in 'traditional' rustic smocks and other garments associated with local customs.

In 1923, the Stoolball Association of Great Britain was founded at Lord's. The Japanese embassy even had a team. The game also spread to other parts of the empire such as Ceylon, and an indoor version of the game called 'stoolballette' was developed for playing during the winter. A stoolball league for elementary schools in East Sussex was established in the 1920s, which continued for a number of decades. This led to conflict between Grantham and those who saw stoolball as essentially a women's game. Nevertheless, during the 1930s there were about 1,000 stoolball teams, mostly based in Sussex and the south-east of England.

Although the Stoolball Association of Great Britain folded in 1942, the National Stoolball Association was founded in 1979. Today there are hundreds of local teams, which play the game with varying degrees of formality in Sussex and adjoining counties.

Sources and Reading:

Gomme, A. B., *The Traditional Games of England, Scotland and Ireland* (London: Thames and Hudson facsimile edition, 1984).
Lowerson, J., 'Sheffield Triumphant: Some Views on Sport and the Regions', *British Society of Sports History Bulletin*, 9 (1989), 2–14.
Lowerson, J., 'Stoolball: Conflicting Values in the Revival of a "Traditional Sussex Game"', *Sussex Archaeological Collections*, 133 (1995), 263–74.
Reeves, C., *Pleasures and Pastimes in Medieval England* (Stroud: Sutton, 1995).
Underdown, D., *Start of Play: Cricket and Culture in Eighteenth-Century England* (Harmondsworth: Allen Lane, 2000).

See also Bittle-Battle, Club Ball, Cricket, Stowball, Stubball

Tony Collins

Stowball

Also known as 'stoball' and 'stopball', but not to be confused with stoolball, stowball was a game both similar to and a forerunner of cricket. 'Stow' and 'stob' are dialect names for a tree stump. The play resembled cricket, with one team batting while the other fielded. The object was also, as in cricket, to score more runs than the opposing team, which was done using the bat to loft the ball over the heads of fielders. The ball was thrown underarm and overs consisted of four balls. The wicket was formed by two wooden staves.

In 1634, the game was denounced by Archbishop Laud for encouraging godlessness among the working classes. Writing in 1686 about his experience of stowball in Wiltshire, John Aubrey noted that the game's players:

> . . . smite a ball, stuffed very hard with quills and covered with soale leather, with a staff, commonly made of withy, about three and a half feet long. The turfe is very fine and the rock (freestone) is within an inch and a half of the surface which gives the ball so quick a rebound. A stobball ball is of about four inches diameter and as hard as a stone.

The bat was light and shaped like a hockey stick, much like the bats and sticks used in bandy and other bat-and-ball games. The sport was popular in Gloucestershire, Wiltshire, Somerset and Devon in the sixteenth century and written records mention it before cricket in the London area.

Sources and Reading:
Brailsford, D., *British Sport: A Social History* (Cambridge: Lutterworth Press, 1992).
Goulstone, J., 'English Folk Games and Sports', *British Society of Sports History Newsletter*, 10 (Autumn 1999), 34–8.
Terry, D., 'The Seventeenth-Century Game of Cricket', *The Sports Historian*, 20 (2000), 33–43.
Underdown, D., *Start of Play: Cricket and Culture in Eighteenth-Century England* (Harmondsworth: Allen Lane, 2000).

See also Stoolball, Cricket, Bandy

Tony Collins

Strike Up and Lay Down

A variation of trap ball, in which the ball is thrown into the air by the batter before it is hit, rather than by a mechanical device.

Sources and Reading:
Encyclopedia of Sports, Games and Pastimes (London: Fleetway, 1935).

See also Trap Ball

Tony Collins

Stroke Bias

A form of foot racing popular in seventeenth-century Kent. A local parish would select 20 of the best runners to race against a team from another parish, although it seems that sometimes up to four parishes would be involved. Each man was paired with one on the opposing team, with the aim of hitting his opponent seven times during the course of the race. Women were also participants in races.

Sources and Reading:
Gomme, A. B., *The Traditional Games of England, Scotland and Ireland* (London: Thames and Hudson facsimile edition, 1984).

Tony Collins

Stroud Throwing Contests

Although its claim to be a traditional sport is open to question, the Stroud Brick and Rolling Pin Throwing Contest is a modern continuation of much older stone-throwing games. It was devised in 1960 when visitors to Stroud in England from Stroud in Oklahoma in the United States suggested an international contest between the citizens of towns named Stroud in Canada, Australia, England and the United States. Each town has six throwers who attempt to throw a 7.5 kilogram brick as far as possible. The contest takes place annually, but each team competes in its own town, the winner being decided through telephone calls between the towns to establish the longest throw.

In 1962, a rolling pin throwing contest was introduced for women. The rules are exactly the same but instead of a brick, a rolling pin weighing 1.5 kilograms is thrown.

Sources and Reading:
Gorini, P., *Encyclopedia of Traditional Games* (Rome: Gremese, 1994).

See also Invented Traditions, Pancake Racing

Tony Collins

Strutt, Joseph

Joseph Strutt (1749–1802), antiquary, author, artist and engraver, was best known for compiling the classic text *The Sports and Pastimes of the People of England* published in 1801. At the age of 14 he was apprenticed as an engraver before becoming a student at the Royal Academy where he was famed for his high-quality work. In 1771 be became a student in the reading room of the British Museum, from where he acquired most of the material for his antiquarian and literary researches. His texts included *Regal and Ecclesiastical Antiquities of England* published in 1773, *Manners, Customs, Arms, Habits of the People of England* published as a three volume set between 1774 and 1776, the *Chronicle of England* (1777–8) and *Dresses and Habits of England* which appeared as two volumes between 1776 and 1779.

He was best known for his text *The Sports and Pastimes of the People of England*, which provides a perceptive insight into aspects of archery, jousting and hunting. It rapidly became the most famous source for this subject, providing unrivalled details of pre-industrial sports and pastimes. The high-quality engravings that accompany the text are Strutt's own work. The text has been widely acclaimed as the most detailed contemporary source of information on these activities, and has been reprinted on numerous occasions.

Following its publication, Strutt embarked upon the task of writing a romance called *Queen-Hoo Hall* which was intended to illustrate the manners and customs of rural society in the fifteenth century. After his death in 1802, the incomplete manuscript was acquired by Walter Scott who compiled a final chapter to the narrative, publishing it as four small volumes in 1808. Two incomplete poems by Strutt called 'The Test of Guilt' and 'The Bumpkin's Disaster' were also published in the same year.

Sources and Reading:
Strutt, J., *The Sports and Pastimes of the People of England* (London: J. White, 1801).

John Martin

Stubball (Wales)

Stubball, or stool-ball, was played in north Wales over the Easter period. It was a variant on the game of fives, and it resembled cricket but without bats and sometimes using a stool instead of a wicket. The game may have been linked with the ancient tradition of 'lifting', which was common among the lower orders and involved raising men or women in a chair from the ground on Easter Monday and Easter Tuesday. This custom is believed to have commemorated Christ's Resurrection.

During the early nineteenth century, both sexes participated in stubball at Oswestry, where games between two districts of the town were played on the streets. The implements used comprised a ball and two bricks or stones, with the latter being placed in the centre of the road around 4 feet apart to form an opening. The object of the game was to pass the ball through this space, which was defended with hands and feet by a member of the opposite side. If the ball was successfully driven through, or caught after being struck, the player standing by the opening was deemed to be out.

Sources and Reading:
Roberts, P., *The Cambrian Popular Antiquities of Wales* (Mold: Clwyd County Council Library and Information Service, 1994; Facsimile edition of original, printed London 1815).

Emma Lile

Swimming

Although swimming can be traced as far back as 2500 BC in other countries and cultures and in various forms related to war, hunting, recreation and sport, records of swimming in Britain followed the arrival of the Romans in AD 55. During their 500 years of occupation of Britain, the Romans established Roman-style civilisation in the communities they conquered. This included building the first bathhouses, some of which included swimming pools. These bathhouses were an integral part of the way of life of the Romans and served their needs for cleanliness and exercise, and they also acted as social clubs.

The Anglo-Saxon heroic poem *Beowulf*, written in the seventh century and known to reflect the history and social structure of the times, makes reference to swimming. The extensive references to the challenges of swimming suggest that those hearing the epic poem would have related to and admired such ability. Through the Middle Ages, swimming continues to receive mention as a necessary skill for those wishing to become knights. The literature of the time records the swimming of the common people in the Thames and their threats to throw the unpopular Cardinal Beaufort into the water to have him 'taught to swim with wings'. Such records would suggest that learning to swim with wings was a normal occurrence with which the ordinary people would associate.

The sixteenth and seventeenth centuries saw an expansion of literature specifically on swimming and an expansion of the references to swimming in all forms of literature. This includes *Colymbetes*, the first text devoted to swimming, by Nicolas Wynman in 1538, and then the more widely recognised and translated *De Arte Nantandi* by English cleric Everard Digby. This was published in Latin in 1587 while Digby was a senior fellow at St John's College, Cambridge.

During this period of the late Renaissance, explorers such as Drake returned to Britain with tales of natives swimming in the tropics. British naval men used swimming to advantage against the Spanish Armada, and John Whitgift, Vice-Chancellor of Cambridge University in 1571, banned swimming by students because of the high accident rate. All information available indicates that swimming continued to occur elsewhere, although there is nothing to suggest mass participation during the period.

In the early nineteenth century there were already a few swimming baths in existence, as well as those baths that related to the activities of the spas. These baths mainly had aristocratic connections. Due to their size, at around 7 to 8 metres in length, they were of limited use for serious swimming. These include the Old Royal Bath in Newgate Street, said to have been built for Charles II, and the Old Roman Bath built by the Earl of Essex in Elizabethan times.

During the first half of the nineteenth century, both sea and river sites became popular with all classes for swimming during the summer months. The interest of George III did much to make the seaside acceptable and promoted the growth of resorts such as Weymouth. The Factory Act of 1833, giving workers the right to some days off, and the later Bank Holidays Act of 1871 combined with the expansion of the railways to make beach bathing a summer activity for the wider population. Bathing machines appeared on the beaches from the late eighteenth century, with towns such as Worthing boasting 60 such machines. These provided direct access into the water, shelter for changing and some protection from prying eyes for modest female bathers.

Groups gathered to swim at suitable areas of rivers and gradually, as enthusiastic and like-minded individuals got together, the early clubs were formed. Crowds of 4,000 would attend the entertainments put on by the clubs at river sites such as the Dee in Aberdeen. These performances included racing, ornamental swimming, comic sketches and mock drownings. Gradually through the 1860s, such activity produced inter-club and open competition, and with that the need for some organising structure for the emerging competitive sport.

In 1869, the first broadly amateur organisation, the Associated Metropolitan Swimming Clubs, was formed 'to promote and encourage a knowledge of the art of swimming'. This slowly evolved from a group representing London clubs to one with wider national representation. It went through several name changes and experienced battles over amateurism and splits in its ranks, but in March 1886 the divergent elements reunited as the Amateur Swimming Association (ASA).

A similar pattern was seen in Scotland, where in 1884 the Glasgow clubs united to become the Associated Swimming Clubs of Glasgow. Over a period of four years it gradually widened its scope to include clubs from other areas of Scotland, and in 1888 it was reconstituted as the Scottish Amateur Swimming Association.

The public schools and the private preparatory schools were probably the first to organise swimming teaching. Sinclair and Henry record the introduction of a rule at Eton, in 1839, requiring all boys to pass a test in swimming prior to being allowed to go boating. The early swimming instruction in such establishments was carried out by the watermen from the rivers, who ensured the safety of pupils in addition to teaching them. Swimming instruction was a feature of the curriculum in the private preparatory schools, but it was much later, well into the second half of the nineteenth century, before any form of physical education and, later still, swimming was included in state schools.

During the mid-nineteenth century, in response to the worsening living conditions (sanitary conditions in particular) in the towns and cities, legislation in the form of the Baths and Wash-houses Act (1846) was passed. This allowed the use of public money for the building of baths and wash-houses. Later, with the Act's revision in 1875, this was extended to the provision of swimming pools. This legislation, prompted by issues of cleanliness and public health, coincided with the worsening of conditions for swimming outdoors due to the pollution of the rivers and coastal areas by industry. With the growth of indoor facilities, the number of people learning to swim and participating increased.

Other events contributed to the profile and popularity of the sport in the late nineteenth century. These included the swimming of the English Channel by Matthew Webb in 1875, which gave much publicity to swimming, while the loss of over 700 lives

in the sinking of the steamboat Princess Alice in the Thames in 1878 led to greater enthusiasm about learning to swim for reasons of safety. In the indoor facility, swimming as a spectacle became increasingly popular as it could be watched in warmth and comfort and was easily accessible to local communities as the new baths were situated in the heart of urban areas. Such entertainments were also timed to take place on midweek evenings and thus did not clash with football, which was the main spectator sport at the time. Weekly papers such as the *Swimming Record and Chronicle of Sporting Events* record the many events that were taking place. The issue of 2 August 1873 shows nine events in London the following week, including Johnson v 'Unknown' and the St Pancras Club Captaincy Race, both at Hendon, the final heat of the Clothes Handicap at City of London Baths, the final heat for Mr White's prizes at Lambeth Baths and the Serpentine Club's Challenge Cup. The evolving governing body organised the national events, with ASA National Championships increasing from one event (the One-Mile Championship) in 1869 to eight events in 1900, and to eighteen events in 1920.

The involvement of large numbers of women in swimming activity was hampered by Victorian attitudes to women as the weaker sex and to issues of decency relating to dress. Prior to the nineteenth century, both sexes swam naked in different outdoor venues. This practice came under pressure due to Victorian morals and standards of respectability. The clothing for women varied from a lightweight but all-covering gown, which floated up once in the water and clung to the body once wet, to heavy navy serge dresses with petticoats that did little to encourage activity in water. As swimming activity moved indoors, men continued to swim naked. Pressure for men to wear costumes, often related to the presence of female spectators at the 'swimming entertainments', arose during the 1860s and 1870s. The ASA introduced legislation about costumes for men in 1890 and amended it to include regulations for costumes for women in 1899. The ASA included women's championship events from 1901, when there was a 100-yards national championship. The puritan attitudes of the Victorian era persisted until well into the twentieth century, with males and females being obliged to swim either at separate times or in separate pools. This improved slightly around 1914, but only in 1925 did the legislation of the Public Health Act take over from the attitudes surrounding the issue.

By the twentieth century, most towns with over 20,000 inhabitants had a pool. The system of keeping the water clean was still the 'fill and empty principle'. This involved filling up the bath at the start of the week and letting it become dirtier due to use until, usually by the end of the week, the bottom of the bath could not be seen. Only then would it be emptied and refilled. This system continued until about 1920 when filtration-based water purification systems became available, which significantly improved the water quality and swimming conditions. Clubs were plentiful by the beginning of the twentieth century. Baths such as Islington had 100 clubs in 1913, serving the competitive, social and recreational needs of the local population.

Sources and Reading:
Amateur Swimming Association, *Minute Books, 1869–1903*.
Bilsborough, P., *One Hundred Years of Scottish Swimming* (Edinburgh: Napier Polytechnic, 1988).
Campbell, A., *Report on Public Baths and Wash-houses in the United Kingdom* (Edinburgh: Edinburgh University Press, 1918).
Keil, I. and Wix, D., *In the Swim: The Amateur Swimming Association from 1869 to 1994* (Loughborough: The Swimming Times, 1996).
Orme, N., *Early British Swimming 55 BC–AD 1719* (Exeter: University of Exeter, 1983).
Searle, M., *Bathing Machines and Bloomers* (Tunbridge Wells: Midas, 1977).
Sinclair, A. and Henry, W., *Swimming* (London: Longmans, 1893).
Thomas, R., *Swimming* (London: Sampson Low, 1904).

See also Swimming (Wales)

Win Hayes

Swimming (Wales)

Swimming has been practised in Wales since ancient times, when it was considered an essential skill for crossing the country's many rivers. Medieval poetry refers to the art, and it constituted one of the 24 ancient feats first recorded in print around 1500. A sea-bathing craze at the end of the eighteenth century pre-dated the rise of competitive swimming, which flourished with the opening of indoor baths from the late nineteenth century onwards. Sea-swimming was also popular during the nineteenth century, be it in the form of ornamental displays, head-to-head contests (often for monetary prizes) or, sometimes, rather unusual long distance challenges. An example of the latter took place in north Wales in 1824, when an individual swam from Caernarfon to Anglesey and back three times, taking with him on the third occasion bread, cheese and a bottle of brandy, which were devoured en route while he floated on his back.

Sources and Reading:
Jones, E., 'Campau Amdrechol y Cymry', *Taliesin*, 8: 2 (1861), 225–32.
Jones, W. H., *Old Carnarvon* (Carnarvon: H. Humphreys, 1881).

See also Swimming

Emma Lile

Sword and Buckler

A medieval game, probably for children, which used imitation short swords and small round shields made of wood. Compton Reeves suggested that some aristocrats of the time disapproved of it because it seemed demeaning to knightly chivalry.

Sources and Reading:
Reeves, C., *Pleasures and Pastimes in Medieval England* (Stroud: Sutton, 1995).

See also Broadsword, Cudgelling and Singlestick

Tony Collins

Tag

A game also known as 'it', 'dobby', 'tick', 'tig', 'touch' or 'touchwood', in which one player, known in the argot of the game as 'it', touches another and rushes off. The newly touched player, who has now become 'it', attempts to touch another, and so on. Most versions incorporate a safety area where players can go and not be touched. The game provides the basis for many other children's games, and also for more-organised variants such as barley break and prisoner's bars.

Sources and Reading:
Gomme, A. B., *The Traditional Games of England, Scotland and Ireland* (London: Thames and Hudson facsimile edition, 1984).

See also Barley Break, Prisoner's Bars

Tony Collins

Taplasau Haf/Twmpathau Chwarae

Secular festivals featuring music, dancing and a varied programme of rural sports, held over the summer weekends. They are known as *taplasau haf* in south Wales and *twmpathau chwarae* in the north. May Day and Midsummer Day were particularly popular occasions for such events, which often centred around a games mound known as a *twmpath*. These outdoor parish activities attracted large crowds of men, women and children, and were popular across the country until about the mid-nineteenth century.

Sources and Reading:
Jones, T., *Y Darian* (12 January 1928; 2 February 1928).
Matthews, E., *George Heycock a'i Amserau* (Abertawy [Swansea]: J. Rosser, 1867).

Emma Lile

Tennis

In the absence of other evidence, the origins of European competitive ball games can be hypothesised on the basis of linguistic analysis and by means of early pictorial representations. From a linguistic analysis of sporting terms it appears that the medieval chivalric tournament traditionally staged in front of a castle gate first served as a model for the ancestor of European ball games, football. Tennis, in turn, can be conceived of as a variety of football played by the medieval clergy in the cloisters of their monasteries. Here, the openings in the colonnaded walks took over the role of the makeshift wooden gates that can be viewed on early pictorial representations of football in Italy (Padua and Venice), and the slanting roofs were indispensable for the service, a feature still characteristic of modern real tennis.

The influence of the tournament is conspicuous in particular sporting terms shared by both medieval football and tennis. The chivalric expression *chase*, for example, which denoted the attack on the gate, reappears in the Italian football of Florence where it came to mean 'goal' (*caccia*), and in all varieties of traditional tennis the world over where it refers to a disputed point. It eventually even yielded the name for the game itself in Flanders (*kaatsen*), Friesland (*keatsen*), fifteenth- and sixteenth-century Scotland (*caich*) and the South American countries of Ecuador and Colombia (*juego de la chaza*).

Medieval tennis was a game for three (or more) players on each side, in which the ball was struck either on the volley or on the rebound with the palm of the hand (hence its ancient French name *jeu de la paume*).

The racket (replacing an earlier hand protection, the glove) was introduced around the turn of the sixteenth century (first mentioned in 1505; the first pictorial representation is on the frontispiece of a moralising treatise in French, *Le Cymetière des Malheureux*, of 1511). Strangely enough, the invention of the net (at first in the form of a line dividing the court) preceded that of the racket, as is evidenced in a political poem by the Burgundian court historiographer Jean Molinet ('Le Jeu de Palme', 1492). Points could be scored by hitting openings in the gallery (the *dedans*, or the winning gallery, the last on the side of the returning party) or in the wall (the grill), or by winning a *chase*. Whereas in modern lawn tennis the ball is dead after it bounces a second time, in medieval tennis it had to come to a stop, after which the spot where it lay was marked. (From the sixteenth century, the spot of its second impact was marked.) This was called a *chase*. Whenever the score was within a point of winning the game (40, originally 45) or whenever two chases had occurred, players had to change ends to contend the chase or chases. To do this, the player who had laid a chase in his opponents' court had to defend it by preventing the ball of his opponents from being stopped (or, in later times, landing) closer to the rear wall than in the case of his own chase.

According to the testimony of a German monk, Caesarius of Heisterbach, tennis seems to have been known in Paris as early as around the middle of the twelfth century. On linguistic grounds, it seems to have originated in Picardy in the north of France, from where it soon found its way to Frisian settlements further north. That is why in modern times the games of Dutch Friesland (*keatsen*), of the Swedish island of Gotland (*pärkspel*) and of Germany's Saterland (played until about 1900, now extinct) constitute the oldest layer of traditional tennis. Of these, the Saterlandic game can be considered the prototype, and the great age of all can be estimated by the absence from them of the traditional scoring method by 15s (possibly based on a French coin used as a wager, the *gros denier*, at first worth 12, then 15 deniers; the number 60

being a boundary in the French numerical system). The scoring method is first mentioned in the English political poem 'The Battle of Agincourt' (soon after 1415).

From France, the game progressed south where in a first wave it reached Italy, Catalonia, the Basque provinces and Spain. On its way south, and after taking root in Provence (*jo de paumo*), its popular variety must have arrived in Italy by 1610 at the latest, when it was described by Italian-born physician Hippolytus Guarinonius. This game has survived in the form of street tennis in Tuscan places such as Vetulonia (*palla*) and in the village of Tavole in the Ligurian Alps (*balun*). Its existence in Catalonia in 1539 is shown by a dialogue in the work of educationalist Juán Luís Vives, and a magnificent illustration of how *el joc de pilota valenciana* was played in former times in Vives' place of birth has survived in a painting by José Brun Albiñana (1881). The modern game in Valencia goes by the name of *les llargues*. The pelota games of the Basque provinces, such as *bote luzea* and *lachoa*, are clearly offsprings of traditional French tennis games, whereas the spectacular Basque game of pelota (whence the *jai alai* of the Americas) is a mixture of these and of the French *jeu de la courte paume* played in covered courts.

Although no traces of the traditional game remain in central Spain, it seems that there was a second wave of movement of the game, and it was taken to the Americas in the wake of the conquistadores. On its way to America, the game was first introduced to the Canaries, where it has in recent times been revived on the island of Lanzarote (*pelotamano*). The game in the Americas has been kept alive by indigenous players in Mexico (Oaxaca; *pelota mixteca*) and in Ecuador and Colombia (*juego de la chaza*).

At an early time, and presumably as a result of the education their sons had received in monasteries, medieval rulers were inspired to build tennis courts of their own, based on the traditional venues in the cloisters. Again the French were in the vanguard. As early as 1316, Louis X died an untimely death as a result of excessive tennis playing.

In the *Avis aus Roys* (*Advice for Kings*, 1360) tennis was recommended as a suitable pastime for the royal offspring, and the usefulness of the game for peers was emphasised in numerous educational treatises of the Middle Ages and the Renaissance. James VI of Scotland (later also James I of England) in his *Basilicon Doron* (1599) recommended tennis to his little son Henry and apparently so whetted his appetite for it that the future Prince of Wales, despite signs of a serious illness in 1612, played an exacting match against Prince Maurice of Nassau, stadholder of the Dutch provinces and champion of the Protestant cause, and shortly afterwards died at the age of only 18. The German emperor Ferdinand I had his first tennis court built in Vienna in 1525, and in Italy Milan's notorious duke Galeazzo Maria Sforza (1444–76) and the d'Este family in sixteenth-century Ferrara were passionate devotees of the game. A member of the latter commissioned Antonio Scaino to write the first treatise on ball-games, including tennis, the *Trattato del giuoco della palla* (Venice, 1555).

It is plausible that as time went on not only the ruling classes (hence 'real tennis' also became known as 'royal tennis'), but also the second best, the courtiers and the *nouveaux riches*, should have striven to master the game. It was the universities and entrepreneurs who ran commercial tennis courts (covered from the seventeenth century onwards) who catered to such ambitions. A special feature of Germany was the so-called *Ritterakademie* (Knights' Academy) which trained the future courtier after the model of the French *galant homme* and for this purpose not only employed professors who taught languages and social sciences, but also a tennis instructor. Although the game of the peerage and rich bourgeoisie began to decline towards the end of the seventeenth century and many courts were put to other uses (not infrequently they were converted into theatres), it nevertheless survived in the form of real tennis in France (three courts in 1997), Britain (twenty courts), the United States (ten courts) and Australia (four courts). The somewhat precarious situation of the game in England at the end of the nineteenth century is best illustrated by the term 'real tennis' itself. This is known to have been used in the 1890s by the Irish lawn-tennis player Harold Sigurson Mahony and reflected the fact that, under the threat of being edged out by the new-fangled lawn tennis, its followers asserted that they were playing the 'real' game.

The modern sport has six national governing bodies: the Tennis and Rackets Association (United Kingdom, founded in 1907, headquarters at the Queen's Club, London); the Australian Royal Tennis Association (Richmond, Victoria); the Canadian Real Tennis Association (Toronto, Ontario); the Comité Français du Jeu de Courte Paume (Féderation Française de Tennis) (Merignac); the United States Court Tennis Association (Bedminster, New Jersey); and the Dutch Real Tennis Association (The Hague, Netherlands). There have been world championship games since around 1750 (when the championship was held by a certain Clerge of France). From 1928 to 1955 the title was held by the legendary Pierre Etchebaster of France. The Men's World Tennis Championship is now organised by the International World Championship Committee and administered by the International Real Tennis Professionals Association. Every two years the champion is required to defend his title against the winner of an elimination series, played between the four leading contenders as defined by the International Rankings list. The Ladies' World Championship was inaugurated in 1985 and is determined by a knock-out tournament every two years. Real Tennis achieved Olympic status only in 1908 (London), when the winner was Jay Gould (USA), although it was also an exhibition sport in 1924 (Paris).

It is clear from the title of his London-based *Court Journal* that Walter Clopton Wingfield, a retired major and a personal acquaintance of the Prince of Wales, was familiar with traditional real tennis when he announced in the spring of 1874 his new invention, 'lawn tennis'. From the old game the successor retained the basic rules (strokes on the volley and the rebound) and equipment (the net, lopsided rackets) and the obligation of serving from one side only (from a 'service crease'), but did away with the overly complicated chase rule, walls and galleries and their hazards and substituted the stuffed balls of old with air-filled rubber balls. These new balls, which could be manufactured as a result of Goodyear's discovery of vulcanisation, bounced well, even on the short-trimmed croquet lawns adjacent to the English manor, the favourite venue for the new society pastime. Wingfield's innovation reached the United States in the year of its invention, 1874, and arrived in France before 1875 and Germany in 1876, when English visitors experimented with it on the lawns of the Royal Victoria Hotel in Bad Homburg. From 1875, the Marylebone Cricket Club assumed responsibility for the new game, and by 1877, the first year of the Championship (Wimbledon), its experts had basically given it its present shape, which included a return to the original scoring by 15s.

In 1888, the English Lawn Tennis Association took over as the governing body. (Its American counterpart, the United States National Lawn Tennis Association, had been founded as early as 1881.) The International Lawn Tennis Federation (ILTF) was set up after the turn of the century, in 1913, with the United States abstaining from joining it because they objected to the Wimbledon tournament having the title of World Championships. The United States became a member in 1923 when all parties were eventually reconciled by the introduction of the four major events in the game, which since the 1930s have become known as the 'Grand Slam' tournaments. Germany, one of the founding members of the ILTF, but at the time banned from the umbrella organisation as a result of the First World War, came away empty-handed in the process. The world team championships, the Davis Cup, was first contended between the British Isles and the United States in 1900, but, contrary to what its inventor Dwight Filley Davis in retrospect claimed in the 1930s, it now seems to have first been suggested by a once famous, but now forgotten, lawn tennis pioneer, the American Charles Adolph Voigt in 1896. Lawn tennis was an Olympic sport from the beginning (Athens, 1896), but was as such discontinued for 64 years after 1924. Olympic tennis was reinstituted in 1988 (Seoul) after professional players had at last been admitted.

Sources and Reading:

Aberdare, Lord, *The Willis Faber Book of Tennis & Rackets* (London: Stanley Paul, 1980).

Best, D., *The Royal Tennis Court. A History of Tennis at Hampton Court Palace* (Oxford: Ronaldson Publications, 2002).

Butler, L. St. J. and Wordie, P. J. (eds), *The Royal Game* (Kippen: Falkland Palace Real Tennis Club, 1989).

Gillmeister, H., *Tennis. A Cultural History* (London: Cassell Academic/Leicester University Press, 1998).

Heathcote, J. M., *et al.*, *Tennis. Lawn Tennis. Rackets. Fives* (London: Longmans, 1890).

Marshall, J., *Annals of Tennis* (London: The Field, 1878; reprint Baltimore: Racquet Sports Information & Service, 1973).

Noel, E. B. and Clark, J. O. M., *A History of Tennis* (London: Oxford University Press, 1924; reprint London: Duckworth, 1991).

See also Handball, Rackets

Heiner Gillmeister

Tennis (Scotland)

The first reference to the *jeu de paume* in Scotland occurs at the end of the life of King James I (1394–1437). James was a prisoner in England between 1406 and 1424 and learned the pleasures of the English court, including its games. When he returned to Scotland he made repeated attempts to control the Scottish barons, and was staying in the Dominican monastery at Perth when their assassins arrived. He tried to escape through an underground vault, but his exit through a sewer was blocked by material he had caused to be put there because it was near the court for the *paume* and balls had been lost down it.

The nature of the *paume* played at Perth is unknown, although its name indicates that it was French in origin. *Catch*, *cache* or *caitch* emerged in Picardy about 1375 and spread over most of Europe. It reached Scotland about 1475 and until the nineteenth century 'catch' was the Scots name for games in which a ball was struck against a wall. The court was the 'catchpool', and there was a catchpool at the Palace of Holyroodhouse in Edinburgh, suggesting that 'catch' may sometimes have been a synonym of tennis, but in other places it was played by boys in the street.

Catch was later called 'handball', and it is sometimes difficult to know whether a particular reference refers to cache or to the football-like game. Although it was probably played all over Scotland, by 1850 its focus was the area east of Kilmarnock. The most important venue was the north wall of Barr Castle, a sixteenth-century tower house in the middle of Galston in Ayrshire. There were no side or end walls, and the ground was of beaten earth. Matches there continued until 1939. The principal fixture was on the Saturday of the week of Glasgow Fair. Irish handball players are known to have been active in Scotland in the nineteenth and early twentieth centuries.

The highly sophisticated game of royal or real tennis, using rackets, was brought to Scotland by King James V who saw it in Paris when he went to marry Magdalene, daughter of François I. James had the court at Falkland Palace built in 1540–1 and it seems to have had its most intensive use in the period before James VI became king of England (1568–1603). Subsequently it fell out of use and much of the stone was removed by the people of the village. It was, however, rebuilt by the third Marquess of Bute in 1896, and is probably the oldest sporting structure in Scotland. Scotland had a second venue at Sun Court, Troon (1905), at present extant but out of use. An odd derivative of real tennis lasted until the latter part of the eighteenth century at Rattray in Perthshire. It was played in the churchyard by two pairs of men, and the method for starting the play was to throw the ball onto the church roof, using it like the sloping penthouse of the tennis court.

Sources and Reading:

Butler, L. St. J. and Wordie, P. J. (eds), *The Royal Game* (Kippen: Falkland Palace Real Tennis Club, 1989).

Gillmeister, H., 'The Origin of European Ball Games: A Re-evaluation and Linguistic Analysis', *Stadion*, 7 (1981), 19–51.

Rodger, R., 'The Silver Ball of Rattray: A Unique Scottish Sporting Trophy', *Proceedings of the Society of Antiquaries of Scotland*, 122 (1992), 403–11, supplemented by Burnett, J., 'A Note on the Silver Ball of Rattray', idem, 128 (1998), 1101–4.

John Burnett

Tennis (Wales)

The game of tennis traditionally played in rural Wales did not resemble the modern form of the game but was probably more akin to fives. Although the familiar small ball was used, there were no demarcated courts and play usually took place, possibly with rackets but sometimes without, against church walls. Tennis is mentioned in a fifteenth-century poem by Guto'r Glyn, and also by the medieval poet Huw ap Elisse who tells of an elderly man recalling playing the game in his youth. Judging by a contemporary account by Rhys Cox, eighteenth-century tennis involved players hitting a ball back and forth against a wall using their hands. Cox describes the game held before the Sunday service in Llanfair-yng-Nghornwy churchyard in Anglesey, in which two teams of ten, occasionally including church officers, competed against each other. Tennis of this nature was popular in parish revels across Wales until their disappearance during the mid- to late nineteenth century.

Sources and Reading:

Cox, Rh., *Lleuad yr Oes* (Swansea: Williams, 1827).

Howells, J., 'The Glamorgan Revel', *The Red Dragon*, 5 (1884), 130–9.

Malkin, B. H., *The Scenery, Antiquities and Biography of South Wales* (London: Longman, 1804).
Williams, I., *Gwaith Guto'r Glyn* (Cardiff: University of Wales Press, 1939).

Emma Lile

Tetbury Woolsack Race

Formerly the centre of the southern Cotswolds' wool trade, the town first held its annual woolsack race in medieval times. Competitors would carry a sack of wool weighing 60 pounds up Gumstool Hill. The collapse of the region's wool trade in the late nineteenth century saw the end of the race. The race was revived in 1973 as a symbol of the town's growing commercial and civic confidence and now takes place every spring bank holiday. Prizes are awarded for team and individual performances. Women also take part in the race, albeit with lighter sacks.

Sources and Reading:
Financial Times (Weekend Magazine) (1 July 2000).

See also Invented Traditions

Tony Collins

Thomas, Catherine

Known as 'Catrin Cwmglas', Catherine Thomas (1761–1837) from Caernarfonshire was renowned for her physical power, which was said to exceed that of many men. The feats of this solidly built individual, whose deep voice and regularly shaven beard hardly exuded femininity, included picking up a 14-stone man and holding him at arm's length over a quay. Catrin Cwmglas also enjoyed fox-hunting and often participated in local hunts. A poem composed on the occasion of her death marvels at her Herculean strength and Amazonian figure.

Sources and Reading:
Bell's Life (26 February 1837).

Emma Lile

Thomas, Daniel

Born in Pontypridd, pugilist Daniel Thomas (1823–1910) showed an interest in fighting from an early age. Following initial professional defeats, he walked to London, where he began earning money by sparring in saloons. His reputation was soon enhanced by his victory over Englishmen such as John Brookes, the 'Norwich Champion', and during the 1850s Thomas, known as 'Dan Pontypridd', was one of the better-known British fighters.

Sources and Reading:
Jones, T., *Hen Faledi Ffair* (Talybont: Y Lolfa, 1970).

Emma Lile

Thrashing the Hen

Found in Essex and Sussex until at least the 1830s, this was a variation on cock throwing which saw a hen placed in a sack and carried around on the back of a man known as the 'hoodman', who had bells tied to his coat-tails. The other participants were blindfolded and had to try to beat the hen to death with sticks.

Sources and Reading:
Hone, W., *The Every-Day Book* (London: Thomas Tegg, 1830).
Whitlock, R., *A Calendar of Country Customs* (London: Batsford, 1978).

See also Cock Throwing

Tony Collins

Throwing and Bowling Games (Scotland)

In 1801, Joseph Strutt demonstrated that in England, a wide range of bowling and throwing games had been played over the centuries. Unfortunately, far less evidence for these games in Scotland survives. Similar games must have been equally popular in Scotland, though being a much poorer people the Scots are likely to have favoured those that did not need implements to be specially made.

Pennystanes is the earliest throwing game known in Scotland. It was a simple game in which stones the size of a penny were aimed at a mark in the ground. It was archery without bow and arrow. John Barbour, in his epic poem *The Brus* [Bruce] (*c.*1375), describes a short distance with the words 'The way was nicht ane pennystane cast'. It seems to have been widely popular: it was a Scots expression for 'a stone's throw'. Pennystanes was not played after the 1820s, but it evolved into quoiting and curling. The first record of 'kittis' (quoits) was at Leith in 1631, and the notably similar word 'cuting' was used for the winter game from the sixteenth century to the second quarter of the nineteenth, when it was replaced by 'curling' which had itself been first recorded in 1620, and had been used as a synonym for cuting.

In quoiting, the thing thrown, an iron ring weighing typically 10 pounds (4.5 kilograms), was a product of the Industrial Revolution. In the first quarter of the nineteenth century, people of some wealth were quoiters: the Six-Feet Club, made up largely of Edinburgh lawyers, included quoiting among its events. Soon it was clear that labouring men, used to hard physical work, were the ones who had the strength to throw a quoit accurately for an hour or more. The commonest competition was the individual knockout, often held as part of a larger general games day. Occasionally it

received patronage from the landed gentry, but more often working men organised it themselves. In the middle of the nineteenth century the miniature silver quoit (or very occasionally a gold one), to be worn like a medal, achieved some vogue as a prize, but money prizes were more usual. It was the leading gambling sport in Scotland. Quoiting was equally popular among urban industrial workers and farm servants: the latter tied their quoits to the harrow to shine them for public competition. The best players were national figures, such as Willie Waters of Lochgelly in the Fife coalfield, around 1900. Before a match he placed his gold watch on the pin and then ringed it with a quoit, thus establishing psychological domination over his opponent. A generation earlier, Thomas Walkinshaw of Carnwath in Lanarkshire had begun as a farm labourer, but his winnings enabled him to reach one of the peaks of popular culture: he became landlord of the inn at Carlops on the Edinburgh–Dumfries road.

Unlike bowling, quoiting did not require a rink to be maintained to rigorous standards: matches could be held where it suited the participants. When bonnet-dressers from Stewarton and Kilmarnock met for a 12-a-side match in 1863, they played beside a bridge halfway between the two towns.

Quoiting remained popular until the 1950s. By this time the Scottish Quoiting Association held a loose control over activity and organised an annual match against Wales. The *Daily Record*, produced in Glasgow, supported working-class culture and from the 1920s it sponsored a national competition. The rapid decline of quoiting had several related causes: less heavy manual labour for men, the softer attractions of motoring and the television, and the decline of mining and farming communities.

Skittles were known in Scotland as 'kyles' (from the French *quilles*). King James IV is known to have played it in 1496. A set of skittles found in a peat bog at Ironmacannie in Galloway in 1830, now in the National Museums of Scotland, have been shown by radiocarbon dating to have been made between 1500 and 1700. In 1695, the town

As well as jousting, other important sports included the tourney, which saw knights on horseback fight each other with blunt swords. The fight would take place in a large pen formed by posts and rails, the two knights would at first be separated by a cord which would be cut when the tourney started. The fight would continue until ended by the judge or, less likely, when one knight surrendered.

Barriers was another form of combat sport often seen as tournaments. Two sets of men would be placed in a square stockade, where they were separated by a long bar 3 feet high to stop them grabbing hold of each other. Men from each side would then fight opponents on the other side with wooden spears and swords until one gave in or the judges ended the fight. It was forbidden to touch the bar or to reach or attack underneath it.

Running at the ring, also known as tilting at the quintain, was a form of jousting in which a lance was used to unhook a ring from a target while riding on horseback, which was popular among the aristocracy in the sixteenth and seventeenth centuries.

The armour originally used by contestants was generally made of boiled leather, which was hard but much lighter than metal. By the turn of the fourteenth century, metal armour was designed specifically for tournaments, offering greater protection but usually being heavier and more unwieldy than battle armour.

The tournament appears to have developed as a sporting event in northern France towards the end of the eleventh century. This coincided with the development of the couched lance, where the lance was tucked under the right arm to give it more power, as portrayed in the Bayeux Tapestry. Matthew Paris in his thirteenth-century *Chronica Majora* refers to it as '*conflictus Gallicus*'.

The first recorded instance of a tournament in Britain is in a charter granted to Osbert of Arden some time between 1125 and 1150. By the latter part of the century the tournament had become a major part of aristocratic life – indeed, no one who was not a knight could participate – with its most famous practitioner being William Marshall, the future protector of England during the minority of Henry III, who earned a considerable amount of money, not to mention influence, due to his success. Tournaments were staged, like so many other sports, on Shrove Tuesday, but also at Christmas and Easter, as well as at major ceremonial occasions and to mark the end of military campaigns.

The most famous tournament probably took place in June 1467 at Smithfield in London between Anthony Woodville, Lord Scales, the brother-in-law of Edward IV, and Anthony, Count de la Roche, known as the Bastard of Burgundy. Over 400 Burgundians crossed the Channel to see the event, which was opened with great pomp in the presence of the king. As far as can be ascertained from contemporary reports, the two combatants missed each other using lances, drew their swords and in the midst of the fight the count's horse collapsed, pinning him underneath. He refused the king's offer of a different horse and the tournament was suspended until the following day. When they resumed, they fought with axes, Scales landing the telling blow on the count's helmet, and the king declared Scales the winner.

Although such tournaments had a ritual and symbolic meaning, they were not simply demonstrations of chivalry. Deaths and serious injuries were common, and their primary purpose was still military training. Just as importantly, they served as demonstrations of aristocratic power, both in terms of politics and wealth.

Despite this popularity in both England and France, the tournament was frowned upon by the church. In 1130, Pope Innocent II banned tournaments; his edict was only finally revoked in 1316 by Pope John XXII, who saw tournaments as useful training for the Crusades. In 1194, Richard I sought both to legitimise the sport and bring it under royal control by introducing a licensing system. His goal was to use the tournament to improve the military skills of the English and allow them to compete more effectively with the French on the battlefield. He designated five official tournament sites and decreed that any knight wishing to take part in a tournament had to buy a licence, the price of which was dependent on his rank. To bind the nobility closer to the crown, each knight was forced to swear loyalty to the king and, emphasising that Richard saw the tournament as a form of military training, no foreign knights were allowed to compete.

As might be imagined, tournaments involving rival knights often became quasi-political events, with the result having a great deal more significance than the merely sporting. For most of its life the tournament effectively became a proxy for the ongoing battle between the crown and the nobility. During times when royal authority seemed to be under threat from the nobility, tournaments were generally banned or severely restricted to prevent them being used as a military rallying-point for dissident nobles. When the pendulum swung to the monarchy, tournaments were allowed. Richard II revived the sport, staging many lavish tournaments, but following his murder the tournament went into terminal decline. Despite a revival under Henry VIII in 1511, when the tournament became a feature of the ceremonial occasions of his reign, the tournament and its associated events had disappeared by the end of the seventeenth century.

Sources and Reading:

Barber, R. and Barker, J., *Tournaments: Jousts, Chivalry and Pageants in the Middle Ages* (Suffolk: Boydell, 1989).
Carter, J. M., *Sports and Pastimes of the Middle Ages* (Columbus: Brentwood University Press, 1984).
The Encyclopaedia of Sport (London: The Sportsman, 1912).
Reeves, C., *Pleasures and Pastimes in Medieval England* (Stroud: Sutton, 1995).

See also Round Table, Jousting, Tilting at the Quintain

Tony Collins

Training

Modern sports training originated in eighteenth-century Britain in pugilism, pedestrianism and horseracing. All of these were associated with gambling and training stemmed from an awareness that the risk of losing could be lessened by developing specialised techniques (especially in 'scientific' boxing) or by improving fitness, endurance and vigour. Prior to this, competitive events – certainly between humans, perhaps less so for animals – were based entirely on the natural talent of the contestants. Training, designed to improve on these innate abilities, emerged as an aspect of rational behaviour as knowledge increasingly became tied to scientific enquiry and embedded in the process of human reason. Simultaneously, a growing emphasis on achievement in a competitive society created the need to improve performance in sport and brought training to the fore. Indeed it became an integral feature of sport.

Horseracing was the first to develop formalised and documented training methods, possibly because almost from its beginnings the sport involved wagering. The methods were based on humoural theory, which applied both to humans and animals; it held that bodies were comprised of the four humours of earth, fire, water and air, each with associated characteristics of melancholy, choler, phlegm and blood. Racehorse training was aimed at achieving a balance in an animal's humours by removing impediments to its body's functioning through a programme of diet, exercise and, if necessary, medication. Diets were developed to minimise the build-up of gross humours, and if the normal processes of urination, defecation and perspiration did not appear sufficient to remove wastes then exercise (to induce sweating), purging or even bloodletting would be undertaken.

Mewett argues that the methods applied to horses were then adopted (and adapted) to human sporting endeavours, though he acknowledges that former participants, often illiterate, also passed on their own ideas when they became sporting trainers. By the early nineteenth century the primary objective of human training was to improve performance by developing good 'wind', essentially stamina. Its basic components were diet – undercooked red meat, dry bread and old beer, with restricted intake of other fluids – and exercise – walking or running between 20 and 24 miles a day – with additional sweating or purging when deemed necessary.

Sources and Reading:
Collins, T. and Vamplew, W., *Mud, Sweat and Beers: A Cultural History of Sport and Alcohol* (Oxford: Berg, 2002).
Mewett, P., 'From Horses to Humans: Species Crossovers in the Origin of Modern Sports Training', *Sport History Review*, 33 (2002), 95–120.

See also Alcohol

Wray Vamplew

Trap Ball

Broadly speaking, trap ball – which is also known as 'trap, bat and ball' or, in Kent, 'bat and trap' – is a team variation of knur and spell. The 'trap' is a piece of wood on a pivot, with a hollow at one end in which the ball is placed. The batter hits the trap, which knocks the ball into the air, and then while the ball is in the air has to hit it as far as possible. The batter uses a smaller bat than that used in knur and spell.

While one team bats, the other fields, the aim being to catch the ball after it has been hit by the batter or, if it lands without being caught, to throw it back and hit the trap. If the ball is caught, the fielding side goes into bat. If the ball is thrown and hits the trap, that batsman is out and another takes his place. The batsman is also out if the ball touches the trap before or while it is hit.

Joseph Strutt noted that the ball had to travel between two boundaries, precursors of baseball's foul lines; if it did not the batter was out, unlike in modern baseball.

This was unusual for bat-and-ball games of the time. He also pointed to the great skill of the batters, the best of whom could drive the ball 'an astonishing distance'.

The first written mention of trap ball was in West Sussex in the early seventeenth century, and it was popular in Essex. Versions of the game were also traditionally played by women on Shrove Tuesday, Easter Monday and Whitsuntide at Bury St Edmunds and Chester. It is still played in parts of Kent today, where there are a number of pub-based bat and trap leagues.

Sources and Reading:
Gomme, A. B., *The Traditional Games of England, Scotland and Ireland* (London: Thames and Hudson facsimile edition, 1984).
Goulstone, J., 'English Folk Games and Sports', *British Society of Sports History Newsletter*, 10 (1999), 34–8.
Strutt, J., *The Sports and Pastimes of the People of England* (London: J. White, 1801).

See also Knur and Spell, Strike Up and Lay Down, Tip Cat

Tony Collins

Troap

A game for two people using curved sticks or bandies and a piece of wood called a 'nacket'. One player attempts to hit the nacket to a line at the other end of the ground. The opponent, standing between the striker and the line, tries to throw the nacket back to the line where the striker stands. If the thrower succeeds, they take the place of the batter; if not the distance between the striker and where the nacket landed is measured by lengths of a stick; the number of lengths are counted as points for the striker.

Sources and Reading:
Gomme, A. B., *The Traditional Games of England, Scotland and Ireland* (London: Thames and Hudson facsimile edition, 1984).

Tony Collins

Troco

Also known as lawn billiards, troco appears to have become popular as a country-house game in the nineteenth century. As the name implies, it was similar to table billiards in that players had to use a wooden cue to propel a ball through an iron ring in the middle of a circle. An opponent would attempt to prevent that from happening by using the ball to cannon off the other. Points were awarded for cannons, for getting the ball through the ring and, the hardest skill to master, cannoning the ball through the ring off an opponent's ball.

The game was also played in pubs with large lawns, but appears to have virtually died out by the Second World War. A version is still played in Belgium, where it is known as *beugelen*.

Sources and Reading:
Taylor, A., *The Guinness Book of Traditional Pub Games* (London: Guinness, 1992).

Tony Collins

Trotting

Trotting matches were held during the nineteenth century and were particularly popular with farmers and tradesmen. They often took place in conjunction with horseraces and athletic sports, and trotting contests for wagers were also known. In 1829, a trotting match for 100 sovereigns between Mr Bonner's Glamorgan pony and Mr Perry's Flintshire pony was reported in the *Monmouthshire Merlin*, with the animals trotting in harness over a course of 10 miles before large crowds of spectators. Several trotting events against the clock were recorded, such as the attempts by Mr Platt of Bangor in Gwynedd in 1833 to trot 1 mile in 3 minutes and by Mr Bagnell of Llanfoist in Gwent in 1838 to trot 2 miles in 8 minutes; both of which were unsuccessful.

Sources and Reading:
Monmouthshire Beacon (29 September 1838).
Monmouthshire Merlin (27 June 1829).
North Wales Chronicle (15 January 1833).

Emma Lile

Trunket

A game similar to cricket but using a short stick as a bat and two holes in the ground instead of wickets. The batsman is out if the ball is caught on the full or if the ball is thrown or placed in the hole while the batsman is running.

Sources and Reading:
Gomme, A. B., *The Traditional Games of England, Scotland and Ireland* (London: Thames and Hudson facsimile edition, 1984).

See also Cricket

Tony Collins

Tug of War

Despite seemingly being an archetypal English village pastime, few written records of tug of war exist. Clearly it is related to many activities of the pre-industrial era, especially those of a military or naval nature, but it appears that it survived more as an informal activity than as a formal sporting contest.

One of the few examples of a traditional tug of war contest can be seen in the game played at Ludlow in Shropshire on Shrove Tuesday. In this version, each end of the rope has the colours of the pulling team attached and the goal is to dip the end of the rope, the 'knob', in the stream. Legend has it that the rope-pull has its origins in Henry VI's siege of the town, when a struggle broke out between supporters of the king and those supporting the Duke of York.

However, this may well be a more modern development of an older tradition in

Ludlow. Writing in 1826, a correspondent to William Hone's *The Every-Day Book*, described the event:

> On Shrove Tuesday, the corporation provide a rope three inches in thickness, and in length thirty six yards, which is given out by a few of the members at one of the windows of the Market Hall at four o'clock, when a large body of inhabitants, divided into two parties (the one contending for Castle Street and Broad Street wards, and the other for Old Street and Corve Street wards), commence an arduous struggle, and as soon as either party gains the victory by pulling the rope beyond the prescribed limits, the pulling ceases.

The first set of rules for the sport was drawn up in 1879 by the New York Athletic Club. It was recognised by the Amateur Athletic Association in 1880, which drew up its own rules in 1887. Between 1900 and 1924 it was an Olympic sport, although in 1908 the British team's win was tarnished by accusations that they had used illegal spikes on their shoes.

Tug of war declined as an athletic sport in the interwar years and became regarded as a fun event for local fairs and fetes. Despite this, the sport has retained a loyal following. The Tug of War Association was founded in 1958 in England and arranges the sport's annual championships.

Sources and Reading:
Day, B., *A Chronicle of Folk Customs* (London: Hamlyn, 1988).
Hone, W., *The Every-Day Book* (London: Thomas Tegg, 1830).

Tony Collins

Tutt Ball

A version of stoolball or pize ball which was played in the Holderness area to the east of Hull (and also at a girls' school in Shiffnal) in the mid-nineteenth century. All the players except one stood behind a line; the remaining player threw the ball to the other players, who had to try to hit the ball using their hands. As soon as the ball was hit, the hitter had to run to one of three 'tutts' (bases) set up as in rounders. The throwing player had to catch the ball or, failing that, throw it at the hitter while she was running between tutts. If successful, the thrower joined the rest of the players and the out hitter became the thrower.

Sources and Reading:
Cooper, Q. and Sullivan, P., *Maypoles, Martyrs and Mayhem* (London, Bloomsbury: 1994).
Gomme, A. B., *The Traditional Games of England, Scotland and Ireland* (London: Thames and Hudson facsimile edition, 1984).

See also Cricket, Pize Ball, Stoolball

Tony Collins

Wales

The Welsh have long stretched their bodies to improve physical fitness, for activities such as running, jumping and throwing are inherent to mankind. As early as the twelfth century, the chronicler Geraldus Cambrensis viewed mountain climbing and loping through forests as means of enhancing one's stamina on the battlefield and described the 'light and active' Welshman who thrived on a military upbringing and devoted himself to 'arms and leisure'. During the medieval period, sports and warfare were intimately connected and athletic proficiency regarded as advantageous, not only for combat, but also to successfully negotiate the nation's difficult terrain. As youths were legally obliged to master the longbow technique, developing efficient weaponry prowess was essential, and intensive training regimes provided ideal preparation for war. Activities such as wrestling, putting the stone and fighting with stone and buckle were practised regularly to provide the strength needed to draw heavy bows and hurl javelins and the endurance required by foot soldiers.

It is difficult to determine when sports came to be enjoyed solely as healthy recreations rather than as adjuncts to war. That there must have been an overlap is reflected by the fifteenth- and sixteenth-century praise poetry, in which patrons were extolled, not only for their fighting ability, but also as athletic champions who were masters of the 24 ancient Celtic feats. First mentioned in writing around the sixteenth century, these included 12 sporting elements, however uncertainty still prevails as to whether they were intended as military training, or as sports contests pure and simple. While the use of bows, arrows and swords in some of the feats implies a distinct military connection, at times of widespread peace they would have been performed entirely for leisure. The combination of mental and physical challenges offered by the feats, such as swimming, horse riding, tuning the harp and writing poetry, contributed to a state of general health and fitness, and a command of the 'twenty-four' was considered an achievement of great renown.

When the possibility of war diminished with the subjugation of Wales by Edward I in 1282, the nation grudgingly accepted English dominance and control and, apart from occasional unrest (notably the revolt of Owain Glyndŵr during the early fifteenth century), settled into a relatively peaceful period. For the masses, pre-industrial daily life revolved around the calendar, with work dictated by the changing seasons. The drudgery of physical labour was only accorded temporary respite by the annual feast days, which were spent drinking, feasting and participating in an array of traditional customs and recreations. Of pagan origins, these latter activities were later adopted by the Church and used to commemorate significant occasions in the Christian year, such as Christmas, Easter and Whitsun. Sports and games were significant elements of the seasonal festivals and were enjoyed by men and women, young and old. Parish celebrations focused on the church, not only for religious reasons, but also as a convenient venue for the various games played.

The church was an important social centre, especially following the service on a Sunday. The sports, along with other secular activities, such as dancing and dramatic items, took place on the north side of the churchyard, as this was an area of unconsecrated ground, and stone seats were often found there to accommodate spectators. Many a gravestone was broken owing to the revelry of recreational pursuits, and wooden shutters were invariably placed on the windows to protect the glass from any ball games. Fives, a game similar to the modern squash but using hands in place of rackets, was particularly popular in the churchyards, with the buttressed north walls and occasionally the towers acting as ideal playing courts. Arrow-mark grooves in many church walls signified the prevalence of archery, while churchyard cockfighting sites drew crowds from near and far to witness the great mains. Until the discouragement of sporting activities with the religious revivals, priests – who were known to participate, act as referees, and announce forthcoming events from the pulpit – often encouraged them.

One of the most popular festivals in the Welsh rural calendar was the *gwylmabsant*, or commemoration of the local parish saint. Rooted in religion, this annual celebration developed from a dedication through prayer to a programme of recreational pastimes, and some of the earliest references to athletic sports played purely for pleasure are those alluding to *gwylmabsant* games. By the eighteenth and nineteenth centuries, *gwylmabsant* festivals were widespread, and people travelled from afar to attend the proceedings. According to author Benjamin Malkin, writing in 1803, the Radnorshire parish revels 'rendered a kind of circus for every sport and exercise', while a Vale of Clwyd parson, mentioned by the author Elias Owen in 1886, claimed that wakes 'gave an individuality to parochial life and fostered parish patriotism'.

Among the games regularly contested were a selection of athletic sports, ranging from the straightforward running races to old women's grinning matches and blindfold wheelbarrow-driving. Typical of rural sports were those of Llangyfelach near Swansea in 1780, which continued for three days; they featured a women's race for a smock and petticoat, flinging the bar for a silver plated mug, eating a hot hasty pudding for a silver tablespoon, and a bull bait, with a bull calf going to the owner of the best baiting dog. Animal sports were a familiar scene – particularly cockfights, on which large amounts of money were wagered. Birds were specially trained for the contest, and the owner of a victorious cockerel earned high regard in the vicinity.

The popular team sport of football instilled a sense of community worth as well as interparish rivalry and matches were often played over Christmas, New Year and at Shrovetide. Owing to a lack of predetermined rules, games tended to degenerate into chaos, and, with football offering an irresistible combination of sport and brutality, matches usually attracted large crowds of spectators. *Cnapan*, a precursor of football and rugby unique to Wales, was also rather violent. Described in detail in George Owen's *Description of Penbrokshire* in 1603, the game involved the carrying of a ball as far as possible by one team into the opponents' district. Fighting was commonplace and players were frequently injured. Another renowned Welsh team sport, which continued in some areas until the late nineteenth century, was bando. Particularly popular in Glamorgan, bando was similar to the modern game of hockey, and teams used clubs to attempt to score by driving a ball into a goal. Bando contained elements that were constant lubricants of sport across the centuries, and which foresaw the coming of organised sports. These included an agreed number of players, a fixed area of play, teams differentiated by colours (such as the red and white favoured by the Margam side in west Glamorgan), gambling on the result, crowds of spectators and matches well-patronised by brewers.

Owing to the combination of betting, feasting and consumption of alcoholic drink, it was not surprising that parish festivals built up a reputation for their rowdiness. Publicans often played a significant role in organising and promoting sports events, and many cockfights, running races and the like were arranged over the bar. Sports events were considered useful methods of increasing trade, as thirsty athletes and spectators poured in to spend their money or to place a wager. The games contested were invariably rather high-spirited affairs, and, as there were no written rules, these would be decided informally before the start of a match. As many sports were localised activities, rules usually differed from place to place, leading to disagreements when one parish competed against another.

From the eighteenth century onwards, religious leaders and others increasingly voiced concern regarding the unlicensed revelry and alcoholic overindulgence commonly occurring at the festivals, as well as the doubtful benefits of the games themselves. The Methodist and other religious revivals which swept across Wales from the mid-eighteenth century until the turn of the twentieth century attacked sporting activities indiscriminately as worthless and sinful. Such condemnation followed on from the Puritan movement in England in the seventeenth century, when cruel animal sports such as bull baiting and cockfighting were severely censured. Physical recreation was viewed by some as a great threat to the morals of the population, with eminent religious figures such as Thomas Charles and Griffith Jones seeking to suppress impious fairs and festivals, the former depicting Wales in 1799 as 'sunk in superstition and vice'. Consequently, parishioners turned increasingly to churches and chapels for release and salvation, and as prayer meetings were sometimes purposely arranged to clash with sports days, religion became a potent force in the latter's eventual decline.

While the lower orders eagerly anticipated the seasonal festivals, the gentry of pre-industrial Wales followed their own sporting programme. Sport was a passion for the moneyed classes and many viewed their own exclusive activities as visual confirmation of the vast difference between themselves and the supposedly 'inferior' classes beneath them. The prevailing chasm between the classes was largely due to the presence of the game laws, which restricted field sports to a tiny minority and legally entitled country gentlemen to shoot or hunt game to their hearts' content, away from the lower orders. Having first emerged in Wales during the fifteenth century, the gentry, along with a lesser number of aristocracy, controlled Welsh society until roughly the 1870s. As wealth lay in the ownership of land, the gentry, with their large estates (which were transferred down the male line), were the main employers. Rents supplemented their income and, with no business or employment demands, they enjoyed a lavish lifestyle, receiving a privileged education and enjoying an endless round of country sports. Financial assets determined one's leisure pursuits, and those enjoyed by the gentry, such as archery, shooting and hunting, openly displayed wealth and opulence, be it in the clothes worn or the money spent on improving the breeding of horses and hounds. Both men and women participated, and the latter, although usually admired for their appearance rather than athletic competence, frequently graced events with their presence. A female's sports experience differed markedly according to her social background, and while the lower-class woman both worked and, when given the opportunity, played hard, the gentry woman led a largely sedentary existence, providing virtually no contribution toward the running of society. For the charming and delicate upper-class female, only certain sports were deemed suitable; archery, for example, with its poise and deportment and absence of hurried, sudden movements.

Horseracing was enjoyed by both men and women and, since medieval times, swift horses were regarded as prize possessions and essential for cavalrymen who wished to escape the enemy during battle. While it may be assumed that horseracing for amusement's sake took place at this time, the sport became more organised during the Tudor period and was a favourite with royalty and the local gentry. The number of flat-racing courses in Wales increased significantly from the late eighteenth century onwards, and, by the early nineteenth century, competitions were enjoyed throughout the country. Horseracing's fortunes depended primarily on whether sufficient gentry subscriptions were raised by the organisers, for it was extremely costly to maintain courses, provide prize money and see to a programme of social entertainments. Wealthy members of society regarded it as their duty to exercise patronage at race fixtures, for it was essential for them to appear generous and supportive of local events.

Despite the socially exclusive nature of many of their activities, the gentry did not, initially at least, ignore folk sports. Until the mid-nineteenth century they regularly attended parish events, and mixed with the lower classes to enjoy such pursuits as fistfighting and cockfighting, often gambling heavily on their outcome, as well as acting as patrons and donating prizes. A general abandonment of popular culture by the upper classes from around the 1860s onwards (a trend which had already been taking place across continental Europe), along with the development of organised sports during the mid- to late nineteenth century, meant that gentry interest in traditional pursuits dwindled and gradually disappeared. Whereas once they had accepted the activities despite their often brutal nature, now they adopted a new morality and respectability, and became more selective in their rural pursuits.

With the onset of industrialisation and the extensive urban growth during the early nineteenth century, by the 1840s Wales had plunged into an agricultural depression. As the century progressed, society was transformed by developments in the production of coal, iron and copper and the subsequent restructuring of work patterns. An increased preoccupation with organisation also manifested itself in games and customs, which, like the working day itself, lost their spontaneity and adopted new sets of predetermined rules and strict regimentation. Modern versions of old games were created to suit the social climate, and although boisterous seasonal customs did not vanish completely, their former informality was no longer acceptable in an environment dominated by order.

For a time, folk sports coexisted with organised games. Some activities, such as professional pedestrianism, a forerunner of modern athletics, straddled old and new as it adopted new rules and regulations yet maintained elements of the rougher calendar customs, such as match fixing, riots among spectators and a preponderance of betting. The competing athletes continued a tradition of impressive running performances, most notably those of the legendary Griffith Morgan, better known as Guto Nyth Brân, who, during the eighteenth century, beat several English champions and even recorded a victory over a horse. His feats rivalled those undertaken in pedestrianism, which peaked in Wales during the mid-nineteenth century, and included running and walking events of varying types and distances. From 100-yard sprints to 1,000-mile walks, pedestrian events, which were open to all classes, were either held within the new towns, or equally well on the countryside's turnpike roads and fields.

Other modern sports grew out of the old folk versions. The game of cricket may well have evolved in south Wales from folk games that used some kind of bat or stick, such as bando. During the eighteenth century these would have been played in churchyards or on common land and were rather spontaneous in nature. Gradually, more formalised versions would have emerged. The first written reference to cricket in Wales is in a manuscript of 1783, which records a game near Carmarthen. This involved members of the local elite, and it was the gentry who standardised what had commenced as a folk sport. A set of rules was essential, not only for local matches but also for games against teams from England, and by the mid-nineteenth century many cricket clubs had been founded in the industrial south. The construction of railways on a national scale in the 1840s and 1850s made it easier for clubs to play each other regularly. Although cricket was initially exclusively a sport for the wealthy, as a subscription rate was attached to each club, with the growth of workingmen's teams during the 1870s and 1880s it spread downwards and began to be played in most towns and villages.

The restructuring of society during the second half of the nineteenth century was reflected in sport by the formation of governing bodies. Organisations such as the Football Association of Wales (1876) and the Welsh Rugby Union (1881) were formed to standardise games and to ensure consistency throughout the country. The most important factor behind the spread of organised sports was the coming of the railways, enabling faster and cheaper travel across the country. While the new games were created by the middle classes, they soon filtered down to the lower orders, who began to regularly journey by train to support their team.

Well into the nineteenth century, religious leaders continued to warn society of the supposed evils of games, and their perceived detrimental effects were the subject of many lectures and discussions. Consequently, pressure from the churches and chapels, along with the onset of industrialisation and the development of modern sports, contributed greatly to the eventual disappearance of rural festivities. Contemporary literature highlights the decline of seasonal celebrations during the 1870s and, although in some cases *gwylmabsantau* continued to be held in parallel with formalised athletic events, the march of industrialisation and urbanisation generally transformed agricultural areas. The folk game of bando ended in Margam around the 1870s when two industrial plants were opened in the area and Aberafon Rugby Football Club formed. Following the passing of the County Councils Act in 1888, the increased powers granted to local government led to further standardisation of recreational forms; time-honoured ways of rural life became casualties of social and legislative change. As the population in the industrialised areas steadily rose, so a large section deserted the countryside and all the customs and recreations associated with it.

Sources and Reading:
Hignell, A., *A 'Favourit' Game: Cricket in South Wales before 1914* (Cardiff: University of Wales Press, 1992).

Lile, E., *Athletic Competition in Pre-Industrial Wales*, M.Phil. dissertation, University of Birmingham, 1994.

Moore-Colyer, R. G., 'Gentlemen, Horses and the Turf in Nineteenth-Century Wales', *Welsh History Review*, 16: 1 (1992), 47–62.

Suggett, R., 'Festivals and Social Structure in Early Modern Wales', *Past and Present*, 152 (1996), 79–112.

Waddington, H. M., 'Games and Athletics in Bygone Wales', *Transactions of the Honourable Society of Cymmrodorion* (1953), 84–100.

Williams, G., *1905 and All That: Essays on Rugby Football, Sport and Welsh Society* (Llandysul: Gomer, 1991).

Emma Lile

Wallops

A form of skittles played in north-west Yorkshire in which a 4-feet-long wooden 'walloping stick' is thrown at nine skittles arranged in a square.

Sources and Reading:
The Encyclopaedia of Sport (London: The Sportsman, 1912).

See also Skittles

Tony Collins

Walton, Izaak

Izaak Walton (1583–1683), author of the famous classic treatise on angling, *The Compleat Angler*, was born at Stafford in August 1593. He worked in London as an ironmonger and become a friend of Dr John Donne, vicar of St Dunstan's. In December 1526 he married Rachel Floud, a great-great-niece of Archbishop Cranmer. Following her death in 1640, he married Anne Ken, the pastoral 'Kenna' of the angler's wish. After the Royalist defeat at Marston Moor, he retired from business in the 1650s and compiled a treatise that would earn him immortality.

The Compleat Angler, or, the Contemplative Man's Recreation – Being a Discourse of Rivers Fishponds and Fishing not Unworthy of the Perusal of Most Anglers was published in 1653. It was a combination of manual and meditations, focusing on the story of a fisherman Piscator, who is Walton, conversing with a huntsman, Viator. They travel along the River Lea on the first day of May, conversing about the merits of their different activities. The text is interspersed with songs and ballads and quotations from other writers, and gives an insight into the pleasures of fishing in the near idyllic countryside alongside the English rivers of the seventeenth century.

It proved so popular that a second edition, largely rewritten, was published two years later. In order to counter the objection that Piscator had dominated the discourse, Walton also introduced the falconer Auceps and changed Viator to Vetator. This was followed with a third edition in 1661, a fourth in 1668, and a fifth in 1676. By this time, the original 13 chapters had expanded to 21, and a lengthy section on fly-fishing on the River Dove, a subject which the author knew little about, was added.

The *Compleat Angler* is the most famous book ever written on angling and has been through more than 300 editions since it was first published. The most popular old copy of the work is John Major's second edition, published in 1824. Walton's biography is prefixed to an edition of his text compiled by Sir Harris Nicholas in 1836.

Walton was also a writer of some reputation on other topics, having compiled a biography of Sir Henry Wotton in 1649. His poems and extracts of prose were collected in 1878 under the title of *Waltoniana*. Walton died at his daughter's house in Winchester and was buried at the cathedral. He left his property in Stafford to the poor of his native town.

Sources and Reading:
Major, J. (ed.), *The Compleat Angler* (Second edition) (London: 1824).

Martin, S., *Izaak Walton and his Friends* (London: Chapman and Hall, 1903).

Walton, I. and Cotton, C., *The Complete Angler*, (London: Wordsworth Classics, 1996).

John Martin

Wedding Games (Wales)

Traditional wedding celebrations in Wales often included numerous games and sports, along with singing, dancing and general feasting. One of the most popular activities was the horse or foot race, which began immediately following the matrimonial ceremony. Competitors raced from the church door to the bride's house, not only to be first to the wedding feast, but also to win the wedding cake. The prevalence of such races on horseback led to claims that these events constituted the forerunners of the steeplechase.

It was customary at many a wedding for the groom and his fellow horse riders to negotiate the quintain: a tall post on top of which was a freely rotating crossbar with a sandbag attached to one end and a wide board to the other. While less-talented riders were dismounted by the swinging sandbag, much to the amusement of spectators, skilled horsemen hit the flat board with their spears and felt only the wind of the sandbag in their hair as they continued on their journey. Those who stayed seated proceeded to the bride's house and on arrival played music and recited poetry in the hope of being let in.

Sources and Reading:

Owen, T. M., *The Customs and Traditions of Wales* (Cardiff, University of Wales Press, 1991).

Pritchard, W., 'Anglesey Folklore', *Anglesey Antiquarian Society and Field Club Transactions* (1914), 35–70.

'S. E.', 'Arferion Priodasol y Cymry', *Y Frythones*, 13 (1891), 204–7.

Emma Lile

Welsh Feats (Ancient)

'Y pedwar camp ar hugain' (the 24 feats) comprised a set of mental and physical challenges designed to enhance one's character and produce a fully rounded individual. While the earliest written reference to the feats appears in the Peniarth manuscripts dating from around 1500, uncertainty prevails regarding their exact origin. It is also debatable whether the 12 athletic elements of the feats were devised solely as military training, as physical contests in their own right, or, as is most likely, a combination of both. Warriors certainly participated in such endeavours to improve their overall health and fitness, and would surely have continued doing so purely for pleasure and enjoyment in more peaceful times.

The 24 feats were divided into *gwrolgampau*, *mabolgampau* and *gogampau*, which covered a range of domestic and literary tasks, rural sports (such as fishing and falconry), weaponry exercises (including archery) and rigorous athletic pursuits. These latter activities, which included throwing, horse riding, running, jumping, swimming and wrestling, required considerable strength and stamina, and were extremely highly regarded in society at large. Trials in these six events were regularly contested, as competitors stretched themselves to their physical limits in order to outperform their rivals and claim the undisputed title 'champion of the feats'.

Several fifteenth- and sixteenth-century Welsh poems mention the 24 feats, and as recently as the nineteenth century the poet and antiquary Iolo Morganwg recognised their importance in releasing the qualities of alertness, power and understanding necessary for a full life. Only equal training in both mind and body could produce complete human beings, who were attentive, observant and prepared for any eventuality.

Sources and Reading:
Jones, E., 'Campau Amdrechol y Cymry', *Taliesin*, 8: 2 (1861), 225–32.
Lile, E., *Athletic Competition in Pre-Industrial Wales*, M.Phil., University of Birmingham, 1994.

Emma Lile

Whippet Racing

Common in the early part of the twentieth century in the industrial regions of the north of England and Scotland, whippet racing developed in response to the decline of rabbit coursing in the late Victorian period. The whippet itself is a cross between a greyhound and a terrier, which presumably explains its combination of speed and tenaciousness.

Quite accurately, if somewhat patronisingly, *The Encyclopaedia of Sport* summed up its appeal in 1912: 'it gives the average working man the opportunity of backing his fancy in the betting rings, which are as inseparable adjuncts of dog racing grounds as they are of racecourses'.

Whippet races were traditionally held on straight courses 200 yards long. Each whippet races towards a rag held by their owner or other member of their team, known as the 'runner up'. There are no starting traps; the dogs are held by a 'slipper' until the starting pistol is fired, upon which they release the dog.

Like many other sports, especially quoits, whippet racing was especially popular among miners and reached its heyday in the interwar years.

Sources and Reading:
The Encyclopaedia of Sport (London: The Sportsman, 1912).
Martin, L., 'Sport in Cumbria, c. 1870–1939', *British Society of Sports History Bulletin*, 9 (1989), 51–62.

See also Coursing

Tony Collins

Wildfowling

Wildfowling is a specialist branch of shooting that traditionally involved the pursuit of wild ducks and geese on marshes and foreshores. The birds were shot on their flight lines at dawn and dusk, or on their feeding grounds by using decoys to attract them. Unlike the other forms of shooting, its success depends as much on the wildfowler's understanding of the habits and habitat of their quarry as on their marksmanship. It is a physically demanding sport, and requires significant skill at identifying the quarry and an appreciation of the importance of tides and weather conditions. The success rate in securing quarry is very uncertain, hence the term 'wild goose chase'. The increase in the artificial rearing and stocking of inland waters with ducks since the 1970s has led to an expansion of the sport.

Puntgunning was a traditional form of wildfowling; sportsmen crept up on the birds by lying in a flat-bottomed, shallow, canoe-type boat before shooting at them with specially designed large-bore muzzle-loading guns.

Before the Second World War, wildfowling provided a precarious way of earning a living for a select band of professional shooters willing to brave the crawling tides of winter dawns and moonlit nights. The decline in the number of wildfowl and the prohibition of the sale of dead wild geese in the 1960s undermined wildfowling as a commercial activity and led to it becoming the preserve of enthusiastic amateurs.

Whilst not technically classified as game, ducks and geese are also protected during close seasons and by legislation which proscribes the killing of certain species. Government also has the power to impose a ban on the shooting of all types of wildfowl during periods of exceptionally bad weather. Most participants in the sport belong to wildfowling clubs affiliated to the British Association for Shooting and Conservation, which deals with this branch of shooting.

Sources and Reading:
Begbie, E., *Modern Wildfowling* (Shrewsbury: Swan Hill Press, 1990).
Humphreys, J. and Bown, D., *Shooting Skills: Rough and Wild Shooting* (London: Cassell, 1995).
Wilcock, C., *The ABC of Shooting* (London: Deutsch, 1975).

Websites:
www.wildfowling.co.uk
www.wildfowling.com
www.irishfieldsports.com/fowling

Nicholas Goddard
and John Martin

Women

Women's involvement in sport in pre-industrial times was shaped by the subordinate role they occupied in society. Viewed as inferior to men, both legally and physically, they were generally denied the access to recreation and sporting activities that men took for granted. The fact that many sports were adjuncts to military training, from which women were excluded, further reduced the opportunities for them to participate in sport.

Probably the most noted involvement of upper-class and aristocratic women in sport in medieval times was their attendance at tournaments, where their presence was essential as part of the courtly and chivalrous ritual of the event. By the sixteenth century there is some evidence that women took part in hunting; Elizabeth I certainly participated in the sport, and also in horse riding and falconry.

For working-class women, the double burden of child-rearing and agricultural labour reduced any leisure time to a minimum. Nevertheless, it appears that their participation in the work of their communities also provided opportunities for them to take part in some of the sports that were parts of the festivals and holidays of the rural year.

Even as early as the fourteenth century, some games were identified as being particularly popular with women. Pat ball, a game which involved two people hitting a hollow ball between each other, was identified as being a game played widely by girls and young women. In the same century, games like prisoner's bars were also popular with women and featured the beginning of mixed participation. Women were regular swimmers too, even in medieval times. As early as 1244 a woman was recorded as drowning while swimming alone.

Possibly the most common sporting events for women were smock races, in which women would run against each other for a prize, usually, as the name suggest, some form of smock. In some areas the smock race was known as 'running for shifts'. Many May Day or other summer festival sports included smock races, which were sometimes divided into age categories, with the races featuring young women or old women being the most popular.

Although there was undoubtedly an element of ridicule in some events staged for women, many race organisers did take women's participation seriously. Stroke bias running between parish teams in seventeenth-century Kent included women as legitimate contestants. The popularity of athletic running for women grew in the eighteenth century and events for women were often staged side-by-side with those for men. For example, in 1739 Marlborough staged two one-mile races, one each for men and women, the entrance fee was two shillings and sixpence for male runners but only a shilling for female athletes.

Women of the working classes were also involved in many of the boisterous and occasionally riotous pastimes of working-class men. For example, a description of bull running in Stamford in the eighteenth century demonstrates that women of all ages were keen participants: 'hivie, shivie, tag and rag, men, women and children of all sorts and sizes, with all the dogs in the town'.

Indeed, the reformers of the early nineteenth century often pointed to the danger to the morals of young women posed by traditional sports. During the late eighteenth century there were even examples of women boxing, although these seem to be commercial enterprises staged by businessmen who expected the novelty of the event to attract large crowds. The fact that many sporting events were accompanied by drinking and licentiousness was highlighted as one more reason, alongside public disorder and business efficiency, why such sports should be curbed.

Women also sometimes participated in games of folk football. A correspondent to *Baily's Magazine* in 1868 quoted an old rhyme to demonstrate that football had also been traditionally popular with some young women:

> Young men and maids,
> Now very brisk,
> At barley-break and
> Football frisk.

There are a number of accounts of women taking part in football games, and Sir Frederick Morton Eden notes in his *Statistical Account of Scotland* that in the 1790s a match between married and unmarried women took place every Shrove Tuesday in Midlothian.

As well as football, women and girls also took part in cricket: the fact that over-arm bowling was reputedly invented by a woman demonstrates that women players were not unheard of. Indeed, there is a long tradition of women playing bat-and-ball games, such as trap ball, in which there was a six-a-side competition for women in Bury St Edmunds every Shrovetide, Easter Monday and Whitsuntide. Perhaps the most notable example is stoolball in Sussex, which in the late nineteenth century appears to have been almost exclusively a female sport.

The sport which has possibly the longest organised association with women is archery. From the mid-eighteenth century, archery became increasingly popular with upper-class women. Women were first admitted to the Royal British Bowmen archery club in 1787 and by the early nineteenth century there were a number of women's archery competitions in Britain; for example, in 1825 the women's contest at the Derbyshire Bow Meeting at Keddleston was won by a Miss Bent, who received a gold medal for her victory. Joint archery meetings at which both men and women competed were common in the 1820s. Writing in the 1830s, Pierce Egan noted that archery 'has been the favourite recreation of a great part of the female nobility, the only field diversion they can enjoy without incurring the censure of being thought masculine'.

The fear of masculinity becoming entwined with femininity, to the detriment of the latter, was to haunt sport throughout the nineteenth and much of the twentieth centuries. It provided the rationale for Muscular Christians and other leaders of sporting bodies to prevent or restrict the participation of women in many sports. Indeed, it is interesting to note that revived and invented 'traditional sports', such as pancake racing and the Stroud rolling pin throwing contest, reasserted stereotypical roles for women, most commonly those derived from the kitchen, which sports such as smock racing and bull running did not necessarily portray.

Sources and Reading:

Egan, P., *Book of Sports* (London: Thomas Tegg, 1832).

Guttmann, A., *Women's Sports: A History* (New York: Columbia University Press, 1991).

Hargreaves, J., *Sporting Females* (London: Routledge, 1994).

Hone, W., *The Every-Day Book* (London: Thomas Tegg, 1830).

Malcolmson, R., *Popular Recreations in English Society 1700–1850* (Cambridge: Cambridge University Press, 1973).

Parratt, C. M., *'More than Mere Amusement': Working-Class Women's Leisure in England, 1750–1914* (Boston: Northeastern University Press, 2001).

Tony Collins

Wrestling

Without doubt one of the oldest of the world's sports, organised wrestling has been in existence in varying forms at least since the beginnings of early Egyptian civilisation. It also took place in ancient Assyrian, Babylonian and Chinese societies, although it is probably most associated with Greece, having been introduced in 704 BC to the ancient Greek Olympics. Two Roman emperors, Commodus and Maximiam, were renowned for their wrestling abilities.

Although professional and elite wrestling competitions appear to have died out with the decline of the Roman Empire, the sport continued to be enjoyed throughout the Middle Ages and grew in popularity in Britain during that time. From the thirteenth century, annual wrestling competitions were held outside the walls of London on the festival of James the Apostle, 25 July, for the prize of a ram. The intensity of feeling for the sport ran so high that a dispute over the result of a match in 1222 led to riots in the city. The fourteenth century saw regular competitions between officials of the City of London and those from outlying areas, such as Westminster. Clerkenwell was a popular location for major wrestling contests. Wrestling's appeal also began to extend to the upper classes of society: legend has it that England's Henry VIII fought France's Henry I on the Field of Cloth of Gold.

However, wrestling was not without opponents. Many sections of the Church disapproved of wrestling, for reasons of both public order and morality. In 1197, 100 spectators and participants were whipped for staging and watching wrestling in St Albans Abbey churchyard. The Synod of Ely forbade clergy from participating in wrestling in 1364. In the mid-fourteenth century, the Archbishop of York banned wrestling and the Dominican preacher John Bromyard attacked it for being a 'foul and unthrifty occupation'.

Nevertheless, this appears to have done little to reduce wrestling's popularity, and by the seventeenth century it had become one of the most popular spectator sports, fuelled in part by the growing commercial opportunities offered by sporting contests. The diarist John Evelyn recorded a February 1667 visit to a wrestling match in St James's Park, which was attended by the king and various other nobles, between wrestlers from the south-west and the north for a stake of £1,000. As can be imagined, betting was an important factor in the popularity of wrestling matches, even outside of urban areas: 'many Hundred Pounds' were won and lost in wagers at a wrestling match at Botley in Berkshire in 1737 which, it was claimed, attracted a crowd of over 10,000.

By the eighteenth century, the sport in Britain had developed distinct regional styles, most notably the Cornish, Cumberland, Devonshire and Lancashire variants. There was also a Norfolk version, Charles Layton's guide to its rules being published in the 1830s. Wrestling appears to have been popular throughout England and few local fairs were complete without a wrestling contest. In London, wrestling's heyday was in the 1820s and 1830s. Many tournaments were organised on pub bowling greens and on cricket grounds, with silver cups and stakes of up to £40 to be won by the wrestlers. Like prizefighting of the time, the organisation of wrestling was centred on pubs, the most important for wrestling being Tom Rouse's Eagle Tavern on the City Road.

Much of wrestling's support was based on exiles from the south-west and north-west of England who were keen to continue practising or watching the sports of their county of origin. For example, in 1829 200 men from the north-west entered a Cumberland wrestling tournament to win a silver cup worth £20 at the Eyre Tavern in St John's Wood. London was not alone in attracting large crowds for wrestling. In 1826 an estimated 30,000 people saw the Cornish champion Polkinghorne defeat the Devonian champion Cann at Devonport.

As with prizefighting, supporters of wrestling were keen to link its popularity with the sense of national triumphalism felt following the defeat of Napoleon. Writing in 1832, Pierce Egan argued that:

> . . . within it [wrestling] we view all the remains of that chivalric spirit, which has distinguished the most celebrated conquerors in all ages . . . it is to that generous spirit of emulation which animates the wrestler to acquire celebrity in the ring, that we are indebted for the glorious victories of Agincourt, Trafalgar, Waterloo, etc.

Nevertheless, by the 1840s wrestling was in decline, not just in London but also in Devon, where the local form of the sport, which was notorious for the emphasis placed on kicking an opponent, began to die out and be replaced by its Cornish rival. As well as in Cornwall, the sport retained its strength in the north-west under Cumberland and Lancashire rules.

As with almost every sport, wrestling benefited from the growth in leisure time and rise in living standards from the 1870s. Wrestling matches were staged in music halls, by local publicans and as sporting events in themselves. Glamour was added to the sport by frequent tours by American wrestlers, such as Tom Jenkins and Frank Gotch, the sport having risen to great heights of popularity in the United States.

The commercialism and mass popularity of the sport caused great concern to those sections of the middle classes who took an interest in wrestling, and who feared for what they saw as its noble Greek traditions. The inclusion of wrestling in the first modern Olympic Games in 1896 gave a new impetus to amateur wrestling. This was strengthened in 1921 with the formation, inspired by the success of wrestling at the Olympics, of the international amateur wrestling federation, the Fédération Internationale des Luttes Amateurs.

Alongside this strengthening of the amateur sport, professional wrestling continued to grow in the interwar years, and it was given further impetus from the 1950s when the new ITV television channel began broadcasting it regularly on Saturday afternoons. Caught between amateurism, an increasingly pantomime-like professional game and the popularity of martial arts such as judo and karate, the traditional forms of wrestling fell into a steady, although not terminal, decline.

Sources and Reading:

Brailsford, D., *British Sport: A Social History* (Cambridge: Lutterworth Press, 1992).

Egan, P., *Book of Sports* (London: Thomas Tegg, 1832).

The Encyclopaedia of Sport (London: The Sportsman, 1912).

Kent, G., *A Pictorial History of Wrestling* (London: Spring, 1968).

Litt, W., *Wrestliana* (Whitehaven, 1823).

Malcolmson, R., *Popular Recreations in English Society 1700–1850* (Cambridge: Cambridge University Press, 1973).

Reeves, C., *Pleasures and Pastimes in Medieval England* (Stroud: Sutton, 1995).

See also Cwdwm Braich, Cwdwm Cefn, Grasmere Sports, Morpeth Olympic Games, Wrestling (Cornish), Wrestling (Cumberland), Wrestling (Devonshire), Wrestling (Lancashire)

Tony Collins

Wrestling (Cornwall)

Cornish wrestling is a sport unique to Cornwall. Although a similar form is found in Brittany, it was most likely introduced by people from Cornwall during the Celtic period, between the fourth and seventh centuries AD. There was also a variant in Devon, which died out at the end of the nineteenth century. The most distinctive features are the absence of grappling on the ground, as with other styles, and the use of a short, loose, coarse canvas jacket on which all grips are taken.

Victory is achieved when one wrestler 'backs' his opponent. To gain a 'back' a wrestler must throw his opponent onto his back so that at least three of four 'pins' (shoulders or hips) simultaneously touch the ground. If no back occurs in the allotted time, the bout is decided on points, according to the number of pins that touch the ground, or in favour of the wrestler who shows the most 'play'. Three 'sticklers' – so called as each carries a ceremonial stick, which is placed under a 'backed' wrestler to adjudge the number of pins down – control the contests. They also ensure fair play, decide which throws merit points, and when a foul is committed.

The origins of the sport are uncertain, although there is compelling evidence to suggest that the Irish introduced it into Cornwall with the early Christian missions. The first mention of wrestling in the British Isles is in the *Book of Leinster*, which records that it formed part of the Tailtean Games in County Meath, dating back to 2000 BC. What is certain is that by the beginning of the eighteenth century the sport was a widespread 'traditional' activity, deeply rooted in the local culture, and there is sufficient evidence to demonstrate that it was Cornwall's most popular sport.

Cornish wrestling reached its height of popularity during the early decades of the nineteenth century, when numerous tournaments, offering very lucrative prizes and attracting large numbers of wrestlers and thousands of spectators, were organised during the summer months throughout the county, especially at the many fairs, holidays and feast days. It was particularly associated with copper and tin miners, who were attracted by the large money prizes offered by the organising committees (which were often initiated by local publicans).

The sport's popularity also spread to London, where entrepreneurial landlords of such establishments as the Eyre Tavern in St John's Wood and the Brecknock Arms in Camden Town regularly offered large money prizes for wrestling in the Cornish style. These contests, which were common between the mid-1820s and the 1850s, often attracted wrestlers from Cornwall and Devon, who used the occasions to maintain an age-old rivalry. For this brief period, the names of the best wrestlers also became known nationally as the bouts were advertised and reported in *Bell's Life in London*.

Cornish wrestling suffered a decline in popularity, both in terms of participants and spectators, during the latter decades of the nineteenth century, and by the beginning of the twentieth century had almost completely died out. This was largely due to the economic decline of the Cornish mining industry, which led large numbers of Cornwall's economically active young men to migrate, mainly to mining settlements as far afield as Australia, the United States and South Africa. Cornish wrestling tournaments were soon introduced to these areas, and were still active well into the twentieth century. Other factors leading to the decline of Cornish wrestling were the growth of 'faggotting' (the agreement between wrestlers to fix results and share the prize money), the growth of counter-attractions such as cricket and rugby, and a general shift of attitudes away from traditional activities (largely led by the Methodists, who had come to be a dominant force in Cornwall).

During the 1920s Cornish wrestling underwent something of a revival, with the establishment of the Cornish Wrestling Association in 1923 and the introduction in 1928 of regular tournaments between teams of wrestlers from Cornwall and Brittany. This formed part of a more general 'Celtic revival', led by the same middle-class scholars also involved in music, literature, the Cornish language and the creation of the Cornish *Gorseth*. However, these efforts were not able to reverse an almost terminal decline into obscurity.

Although today there are only a handful of wrestlers, competing in a small number of tournaments, watched by a dwindling set of supporters, Cornish wrestling is unlikely to die out completely, largely because it has such strong ties to a very distinct and separate cultural identity.

Sources and Reading:
Johns, C., *Cheer Like Mad for Cornwall: The Story of Cornish Wrestling* (St Austell: Johns, 1995).
Kendall, B., *The Art of Cornish Wrestling* (Launceston: Federation of Old Cornwall Societies, 1990).
Kent, G., *A Pictorial History of Wrestling* (London: Spring Books, 1968).
Tripp, M., *The Socio-Genesis of Cornish Wrestling*, M.Sc. dissertation, Leicester University, 1996.

See also Wrestling, Wrestling (Cumberland), Wrestling (Devonshire), Wrestling (Lancashire)

Mike Tripp

Wrestling (Cumberland)

A form of wrestling unique to the Cumberland and Westmorland area of north-west England which, it is claimed, is of Celtic origin. The wrestlers clasp hands behind each other's back, with one arm over the shoulder and one arm below. The chin rests on one of the opponent's shoulders. The object is to throw one's opponent on to the floor. A contest is decided by one fall.

Because of the style of wrestling, matches tended to be fairly static, as each wrestler struggled to increase his grip and maximise the leverage on his opponent. An 1857 contest between Thomas Longmire and Richard Wright lasted around 5 hours, not least because the £100 prize money meant that neither was prepared to take a risk and lose the match. Throughout its history the sport has continually sought to reduce the opportunities for such stalemates through subtle rule changes.

Cumberland wrestlers wear a white or pale pink singlet, with dark trousers over long underpants. Although assumed to be a traditional costume, in reality it was introduced in the mid-Victorian period; previously, wrestlers would simply discard their outer garments for the match.

Cumberland wrestling champions have traditionally been awarded a leather belt. Its most famous champion in the pre-modern era was Thomas Longmire in the 1820s. George Steadman won the heavyweight championship 14 times between 1872 and 1900, having started his wrestling career in 1862, although it was common for men to continue wrestling into their 40s. Douglas Clark, the Huddersfield and Great Britain rugby league forward, was one of the sport's dominant wrestlers in the periods immediately before and after the First World War.

The origins of this style of wrestling appear to date back to the fifteenth century. It was certainly a major spectator sport in the region in the early eighteenth century, and by the early nineteenth century matches and tournaments could attract five-figure crowds. The 1830s saw the sport undergo a period of growth, until it began to fall in popularity from the 1870s. Even so, the sport's historic popularity had also led to an expansion of its appeal. In London it had commanded the attention of exiles and followers of other forms of wrestling since the eighteenth century and Good Friday matches had been organised since at least the 1820s. It also spread to Lancashire and the north-east, where it found great popularity as the central attraction of the annual Morpeth Wrestling and Athletic Games, which were founded in 1873 and lasted until 1958 (latterly being known as the Morpeth Olympic Games).

It underwent another boom at the turn of the twentieth century and by 1910 it had established training 'academies' in 30 towns across the north of England and the Scottish Borders. At the same time, around 400 meetings were held annually, ranging from Blackpool in the south to Bridge of Allan in the north.

Throughout its history, Cumberland wrestling has been a semi-professional sport. Much of its revival in the early nineteenth century seems to be linked to the increase in the value of prize money available. In 1811 a prize of 20 guineas was offered at a match in Carlisle, but by the 1860s over £100 annually was being offered in prize money for tournaments there. Much of this money was offered by members of the local gentry who patronised the sport.

Historically, one of the major concerns of the sport has been to ensure transparency of competition and to stop the fixing of matches, a practice known locally as 'barneying'. In 1859, anyone found guilty of such corruption was barred from all Cumberland wrestling competitions. Even as late as the 1940s, a number of matches were suspected of being fixed, but the decline of the sport from the 1950s, together with the consequent fall in the value of prize money, removed much, if not all, of the incentive for barneying.

The first governing body for the sport was formed in 1809 as the Carlisle and Cumberland Wrestling Association, although its influence was patchy and its authority not universally acknowledged. In the 1870s, in order to give itself wider appeal, it changed its name to the Cumberland and Westmorland Wrestling Association. When it began to incorporate other athletic events into its activities in the 1890s, and in an attempt to broaden its appeal, the name was changed again in 1899 to the Northern Counties Wrestling and Athletic Association. In 1906 it became the Association Governing the Cumberland and Westmorland Style of Wrestling. This signalled the consolidation of the association's authority over all wrestling in the region. In 1910 it could boast that around 400 wrestlers were officially registered with it.

The sport survived throughout the interwar years and, as with many sports, experienced a surge in popularity in the late 1940s. But from the 1950s, Cumberland wrestling began to decline in popularity and in the number of participants. Even in the 1930s it had started to lose its appeal to more nationally-based sports, especially boxing, and it suffered from a general decline in

regional identity spurred by the growing dominance of a national sporting culture through radio, newspapers and army service.

Today, it exists as a popular sport in small pockets of the north-west. To some extent its continued presence in the sporting consciousness is due to its status as a traditional regional sport and to the role that it plays in the heritage industry of the Lake District. Matches still take place at local carnivals and agricultural shows, as well as at the annual Grasmere Sports festival, and are promoted as part of a tourist package to attract visitors to the region. Despite the sport's decline, the respect in which it is still held can be gauged by the fact that the Grasmere Sports continue to this day to attract wrestlers from all over the world.

Sources and Reading:

Day, B., *A Chronicle of Folk Customs* (London: Hamlyn, 1988).

The Encyclopaedia of Sport (London: The Sportsman, 1912).

Huggins, M., 'The Regular Re-invention of Sporting Tradition and Regional Identity: Cumberland and Westmorland Wrestling, c. 1800–2000', *Sports Historian*, 21: 1 (2001), 35–55.

Martin, L., 'Sport in Cumbria, c1870–1939', *British Society of Sports History Bulletin*, 9 (1989), 51–62.

See also Grasmere Sports, Morpeth Olympic Games, Wrestling, Wrestling (Cornish), Wrestling (Devonshire), Wrestling (Lancashire)

Tony Collins

Wrestling (Devonshire)

Devonshire wrestling was a close relative of Cornish wrestling which flourished until the mid-nineteenth century. Its chief defining characteristic was that it allowed kicking below the knee with the heel or toe, known locally as 'showing a toe'. To increase the impact of the kick, the wrestlers would traditionally wear a boot which had been soaked in bullock's blood and hardened through baking.

As in Cornish wrestling, which did not allow any form of kicking, wrestlers wore a loose-fitting linen jacket, which had to be held by the opponent for a fall to be recognised. Only a three-point fall counted as a scoring fall; this occurred when both shoulders and one hip or both hips and a shoulder touched the ground. The difficulty of achieving this meant that contests could last for over an hour, and also that three referees were needed to adjudicate on throws. The referees, as in Cornwall, were known as 'sticklers', which may be the origin of the phrase 'a stickler for the rules', especially given that the rules governing falls were so precise. In contrast to Cornish wrestling, in which prizes tended to be given in kind (for example, in the form of a hat, waistcoat or pair of gloves), cash dominated the Devon scene.

The sport reached it heyday in the 1820s and 1830s, when it became dominated by its most famous practitioner Abraham Cann, the self-proclaimed wrestling Champion of All England. Such was his prowess that in 1826 he was backed against any man in England for £500. His battles with the Cornish champion Polkinghorne, especially that of 1826 when 30,000 people saw the Cornishman defeat him at Devonport, became famous throughout the south of England. A description of a match featuring Cann which took place at the Eagle Tavern in London's City Road can be found in the *London Magazine* of October 1826.

As the Cann v Polkinghorne bout demonstrates, despite their differences over kicking, Cornwall v Devon competitions were common, both between teams and their respective champions, and were held in London from at least the 1810s up until 1848, although by that time the Devonshire shoe was forbidden. These contests were not without controversy, however, as the different styles of the wrestlers often led to crowds disputing the referees' decisions.

By the end of the 1830s, Devonshire wrestling was in decline, partly due to changes to the social conditions that previously allowed it to flourish – for example, it has been especially associated with local rural feasts and holidays – and allegations of match-fixing, but also because it appeared to be needlessly violent, especially when compared with other styles of wrestling. In 1835, Thomas Shapter's *Medical Topography of Exeter* noted that wrestling in Devon differed from other forms 'in as much as the cruelty of kicking the shin is permitted; a custom which is very prolific of obstinate ulcered legs in after years'. Broken legs were also common, and the constant kicking of the shins also meant wrestlers would often retire from a bout before a fall had been recorded, undermining the supposed goal of the contest. By the mid-1850s, matches were being organised which forbade kicking, putting the sport on a course for integration with Cornish wrestling. Certainly by the time that Abraham Cann died in 1864 the sport was virtually dead, and the end of the nineteenth century saw it completely integrated with the style of its neighbour and former rival.

Sources and Reading:

The Encyclopaedia of Sport (London: The Sportsman, 1912).

Hone, W., *The Every-Day Book* (London: Thomas Tegg, 1830).

Porter, J. H., 'Devonshire Wrestling in the Nineteenth Century', *British Society of Sports History Bulletin*, 9 (1989), 19–38.

See also Purring, Wrestling, Wrestling (Cornwall), Wrestling (Lancashire)

Tony Collins

Wrestling (Lancashire)

Also known as 'catch-as-catch-can' wrestling, this form of wrestling is traditional to Lancashire. In the first half of the twentieth century it was popular enough to support both professional and amateur wrestlers; it was most popular in the mining areas, and even today it retains a following in and around the Wigan area.

The object is to gain a requisite number of falls, a fall being defined as when the two shoulders of an opponent are made to touch the floor simultaneously. Other than throttling and limb-breaking holds not being allowed, there is a minimum of restrictions in the rules. Unlike other forms of wrestling, struggling on the ground is allowed.

Of all the versions of wrestling, Lancashire wrestling had the greatest reputation for brutality, although this may have been based as much on prejudice against the men who took part, and their spectators, as on the nature of the sport itself. Indeed, the Lancashire style of wrestling is very similar to the freestyle wrestling seen at the Olympic Games and, shorn of its theatre and dubious sporting value, to modern professional wrestling.

Sources and Reading:
Encyclopedia of Sports, Games and Pastimes (London: Fleetway, 1935).

See also Wrestling, Wrestling (Cornish), Wrestling (Cumberland), Wrestling (Devonshire)

Tony Collins

Wrestling of Breeches (*Codwm Clos*)

This was a form of wrestling in which competitors grabbed each other by the waistband, as opposed to the usual method of by the neck.

Emma Lile

Yachting (Scotland)

Yachting in Scotland effectively began with the founding of the Royal Northern Yacht Club in 1824. The club was initially based both on the Firth of Clyde and on Belfast Lough, but the two components split up in 1826. As the century progressed the number of yachts increased (though on average they became smaller), and the number of clubs also increased. The second important club was the Royal Clyde, established in 1856; it was to amalgamate with the Royal Northern in 1978. Events proliferated. By the 1880s the Clyde had become an international centre for yachting, and the 'Clyde Week' at the beginning of July expanded into the 'Clyde Fortnight'. It combined the highest standard of competitive sport with dinners and balls in the evenings. The yachts were crewed by professional sailors, often fishermen who welcomed good wages plus tips for the summer.

In this competitive environment, the most innovative Scottish designer was George Lennox Watson (1851–1904), son of a Glasgow physician, who was trained on the Clyde. He was one of the first to apply to yachts the mathematical principles of hull design that were being worked out by William Froude (1810–79) for the Royal Navy and by W. J. Macquorn Rankine (1820–72) at Glasgow University. Watson designed four Americas Cup challengers, and perhaps his most successful vessel was *Britannia*, built for the Prince of Wales in 1893. These large yachts had a notable ability to sail in heavy weather. In 1901, two boats designed by Watson, the cutter *Kariad* and the yawl *Sybarita*, raced in mountainous seas from Rothesay to Ailsa Craig and back, a distance of 75 miles; they averaged 12.3 knots, and several steam yachts were unable to keep up with them. During Clyde Fortnight, crowds watched the racing from the shore and from pleasure steamers. When *Britannia* raced the Kaiser's yacht in 1896 there were said to be 100,000 spectators.

Watson was a consulting naval architect, but his rival William Fife II was both a designer and a builder of yachts. Fife produced *Shamrock* and *Shamrock III* for the Glasgow grocer Sir Thomas Lipton, though the closest Lipton came to winning the Americas Cup was in 1901 with *Shamrock II* which had come from Watson's drawing board. Fife was one of a family who ran a boatbuilding yard at Fairlie from about 1800 to 1939: one of their products can be seen in miniature as the weathervane on Fairlie parish church. In 1908, and for the only time, an Olympic event was held in Scotland: 12-metre yachting, which was won by a Clyde-built boat, skippered by her designer, Sir Thomas Glen Coats.

From the beginning of the twentieth century, the number of smaller boats being sailed increased significantly, just as it did in other parts of Europe. The Clyde's long shoreline, the dozens of villages (each with at least one pier), the magnificent scenery, the firth's closeness to Glasgow and its strong maritime tradition, all contributed to making it a major centre for sailing.

For a brief period, the Royal Northern Yacht Club also held steamer races. However, before the start of the 1835 event the boiler of the *Earl Grey* exploded. It was obvious that her safety valves had been screwed down in order to raise extra steam pressure, and so the formal racing of steamers was abandoned. Informal racing, however, remained a central part of Clyde steamer services in the summer, as ships competed for prestige and a berth at the next pier.

Sources and Reading:
Blake, G. and Small, C., *Cruise in Company: History of the Royal Clyde Yacht Club* (Glasgow: Royal Clyde Yacht Club, 1959).
McCallum, M. F., *'Fast and Bonnie': A History of William Fife and Sons Yachtbuilders* (Edinburgh: John Donald, 1998).

John Burnett

Yachting (Wales)

The earliest Welsh yachting club was founded at Beaumaris in 1825 and entitled the Royal Anglesey Yacht Club. There followed numerous other clubs, including the Royal Welsh (Caernarfon, 1848), the Bristol Channel (Mumbles, 1875), the Exchange Club (Wrexham, 1876) and the Penarth Yacht Club (1880). Clubs tended to cater for the middle and upper classes, and membership was restricted by the charging of a significant annual subscription fee. The two Cardiff clubs, the Cardiff and County (1876) and the Cardiff Exchange Club (1866), charged annual subscription fees of six guineas and three guineas respectively, with the former demanding an additional entrance charge of ten guineas. Such strict monetary regulations meant that by 1896 Wales had a combined national yachting club membership of a mere 518.

Sources and Reading:
Breen, A. M. O., *Drinking Clubs in South-East Wales 1881–1921*, M.A. dissertation, University of Wales, Cardiff, 1991.

Emma Lile

Yards of Ale

A drinking contest in which competitors try to drink beer as quickly as possible from a long thin glass shaped like a horn with a bulb at the end. It is, as the name suggests, a yard long and contains approximately 1½ litres of beer.

Sources and Reading:
Gorini, P., *Encyclopedia of Traditional Games* (Rome: Gremese, 1994).

Tony Collins

Index

Page numbers in **bold** type indicate main entries